D1427300

'[Leaming] handles with expertise Monroe's relations with the film moguls, the triangle between Monroe, Kazan and Miller, and also the degree to which Miller's marriage to Marilyn influenced his work. She presents a convincing portrait of Monroe as victim, exploited, abused and betrayed by men' *Daily Telegraph*

'Engrossing. Restores Marilyn's humanity. Leaming has a sure dramatic instinct. A gripping and corrective book' *New York Times Book Review*

'Barbara Leaming [is] the most meticulous of all current Hollywood historians ... [she] makes a powerful case for Monroe as a serially abused woman destroyed by the man she most loved ... Leaming does not shirk from recording much of the hostility Marilyn provoked ... This is ultimately a biography about betrayal, and Leaming writes it with all the cool efficiency of a court reporter' *Sunday Times*

'First-rate. A sympathetic, gracefully written study of an American legend' *People*

'Do we need yet another book on Marilyn Monroe? Well, yes, provided it's by ex-Professor Leaming, renowned for her excellent biographies of Orson Welles, Hayworth, Hepburn *et al* ... Doomed, plucky, exasperating – a convincing portrait' *Time Out*

'Everyone ought to own one book on Monroe. Go to Barbara Leaming's *Marilyn Monroe* if you are still under-rating her dependence on drink and drugs or still think she was bumped off. You'll end this well-written life with a different view' *Sunday Times*

Barbara Leaming is the author of *Orson Welles: A Biography*, written with Welles's co-operation, as well as the bestselling *Katharine Hepburn*. She was for many years Professor of Theatre and Film at Hunter College in New York City. Her articles have appeared in *Vanity Fair* and the *New York Times* magazine. Barbara Leaming lives in Connecticut.

By Barbara Leaming

Polanski: A Biography
Orson Welles: A Biography
If This Was Happiness: A Biography of Rita Hayworth
Bette Davis: A Biography
Katharine Hepburn
Marilyn Monroe
Mrs Kennedy: The Missing History of the Kennedy Years

MARILYN MONROE

✦

BY

Barbara Leaming

ORION

An Orion paperback
First published in Great Britain by Weidenfeld & Nicolson in 1998
This paperback edition published in 1999 by Orion Books Ltd,
Orion House, 5 Upper St Martin's Lane, London WC2H 9EA

Second impression 2002

A CIP catalogue record for this book
is available from the British Library.

ISBN: 0 75282 692 1

Printed and bound in Great Britain by
Clays Ltd, St Ives plc

Contents

Illustrations

Marilyn with George Cukor and Yves Montand on the set of *Let's Make Love* (John Springer/Corbis–Bettmann)

Marilyn and Arthur with John Huston on location for *The Misfits*, 1960 (UPI/Corbis–Bettmann)

Marilyn leaves Columbia–Presbyterian Hospital, March 1961 (*Daily Mirror*/Corbis–Bettmann)

Marilyn with Joe DiMaggio in Florida, March 1961 (UPI/Corbis–Bettmann)

Marilyn and Joe DiMaggio board the plane back to New York, April 1961 (UPI/Corbis–Bettmann)

Marilyn, Elizabeth Taylor and Dean Martin watch Frank Sinatra perform in Las Vegas, June 1961 (UPI/Corbis–Bettmann)

Marilyn with Peter Lawford (Patricia Lawford Stewart/Corbis–Bettmann)

Marilyn sings "Happy Birthday" to President John F. Kennedy at Madison Square Garden, May 19, 1962 (UPI/Corbis–Bettmann)

Marilyn poses nude on the set of her final film, *Something's Got to Give*, May 1962 (UPI/Corbis–Bettmann)

Marilyn's death is announced in Times Square, August 5, 1962 (UPI/Corbis–Bettmann)

Joe DiMaggio at Marilyn's funeral, August 8, 1962 (UPI/Corbis–Bettmann)

Arthur Miller and Elia Kazan during preparation for *After the Fall* (UPI/Corbis–Bettmann)

Marilyn blows a kiss (UPI/Corbis–Bettmann)

Time is short, baby, it betrays us
as we betray each other.

—TENNESSEE WILLIAMS

PART ONE

✦

+ O N E +

On January 16, 1951, a black Lincoln convertible pulled into the driveway at 2000 Coldwater Canyon Drive in Beverly Hills. Arthur Miller and Elia Kazan had just traveled cross-country by train from New York. Miller, tall and lean, had a dark, angular, weathered face and a receding hairline. Kazan, known as Gadget or Gadg to his friends, was small with a large nose and a mop of wavy black hair. The men were in Los Angeles to set up their first film together. Miller had written a screenplay for Kazan to direct, and both had a great deal riding on the venture. But already there was a serious problem. On the train, Kazan had read the most recent draft of *The Hook*, a story of union corruption on the Brooklyn waterfront, and he'd been disappointed by what Miller had accomplished so far. Kazan made it clear that the script needed to be much better.

Greeted at the front door by a servant, Miller and Kazan entered the home of Charles Feldman, a prominent Hollywood agent and independent film producer. He was producing Kazan's latest project, the film of Tennessee Williams's *A Streetcar Named Desire*, starring Marlon Brando and Vivien Leigh. As Feldman told his friend and investor Joseph P. Kennedy, he believed that Kazan's work had been outstanding. Shooting had been completed before the holidays, but some post-production work remained to be done. Feldman, away on business and anxious to keep the director happy, had offered Kazan the run of his art-filled house. An inveterate collector, Feldman purchased paintings and bibelots in quantity, often sight unseen. The furniture, mostly English antiques and modern pieces, was kept to a minimum to emphasize the Chagalls, Renoirs, and Toulouse-Lautrecs that covered the walls. There were Thai bronze Buddhas. There were Ming and Sui stone heads. There were T'ang and Chou horses and birds.

In the garden, steps led up to a heated swimming pool, beside which Miller set up his typewriter on a glass table. To understand the strain he was under, it is essential to keep in mind that *The Hook* was not just any screenplay. It was to be the work with which Miller followed *Death of a Salesman*, which had been a huge success on Broadway in 1949, directed by Kazan. Many critics thought the thirty-three-year-old Miller had written *the* great American play, and some pronounced it the century's finest drama. There was a price to be paid for acclaim of that magnitude. After the premiere, Miller confided to his producer, Kermit Bloomgarden, that he knew he was going to have a hell of a time topping that. Indeed, there had been moments when Miller wondered whether he would be able to write another play at all.

As Kazan perceived, Miller was not a playwright who invented stories. He needed to find his material in his own life. Yet *The Hook* was not based on anything Miller had actually experienced. The screenplay did not come out of a crisis that he himself had endured, and as a result he did not completely trust it. Miller began to worry that for a man his age, he had not lived enough. Yet the pressure was on to revise quickly while they pitched to Twentieth, Warner Bros., and Columbia Pictures. Unfortunately, Miller was not like his rival Tennessee Williams, who could work anywhere, under almost any conditions. He was a creature of routine, who found it difficult to write in unfamiliar surroundings.

Adding to the playwright's pressures was the threat of losing Kazan. In a period dubbed by the critic Brooks Atkinson "the Williams–Miller era," Kazan seemed at times to enjoy playing each against the other. Kazan, wavering provocatively between the two, had finally chosen to film *A Streetcar Named Desire* instead of *Death of a Salesman*. Afterward, when Williams had had every expectation that Kazan would do his new play, *The Rose Tattoo*, on Broadway, the director jumped ship at the last minute, going off to Los Angeles for *The Hook*. Evidently, Kazan was not about to give either playwright reason to take him for granted. Always the director, he controlled people and situations; he didn't like being controlled by them.

Kazan was then probably the most powerful director in America. On Broadway, he had directed three Pulitzer Prize-winning plays. His association with Miller and Williams had earned him a reputation for being a playwright's director, but he was also clearly an actor's director. His work with Marlon Brando in the first stage production of A Streetcar Named Desire in 1947 had broken exciting new ground. In Hollywood, he'd negotiated a six-picture, non-exclusive deal with Twentieth Century–Fox, at the highest per-picture director's salary the studio had ever agreed to pay. Kazan had already won an Academy Award as Best Director for Gentleman's Agreement, but it was Streetcar, on which the advance word was spectacular, that promised to be his watershed. Before that, despite the Oscar, Kazan had confided in Williams that he didn't really know how to make films yet. In Streetcar, Kazan demonstrated the mastery he so often showed on stage. The Hook was particularly important to Kazan, since he needed to follow Streetcar with another great film; that's why the current draft had been such a big disappointment. As it was, the script wasn't going to give either man what he needed.

There was an even greater pressure burdening Kazan. The House Un-American Activities Committee, which since 1938 had been attempting to document the Communist infiltration of American film and theater, was preparing to launch motion picture industry hearings in March. Its investigations had been given new and vigorous life by America's entry into the Korean War in 1950. Having belonged to the Communist Party for about nineteen months between 1934 and 1936, Kazan figured it was only a matter of time before HUAC summoned him. He was visible. He was successful. He was very much in demand. Those qualities made him a prime target for a committee whose raison d'être, in large part, was publicity. "If they call me, I'll tell them to go fuck themselves," Kazan vowed to Kermit Bloomgarden. If he did that, his Hollywood career would be destroyed. The inevitability seemed to shadow Kazan's every action.

The climate of fear in Hollywood also had an impact on the particular project he and Miller were selling. When they met with Darryl Zanuck in his high-domed office at Twentieth Century–Fox, the production chief turned down The Hook because of its politically sensitive subject matter. Zanuck, though eager to begin Kazan's next film, wouldn't touch Miller's script, concerned as it was with unions and labor. Abe Lastfogel, Kazan's agent at William Morris, left the meeting and went directly to Warner Bros. to try his luck there.

Meanwhile, Kazan had something else he wanted to do on the Fox lot. Ostensibly, he took Miller to the set of As Young as You Feel to visit the director, Harmon Jones, who had previously worked as Kazan's film editor. But the real reason was to see a girl he had heard about from Charlie Feldman. The detour offered a way to blow off some of the tension.

Before Miller and Kazan actually saw her, her name echoed through the studio. "Marilyn!" an assistant shouted frantically while Jones told Kazan about the trouble he'd been having with the twenty-four-year-old actress. She was forever disappearing from the set. Worse, when she returned, her eyes were often swollen from crying, making it difficult to film her. Fortunately, her role was a small one. This was to be her final day, if only Jones could get the shots he needed. She appeared at last, her skin-tight black dress disclosing a body perfect even by Hollywood standards. She had blue-gray eyes, a turned-up nose, and luminous white skin. She wore her fine blonde hair pinned on top of her head.

Marilyn Monroe was in crisis. When she finished work on this picture, she had no further assignments. After today, she had nothing to do and nowhere to go. A career that meant everything to her might well be over. Though Marilyn was under contract to Twentieth, Darryl Zanuck, who loathed her, was unlikely to pick up her option in May. Though she had signed a three-year contract with the William Morris Agency as recently as December 5, suddenly no one there would take her calls. Marilyn felt as if she were about to fall off the face of the earth.

Highlighting Marilyn's predicament was the fact that she had just had the best year of her professional life. She owed it all to Johnny Hyde, a partner and senior agent at William Morris. For two years, he had worked tirelessly on her behalf. Very much in love with Marilyn, the dwarf-like agent believed in her, and in her dream of being a star, as no one had done before. He was even rumored to have personally under-written the new contract he had negotiated for her at Twentieth. Before meeting Johnny, Marilyn had briefly been under contract at both Twentieth and Columbia, but neither studio had kept her on. Hyde was determined that things were going to be different this time.

For a while, it seemed they would be. By 1950, Hyde's efforts had begun to pay off. Marilyn attracted attention in small but showy roles in John Huston's The Asphalt Jungle and Joseph Mankiewicz's All About Eve.

It was thanks to Johnny that she had an opportunity to work with the best directors; it was thanks to Johnny that she knew who the best directors were. But just when all that she had been working for finally seemed within her grasp, the fifty-five-year-old Hyde had a fatal heart attack in Palm Springs on December 18. Marilyn had refused to join him there for the weekend. She blamed herself for his death. The day after Hyde's funeral, Marilyn attempted suicide, swallowing the contents of a bottle of barbiturates. Though a roommate discovered her in time, in the days and weeks that followed she never really came back to life. With no one to fight for her anymore, Marilyn seemed to have given up. In January, she reported for work on *As Young as You Feel*, the last film Johnny had arranged for her, but from the first it was evident that she was merely going through the motions.

Miller and Kazan watched her struggle through a scene. Between takes, she fled to a dark, deserted sound stage littered with office furniture. When Kazan caught up with her, he found her in tears. They had met before, though he assumed she didn't remember—Marilyn and Johnny had once had dinner with Kazan and Abe Lastfogel, Hyde's partner at William Morris. Now, Kazan offered consolation for Johnny's death. Marilyn looked away, far too upset to reply. She returned for another take. When she finished, Miller looked on as Kazan asked her to dinner. Marilyn said no, and the men went off to the studio cafeteria.

So that was it for Marilyn. Her work on the picture was done. There seemed to be nothing left for her at Twentieth. Since Johnny's death, her phone had rung constantly, but it was always Charlie Feldman or one of the other men in their group, each of them eager to be first to sleep with Johnny's girl before passing her on to the others. The only sign that anyone else remembered her was a package from Johnny's family, containing a stack of nude photographs of Marilyn that had been discovered in the top drawer of his bureau. As Marilyn's recent behavior suggested, part of her just wanted to curl up and die.

But Kazan's fortuitous arrival indicated that this was no time to indulge in self-pity. Whatever Kazan may have thought, Marilyn knew exactly who he was. As it happened, she had previously encountered him not once but twice. The previous August, Johnny Hyde had taken her to Danny Kaye's party to welcome Vivien Leigh to Hollywood for *A Streetcar Named Desire*. Kazan, Leigh's dinner partner, had been very much the power player in the room that evening. Now, at a moment when Marilyn seemed about to lose everything, the important director had walked into her life. On the Fox lot, Kazan was known to be casting the film *Viva Zapata!*, then being written by John Steinbeck. If Marilyn failed to seize the opportunity, it might not present itself again. It didn't matter that she was mentally and physically exhausted. Marilyn, through an act of will, pulled herself out of the mists of the depression that had engulfed her. Soon, she was on her way to the studio cafeteria, having decided to find Kazan and say yes to his dinner invitation.

Marilyn began to spend nights in Kazan's room at Feldman's, while Miller slept alone in a room down the hall. By day, Miller, powerfully attracted to Marilyn himself, swam laps in the pool in an effort to cool off. Marilyn, appointed "mascot," accompanied Kazan and Miller on their rounds with *The Hook*. She loved Gadg's idea of playing a practical joke on Harry Cohn, the production chief at Columbia. Kazan would introduce Marilyn as his private secretary, Miss Bauer, who was there to take notes on Cohn's reaction to the script. In fact, she and Cohn had met in the past, when he had banned her from the lot after she refused to accompany him on a yacht to Catalina Island. Marilyn's rage over the incident had festered, and now she welcomed an opportunity to laugh at his expense. Despite her carefully cultivated soft, breathy voice, Marilyn was full of anger. As it turned out, going to Harry Cohn's office may not have been such a good idea after all; inevitably, the visit reminded Marilyn that without Johnny Hyde's protection, she faced the loss of yet another studio contract.

By the time Charlie Feldman returned from New York on Sunday, January 21, Marilyn appeared to have lined up a new protector. Feldman had to give the devil her due—she had worked quickly, replacing Johnny with Kazan. Feldman was a bit of a dandy, sporting a Clark Gable mustache and a gold signet ring on his right pinky finger; he had planned to be the first to take Johnny's girl to bed, but he accepted defeat gracefully. When he drew up a guest list for a buffet dinner party in Miller's honor,. he listed Marilyn simply as Kazan's girl; that being her current identity, no other name seemed necessary.

All week the house in Coldwater Canyon was a hive of activity in anticipation of Friday night. A dance band was hired. Heaping platters of beef tenderloin, chopped chicken liver, and marinated herring were ordered from the Hillcrest Country Club. Miller had been having trouble with his wife back in Brooklyn, and Kazan, who also had a wife in the east, had resolved to get him a girl in California. So the party was conceived as what Feldman and his friends called a stag. Feldman put together similar parties for Joe Kennedy's son Jack when he was in town. Men, whether married or not, came alone. Girls, as they were designated, arrived in their own cars. That way the men would not be required to take them home afterward. Marilyn knew that Feldman's friends Raymond Hakim and Pat De Cicco, both of whom had also been hounding her since Johnny's death, would be at the stag. But she had every reason to expect that Kazan's presence would force them to keep their distance. Hakim was an Egyptian-born film producer, De Cicco a procurer for Howard Hughes and other wealthy men in Hollywood.

Friday arrived and Kazan decided not to take Marilyn to the party after all, claiming to have some business to attend to. In fact, he went off to meet another girl. At the last minute, Miller was assigned to Marilyn as his substitute. She knew precisely what that meant, of course. She had slept with Kazan, then been passed on to the next guy. When Miller called to say he would pick her up, Marilyn, well aware of how these things worked, said it wouldn't be necessary. She could get to Feldman's on her own. To her astonishment, the gravel-voiced Miller insisted.

The actress Evelyn Keyes had had dinner with Feldman and Joe Schenck, an executive producer at Fox, two nights previously. In the course of the evening, Feldman invited her to the party for Arthur Miller. Witty, intelligent, well-read, and recently divorced from John Huston, Keyes was very much interested in meeting the author of *Death of a Salesman*. But when Miller appeared on Friday night, there could be no mistaking that he was "totally wrapped up" in Marilyn Monroe. "I don't think he ever looked my way," Keyes recalled. Marilyn, as she made her entrance, resembled nothing so much as "the prow of a ship." She was "all front." She actually seemed to lean forward as she walked, her breasts "in advance."

Marilyn must have been nervous coming into that crowded, dimly-lit, music-filled room. She knew that Feldman, Hakim, De Cicco and the other men would all be laughing at her. She knew that it was obvious she had already been passed on. She knew people were saying that she had been foolish to have repeatedly turned down Johnny Hyde's proposals of marriage; and in the light of current circumstances, it crossed her mind that perhaps they were right.

Soon, they were seated on a sofa, Miller leaning slightly toward her. Evelyn Keyes observed them there. Miller, utterly absorbed, watched Marilyn as though he were "studying this phenomenon." After they had talked a while, Marilyn, who believed that men only like happy girls, kicked off her high-heeled shoes and tucked her slender legs under her. Miller told her about his troubles with his wife. Marilyn would not have been surprised if he had asked her to come to his room or to the car. Probably, she would have accepted. Instead, he took her big toe in his fingers and squeezed gently.

Kazan came to the party late, his date having failed to work out. At this point, Marilyn was his to reclaim if he wished. As far as anyone was concerned, she was still Kazan's girl. Miller had merely been his stand-in. But once Kazan saw Arthur and Marilyn dancing together, he pretended to be weary and asked his friend to see her home. On the way back to her apartment, Miller again made no move to sleep with her, though he desired her very much. Marilyn, accustomed to being pawed by men, interpreted his shyness and awkwardness as a sign of respect. No man, not even Johnny Hyde, had ever treated her like that.

Miller feared where this was headed. Being true to himself meant a great deal to him. He thought of himself as a man of conscience. He thought of himself as a man guided by moral principles. In his notebook, later, he would meditate on the inadequacy of guilt as a basis for morality. He sincerely wanted to do the right thing. How could such a man betray his wife, the mother of his children, the woman who had supported him when he was a struggling writer? Miller, torn, returned to New York the following day.

His departure left Marilyn in a quandary. She told herself that she was in love with Arthur Miller. But it was Kazan who would be staying on at Feldman's. Had the director really passed her on, or would he expect their arrangement to go back to what it had been before that night? Marilyn couldn't wait to see Miller again, but she also didn't want to give up the chance to be cast in one of Kazan's films. She had to decide what to do about Kazan.

+   +   +

Arthur Miller had gone back to a world that Marilyn could hardly imagine. His life in New York and Connecticut had almost no reality to her. At the same time, Miller can barely have comprehended the world Marilyn came from. He knew nothing of the bleak, impoverished, violent childhood in the Los Angeles area that had fueled her hopes and dreams.

Marilyn wanted to be a movie star so very badly because it was the only way she knew to escape a chaotic, nightmarish existence that constantly threatened to draw her back in. From the time she was a little girl, passed from one grim foster home to another, that dream had given her a reason to go on living. Of course, many children in those circumstances fantasize about a film career. In Marilyn's case, the accident of geography, the fact that she grew up in and around Hollywood, made her dream seem achingly within reach.

Marilyn, then called Norma Jeane Baker, spent her earliest years in Hawthorne, a suburb of Los Angeles. She had been farmed out to a foster family by a sick mother, who was barely able to make ends meet with various low-end jobs in the film industry. Norma Jeane's life had nothing to do with the movies. Because of her foster parents' strict religious beliefs, movies were never mentioned. All that changed, however, when Norma Jeane, aged seven, went to live briefly with her mother, Gladys Baker. Hardly had mother and daughter settled in when Gladys became ill again and had to be hospitalized. Responsibility for Norma Jeane fell on Gladys's best friend, Grace McKee, who worked with her in a film laboratory. It was "Aunt Grace" who first encouraged Norma Jeane to believe that she was destined to be a star like Jean Harlow.

Indeed, Grace was the only person in the child's life who seemed to take any interest in her whatsoever. She was the only person to believe in Norma Jeane. But for all the cheerleading, Grace was in no position to care for a little girl. So Norma Jeane went back to living in a series of foster homes until Grace ran out of families with which to place Gladys's daughter. The Los Angeles Orphans Home, an enclave of red-brick buildings on North El Centro Avenue, was the only remaining option.

On September 13, 1935, Grace led nine-year-old Norma Jeane to the orphanage door. When the child saw the huge black sign with gold lettering, she shrieked that there must be some mistake. She was not an orphan and did not belong here. Grace had to drag her, screaming and kicking, inside. Norma Jeane had endured poverty. She had endured being treated by certain families as little more than an indentured servant. She had endured having no real home of her own. But finding herself locked in an orphanage was another matter entirely. As far as the child was concerned, it meant that she really was no one in the world. And that feeling of utter worthlessness hurt more than anything ever had in her short life.

On the first night, a tearful Norma Jeane was assigned to one of twenty-seven metal beds in a huge dormitory. After the lights went out, she slipped out of bed and went to the window. In the distance, she could see the water tower at the Gower Street studios of RKO Pictures. The sight comforted her, partly because she remembered entering the studio gates with her mother, who had once worked there. But even more, it was a symbol of the glittering fairy-tale kingdom which Grace had often promised she would one day inhabit. In the nights that followed, Norma Jeane made a point of always taking a peek at the water tower before she tried to sleep. At a moment when the sad, lonely little girl was on the brink of utter despair, that sight, and the hope it represented, provided a lifeline.

Almost every weekend, Grace, who had been appointed Norma Jeane's legal guardian, would show up at the orphanage. She brought gifts of lipstick and rouge. Before Norma Jeane was ten, she had grown accustomed to being coiffed and made up by Grace as though she were an adult. Grace, harping on the fact that Norma Jeane resembled a little movie star, regularly took her to the movies—less for entertainment than for instruction. She inculcated the child with a powerful sense of what her future must be.

Shortly before her eleventh birthday, Norma Jeane went to live in Van Nuys with Grace and her fourth husband, Erwin "Doc" Goddard, a sporadically employed aircraft worker. But the arrangement did not last. Doc, who drank heavily, made sexual advances to Norma Jeane, so Grace shipped the child off to other foster homes. By the time Norma Jeane was twelve, she had been assaulted in at least two of these homes, and possibly others. Time and again, Grace had to find another family to take her in. That in each instance it was the victim, not the victimizer, who was expelled sent a powerful message to Norma Jeane: She had to be punished because somehow she had brought the attack on herself.

Through all this horror, one thing appeared to sustain the poor, abused child. Under Grace's tutelage, she had become completely absorbed by the fantasy of the movies—a world of glamor and beauty that bore no relation to her own existence. Yet that fantasy seemed attainable, if only because she had spent her entire life within a few dozen miles of Hollywood. And it clearly helped that Grace believed in her to the extent that she did. No matter how dreadful Norma Jeane's day-to-day reality, Grace persisted in her promises that the future would be different: One day Norma Jeane would be a star, and no one would dare mistreat her again.

That fantasy gave Norma Jeane hope, but it also confused her. Grace was sending mixed signals. On the one hand, Grace repeatedly communicated that Norma Jeane had been thrown out of Grace's own and other households because she had behaved provocatively. On the other hand, Grace encouraged her to believe that it was precisely her beauty and sexuality that would eventually win her better treatment. Norma Jeane would later be rewarded for the very behavior that had previously elicited punishment. Further confusing the child was the fact that the abuse she had endured had been her only experience of power. Terrible as those experiences were, they suggested that Norma Jeane had the ability to attract attention in a world that was otherwise indifferent to her. All the talk of becoming a movie star reinforced the child's sense that her sexuality was the one form of power she had.

When Norma Jeane was fifteen, it was Grace—of all people—who trod on the dream she had done so much to create. Grace announced that she and Doc were moving to West Virginia and could not take Norma Jeane with them. She offered Norma Jeane a choice: either she married a young man Grace had selected, or she would have to return to the orphanage. The prospective bridegroom was James Dougherty, the twenty-one-year-old son of a former neighbor. Norma Jeane chose marriage, though that meant dropping out of high school before she had completed her sophomore year. On June 19, 1942, three weeks after her sixteenth birthday, Norma Jeane Baker married Jimmy Dougherty. She seemed to forget about the movies, apparently forever. Jimmy was a kind, decent man; he gave his young bride so much attention that she didn't seem to mind that her dream had been put aside. Maybe the attention would do after all.

Norma Jeane might well have remained a housewife in the San Fernando Valley for the rest of her life if World War II had not intervened. The young husband left his job at the Lockheed aircraft factory to join the Merchant Marine. In spring 1944, he shipped out. Like many wartime wives, Norma Jeane went to live with her husband's parents and found a job in a defense factory. The Radio Plane Company produced the radio-controlled small airplanes that Army gunners used for target practice. Jimmy's mother was employed as a nurse in the infirmary. Seventeen-year-old Norma Jeane worked on the assembly line, first as a chute-packer, later as a glue-sprayer.

In 1945, Army photographers from the First Motion Picture Unit came to Radio Plane to film women in war work. A young corporal named David Conover spotted Norma Jeane and took her picture. When the results came back from the lab, Conover returned to the factory and told her she was pretty enough to model. That was all Norma Jeane needed to hear; in an instant, her old dream of escape had been reactivated.

Conover asked Norma Jeane to pose again. Her husband was due on shore leave just then, so Norma Jeane put the photographer off until Jimmy had gone back to sea. Dougherty left again in June 1945, just as Norma Jeane celebrated her nineteenth birthday. The moment he was gone, she moved out of her in-laws' house, quit her job, and never looked back.

By the end of the month, Conover had taken a set of pictures of Norma Jeane for *Yank* magazine. He showed the photographs to a friend, who in turn put her in touch with the Blue Book Modeling Agency in Los Angeles. The agency passed her on to a film agent, who landed her a screen test at Twentieth Century–Fox. A little over a year after Conover first photographed Norma Jeane, she had divorced her husband, signed a contract at Twentieth, and changed her name to Marilyn Monroe.

On August 26, 1946, Grace accompanied Marilyn to Twentieth. Marilyn was still a minor, so her guardian had to sign the contract as well. Miraculously, everything seemed to be working precisely as Grace had once predicted. In a way, it had all been so easy; from Conover on, everybody had been kind and helpful. Marilyn was confident that she was about to become a movie star at last. In the months that followed, she did whatever Twentieth asked. She worked. She studied. She had her chance, and she applied herself with an earnestness that was disarming. But by the end of the year, Marilyn had had only two bit parts. Worse, when her contract came up for renewal, the studio decided to let her go because production chief Darryl Zanuck thought she was unattractive. On July 26, 1947, when Twentieth notified Marilyn that her option would not be picked up, her film career screeched to a halt. Marilyn could always eke out a living as a magazine model, but that was not the dream Grace had instilled in her. Horribly disappointed, Marilyn was prepared to do anything to get her career moving again.

By the fall of 1947, she had joined countless other starlets, models, and assorted young women on the Hollywood party circuit. Like them, Marilyn hoped to meet someone who could help her get a part in a film. At one of these parties, early in 1948, Marilyn encountered Pat De Cicco. He invited her to one of the town's Saturday-night institutions, Joe Schenck's all-night, high-stakes gin rummy game in Holmby Hills. Marilyn knew exactly who Schenck was. Until only a few months ago, he had been one of her bosses at Twentieth, where he served as an executive producer. Schenck had been board chairman at United Artists in the 1920s and had founded Twentieth Century with Darryl Zanuck in the thirties. When Twentieth merged with Fox in 1935, he had been appointed board chairman.

At sixty-nine, Schenck was said to be one of the richest men in Hollywood. His card games were attended by top studio executives, producers, and directors. De Cicco, Schenck's court jester, provided girls. In exchange for dinner and the chance to meet some of Hollywood's most important players, the women were expected to make themselves available to "Uncle" Joe's friends. When a guest absented himself from the card table, more often than not it was to take a girl of his choice to one of the mansion's many bedrooms.

Marilyn became a regular at Uncle Joe's. Schenck took a special liking to her, and soon she came to be known as "Joe Schenck's girl." She stood behind his chair as he played cards. She served drinks and emptied ashtrays. Before long, Marilyn was at the house several nights a week for dinner. To keep the old man happy, she even briefly moved into the guest cottage in order to be nearby when he wanted her at night. Uncle Joe repaid Marilyn by persuading Harry Cohn to sign her to a six-month contract. She started at Columbia Pictures in March 1948.

At the studio, Marilyn fell in love with Fred Karger, a vocal coach who had been assigned to work with her. Swept away by her feelings,

Marilyn informed Uncle Joe that she could no longer live at the estate; she moved to an apartment of her own. Karger, however, was less serious about the relationship than she was. Marilyn desperately wanted to marry, and she was crushed when Karger announced that he didn't feel comfortable with her as a stepmother for his child from a previous marriage. Nonetheless, Marilyn's devotion to Karger meant that she turned down an invitation to spend the weekend on Harry Cohn's yacht, and that killed any chance she might have had of being kept on by Columbia after her contract expired on September 9, 1948.

So Marilyn was back on the party circuit—except this time she no longer had the protection of being Joe Schenck's girl. When Marilyn attended Uncle Joe's parties, or accompanied him to Palm Springs for the weekend, he was happy to pass her around to friends. There were plenty of men willing to take Marilyn upstairs for half an hour, but no one seemed even remotely interested in casting her in a film. Though Marilyn regularly passed in view of some of Hollywood's best directors and producers, no one guessed her potential. No one suspected she was star material. Most didn't even think she was worth a second look. She appeared indistinguishable from all the other girls. When Marilyn approached Howard Hawks one weekend in Palm Springs, the director made it clear that he saw nothing special about her. He thought she was stupid and told her so. He wasn't even interested in a sexual encounter.

Though Marilyn did her best to play the happy girl, the party circuit was a brutal, degrading, sometimes dangerous business. At times, the men become violent. On one occasion, Marilyn found herself in a bedroom, with two men holding her down while a third tried to rape her. Somehow, she managed to break free, but the incident recalled the sexual assaults she had endured as a child, when Grace taught her to believe that somehow she had provoked the violence. Marilyn had come to these parties seeking help and attention. She had no illusions about what most of the guests expected from her and the other girls. She knew the risk of being attached to no particular man. She knew that once she was no longer Joe Schenck's girl, she was up for grabs—or, at least, that was the way most men in this milieu perceived her. So on one level Marilyn believed she had brought the incident on herself. But on another she knew better, and she was filled with rage at the men who had done this to her.

Everything changed for Marilyn, however, at Sam Spiegel's New Year's Eve party in Beverly Hills on December 31, 1948. Recently, Marilyn had established herself as one of the producer's "house girls." Spiegel's parties were famous for—in the words of Orson Welles—"the best delicatessen and the best whores" in town. Indeed, some of the "house girls" were actually prostitutes hired by Spiegel to entertain his guests; others were starlets who hoped to advance their careers by catering to the needs of Spiegel's rich and powerful friends. An invitation to Spiegel's New Year's Eve gala was one of the hottest tickets in Hollywood. That year, the guests included the directors Otto Preminger, William Wyler, John Huston, Henry Hathaway, Jean Negulesco, Anatole Litvak, and many others.

One prominent guest, Johnny Hyde, was not in the best of moods that night. Two weeks before, his most important female client, Rita Hayworth, had sailed to Europe with Prince Aly Khan; at this point, it looked as if she had no intention of ever coming back. Harry Cohn, who had Hayworth under contract, was fuming. As Hyde entered Spiegel's house on North Crescent Drive, he seemed preoccupied and even a bit melancholy. Then he spotted Marilyn seated on a barstool across the room, and his demeanor changed entirely. Hyde, who had discovered Lana Turner, had a famous eye for beauty. In a room crowded with directors and producers, he looked at Marilyn and saw what not one of them had even remotely perceived: the makings of a great star.

Johnny Hyde was the first person, aside from Grace McKee, who saw Marilyn as she saw herself. But Johnny, unlike Grace, had the power to make Marilyn's dream a reality. And, despite his poor health, he had the will to keep pushing until others saw her as he did. Johnny's close friendships with many of the most important men in the film industry made it inevitable that eventually he would be able to force one of them to give Marilyn a chance.

The week after Spiegel's party, Hyde invited Marilyn to Palm Springs for a few days. By the time they came back, the little fellow with a taste for tall blondes had fallen hopelessly in love. That was another thing that made Johnny different from anyone Marilyn had ever known in Hollywood. He sincerely cared for her. Certain of his friends and associates laughed that he was obsessed.

Soon, Johnny was taking Marilyn everywhere, in an effort to be certain people saw her. If he had lunch with a client at Romanoff's, more often than not Marilyn would be at his side. If he played poker with the boys, Marilyn would be nearby reading a book. At the card table, he used every opportunity to hint to friends like John Huston and William Wyler that they ought to give the kid a chance. On visits to film studios, Hyde carried a silver film tin containing Marilyn Monroe footage under his arm. "You'll see! They'll all see!" he declared. "This kid has really got it. It's not just her looks, although everybody admits she's a knockout, but she's got the spirit. And she's funny. And a hell of an actress. And what's more important, she wants to do it. She wants to get there and be somebody." Still, no matter how powerful or well-connected Johnny might be, for some time none of his friends was willing to listen.

For her part, Marilyn listened very carefully when Johnny explained his strategy to her. She absorbed all he said. He didn't want to put her in just any film. The kind of "nothing" pictures she had already done would never make her a star. She could appear in a great many such films and still go nowhere. Johnny believed that for Marilyn to realize her dream, she needed a part that would get her noticed. It didn't have to be a large role, just an interesting one, in a picture by an important director.

Finally, Hyde's persistence paid off. With Sam Spiegel's help, he persuaded John Huston to let Marilyn read for a role in his new film. That was the break they had been waiting for. The Asphalt Jungle proved Johnny correct. In due course, some of the very men who had overlooked Marilyn at Hollywood parties were interested in using her. At Johnny's urging, Joseph Mankiewicz viewed a rough cut of Huston's film in early 1950; he promptly offered Marilyn a tiny role in All About Eve. Howard Hawks, once so scornful of Marilyn, fired off a telegram congratulating Huston on his discovery of "the girl." As Johnny never tired of reminding Marilyn, The Asphalt Jungle was the first of her films that mattered.

All About Eve was the second. On the basis of the rushes, Darryl Zanuck agreed to take her back at Twentieth Century–Fox. Hyde negotiated a new seven-year contract that went into effect on May 11, 1950. That same month, the release of The Asphalt Jungle signaled that Marilyn's career had taken off. From here on, Johnny assured her, everything was going to be very different.

But there was a problem. Johnny wanted something in exchange for all that he had done. He wanted Marilyn to be his wife. Marilyn refused. She was perfectly willing to sleep with little Johnny, but she wouldn't consider marriage to a man she did not love. He pleaded; he threatened; he cajoled. He warned that without his help, Marilyn would soon be right back on her ass with all the other girls. Again and again, Johnny threw her out, then took her back in the next day.

By the time *All About Eve* was released in October 1950, Johnny was gravely ill. A doctor had warned him that his sexual relationship with Marilyn was a strain on his already weak heart. Johnny replied that he would rather die than give her up. Mortified by Marilyn's refusal to marry him, he asked Joe Schenck to try to change her mind. Uncle Joe took a practical approach: He informed Marilyn that Johnny was unlikely to live much longer and urged her to marry for her own good. As Mrs. Hyde, she would inherit his palatial home on North Palm Drive in Beverly Hills and much else that he owned.

Still, Marilyn said no. It wasn't money that Marilyn wanted in life but respect; and who would respect a girl if she married a man she didn't love just to be sure she inherited his estate? Yet even as Marilyn said all this, she could not quite bring herself to accept that Johnny really was about to die. And she certainly didn't think it would happen so soon.

Two months later, all at once Marilyn was alone. Yet again, her career screeched to a halt. Yet again, she had no one to turn to. For a time, it seemed to Marilyn that without Johnny she was helpless. Everything good that had happened recently—the films with Huston and Mankiewicz, the new studio contract—had been due to his connections. Marilyn had paid attention to all that Johnny had said. She understood his plan for her. But on her own, Marilyn had no access to the A-list directors Johnny insisted she needed in order to become a star.

When she and Kazan saw Arthur Miller off at the airport in January of 1951, there was not really any question of what Marilyn must do next. Whatever her feelings for Miller, she knew that Kazan was her main chance. Marilyn was prepared to hold onto Kazan in whatever way she could.

+   +   +

The Beverly-Carlton on West Olympic Boulevard had a reputation as a good second-rate hotel where screenwriters took up residence when the studio was not paying the bill. Across the street, an annex offered four apartments on the second floor. Marilyn moved there when Arthur Miller went to New York. She gave no explanation to her roommate and dramatic coach, Natasha Lytess, who guessed that Marilyn required privacy because she was seeing a new man.

The bed, which dominated the tiny studio apartment, was actually a fold-out sofa covered in a nubby beige fabric. Marilyn almost never made it up as a sofa. There were plump, block-shaped bolsters along one gray wall beneath a large unframed mirror. Two low, light wood bookcases, crammed with books and pictures, served as a headboard. On one shelf was the slender red edition of *Death of a Salesman* that Miller had given her. There was a copy of *Focus*, his novel about anti-Semitism. There was a copy of Ibsen's *An Enemy of the People*, a play which Miller had recently adapted for Broadway. Directly over the place where Marilyn slept on a tufted, white satin comforter, a black-and-white photograph of Miller's gaunt face leaned against some books on the lower shelf. She expected him to return soon.

Harry Cohn, nervous about the politics of Miller's screenplay, had submitted it to the Federal Bureau of Investigation for review. He also consulted the labor leader Roy Brewer, of the International Alliance of Stage Employees. In sending *The Hook* out to be vetted, Cohn was almost certainly motivated less by patriotism than by economics. Films that were politically suspect, whether by virtue of their content or of the leftist backgrounds of the people who made them, ran the risk of being boycotted by patriotic and religious groups. The image of pickets at the box office was enough to put off any studio executive. Presumably, Roy Brewer could advise Miller and Kazan on potential problems in the script. Brewer was soon to testify at HUAC on the Communist conspiracy to seize control of the Hollywood labor unions.

Marilyn believed that Miller had gone to New York solely in order to finish *The Hook*. He had been unable to concentrate in Los Angeles. He worked best in a swivel chair at the cluttered desk in his cozy study in Brooklyn or in the ten-by-twelve-foot shack he had built with his own hands on his country property in Connecticut, where he had written *Death of a Salesman*. The moral crisis that, in reality, had sent Miller rushing back to New York would only have made him more attractive to Marilyn. She loved that he hadn't tried to sleep with her, though he clearly wanted to. She was drawn to him precisely because he was a man of conscience. She longed to have someone to look up to. As a moral figure, he seemed capable of absolving her of all she was ashamed of in her past. If he could love her, perhaps she really was worthy of respect. Marilyn, pretending it came from Harry Cohn's secretary, sent a telegram instructing Miller to finish his screenplay and return to Los Angeles.

Meanwhile, she slept with Kazan, who remained in town during February to work on A Streetcar Named Desire. Their sexual relationship did not end now that she had become preoccupied with Arthur Miller. In a curious way, it actually seemed to have intensified. Kazan was precisely the kind of director Johnny had said Marilyn needed. But if she pushed too hard, she might lose him. Kazan had fled once before, when he passed her on to Miller. This time, she had to keep his interest. And in the light of the fact that he knew how much she cared for Miller, she had to prevent his ego from being twisted out of joint; it certainly wouldn't do for a man to think the only reason she was sleeping with him was to get a film role.

Instead of hiding how she felt about Kazan's friend, however, Marilyn talked about it openly and at length. She and Kazan endlessly discussed Miller. She created the impression that in Arthur's absence, Kazan provided a vital link to his world. In a way, of course, he did. She told him what Arthur had said about being unhappy at home, and asked Kazan to help him. On at least one occasion, she even talked about Miller as Kazan made love to her. Miller, evidently, was in both their minds as they tangled on that bed. Afterward, Kazan found himself looking into Miller's eyes on the bookshelf over Marilyn's pillow. It may be that, perceiving the intensity of the men's relationship, Marilyn talked on about Miller because she knew that was the sort of thing Kazan wanted to hear. But why, if she loved Miller, did she leave his photograph in view? Making love under Miller's watchful eyes was every bit as much a gesture on her part as it was on Kazan's. For all of her calculation, perhaps Marilyn, too, was turned on by the idea of the triangle.

Back in New York, Kazan had a wife and children whom he had no intention of leaving. Studio publicity described him as "an ardent family man." Nonetheless, in Los Angeles he went about openly with Marilyn. He told himself that their relationship was not serious. He told himself that he took a European attitude to such matters. Marilyn was great fun, Kazan believed, but she wasn't cut out to be anybody's wife.

Usually, she played a happy girl for him. Yet there were times when she just couldn't bring off the act anymore. There were times when, he sensed, she clung to him as if he were all she had. Kazan, for his part, certainly didn't want any trouble. His marriage had nearly broken up over an affair with the actress Constance Dowling. Though he carried on with many girls, he did not want anything like that to happen again. He made a point of never telling a girl he loved her. Still, Marilyn discovered that Kazan could be tender and compassionate. He was a man of powerful silences. He might say nothing, yet he made his presence strongly felt. One night when she was in despair, Kazan held her in his arms, gently rocking her to sleep.

For the most part, however, the relationship was keyed to Kazan's needs. Marilyn accompanied him to business meetings at Feldman's, waiting contentedly beside the pool until the men were done. She drove up to Santa Barbara with Kazan on February 15 for the test preview of *Streetcar*. The following evening, after dinner at Feldman's, she and Kazan went on to Joe Schenck's. In poor health, Schenck had been recuperating in Hawaii when Johnny Hyde passed away. By the time he returned to Los Angeles, Marilyn, to his dismay, had already taken up with Kazan.

A stack of letters from Miller was accumulating next to his photograph on the shelf above Marilyn's bed. She read by the light of a small, goose-necked lamp. Arthur remained unhappy at home, where he and his wife were on very bad terms. Mary, a lapsed Catholic, was appalled that he might so much as think about sleeping with another woman. And in Los Angeles, he had certainly been tempted. He could say nothing to convince his wife to give him, and the marriage, another chance. She simply refused to believe anything he said.

Yet he had no plans to return to Los Angeles. Roy Brewer demanded that Miller change the union racketeers in his script to Communists. If Miller refused, Brewer threatened to call a strike of projectionists in order to prevent *The Hook* from ever being screened in the United States. Miller abruptly withdrew his script, refusing to make changes that struck him as absurd. Communists, he argued, were virtually nonexistent on the Brooklyn waterfront. He may also have been motivated by his own sensitivity to being subpoenaed by HUAC, Brewer having threatened to launch an investigation of both Miller and Kazan. It seemed to Kazan that the prospect filled Miller with panic.

Though Miller had never been a Communist Party member, he had attended several Communist writers' meetings in 1947. As Miller later disclosed to his attorney, he worried that some of the people who saw him there might have assumed he actually belonged to the Party during that period. Thus, if Miller testified truthfully that he had not been a Party member, there were individuals who, in the belief they were telling the truth, might come forward to say he was lying. He could find himself jailed for perjury. On the other hand, if Miller spoke frankly of his association with the Communist writers, HUAC would require him to establish credibility as a patriot by identifying others who had attended the meetings. That, as a matter of conscience, Miller would not do. As an unfriendly witness—that is, one who declined to name names—he could find himself held in contempt of Congress and imprisoned.

It may be that Kazan, accustomed as he was to being master of his own fate, had arrived in Hollywood with a politically provocative script like The Hook as a way of taking charge, of deliberately causing a subpoena to be issued. The gesture would have been very much in keeping with his insolent, abrasive character. As it was, he was furious when Miller withdrew his script. Kazan had turned down Tennessee Williams's play in order to work on The Hook. He had already devoted a good deal of time and effort to the project. He expected Miller to put up a fight.

Miller preferred to write a new drama. His moral crisis over Marilyn Monroe provided fresh material. As he once said, he could not write about anything he understood completely; if an experience was finished, he couldn't write it. He worked in his smoke-filled, third-floor study from 9 a.m. to 1 p.m. Posters for Death of a Salesman and All My Sons adorned the walls. A small bookcase overflowed with books. Children's voices—the Millers had a small son and daughter—drifted in from other rooms. Frequently, Miller went back to work at night.

In the months after returning from California, he started two plays, both featuring a wayward husband. The first drew on a true story Miller had heard on the Brooklyn waterfront as he researched The Hook. It tells of a married longshoreman who permits two brothers, Italians who have entered the country illegally, to live with him. One brother falls in love with the longshoreman's orphaned niece, also living in the apartment. The longshoreman, filled with incestuous desire for the young woman, betrays both men to the immigration authorities. That makes him a pariah in his community. When Miller had first heard the story several months previously, it hadn't particularly seized his imagination. What did it have to do with him? But now, like the longshoreman, he had been stirred by illicit desire. He hadn't acted on that desire, but he felt guilty all the same. He was part of a sexual triangle, one of two men drawn to the same woman. He knew what it was to think of another man with a woman he himself yearned for. He knew what it was to think of oneself as a betrayer. Yet still the material didn't jell and Miller put "An Italian Tragedy" aside. He would return to it several years later.

Marilyn, whom Miller had known for only a few days, hovered in his thoughts. She remained as much of a fantasy for him as he did for her. In a second work-in-progress, Miller wrote about a Marilyn-like woman of free and open sexuality. Lorraine, as he called her, bids men to abandon their wives and children, but those who are drawn to her come to an unhappy end. One character leaves his wife for Lorraine, who, faithless, later does the same to him. Another husband, protective of his social position, condemns himself to the safety of a cold and loveless marriage.

After six weeks as Feldman's houseguest, Kazan planned to fly home on February 23. Before he left, he made arrangements to shoot *Viva Zapata!*. He agreed to report no later than May 7, with shooting to begin twenty-one days after that. He persuaded Twentieth to pay for his wife, Molly, their four children, and a nanny to come to the location. Obviously, the presence of his family would limit Kazan's ability to carry on with Marilyn.

As the time approached for Kazan to go, Marilyn panicked. She had spent all this time with him, but he had not offered her a role in his new film. Frantic to maintain a connection, she made an uncharacteristic misstep. Marilyn told Kazan that she was pregnant. As though quickly realizing that that was the last thing in the world a married man would want to hear, she tried to reassure him. Marilyn insisted he mustn't worry, whatever that might mean. Later, she wrote to say that she had miscarried. Nonetheless, faced with precisely the sort of trouble he wanted to avoid, Kazan returned to New York determined to mend his ways and be faithful to Molly. Alone again, Marilyn had little choice but to look ahead. Two months had passed since she tried to take her own life following Johnny's death, and now she still had to figure out how to go on by herself.

✦ TWO ✦

At the Beverly-Carlton, flower deliveries accumulated outside Marilyn's door. The blinds remained shut all day, as Marilyn rarely got out of bed before 5 p.m. The phone rang constantly. Hardly had Kazan gone back to New York when all the men started calling again for dates. There was one invitation Marilyn could not refuse, however. She agreed to let Joe Schenck take her dancing at the Trocadero. Uncle Joe had something he wanted to say. He sent a studio limousine for her that night.

Large and bald with a poker face, Schenck was said to resemble Buddha. Lines and shadows were deeply etched around his eyes and bulbous nose. His face seemed always to be twisted in a frown. He and Marilyn were on the dancefloor when he made his pitch. He reminded Marilyn of her circumstances. He said she'd been a fool to turn down Johnny's marriage proposals. He pointed out that in recent weeks she had been wasting her time on a married man.

He urged her not to be just a scalp on a man's belt. He warned her not to allow herself to be used as a spittoon or an ashtray. He stressed that his own situation had changed recently; he was old and in poor health. He alluded to his impotence and said he would understand if as his wife she wanted to sleep with other men. His only stipulation was that Marilyn not have the same fellow twice in a row. In short, Uncle Joe was asking Marilyn to marry him. When he died, which seemed likely to happen soon enough, Marilyn would inherit everything. Marilyn, stunned by the offer, said she needed time to make up her mind.

Back at the Beverly-Carlton, she spent days considering what to do. Of course, Schenck had totally missed the point of her affair with Kazan. It wasn't marriage she had been hoping for; she certainly hadn't expected him to leave his wife. All Marilyn wanted was a part in Kazan's new film. But Schenck would never have understood that. He didn't think she was star material. He'd always thought her dreams unrealistic. Fond as he was of Marilyn, Uncle Joe, unlike Johnny, had never believed in her. He was utterly sincere in the conviction that the best thing that could happen to her was marriage to a wealthy man.

His offer was certainly very tempting. Marilyn still had not heard from the studio or her agents. No one in either place would see her or take her calls. There were no film assignments on the horizon. The way things stood, all she had to look forward to was the termination of her contract. The William Morris Agency was doing nothing for her. As far as Abe Lastfogel seemed to be concerned, now that Johnny Hyde was dead Marilyn didn't exist. Though she wrote to both Kazan and Miller in New York, she really had no idea whether she would ever see either of them again.

For all that, Joe Schenck's marriage proposal only reminded Marilyn of what she had really wanted all along. It brought into sharp focus what her struggle had always been about. Money and security, the things Hyde and now Schenck offered, were never really what she was after. The whole point of getting involved with Johnny, Kazan, or any of the other men in her life had been to help her reach a goal. She wanted to be a person in her own right.

Johnny had often compared Marilyn to Rita Hayworth, but there was a fundamental and revealing difference. Hayworth had been pushed by a father, then by a husband, to pursue a film career that she herself had never really wanted. By contrast, the only person driving Marilyn was herself, and she did so relentlessly. In the end, Marilyn turned down Uncle Joe. Being an important man's wife was never what she'd wanted. If it had been, she would have married Johnny.

Marilyn had chosen her dream over marriage. But she was left to face the probability that she was about to lose the means to realize that dream. She wasn't on any producer's casting list. Darryl Zanuck had sent down word that she was "just a freak" and that he didn't want to waste time on her. For Marilyn, it was no longer a question of being cast in good films by the best directors; the issue was whether she would be assigned to any films at all. In Kazan's absence, Marilyn decided that she had to abandon Johnny's plan temporarily. She had to find some way around Zanuck. She had to get Twentieth to put her in a film—any film. Otherwise, there wasn't a chance that her contract would be renewed.

Marilyn was smart. Though she had rarely said a word at all those endless business lunches Hyde had required her to attend, she had listened carefully. She had often heard him remark that when he wanted something at Twentieth, it could be useful to play the studio's two top men against each other. She'd heard Charlie Feldman and others speak along the same lines. The key to doing deals at Twentieth was to keep in mind that the production chief and the president were fiercely at odds.

Spyros Skouras had been president of Twentieth since 1942, yet he spent little time in Hollywood. The Old Greek, as he was known, preferred to run the business from New York, where he put in sixteen-hour days. A gigantic world map, with bright red stars to indicate Fox offices, was fixed to the wall behind his desk. A framed photograph of his beak-nosed wife, Saroula, dark hair piled on top of her head, leaned against the map on a side table littered with other, smaller family photographs. In front of his desk were a pair of beige club chairs and a large globe. Skouras, a bald, stocky, square-shouldered immigrant, always wore a conservative blue suit with a crisp white linen handkerchief in the breast pocket. His oversized eyeglasses had thick, shiny, black frames. He had a meaty face, with prominent eyebrows and a broad nose. He had coarse, mottled skin and deep, dark creases in his forehead. Impatient, always in a hurry, he was perpetually drumming thick fingers on the slab-like marble desktop. In a Turkish bath that adjoined his office, two masseurs, one on either side, would pound and knead the muscles of his bear-like body while Skouras dictated correspondence in mangled English to a secretary who perched behind a screen. The Old Greek was famous for the ability to fall asleep at will, awakening in a minute or two visibly refreshed, though some business associates believed the whole thing was just an act. He was prone to take a nap when people started to say anything he didn't want to hear.

Darryl Zanuck had little respect for Skouras. Privately, he regarded him as a fool. The production chief prided himself on excluding Skouras from creative decisions, revelling in his power to decide which projects were made and which were not. Calling himself a "one-man show," he made it a point of honor never to send Skouras a script. Zanuck sent finished films to New York, where Skouras, alternating between puffs on his cigar and a sip of Scotch, watched them late at night in his screening room. As long as the firm's chief executive officer remained in New York focused on business matters, Zanuck was content.

That March, Skouras came to Los Angeles for the annual sales conference. Five days of screenings culminated in an exhibitors' luncheon at the studio commissary, where theater owners mingled with Tyrone Power, Susan Hayward, Anne Baxter, and other stars. Zanuck, known as "the Coast," was in attendance, of course, but this was very much New York's show.

Skouras, hoarsely muttering "Won'erful! Won'erful!" as he liked to do, worked the room. He was brilliant with exhibitors. The connection was direct and intense. His eyes shot open. His greeting was electric. He gave them a bear-hug. He kissed them on both cheeks. He inquired about their wives and children by name. He told them about the infestation of Mediterranean worm that had destroyed the family vineyard when he was a boy. He reminded them that he himself had started out in motion pictures as co-owner of a St. Louis theater with his brothers Charlie and George.

After drinks and hors d'oeuvres, Skouras had taken his place at the main table when there was a fuss at the door. All heads turned as Marilyn Monroe burst in, more than an hour late. She appeared to have been sewn into her chiffon and satin black strapless cocktail gown. Someone said that she looked like Cinderella in flight from the pumpkin coach. Marilyn's air of helplessness and bewilderment masked a fierce determination to force the issue of her contract. This was her moment to attract Skouras's attention, and she put on quite a show.

Joe Schenck, also at the main table, watched with the others as Marilyn wiggled toward the first available chair. It was at a table of Midwestern exhibitors. From where Skouras sat he could not hear the conversation, but the theater owners' excitement was palpable.

"And what pictures are you going to be in, Miss Monroe?" one theater owner shouted.

"You'll have to ask Mr. Skouras," Marilyn replied in a wispy voice, at once childlike and seductive.

Skouras, who recognized Marilyn from *The Asphalt Jungle* and *All*

About Eve, demanded to know the same thing. Marilyn Monroe did not have an assignment, Schenck informed him. And her contract was about to come up for renewal. Within seconds, Marilyn was seated to Skouras's right at the main table. Within minutes, Skouras announced that her option was to be picked up. Within hours, he was dining with her at Uncle Joe's. Within days, he ordered studio executives to find new projects for her.

Her first assignment was a small part in *Love Nest*, to be directed by Joseph Newman. As Marilyn knew only too well, it was hardly comparable to the assignments Johnny had secured on her behalf. And it was hardly the sort of film that would get her attention. But at least she had a role, and at least her contract was going to be renewed. With no one looking out for Marilyn at William Morris, Twentieth managed to get away without giving her the yearly raise Johnny had negotiated. She received no credit for the year she had worked and, in effect, she began a new seven-year contract all over again.

Still, Marilyn had cause to rejoice. She had found an important protector at Twentieth. She had bought another year before her option came up again. She had provided herself with another chance to realize her dream. This time, she intended to make full use of the opportunity. During the next twelve months, Marilyn would do everything necessary to transform herself into a star.

✦   ✦   ✦

Kazan's resolve to be faithful to his wife proved short-lived. When he returned to Los Angeles after two months, he began to see Marilyn again. Marilyn was thrilled. Though he had failed to cast her in *Viva Zapata!*, perhaps there would be a role for her in some future Kazan picture. Marilyn had not forgotten Johnny's plan. She was aware that she could be given a great many assignments like *Love Nest* and still not get the attention she needed to become a star. So while it was certainly a triumph to have had her option picked up, Marilyn did not allow herself to be complacent. Either in a Kazan film or by some other means, Marilyn was determined to get herself noticed. The question was, how?

On May 7, Marilyn accompanied Kazan to dinner at Charlie Feldman's. A great deal had changed since the agent had seen her last.

Feldman had certainly never been known to take a professional interest in Marilyn. As far as he'd been concerned, Marilyn had simply been Joe Schenck's girl or Johnny Hyde's girl or Gadg Kazan's girl. She'd been the girl Charlie and his friends had briefly been competing for. But tonight, when she appeared at the house with Kazan, Feldman looked at her with new eyes.

Feldman had heard about Marilyn's new studio contract which, as it happened, was to be finalized in four days. He had heard about her triumph at the sales conference. Most importantly, he had heard about Spyros Skouras's decree that assignments must be found for her. Marilyn was just completing her first such assignment and was already set to begin another, Let's Make It Legal, in June. Skouras, as Feldman knew well, was a powerful ally.

Skouras's professional interest in Marilyn intrigued Feldman, as Johnny's sexual obsession had once made Charlie and his pals want to go to bed with her. For the first time, Feldman regarded Marilyn as someone he would be interested in signing up for Famous Artists, Inc. He made a mental note to send one of his agents to visit Marilyn on the set at Twentieth in order to remind her that she was being poorly served by William Morris.

Feldman's new attitude was a measure of the astonishing degree to which Marilyn had turned her circumstances around. She was flattered by his attentions, but she was also wary. From the first, Feldman had two strikes against him. He was one of the men who'd hounded Marilyn in the weeks after Johnny's death, and he was a close personal friend of Darryl Zanuck's. As far as Marilyn was concerned, Feldman's relationship with the production chief meant that he wasn't to be trusted. For the moment, however, Marilyn carefully kept her reservations to herself. She smiled sweetly. She strove to give no sign of what she was really thinking. In Kazan's presence, she consciously played the happy girl, fearful that she might lose his interest again if she did not.

But her role as the happy girl was far from the truth of Marilyn's existence as she struggled to make use of the opportunity Skouras had given her. To understand the immense pressure Marilyn was under, it's important to remember that in her case succeeding in films was much more than a question of simple ambition. It was a life-and-death matter. As far as Marilyn was concerned, life was not worth living if she failed to win the dignity and respect that came with being a star.

Marilyn might have been given minor roles in a pair of insignificant films, but in her mind everything was at stake. She was convinced that the slightest miscalculation might cause her enterprise to collapse. Therefore, on a film set, Marilyn was terrified of going in front of the camera. She would break out in a rash, vomit, revert to a childhood stammer. She would find a thousand reasons for postponing the moment when she finally had to emerge from her dressing room. The extent to which Marilyn keyed herself up in anticipation of being filmed also accounts for why audiences often couldn't take their eyes off her. Every time Marilyn appeared in a film, she was excruciatingly focused on making that moment happen. For Marilyn, nothing else mattered. At times, she seemed to be acting in a film of her own. Her role might be modest, her line readings inept, yet she communicated through the sheer intensity of her performance.

Marilyn's partner in all this was her acting coach and former roommate, Natasha Lytess. Marilyn had moved to the Beverly-Carlton in search of privacy, but skinny, green-eyed, flamboyant, nervous Natasha became a constant presence there. To account for her temperamental nature, Natasha claimed to be of mixed Russian and French blood. Some people whispered that she was really a German. She was in fact an Austrian Jew, a former actress in Max Reinhardt's company in Germany.

Natasha never complained when Marilyn summoned her by telephone after midnight to go over lines. She didn't seem to mind when Marilyn called her out of her day job as a dramatic coach at Twentieth. She regarded Marilyn as her second daughter and called herself Marilyn's private director. She encouraged people to think of her as Marilyn's right arm. Natasha was Marilyn's teacher, cheerleader, psychiatrist, best friend, handmaiden, slavedriver, and whipping boy, all rolled into one. She told Marilyn that she was too negative. She begged her to discard her insecurity. She implored her to learn to love herself. She informed her that she suffered from a guilt complex. She derided her laziness. She urged her to be strong. She warned her to grow up. When Natasha castigated Marilyn, she insisted that she gave her own daughter the same rough treatment when she misbehaved.

Marilyn's relationship with Natasha was passionate, turbulent, caring, over-the-top, and mutually exploitative. The emblem of that relationship was an antique cameo brooch—a woman's head delicately enclosed in gold—that Marilyn gave her at Christmas, 1950, shortly after Natasha had rescued her from her suicide attempt following Johnny's death. A note in a blue envelope declared Marilyn's belief that she owed Natasha much more than her life. Natasha planned to collect.

Natasha had met Marilyn at Columbia Pictures, where she had been assigned to prepare Marilyn to play a burlesque queen in Phil Karlson's *Ladies of the Chorus*. As a dramatic coach, she was nothing if not critical. She thought Marilyn's gestures tense, inhibited, and unnatural. She hated Marilyn's affectation of refusing to move her lips when she spoke. She found Marilyn's voice so irritating that she asked her to refrain from talking unnecessarily until they had a chance to work together. She had Marilyn slowly read a book to a lamp, emphasizing the first and last letter of each word. Marilyn, who adored working with Natasha, never missed a session.

When Harry Cohn failed to renew Marilyn's contract, she rushed to Natasha's apartment in despair. Marilyn hardly knew her coach, but she had no other friends and nowhere else to go. Marilyn was crying and Natasha guessed that she might be about to try something foolish. Natasha asked Marilyn to do her a favor. She asked her to promise that for the next twenty-four hours she would not be afraid. Years afterward, Natasha traced the start of their friendship to that moment.

Their working sessions exploded with emotion. Both women were totally invested in Marilyn's ability to become a star, and Marilyn was often in tears. Natasha never tired of reminding her that she had picked her up when she was nothing and given her life. Constantly she reiterated that her lessons were more valuable than anything money could buy. She frequently complained that she was humiliated when people gave her credit for Marilyn's sexy mannerisms. It hurt Marilyn when, as she often did, Natasha treated her as though she were an imbecile.

Natasha's attitude toward Marilyn was deeply contradictory. On the one hand, she resented her own dependence on this girl, whom she thought so vulgar and inferior. On the other hand, Natasha spotted something unique in Marilyn, something she believed that she, the teacher, could shape and create. Natasha gave Marilyn books to read: Rilke, Tolstoy, Dostoevsky, and Proust. She made her listen to recordings of Schubert and Brahms. Natasha, confident that she already was somebody, seemed angry that the world no longer treated her as it should.

Marilyn, by contrast, was struggling to become somebody. She wasn't trying to regain her rightful place; she was trying to discover it.

For *Love Nest* and *Let's Make It Legal*, Marilyn insisted on working out her entire performance—every word, gesture, breath, and eye movement—before she even met the director and other actors. She prepared for these small roles as though she had the lead. Natasha discovered early on that Marilyn had an instinct for recognizing when she was doing something right. At the same time, she could detect any kind of falseness in her own performance. It wasn't something Marilyn had learned; she couldn't really explain it. But an alarm just seemed to go off inside her when she finally discovered the correct approach.

Marilyn was a perfectionist—but at immense psychological cost. Sensing that something was wrong didn't mean that Marilyn had any idea of how to fix it. Even if Natasha had been tempted, she would never have suggested that something Marilyn did was good just to make her feel better. Marilyn might have sensed her dishonesty, and that would have been fatal to the partnership. Marilyn was determined to keep working until she got things right; when she didn't, which was quite often, a sense of desperation pervaded the room.

One consequence of all this pressure was Marilyn's increasing dependency on drugs. She haunted the prescription counter at Schwab's drugstore in Hollywood. She couldn't sleep, so she took barbiturates. She felt drowsy, so she took amphetamines. From the time Marilyn began to menstruate, she had suffered severe monthly pain, which doctors later attributed to the presence of endometrial tissue in areas other than the uterus, a condition called endometriosis. As she grew older, not only did the pain increase, but she built up a tolerance to medication, driving her to ever larger doses. She experimented with different kinds of pills. More and more, a diet of painkillers, tranquilizers, and stimulants left Marilyn perilously on edge.

In these months, the photograph of Arthur Miller remained on the bookshelf over Marilyn's bed, a reminder of why she drove herself so hard. She told herself that Arthur might see one of her movies in New York. She imagined he would go to the theater for the other half of a double bill and see her movie by chance.

Miller wrote to Marilyn that, though he wished her the best, he just wasn't the man to make her life work out as she hoped. He suggested

that if she needed someone to look up to, she would be better off choosing Abraham Lincoln. The suggestion, whether he knew it or not, hinted
at his own ambivalence. Miller bore a distinct physical resemblance to
Lincoln. He had poured out his troubles to Marilyn, and no matter how
he tried to put her off, somehow she remained serenely confident that it
was only a matter of time before he would leave his wife for her.

Marilyn continued to discuss Miller with Kazan. As she worked on
the director for a role, she persisted in feeding him details of her troubled
relationship with Miller. Even at a time when Arthur had retreated from
Marilyn's life, the triangle remained a big part of their affair.

After two weeks of rehearsal in Los Angeles, Kazan went off to
shoot *Viva Zapata!* on location in Brownsville and Del Rio, Texas. His
family was due to join him as soon as school let out. Marilyn had previously been scheduled to begin a third picture at Twentieth after *Let's
Make It Legal*, but at the last minute, the film was called off. Though the
cancellation had nothing to do with Marilyn, geared up as she was, the
change of plans upset her terribly. In this state of mind, she turned up
suddenly in Brownsville before Mrs. Kazan and the children arrived.

Kazan had problems of his own just then; it had been widely
rumored that he was about to be called by HUAC. He would be asked
the so-called Big Question—had he ever been a Party member? Though
he had long ago repudiated his connection with the Party, he would then
be asked to submit to the ritual humiliation of identifying other
Communists. If for whatever reason Kazan declined, he faced not only a
jail sentence but also the prospect of being blacklisted in the movie
industry. Still, the feeling on the set of *Viva Zapata!* was that Kazan, so
tough and brash, would refuse to submit.

After Marilyn arrived, it seemed to the actor Anthony Quinn that
Kazan was trying to "negotiate a bizarre little love triangle" consisting of
Marilyn, Kazan himself, and Marlon Brando. In the beginning, it was no
secret that Marilyn was there to be with Kazan. But soon the director
appeared to throw her at Brando, or so it seemed to Quinn, who suspected that Kazan, in the interest of heating up the situation, wanted to
"cross swords with Marlon over his protégée."

This wasn't how Marilyn had hoped to find herself on a Kazan set.
She had wanted to appear in a film of his, not simply to watch him direct.
Nonetheless, the entire experience thrilled her. The chance to observe

Kazan and Brando at work whetted her appetite for a whole different level of filmmaking. On location, Marilyn saw for herself how good Kazan was, and she went home more determined than ever to work with him.

In Los Angeles, Kazan picked up with Marilyn again. She made certain of that. Though his wife and children were installed in a beach house at Malibu, Marilyn often accompanied Kazan to the Fox ranch, where some additional scenes were being shot. Afterward, accompanied by Kazan's friend, the magazine photographer Sam Shaw, they would go to roadhouses to play the jukebox, drink beer, and dance. Shaw, who shot the stills on *Zapata*, was to become Marilyn's close, lifelong friend.

Marilyn seemed to be having fun, but underneath the happy-girl mask she was frantic about Twentieth's failure to give her a new assignment. Had she done something wrong? Had she already blown her chance? What Marilyn didn't know was that the studio was considering a request from RKO to borrow her. Meanwhile, Marilyn was desperate to be doing something to advance her career.

In the absence of the prestigious roles Johnny had prescribed, Marilyn decided to get attention in some other way. Day after day, she turned up at the Fox publicity office, eager for any assignment. She wanted to talk to reporters. She wanted to be photographed. She was willing to pose in any and all circumstances. Posing for still photographs never caused Marilyn the sort of anxiety that going in front of a motion picture camera invariably did. When the studio publicity people had nothing for her, she danced attendance on the show-business columnist Sidney Skolsky, who had an "office" in Schwab's drugstore. Marilyn enlisted Skolsky's help in preparing sympathetic stories about her to feed to the press. Skolsky frequently mentioned "the Monroe" in his own columns and encouraged his colleagues to do the same.

Touched by Marilyn's efforts to get publicity, Kazan asked Shaw to take some pictures for her portfolio. Shaw protested that photographing pretty girls wasn't his line, but Kazan insisted. Marilyn turned up for the shoot in a black gaberdine suit, stiletto heels, and a cute little white beret. Shaw, uncomfortable with the assignment, decided to do the pictures as a satire. He photographed Marilyn, wearing horn-rimmed glasses, reading Vernon Louis Parrington's thick tome on the history of American literature. When Kazan saw what Shaw had done, he was outraged. "You son of a bitch!" Kazan barked. "That's a satirical thing. You're making fun of the kid!" Kazan, almost in spite of himself, seemed really to care about her.

Kazan took his family home on August 11. There was a last-minute censorship crisis over A Streetcar Named Desire, and he needed to be in New York. The remaining post-production work on Zapata could wait until he returned to Los Angeles. While in the east, Kazan met up with Miller, who was once again in crisis. That month, As Young as You Feel had its premiere in New York. Seven months had passed since Miller and Kazan had first glimpsed Marilyn on the Fox sound stage. Almost seven months had passed since Miller had decided to resist his attraction to her and go back to his wife. Miller told Kazan that he had done every-thing he could to save his marriage, but that it was no use. After California, Arthur felt that Mary had shown no willingness to forgive. According to Miller, their household, across the East River in Brooklyn Heights, remained a harsh, cold, loveless place.

When Marilyn heard about Arthur's decision, she rushed to New York to see him. But it was no good. At the last minute, he called off their meeting. He had decided to try yet again with his wife. Marilyn, hurt and humiliated, spent some time at her hotel with Kazan. She flew back to Los Angeles in the morning. By the time she got back, she had filed away the whole Miller episode as something that wasn't going to happen. The fantasy that such a man was going to swoop into her life and fall in love with her appeared to have ended. Marilyn had her work to occupy her. Hardly had she returned to Hollywood when exciting new developments demanded her full attention. Indeed, it appeared that Marilyn's efforts were finally about to pay off.

+   +   +

Suddenly, Marilyn seemed to be making progress on several fronts at once. On August 21, Twentieth officially agreed to loan Marilyn out to RKO, where she was to appear in Clash by Night, a screen adaptation of Clifford Odets's play. Marilyn's assignment was a major breakthrough in two ways. She would be working with Fritz Lang, the director of such classics as Metropolis, M, and Fury, and she would receive star billing, though in fact she was to have only a supporting role as a worker in a fish-canning factory. For the first time, her name would appear above the title, along with those of Barbara Stanwyck, Paul Douglas, and Robert Ryan.

Two weeks after the contracts for the loan-out were signed, Collier's magazine published the first full-scale profile of Marilyn Monroe. The article, "1951's Model Blonde," was an extraordinary achievement for a young actress who, after all, had yet to do a single starring role. From the first, she discovered that she was confident and at ease with reporters in a way that she simply never was on a film set. For the Collier's profile, in the issue of September 8, 1951, Marilyn carefully crafted the story that she would repeat to reporters all that fall. In interview after interview, Marilyn portrayed herself as a courageous little orphan girl, a sort of modern-day Cinderella, whose childhood had been spent being passed from one foster home to another. She painted her youth in the darkest possible tones, leaving readers with the impression that both her mother and father were dead. That last point would soon come back to haunt her, but the immediate effect of all this was to make Marilyn Monroe immensely sympathetic to the public.

The Collier's profile and the many newspaper and magazine pieces that followed encouraged people to root for Marilyn. Readers who had never even seen Marilyn in a film wanted her to succeed in Hollywood, allowing the fairy tale she'd spun to have a happy ending. It quickly became apparent from Marilyn's fan mail at Twentieth that her one-woman publicity campaign was working. Through her own shrewd efforts, she had attracted a huge following that was entirely out of proportion to the small roles she had played to date. Had Twentieth made a mistake in loaning Marilyn out for her first film with star billing? On the basis of all the publicity, even Darryl Zanuck began to wonder.

When Marilyn wasn't preparing for her upcoming film with Natasha, she worked with a second acting teacher, Michael Chekhov. Terrified that she couldn't possibly get through the assignment at RKO alone, she requested permission for Natasha to accompany her. Marilyn's self-reliance in matters of publicity contrasted sharply with her utter dependence on her dramatic coach. Lang permitted Marilyn to bring her on one condition: that Natasha refrain from going over Marilyn's lines at home. He didn't want Marilyn's interpretation of the role to be locked in before she had an opportunity to work with the director and the other actors.

This arrangement was a problem from the start. Lang, attempting to direct Marilyn, initially had no idea that Natasha stood directly behind him. It was a strange sight, almost comical: The director grimly studied Marilyn from his canvas chair as a wraithlike woman with flashing eyes gestured behind his back. Marilyn and Natasha had worked out a code that Natasha compared to the signals between a catcher and a pitcher in baseball. After a take, as Lang clarified what he wanted, Marilyn, barely listening, would surreptitiously glance over his shoulder. Even when Lang wanted to move on to the next setup, if Natasha failed to nod, Marilyn insisted on another take. It took a while before the director figured out what was going on, but when he did he angrily banished Natasha.

Marilyn—an odd combination of fear and ferocity—reacted with horror. She was painfully insecure about her abilities, and believed she needed Natasha to keep going. She was convinced she just couldn't do it alone. Yet she was ready to fight for what she needed, and she was prepared to shut down the production if she didn't get her way. She refused to work without her dramatic coach. Eventually, Jerry Wald, the head of RKO, negotiated a compromise. Natasha could return to the set, but under no circumstances was she to send hand signals to Marilyn.

Word of the trouble Lang was having with Marilyn drifted back to Twentieth, where Zanuck, under pressure from Skouras, was thinking of giving her her first real starring role. The film was Roy Baker's *Don't Bother to Knock*, in which Marilyn would play a beautiful psychotic, reflecting Zanuck's perception of her as sexually dangerous and not a little mad. His view was based on the talk in Hollywood that somehow Marilyn had been responsible for Johnny Hyde's death. Some of Johnny's friends, the screenwriter Nunnally Johnson for instance, liked to say that Johnny had died like a man. Others remarked that poor Johnny, unable to stay away from Marilyn, had screwed himself to death.

Zanuck was by no means convinced that Marilyn was ready—if she ever would be ready—to carry a film. He insisted that she take a screen test. If she did well, she could have the part of Nell, the baby-sitter who nearly murders a child because she believes it poses an obstacle to her love affair. For the moment, the screen test became the focus of Marilyn's existence. She worked round the clock with Natasha to prepare. On the day of the test, Marilyn, terrified of going through the ordeal alone, sneaked Natasha onto the set.

The test, as it turned out, was a success. Zanuck quickly threw another obstacle in her path. Citing the test as evidence that Marilyn didn't need a coach, he refused to allow Natasha on the set of *Don't Bother to Knock*, telling Marilyn that it would lead to chaos if every actor or actress demanded special coaching from the sidelines. He insisted that Marilyn was quite capable of acting in a film under the sole guidance of the director. "You have built up a Svengali," he wrote to her in a memo, "and if you are going to progress with your career and become as important talent-wise as you have publicity-wise then you must destroy this Svengali before it destroys you."

Natasha was in an exceedingly awkward position. What happened at RKO had been of little concern to her. She worked for Twentieth, Johnny Hyde having arranged for her to be hired when he negotiated Marilyn's contract. Darryl Zanuck was Natasha's boss, and she did not want to be in any sort of trouble with him. His references to her as Marilyn's Svengali were alarming. She did not want to risk her job by being seen to interfere between Marilyn and her director

At first, Marilyn agreed to work without her coach, but repeatedly she rushed off the set to call Natasha's office. They reviewed scenes together before Marilyn actually performed them. Meanwhile, Marilyn barraged Zanuck with letters imploring him to allow her to have Natasha. Finally, Natasha received the call she had been dreading. The production was well under way when Marilyn announced that she would not work another day without her coach. Zanuck, with a good deal of film already in the can, had little choice but to agree. Natasha was ordered to report to the Western Avenue stage at once.

Roy Baker, pale and slight, was directing his first film in Hollywood, after having made *I'll Never Forget You* for Fox in England. He was clearly irritated by Natasha, whom he regarded as Marilyn's security blanket. Natasha took Marilyn aside and reminded her of the difficult position she had put her in. In view of Baker's resentment, they must tread carefully. If the director was displeased with their work, Natasha would be crucified.

In the days that followed, Marilyn repeatedly blew her lines. Though she gave the appearance of having come to the set unprepared, in fact, the truth was the very opposite. Marilyn resembled a student who has studied too hard for a crucial test. She knew her lines perfectly well, but when it was time to deliver them, she just blanked out. One had to wonder why Marilyn persisted in putting herself through this anguish. The answer was that her drive to be effective on screen was every bit as strong as her fear and insecurity.

On the last day of filming, Marilyn appeared utterly unfamiliar with the scene she was supposed to be working on. The more the director shouted, the worse she seemed to tense up. Finally, Marilyn announced that she had to confer with Natasha. Baker, exasperated, pointed out that he was quite capable of providing all the help she required. Marilyn, in front of everyone, replied that he wasn't. Baker permitted Marilyn to work with her coach. They shot the scene and it was perfect. Then he marched to the telephone and arranged for Natasha to be dismissed.

These problems notwithstanding, Marilyn's first starring role turned out to be not so bad after all. The consensus at the studio was that she was pretty enough, and that somehow all the frenzy on the set had fed into the unstable character Marilyn portrayed. Zanuck, pleased with Marilyn's performance, decided to look around for another dramatic role for her. Meanwhile, she was given minor assignments in Edmund Goulding's *We're Not Married*, Henry Koster's *O. Henry's Full House*, and Howard Hawks's *Monkey Business*.

A chance for Marilyn to work with Hawks, one of Hollywood's finest directors, was precisely the sort of thing Johnny would have welcomed. Hawks was convinced that "the girl," as he called Marilyn, had enormous potential. He had been tremendously impressed with her in *The Asphalt Jungle*. More recently, Hawks had suggested to Zanuck that she'd been improperly cast in *Don't Bother to Knock*. The significance of *Monkey Business* was not that it got Marilyn noticed, as the Huston and Mankiewicz films had done, but that it presented an opportunity for Hawks to figure out how Marilyn should be used. When he knew that, he'd have the formula that would enable Marilyn to become a star.

Soon after Marilyn began work with Hawks on February 26, 1952, she had an appendix attack. Hospitalized, she refused surgery lest Zanuck pull her out of the film. Marilyn was not about to permit anything, not even excruciating pain, to impede the momentum of her career. Her doctors agreed to freeze the appendix so that Marilyn could finish her assignment. No sooner had she returned to the set, however, than a fresh crisis threatened to derail her. She was summoned to

Zanuck's office, where he and the studio publicity director, Harry Brand, confronted her with information they had received from a UP wire service reporter, Aline Mosby. According to Mosby, Marilyn had posed for a popular nude calendar that adorned the walls of gas stations and barber shops across America. Zanuck warned Marilyn that if the story broke, her career could be destroyed. Every Hollywood contract contained a morals clause which permitted the studio to fire an artist for offensive behavior. Zanuck personally had no objection to the calendar, but if there was a public outcry he would have to dismiss her.

Marilyn admitted to having posed for the calendar in 1949. Unfortunately, Johnny Hyde had been in Europe to attend Rita Hayworth's wedding to Prince Aly Khan, so when Marilyn needed cash she did what she often did in such circumstances—she hired herself out as a model. On this particular occasion, she called up a cheesecake photographer named Tom Kelley, who had previously asked her to pose in the nude. She had refused at the time, but now she changed her mind. He gave her fifty dollars for the session.

The consensus among studio executives was that Marilyn should deny that she was the naked girl stretched out on rumpled red velvet. When she sought his advice afterward, Sidney Skolsky recommended the opposite. He urged Marilyn to be honest about what she had done and told her to give the story exclusively to Mosby, who, besides having tipped off the studio about the calendar, had written a warm account of Marilyn's childhood a few months previously. Harry Brand, alone among Fox executives, supported Marilyn's decision to tell the truth. As for Marilyn herself, not only was she brilliant with the press, but she knew how good she was. Better yet, she was capable of masking that confidence so that everything she said appeared to be utterly innocent and uncalculated.

"Oh, the calendar's hanging in garages all over town," Marilyn told Mosby over lunch. "Why deny it? You can get one anyplace. Besides, I'm not ashamed of it. I've done nothing wrong. I was told I should deny I'd posed . . . but I'd rather be honest about it."

When Mosby's story appeared in newspapers on March 13, 1952, the overwhelmingly favorable public reaction was a testament to the publicity campaign that Marilyn had launched in *Collier's* magazine five months previously. People had nothing but sympathy for the heroine of "the greatest Cinderella story in Hollywood history." To judge by the fan letters with which Twentieth was inundated, the self-styled "courageous little orphan girl" could do no wrong.

Two days after the Mosby piece, Marilyn, taking no chances, seized an opportunity to endear herself further to the American public by going on a blind date with Joe DiMaggio. She and Skolsky agreed that there could be no better character reference than the nation's favorite athlete-hero, and he planned to break the news in his column. DiMaggio, who had retired from baseball three months previously at the age of thirty-seven, was known as the greatest living ballplayer. He was idolized and revered. If "the last American knight" thought Marilyn Monroe a fine decent girl, what could anyone else say against her?

The meeting took place the following Saturday night at the dimly-lit Villa Nova restaurant on the Sunset Strip. DiMaggio preferred dark restaurants. The date had been arranged by David March, who hoped to be hired as Marilyn's business manager. DiMaggio, fascinated by a publicity photograph of Marilyn in brief white shorts, a snug sweater, and open-toe high heels, posing with a baseball player named Gus Zernial, had asked his friend March for an introduction. Under other circumstances Marilyn might not have agreed, but at the moment the potential for publicity was irresistible.

DiMaggio, nursing a sweet vermouth on the rocks in the last booth on the left, was tall and long-boned, with wavy, precisely parted, graying hair and flaring nostrils. It was said that DiMaggio's profile came to a point at the end of his nose. He had sad brown eyes, long eyelashes and a conspicuous overbite. He had broad shoulders and massive, strong arms, with enormous wrists. He chain-smoked Camels as he waited, wearing a gray flannel suit, a white shirt, and a blue polka-dot tie. He was graceful and subdued. There was a poignant air of remoteness about him. The sportswriter Jimmy Cannon, one of DiMaggio's closest friends, once described him as one of the loneliest men he'd ever met, adding, "I doubt if anyone fully understands his lonely character."

The dinner was arranged for 6:30. David March and his girlfriend, sipping dry Martinis, were sitting with DiMaggio when Marilyn walked in, two hours late. DiMaggio bashfully told Marilyn that he was glad to meet her, his strident voice competing with the schmaltzy Italian music on the sound system. His long face was oddly expressionless, a reminder of why some people called him Dead Pan Joe. Instead of the garishly-dressed sports figure Marilyn had expected, DiMaggio reminded her of a steel magnate or a Congressman. His endearing shyness reminded her of Arthur Miller.

"There's a blue polka dot exactly in the middle of your tie knot," she said, in an effort to break the ice. "Did it take you long to fix it just that way?"

That was virtually the extent of their conversation. DiMaggio never talked much, leading a friend to remark once that when Joe said hello, it was a long conversation. March told some funny stories about his experiences in Hollywood and Mickey Rooney bounded over to display his knowledge of DiMaggio's feats on the baseball field. Ignoring hints and signals that he ought to leave, Rooney monopolized his hero for most of the evening. After about an hour and a half, Marilyn went home. DiMaggio called the next day to ask her to dine with him alone. She refused, DiMaggio persisted, and finally Marilyn agreed to an intimate dinner with him on Wednesday the 19th.

By March 17, when Skolsky revealed to America that Marilyn was dating Joe DiMaggio, there was no question at Twentieth that she had turned the nude calendar scandal into perhaps the greatest publicity coup in Hollywood history. Marilyn hadn't distinguished herself on screen yet, but as each day passed she was becoming an increasingly valuable commodity. Everyone at the studio would have known exactly what it meant when Charlie Feldman arrived on the set of *Monkey Business* on March 18 to see Marilyn. Ordinarily he would have sent one of his staff to court a new client. That he came himself, and that he talked quietly with Marilyn for a long while on the fringe of the set, was a sure sign Feldman was concerned that every agency in town would soon be after her.

The day Feldman went to see Marilyn, he was in an exceptionally good mood. *A Streetcar Named Desire*, which had opened to critical acclaim in September, was nominated for twelve Oscars. The awards ceremony was two days away, and Feldman and Jack Warner predicted that the picture would sweep the major awards. In addition, Feldman was sure this would be the first time all four acting citations went to one film.

Since the New York critics had chosen *A Streetcar Named Desire* as their best picture of the year, Warner, who had backed the film with

Feldman, had virtually been begging Williams and Kazan to do another project for him. The playwright and the director were both very hot at the moment. When they couldn't come to Los Angeles, Feldman and Jack Warner went to New York. In discussions with Audrey Wood, Warner emphasized that he didn't just want to make a deal, he wanted to make an "important" deal. Feldman knew that Warner was prepared to pay handsomely for *Baby Doll*, the screenplay Williams was writing in close consultation with Kazan, based on his one-act plays *27 Wagons Full of Cotton* and *The Unsatisfactory Supper*.

Marilyn wasn't surprised when, just as she was preparing to go out on her second date with Joe DiMaggio, she had a call from Kazan, who had arrived from New York and checked into the Bel Air Hotel. Tennessee Williams was staying there, too, along with his agent, Audrey Wood, and her husband. Wood had arrived in Los Angeles determined not to show Warner the screenplay-in-progress until there was a signed contract, though she brought a typed copy just in case. Fortunately, Warner seemed even more anxious than she to put a deal in place.

One might have expected Kazan to be on top of the world. In private, however, he was in turmoil. HUAC was again holding hearings about the entertainment world. The trio of Kazan, Clifford Odets, and Lillian Hellman, all former Communist Party members, came from Broadway's upper echelon. They were precisely the sort of successful, prosperous people who tended to be friendly witnesses, if only because they had so much to lose. All three of them would be called in this round of hearings. Indeed, Kazan had already been interrogated. On January 14, 1952, in secret testimony in Washington, D.C., Kazan admitted to having briefly been a Communist but refused to identify other Party members. Afterward, he had chest pains. His hands trembled. He had difficulty sleeping. He worried that if Jack Warner learned about his refusal to name names, the deal would be off. Back in New York, Kazan had been summoned by Spyros Skouras, who urged Kazan to change his HUAC testimony. He offered personally to accompany Kazan to Washington, and made it clear that if Kazan failed to name names, he would never direct another Hollywood film.

Kazan had a great deal on his mind as he arrived in Los Angeles on March 19. When he picked up a copy of that day's *Hollywood Reporter*, his worst fears were realized: "Elia Kazan, subpoenaed for the

Un-American Activities Committee session, confessed Commie membership but refused to supply any new evidence on his old pals from the Group Theater days." Aware of the impact the item was likely to have, he telephoned Marilyn as a way of forgetting his troubles. She seemed to occupy another plane of existence, one that had nothing to do with HUAC. She was on her way out to a dinner date, she explained, but she would come to the Bel Air Hotel afterward. He left the door unlocked and fell asleep.

Marilyn spent the evening with Joe. Finally, she entered Kazan's room at 3:30 a.m. and crept into bed. At this point, she knew nothing of the film he was supposed to be setting up with Warner. She was unaware that he had in his hands the project she longed for, with a lead role that would have been perfect for her. Excitedly Marilyn told him that after tonight she didn't plan to see him again. She had found the man she wanted to marry. Naturally, Kazan assumed she meant Arthur Miller.

"He comes all the way down from San Francisco just to have dinner with me," Marilyn added, "and we haven't even done it yet!"

Kazan, puzzled, asked who she was talking about.

"Joe," said Marilyn. "He wants to marry me, and I really like him. He's not like these movie people. He's dignified."

Kazan listened to Marilyn chatter on about Joe DiMaggio; then he made love to her.

The next day, instead of the sweep Charlie Feldman and Jack Warner had predicted, A Streetcar Named Desire won four awards: Vivien Leigh for Best Actress, Karl Malden for Best Supporting Actor, Kim Hunter for Best Supporting Actress, and Richard Day and George James Hopkins for Best Art Direction and Set Decoration. An American in Paris was named Best Picture, and A Place in the Sun picked up the prizes for direction and writing. Humphrey Bogart, in The African Queen, won for Best Actor. Feldman was convinced they had been robbed. Worse, Hollywood's attitude to Kazan appeared to have changed overnight. The item in the Hollywood Reporter had been devastating. Overnight, Jack Warner lost interest in Baby Doll. Overnight, the director everyone wanted to work with became a pariah.

Marilyn's resolve not to see Kazan again proved short-lived. That evening she was his date at what was to have been a post-Academy Awards celebration at Charlie Feldman's house. He needed comforting, so once again Marilyn played the role of Kazan's girl. Her willingness to accompany him suggested that she might have a harder time than she had anticipated keeping her vow to break off with him. Had he been given the green light on *Baby Doll*, one wonders whether she would have been able to stay away at all.

+   +   +

When Kazan left Hollywood, Tennessee Williams had the impression that he was going to continue to refuse to disclose the identities of fellow Communist Party members, whatever the cost. Williams admired Kazan's courage and sense of honor. At home with Molly and the children, however, Kazan began to waver. One afternoon, Kermit Bloomgarden heard pebbles clattering against the window of his second-floor office overlooking Broadway. He glanced out and saw Kazan, who had an office in the same building, standing on the sidewalk, waving to him to come down. Over coffee at Dinty Moore's nearby, Kazan indicated that he might be about to do as Spyros Skouras demanded. Kazan's hair had started to go gray. Heavy lines had formed around his mouth.

Bloomgarden, who had known Kazan since the Group Theater and had produced *Death of a Salesman*, which Kazan had directed, was horrified by what he heard. He said little until the end, and then stated his position.

"We bring our children up not to tattle."

Kazan made the rounds of the friends and associates he would be required to name. These included Paula Strasberg, who had nearly broken up Kazan's marriage by telling Molly about his affair with Constance Dowling, so there can have been little love lost there. But there was also his great friend Clifford Odets. Powerful feelings flowed between the two men. They were always very physically affectionate with one another, leading a good many people to mistake them for lovers. Since 1939, Odets had lived in daily terror of being exposed as a Communist, but now he and Kazan agreed to name each other. Odets would testify privately on April 24, and publicly in May.

On a dark, rainy morning in early April, Arthur Miller drove from Roxbury to Kazan's farmhouse at Newtown, Connecticut. Having already talked to Bloomgarden, he guessed what he was about to hear.

The rain stopped and the sun came out. As they walked together in the fragrant woods, Kazan told Miller of his decision to name names. Miller put his arm around Gadg and awkwardly pressed the side of his body against his friend. The gesture was familiar. It was the same tense, guilty gesture Miller performed when, called on to embrace a young woman, he did so while turning his body to the side.

Miller had been thinking a lot about guilt lately. His encounter with Marilyn Monroe continued to preoccupy him. In a thin, brown, wire-bound composition book, he had been taking notes on a contemporary play about adultery he hoped to write. The notebook contained ideas and snippets of dialogue. Possible titles included "The Men's Conversation" and "Conversation of Men." The protagonist, Quentin, has recently had an adventure that causes him to confront how much he despises married life, which he compares to a trap. His wife, refusing to forgive, declares that the man she knew could never transgress as Quentin has done. She insists that he crush his daimon—that is, his desire for sex outside the marriage. Quentin longs to free himself of the need for his wife's acceptance and the respectability she represents. Only when it is possible to leave will his decision to stay have any meaning. Quentin seeks a way to remain in the marriage not simply because that is what his wife demands but because that is what he chooses. At the same time, he wonders whether he really wants to abandon the possibility of ever experiencing ecstasy again.

Miller did not progress beyond these notes. Though he customarily found his material in his own life, perhaps he was just too close to it here. He was still in the marriage he was trying to write about. In his notebook, he was working out his own problems rather than those of a fictional character. The wife was transparently Mary. Quentin's dilemma was transparently Miller's.

After hearing what Kazan had to tell him, Miller drove directly to Salem, Massachusetts, to research a new play. Since 1950, Miller had wanted to write something about the Red hysteria. He studied Marion Starkey's *The Devil in Massachusetts* and saw a parallel between the Salem witchcraft trials of 1692 and the hunt for Communists in America. At one point he had given a copy of the book to Kazan, with an eye to their doing a play together. Not until Miller actually went to Salem, however, did he see a way to personalize the material, to make it his.

Poring over old court records, he imagined there might have been an affair between John Proctor and a young servant girl named Abigail Williams, who went on to accuse Proctor's wife, Elizabeth, of witchcraft. In this story, Miller discovered an armature for the adultery play he wanted to write. The historical characters and setting provided the distance that his earlier effort lacked, and the adultery theme invigorated the political, witch-hunt material with a deeply-felt conflict of his own. In his notebook, the playwright skipped three pages and started to take notes on a scene in which Abigail attempts to seduce John Proctor. Those lines were the germ of *The Crucible*.

On April 10, Kazan went to Washington, D.C. to reopen his HUAC hearing. Kazan, who took pride in his ability to conceal his feelings, made it clear that he had returned not because anyone had forced or threatened him, but because he wanted to—he was fully in control. He insisted on testifying in writing. That way he would say precisely what he chose to say and no more. The committee didn't object, so long as he did as they asked and named names.

Kazan identified eight of his former colleagues at the Group Theater, including Paula Strasberg and Clifford Odets. He detailed his own association and disenchantment with the Communist Party. Then he underscored his reasons for breaking with the Party. "The last straw came when I was invited to go through a typical Communist scene of crawling and apologizing and admitting the error of my ways." Kazan seemed unaware that this sentence was shot through with irony. Wasn't crawling, apologizing, and admitting the error of his ways precisely what HUAC had required him to do? In a gesture that irked some people far more than his having named names, Kazan, unbidden, went on to catalogue play by play, film by film, his entire directorial output. He aimed to show that as an artist he had consistently upheld all-American values. It was one thing to have submitted under duress. It was quite another to have gone to such elaborate lengths to justify his own act of betrayal.

For all the talk of duty, the final, seemingly perfunctory and anticlimactic sentence of Kazan's testimony pointed to a very different reason for his change of heart. "I have placed a copy of this affidavit with Mr. Spyros P. Skouras, president of Twentieth Century–Fox."

On May 19 and 20, Clifford Odets gave a comparable performance, naming names and chronicling his own disenchantment with the

Communist Party. Of the elite Broadway trio, only Lillian Hellman declined to be intimidated. She faced HUAC on the 21st. A controlling, abrasive, outspoken character rather like Kazan, she, too, chose to read a carefully-crafted letter to the committee. Unlike Kazan, however, Hellman refused to name names, declaring memorably, "I cannot and will not cut my conscience to fit this year's fashions."

Tennessee Williams, insisting he wasn't a political person, declined to take a position on what Kazan had done. Privately, Williams told his friend Maria Britneva that human venality was something he always expected and forgave. Kazan published an advertisement in the *New York Times* to defend what he had done and to urge others to do the same. It was rumored to have been paid for by Skouras. Williams, full of compassion, told Audrey Wood that the advertisement was a sad comment on the times. Some of Kazan's other friends were less forgiving. A few months after his testimony, Kazan was on his way out of his office building when he encountered Miller and Bloomgarden. The playwright and the producer, on their way in, pointedly ignored him.

Kazan's testimony also brought closure to his relationship with Marilyn. After the strain of the HUAC testimony and its aftermath, Kazan chose to shoot his next picture for Twentieth in Europe. It would be some time before he returned to Hollywood. As a result, Marilyn never had an opportunity to find out whether she really would have held to her decision not to see him again. Kazan's prolonged absence cleared the field for Joe DiMaggio.

+ THREE +

At last, Darryl Zanuck announced that he had found a second starring role for Marilyn. Ignoring the conversation he'd had with Howard Hawks, he put her in another drama, but this time, in keeping with the splash the calendar scandal had made, the film was to be a much larger, more expensive production than *Don't Bother to Knock*. Marilyn was to play a murderess in Henry Hathaway's *Niagara*, to be shot on location at Niagara Falls. She was very excited. Another big role meant that her career was really taking off. Expecting to begin pre-production at the end of May, Marilyn checked into Cedars of Lebanon Hospital as soon as she finished *Monkey Business*.

On the morning of April 28, 1952, Marilyn's appendix was removed. When a nurse wheeled her back into her room, it was filled with dozens of roses from Joe, who was then away in New York. Slugger, as Marilyn called DiMaggio, had spent a good deal of time lately at her book-filled studio apartment. She said he was the best lover she ever had.

Within hours of surgery, Marilyn received word that a new scandal was brewing. The news came as a complete shock. Erskine Johnson of the *L.A. Daily News* had contacted Twentieth Century–Fox with information that Marilyn's mother, a fifty-year-old former mental patient, was very much alive. In other words, it appeared that Marilyn, the self-styled courageous little orphan girl, had misled the press, and this time she was not going to be able to handle the matter as blithely as she had the question of the nude calendar. In some quarters, Marilyn was being accused of having lied to her fans. Would the public turn on her? Marilyn, ever watchful for threats to her dream, had reason to fear that the bad publicity would jeopardize her role in *Niagara*.

In addition to her concerns over the film, Marilyn worried that reporters might actually seek out her mentally ill mother, who was then living with Grace and Doc in Van Nuys. It had been Grace who advised Marilyn to claim that her parents were dead. Better to lie, she counseled, than to allow people to find out about Gladys.

In the beginning, Norma Jeane hadn't even known that Gladys was her mother. For her first seven years, she had lived in a six-room house in Hawthorne with a religious couple named Wayne and Ida Bolender, who took in foster children to augment Wayne's salary as a mailman. Every so often a small, strange, silent woman visited Norma Jeane in the living room, which was decorated with a red print rug, a ramshackle piano, a coffee table piled with religious books, a pair of ceramic cry-baby dolls, and an old rocking chair. "The woman with the red hair," as Norma Jeane called her, was Gladys Baker. Norma Jeane feared and dreaded her visits, which recalled her earliest, inexplicable memory—Gladys's attempt to smother her in her crib.

Once, when Ida Bolender was giving Norma Jeane a bath, the three-year-old called her "mommy."

"I'm not your mommy," Ida corrected her. "Call me Aunt."

"But he's my daddy!" said Norma Jeane, pointing to Wayne.

"No, we're not your parents," said Ida. "The one who comes here with the red hair, she's your mother."

Gladys was born in Mexico on May 27, 1902. Her mother, Della May Monroe, was later diagnosed as suffering from manic-depressive psychosis. Her father, Otis Elmer Monroe, an American house-painter who had crossed the border in search of employment, had syphilis. Soon after Gladys's birth, the Monroes returned to California, where Della gave birth to a son, Marion, in 1905. Syphilis caused Otis's mental health to deteriorate, and in 1908 he entered Southern California State Hospital in Patton. Suffering from dementia in the final stages of syphilis, he died on July 22, 1909.

Della, lamenting that Gladys and Marion would no doubt wind up in a mental institution like their father, remarried. Her second husband, Lyle Graves, had a drinking problem and a violent temper. In one outburst, he hurled Gladys's pet kitten against a brick wall. The cat died and

Della fled with her children. She sent Marion to live with relatives and found a one-room apartment in Venice. The landlord, thin-lipped, jug-eared Jap Baker, hired her to manage the property while he operated a game concession at the beach. Before long Della had a new boyfriend, Charles Grainger. She wanted to move in with him, but he objected to her daughter's presence.

By this time, Gladys, fine-boned and barely five feet tall, had full high breasts, a long narrow tapered back, and rounded hips. Her reddish hair fell back in waves from her prominent widow's peak. At fourteen, Gladys became pregnant by her mother's twenty-six-year-old employer. Instead of being upset, Della instantly saw a way to realize her dream of moving in with Charles Grainger. Ten days before Gladys's fifteenth birthday, Della, giving the child's age as eighteen, signed her daughter's application for a marriage license.

The marriage was calamitous from the first. Gladys was unprepared for the responsibilities of motherhood, and Jap Baker proved to be a violent drinker like her stepfather. Gladys's first child was the ill-fated Robert Kermit Baker, whom they nicknamed Jackie. There followed a daughter, Berniece.

Gladys was nineteen, her hair bleached to a light shade of blonde, when Jap drove them in an open car to see his family in Flat Lick, Kentucky, near the Tennessee border. On the way up into the southeast mountains, Jap and Gladys quarreled fiercely. They failed to notice when three-year-old Jackie, sitting alone on the rear seat, tumbled out of the car. The boy's hip injuries left him permanently lame. The quarreling continued in Flat Lick, where Gladys, wearing a tight dress, disappeared into the mountains with Jap's older brother. When Jap found her, he whipped her with a leather bridle. Gladys escaped finally and ran into town, displaying her bloodied back to anyone who would look. She shouted at passersby that she was frightened of her husband. On the way home to California, Jap pulled over on a desolate road in Arizona. He dragged Gladys out of the car and pounded her head with his fists.

Gladys divorced Jap and was awarded custody of Jackie and Berniece. Jap, pretending to take the children for the weekend, kidnapped them to Flat Lick, believing that they would be better off raised by his own mother. Gladys pursued Jap, but no one would help her get her children back. Flat Lick was Jap's turf and everyone seemed to take his side. Gladys supported herself by cleaning houses in Flat Lick for a time, but after Jap married a local widow—one of the people to whom Gladys had displayed her bloodied back—Gladys returned to California to start a new life alone.

In Los Angeles, Gladys found work as a negative cutter at Consolidated Film Industries—thus the persistent smell of glue that her daughter remembered years after—and there she met Grace McKee, who became a lifelong friend. Under the influence of Grace, a peroxide blonde, Gladys changed her hair color to bright red. The women, who shared an apartment in Silverlake, caroused with a good many men from the film lab and the studios. On October 11, 1924, Gladys married Martin Edward Mortenson, a meterman, but walked out after four months and moved back in with Grace.

In the fall of 1925, Gladys became pregnant, possibly by Stanley Gifford, her lab supervisor. Gifford, recently divorced, would not acknowledge the child or help Gladys. Though Mortenson had filed for divorce on grounds of desertion, he was still legally Gladys's husband and therefore by law the father, unless someone proved otherwise. Gladys dealt with the fact of her pregnancy alone; she did not even tell Grace, and her own mother had gone off with Charles Grainger to the Far East. At 9:30 a.m. on June 1, 1926, four days after her lonely twenty-fourth birthday, Gladys gave birth to Norma Jeane in the charity ward of Los Angeles General Hospital. Oddly, she listed Norma Jeane as her third but only living child, and gave the father as Edward Mortenson, address unknown. Discharged from the hospital, Gladys went directly to a furnished room. For lack of a crib, the baby slept in a dresser drawer. Eventually, Gladys had to go back to work, so she placed Norma Jeane with the Bolenders, who lived across the street from Della's bungalow in Hawthorne. She paid them $25 a month.

When Della returned alone from the Far East, she seemed totally mad. There were disturbing incidents. On one occasion, Ida Bolender watched in horror as Norma Jeane's grandmother ran across the street naked and tried to kick down Ida's door. Finally, on August 4, 1927, when Norma Jeane was fourteen months old, Della was removed to Norwalk State Hospital, where she died in a straitjacket nineteen days later.

"We have to watch that one very carefully," Ida said of Norma Jeane to her husband. Ida tapped her temple and spun her finger round and round. "It's in her family, you know."

No wonder Norma Jeane was afraid of the woman with the red hair.

When Gladys took Norma Jeane to her apartment for short visits, Gladys sat rigidly. She rarely talked. She never smiled. She was acutely sensitive to sound, and the tiniest noises seemed to overwhelm her. When her daughter tried to lose herself in a book, Gladys complained about the noise of the turning pages.

On the wall in Gladys's bedroom, where Norma Jeane liked to hide in the closet, hung the framed photograph of a man who bore a distinct resemblance to Clark Gable. When her daughter asked who the man was, Gladys claimed that he was Norma Jeane's father. The image, shadowed in memory, haunted Norma Jeane for the rest of her years.

Norma Jeane picked up a stray dog who came to live with her at the Bolenders. She called her pet Tippy, and she was devoted to him. Every morning the little black-and-white dog followed her to the Washington School, waiting outside until she was finished. When Norma Jeane was seven, a neighbor attacked Tippy with a garden hoe, and, in front of the screaming child, sliced the dog in two. The incident appears to have triggered Gladys's memories of her own pet kitten being hurled against a brick wall by her stepfather. Suddenly, Norma Jeane, already traumatized, found herself being removed from the Bolenders.

Though Gladys had never told Norma Jeane about her brother and sister, she had a fantasy of buying a house where she would raise all three of her children. In fact, she had lost touch with Jackie and Berniece, and thus was unaware that Jackie had died in 1931. In the years since Gladys had left Flat Lick, her son had led a pitiful existence. He had difficulty walking, one leg being shorter than the other. He lost an eye when a firecracker exploded. He had kidney trouble. Jap Baker, instead of taking him to the hospital, insisted on trying to catheterize the boy at home, and he died of kidney failure soon afterward, aged fourteen.

At the time Norma Jeane came to live with her, Gladys was working at Columbia Pictures with Grace and had managed to save some money. Though Grace warned her that staff cuts were threatened, Gladys made a down payment on a bungalow near the Hollywood Bowl in the summer of 1933. When Gladys did indeed lose her job, there was no choice but to rent out part of the bungalow to an English couple, who worked as film extras.

The responsibility of a home she could barely afford and a child she had no idea how to care for plunged Gladys into a deep depression. The news that her maternal grandfather, Tilford Hogan, had hung himself in Linn County, Missouri, confirmed her fears about the family fate. Gladys had hallucinations. Lying on the living-room sofa, kicking and screaming, she imagined that someone was coming down the staircase to murder her. One morning in January 1935, Gladys woke up in Norwalk State Hospital, where her mother had died in a straitjacket seven years previously. Doctors listed her condition as paranoid schizophrenia; Grace told Ida Bolender that a portion of Gladys's brain had collapsed. From then on, Grace never tired of repeating that she had warned Gladys against taking on too much responsibility, such as buying a house and trying to care for Norma Jeane.

Before Norma Jeane married Jimmy Dougherty, Grace instructed her to disclose that she was illegitimate and that the Mr. Mortenson listed on her birth certificate wasn't her real father. So Dougherty knew something of her background and of the mother who, following an escape attempt, had been transferred to Agnews State Hospital in San Jose. Gladys tried to kill herself at least twice. Once, she stuffed a bed-sheet down her throat. On another occasion, she jabbed the blue vein in her wrist with a hairpin. Dougherty knew that Norma Jeane worried about the fate that had befallen both her mother and her grandmother; and he knew, having once casually told Norma Jeane she was crazy, never to utter that painful word again.

Dougherty was on shore leave from the Merchant Marine when Norma Jeane asked him to accompany her to the bus stop where she was to pick up Gladys, who had finally succeeded in her bid to be released from the state hospital. Dora Hogan Graham, Della's sister, had petitioned the authorities on her behalf, and Gladys agreed to live with Aunt Dora in Portland, Oregon, for at least a year as a condition of her release. En route, she stopped off to visit Norma Jeane, whom she had seen only once in eleven years. When Gladys stepped down from the bus, her appearance came as something of a shock. For reasons that no one could explain, the former mental patient was dressed as a nurse, in a white nylon dress and a nurse's white stockings and shoes.

One year previously, Norma Jeane had quietly visited Agnews. Her husband, apparently, didn't know about the trip. She drove out there with high hopes, but they were quickly dashed. On seeing Gladys, she did not have the feeling, "This is my mother." Gladys wasn't even the woman with the red hair anymore, her hair having turned to salt and pepper. Confronted with someone who seemed less like her parent than Grace did, Norma Jeane, desperately disappointed, never went back. Gladys was a stranger to her. In a sense, that was what she had always been. As Norma Jeane later said, part of her wanted to be with her mother, yet part of her remained afraid.

Norma Jeane loved and loathed, was drawn to and repelled by her mother, all at the same time. On the one hand, Grace's litany that too much responsibility had caused Gladys's breakdown made Norma Jeane feel guilty. On the other hand, she could never expunge the memory of fighting for her life as Gladys tried to smother her in her crib.

Had Gladys really attempted to murder Norma Jeane? It's impossible to say. One can only know that the mentally unstable Gladys communicated, in one way or another, a wish that Norma Jeane had never existed. In a child's mind, it would be a short way from that to her mother's wishing her dead. Whether or not the incident actually occurred, Norma Jeane believed it had. And Norma Jeane believed something else: that her mother associated her with sin, with badness, with evil. Gladys had somehow communicated the notion that as an illegitimate child Norma Jeane was the embodiment of her own sins and had to be snuffed out. Subsequently, when Norma Jeane was expelled from several foster homes after being sexually assaulted, the punishment seemed to validate Gladys's claim that she was intrinsically bad.

Dougherty noted how much mother and daughter looked alike. They had the same eyes, forehead, and hairline. In Gladys, Jimmy believed he saw an image of what his wife was going to look like in her forties. In Gladys, Norma Jeane saw an image of everything she wanted to escape.

Seven years later, as Marilyn lay in the hospital, her mother remained a grim reminder of the past and a terrifying intimation of the future. Gladys, who continued to dress as a nurse, had remarried. She soon discovered that her husband, John Eley, hadn't bothered to divorce a previous wife in Boise, Idaho, so she left him and moved in with Grace and Doc. Gladys, having found religion, strongly disapproved of her daughter's movie career. The publicity surrounding Marilyn's nude calendar had distressed her greatly. Gladys was a bomb waiting to explode. Eley's death on April 23, 1952, five days before Marilyn had her appendix removed, lit the fuse. There was no telling what might happen if Gladys saw newspaper articles that disclosed her existence, or worse, if reporters located her in Van Nuys.

In an effort to control any damage to her career, Marilyn released a written statement to the press: "My close friends know that my mother is alive. Unbeknown to me as a child, my mother spent many years as an invalid in a state hospital. I was raised in a series of foster homes arranged by a guardian through the County of Los Angeles and I spent more than a year in the Los Angeles Orphans Home. I haven't known my mother intimately, but since I have become grown and able to help her I have contacted her. I am helping her and want to continue to help her when she needs me."

The public seemed to accept Marilyn's explanation, which appeared in newspapers on May 3. Soon afterward, Marilyn, having saved herself yet again, began preparations for *Niagara*.

+   +   +

Marilyn reported to the studio on May 21, 1952, for color and wardrobe tests. When she finished, instead of going directly to the location with Henry Hathaway, her co-star Joseph Cotten, and the rest of the cast and crew, Marilyn flew to New York to spend a few days with Joe DiMaggio. Much of that time was devoted to hanging out with Joe and his entourage at Toots Shor's saloon on West 51st Street. It was Marilyn's initiation into a world unlike any she had ever known.

The sportswriter Red Smith called Toots Shor's "the mother lodge." Others described it as "a boys' club" or "a gymnasium with room service." Jimmy Cannon called it "a joint where men come to brag when they're proud and to fight the sorrow when it's bad." Shor himself, a fat, garrulous, pink-faced, crinkly-eyed former speakeasy doorman and bouncer, referred to his establishment as "the store." He and DiMaggio were so close that one regular customer compared them to a pair of "lopsided Siamese twins."

On entering Toots Shor's, the first thing one noticed amid the stifling swirl of cigarette and cigar smoke was the immense circular bar where patrons stood six deep. They were a hard-drinking, boisterous, argumentative, sports-obsessed group. The noise was often deafening. They debated and pontificated, they waved their hands about grandly, they mimicked sports plays, they knocked over a good many high-priced drinks. They engaged in bottle bouts, raucous contests to determine who could guzzle the most booze. In the distance, one caught a glimpse of the large, clamorous, brightly-lit dining room. Sports paintings adorned brick walls. Waiters ferried huge platters of food that almost everyone admitted was terrible. On one occasion, Jackie Gleason actually sent out for several pizzas.

"Had to do it," said Gleason as a delivery boy brought the white boxes to his table. "Can't stand the food here."

You didn't come to Toots Shor's for the food. You came to soak in the atmosphere. You came to talk sports. You came to rub elbows with Ernest Hemingway at the bar. You came to be affectionately insulted by the proprietor: "Get outa my joint, you lousy, creepy, filthy bum!" For certain people in the sports and newspaper crowd, such abuse was a sign of recognition, a badge of honor. A young sportswriter knew he was on the way up when Shor growled that he was nothing but "a piece of raisin cake."

You came to Toots Shor's to watch DiMaggio and his entourage at Table One, the first to the left of the bar. You didn't dare approach, however. If you did, Toots really would kick you out. An invisible wall protected Table One from the rest of the dining room. Everyone knew the rules: Look, listen in if you can, but don't bother the Yankee Clipper. When DiMaggio's first wife, Dorothy Arnold, divorced him in 1944, one of the problems she cited was that instead of coming home to his West Side penthouse, he spent too many evenings with his pals at Toots Shor's.

DiMaggio did like to hang out with the boys. Yet even with close friends, he never said much. Jimmy Cannon, who always sat at Table One, noted that DiMaggio was "more a spectator than a participant in any group." He was "concealed and withdrawn." He watched, he listened, sometimes he cleared his throat. When Jackie Gleason, who called him Fungo, joined the group, perhaps he even laughed. Though DiMaggio tried not to show it, his shyness caused him considerable pain. Once, as the Yankees pitcher Lefty Gomez regaled the table with funny stories, DiMaggio sadly remarked to Toots, "I wish I could be like Lefty, but I can't."

DiMaggio may have been lonely, but he was rarely alone. Wherever he went, including the trip to Los Angeles to have dinner with Marilyn, he was accompanied by an overweight, stumpy, ill-mannered little man with eyeglasses. George Solotaire, proprietor of the Adelphi Theater Ticket Agency, was DiMaggio's best friend, gofer, valet, dinner partner, and—though Solotaire had a wife and child in Bronxville—sometime roommate. When Joe was hungry, Solotaire fetched sandwiches from the Stage Delicatessen. When his suits were dirty, Solotaire took them to the cleaners. When he went on a trip, Solotaire packed the suitcase. Solotaire's feelings were hurt when a newspaper article identified him as nothing more than "a coat hanger for Joe," but there was truth in the characterization.

Solotaire played the Little Guy to DiMaggio's Big Guy. They were inseparable. Patrons of the Stage Delicatessen would watch in fascination as the pair ate dinner in uninterrupted silence. Solotaire arranged dates for DiMaggio and pried girls loose when Joe tired of them, usually after the second outing. Sometimes he even accompanied Joe on a date, pulling out a chair for Joe—not the lady—to sit down. At Table One, his tongue oiled by a few drinks with Toots, Solotaire became talkative.

"J. P. Morgan once called for tickets to the same show for seven straight Saturday nights," he would say.

"How come?" asked Joe, though they all must have heard the story countless times.

"It wasn't the music. He had an eye for a broad in the chorus line."

Women, in Toots Shor's world, were broads, or, if you happened to be married to one, the missus. Shor discouraged women from patronizing the store. The maître d' gave women a chilly reception, but once inside they were treated respectfully. One night, Shor ejected his friend Ted Husing, a sportscaster, for uttering the words "damn" and "hell" in front of some women. A regular customer was permitted to bring the missus once or twice, but no more. To do so would be to lose face. DiMaggio, it was said, avoided bringing women to Shor's. That is, until he met Marilyn.

Toots believed a woman's presence was inhibiting to "our kind of bum." She spoiled the fun just by being there. But Marilyn was with Joe, so Toots, who fawned on the man, did everything in his power to accommodate her. He gave them a special table of their own, but the invisible wall he put up around it could hardly protect Marilyn from being stared at by other customers.

DiMaggio was used to being stared at. He was used to having all the other customers at the Stage Delicatessen turn their chairs slightly to observe the baseball god maul a sandwich. He was used to people brushing past his table for no other reason than to get a closer look. Probably he liked the attention. DiMaggio, who, after a game, would scrutinize his own image in the locker-room mirror for as long as it took to get the parting in his pomaded hair just right, was not without a certain narcissism.

Yet the idea of a bunch of other men looking at Marilyn—his girl—violated his sense of dignity. And dignity was very much what Joe DiMaggio was about. Fearful of embarrassing himself, DiMaggio tried never to display his feelings, but people sensed his carefully-concealed annoyance. Even when Marilyn accompanied him to Yankee Stadium, he was distressed when she chatted with team members in the stands before the game. It may have been the first indication of the fierce possessiveness that was to blight his relationship with Marilyn. Soon there were others.

He didn't think much of her movie career. He didn't respect her ambitions. He didn't believe she had any talent. He resented the time she devoted to her work. He thought her success was totally based on sex appeal. The moment the studio ceased to find her sexy, her career would be over. And what was she going to do then? He sincerely thought she'd be better off getting married and having kids.

"I'll take care of you," he told her. "Show business isn't any business for a girl like you."

Dorothy Arnold, a minor film actress, had left behind a failed career to become the first Mrs. DiMaggio, and Joe couldn't understand why Marilyn refused to do the same.

"She's a plain kid. She'd give up the business if I asked her," DiMaggio, full of pride, insisted to Jimmy Cannon. "She'd quit the movies in a minute. It means nothing to her."

DiMaggio, of all people, should have known what the movies meant to Marilyn. The man who once said, "A ballplayer's got to be hungry to become a big leaguer, that's why no boy from a rich family ever made the big leagues," should have understood why Marilyn wanted so desperately to be a star.

DiMaggio had once been the most graceful of players. Toots Shor used to say that Joe even looked good when he struck out. DiMaggio's movements, wrote Jimmy Cannon, seemed to have been "plotted by a choreographer concerned only with the defeat of awkwardness." But now, in his new job doing pre- and post-game television interviews for the Yankees, the "deft serenity" which he had projected on the baseball field deserted him. As an interviewer, he was rigid and unnatural. His stage fright was painfully obvious, and it was clear that he didn't like to talk on camera any more than he did off. He read scripted lines clumsily and, though the show went out live, he couldn't improvise. On one occasion he refused to go on unless the opening cue card, which had been lost, was found. It read, "Hi, I'm Joe DiMaggio. Welcome to the Joe DiMaggio Show."

DiMaggio, Toots Shor once said, liked to do things well or not at all. That's why he quit baseball when his body started to wear out. That's why his television show was so embarrassing; it felt like a fall from grace. And that, probably, is why his relationship with Marilyn was so painful. He couldn't seem to understand why it failed to live up to his ideal. DiMaggio had difficulty accepting that in life he might never achieve the perfection he had known in baseball.

Even when DiMaggio was still playing ball, his "deft serenity" on the field did not necessarily carry over into human relations. DiMaggio had a poor boy's rage which never left him. He was tormented by fears that he was being taken advantage of. He was constantly testing everyone's loyalty. He was always on the lookout for what a person or an organization wanted from him. He hated the feeling that he was being used. It was a feeling he seemed to have often. DiMaggio engaged in messy, acrimonious contract disputes that led some journalists to call him arrogant. He was acutely sensitive to what other people thought of him—"I know people who meet me go away saying to themselves that I'm a swell-headed Dago," Joe once told Toots Shor—but he persisted. Salary was not really the issue. Toots Shor, who knew DiMaggio better than most, put it best: "It wasn't just the money, it was pride."

DiMaggio's attitude would begin to show itself in Marilyn's, and be reflected in her actions. They shared a thick streak of suspiciousness, and because Joe was an outsider in Hollywood who wanted nothing from her but love, Marilyn believed she could trust him. DiMaggio may have had little regard for Marilyn's work, but more and more he would have a significant impact on how she handled her career.

+   +   +

In June, Marilyn crossed the New York border to Canada for several weeks of location shooting. Before she even had a chance to get started, however, there was concern back at the studio that casting her in *Niagara* might have been a mistake after all. Zanuck's upset had nothing to do with whether she could handle the role of Rose Loomis, a faithless wife who plans to kill her husband. Instead, he was puzzled by the disappointing box-office receipts of *Don't Bother to Knock*. At Twentieth, Marilyn continued to receive an enormous volume of fan mail, but many of the people who had been drawn to Marilyn's publicity clearly were not going to see her films. Considering her popularity, she just wasn't drawing the audiences she should. As a businessman, Zanuck knew that something was very wrong. He decided to discuss the problem with Howard Hawks, who had previously expressed reservations about the kind of roles in which Marilyn was being cast.

"Howard, we ought to have a great big star here and we're losing money," said Zanuck. "What the hell is happening?"

"Darryl," Hawks replied, "you're making realism with a very unreal girl. She's a completely storybook character. And you're trying to make real movies."

"What should she do?"

Hawks suggested that Marilyn would be much more effective in musical comedy than in gritty melodramas like *Don't Bother to Knock* and *Niagara*. Specifically, he mentioned a property that Twentieth already owned. *Gentlemen Prefer Blondes*, based on a novel by Anita Loos, had been a big hit on Broadway starring Carol Channing. Twentieth had originally purchased the property as a potential Betty Grable vehicle. Hawks insisted that Marilyn would be perfect as the gold-digger Lorelei Lee.

"She couldn't do that," said Zanuck, referring to a role that required singing and dancing.

"The hell she can't," Hawks replied.

Zanuck, unconvinced, asked who Hawks would use for the other girl in the story. Hawks said it wouldn't be a problem to borrow his friend

Jane Russell from Howard Hughes. If Marilyn Monroe's name on a marquee didn't bring in audiences, Russell's certainly would. Zanuck, his fears somewhat put to rest, asked Hawks to direct *Gentlemen Prefer Blondes*. Yet he remained nervous that Marilyn wouldn't be able to carry it off.

As it happened, by the time Marilyn received her next assignment she was already instinctively moving her performance in *Niagara* away from the "realism" that Hawks thought all wrong for her. From the moment she began her first scenes with Joseph Cotten and Jean Peters, it was obvious that Marilyn was over-playing, making her murderess anything but real. Her role in *Niagara* was bigger, flashier, and more glamorous than anything Marilyn had done before, affording her an opportunity to push her sexuality to the extreme. Again and again, Marilyn seemed to calculate just how far she could go; then she went several steps further. Her Rose Loomis is larger than life, almost a cartoon of a woman. Everything about Rose—her walk, her husky voice, the tightness of her scarlet dress—is exaggerated. She is a figure in a nightmare. Marilyn might have been demolished playing opposite the skilled, experienced Joseph Cotten; instead, her gaudy, over-the-top performance blasted him off the screen. Henry Hathaway, studying the rushes, realized that it was impossible to take one's eyes off her.

Hathaway, notorious for shouting and cursing at actors on the set, became a teddy bear with Marilyn. He worried that she was driving herself too hard. In addition to her work on the film, she accepted a great many requests for interviews and publicity photographs. It seemed never to occur to her to say no to the studio publicity office, though the long hours she spent on these assignments devoured the very minimal time she had to rest. Hathaway was horrified by how much was being demanded of her, and by how oddly alone and unprotected she seemed.

Finally, Hathaway asked Marilyn where her agent was. Didn't she have someone to tell these guys to lay off while she was working? Marilyn explained that since Johnny Hyde's death, no one at William Morris, where she remained under contract, seemed to remember that she was alive. Hathaway, in a stern but fatherly way, advised Marilyn that she had better understand that after *Niagara*, all this was going to get much worse. He told her how she was coming across in the rushes. Predicting that the film was going to be a very big hit for her, Hathaway advised

Marilyn to get some help, and he urged her to do it before the roller-coaster ride began. The kind of success that awaited her was not something she was going to be able to handle on her own.

When the company moved back to Los Angeles, Marilyn took a six-month lease on a little house in the Hollywood Hills, not far from the place where Gladys had once tried to make her fantasy of creating a home for herself and her little girl come true. Now, like her mother, Marilyn seemed to find the responsibility of even a rented house an unbearable psychological burden. Insisting that she wasn't ready for it at a moment when she had so much work to do, she moved to a suite at the Bel Air Hotel.

By this time, as Jimmy Cannon wrote, Marilyn Monroe and Joe DiMaggio had become the "whole country's pets," endlessly photographed and written about. But as Marilyn was beginning to recognize, the truth of their relationship was considerably more complex than the idealized version in the press. While it was wonderful finally to have a strong, dependable figure like Joe in her corner, the fact remained that he resented her work. And while in the beginning Marilyn had brought Joe into her life as the man who was going to tell the world that she was a good girl, lately he'd also been sending out a very different message. Much as Joe loved Marilyn and wanted to marry her, part of him remained very critical and disapproving. At times, he seemed to disparage almost everything she did. He was determined to change her. He complained that her clothes were immodest. He complained that the parts she played were vulgar. When Marilyn flew to Atlantic City for the premiere of *Monkey Business*, Joe exploded over a particularly revealing publicity photograph of her in a low-cut dress. Unwittingly, Joe activated Marilyn's most deeply-rooted fears and insecurities. Since childhood she'd been intent on proving that she wasn't bad, yet here was Joe, apparently with the best will in the world, constantly suggesting the very opposite.

Marilyn began to pull back from the relationship, but Joe wasn't about to give up. He was in California with her every chance he had. His ten-year-old son, Joe, Jr., whom he adored, attended the Black Rock Military Academy in Los Angeles, and he wanted Marilyn to get to know the boy. That made Marilyn think that perhaps she'd been wrong; if a man wants you to spend time with his children, he must respect you. So

Marilyn happily spent several hours at the hotel pool with Joe, Jr., who found her irresistible. Children always loved Marilyn, because she spoke to them as equals. But the day had an unhappy ending. When Joe, Jr.'s mother read a newspaper account of the visit, she went wild.

Dorothy's second marriage, to a stockbroker, had ended in divorce two years previously, and after that there had been talk of a reconciliation with DiMaggio. Joe, apparently, had never gotten over Dorothy and welcomed a second chance. The couple spent a snowbound weekend together in Nevada, and Dorothy announced in the press that she was considering a second marriage to Joe. But just when she decided that, yes, she very much wanted to be Mrs. Joe D. again, Marilyn appeared on the scene and the choice was no longer hers. Humiliation, no doubt, accounted for the angry charges she hurled at her former husband. "I must think of my son's emotional security," Dorothy declared when she went to court to limit DiMaggio's visitation rights because he had exposed the boy to an improper environment. "Although good heavens, I'm not a jealous woman, the straw that broke the camel's back was when he took him to the Bel Air Hotel pool with Marilyn Monroe."

Dorothy's attack had been aimed at Joe, but the real victim was Marilyn, who was devastated by her remarks. Marilyn was already being pulled in two directions about Joe, but this incident seemed to make up her mind. There could be no question of marriage right now. She would keep Joe in her life, certainly, but her focus, whether he liked it or not, must be on work.

By October, as people at the studio began to have a first look at *Niagara*, everyone seemed sure that this was going to be Marilyn's breakthrough. Yet she still had not done anything about a new agent. Hathaway persistently reminded her that she needed someone to look out for her interests. Finally, with the Hawks film about to start in November, she decided to act, and instructed her lawyer to write the long-postponed letter firing William Morris. She planned to sign with Charlie Feldman. In the last months, the regular visits from Feldman's minions had made it obvious that Famous Artists was eager to have her as a client. She remained far from sure that she trusted Feldman, but at least she'd made a decision. Feldman himself was in New York at the moment, so she told Jack Gordean, one of his agents, that the letter had gone out and asked him to come by the studio for a drink. Gordean called to tell Feldman what had happened. Feldman, delighted, was determined to sign Marilyn before Hawks started filming.

When Gordean arrived, Marilyn said she preferred to wait a few days. She quoted Feldman; she said he had told her that for appearance's sake she ought to wait five or six days after leaving one agency before signing with another. When her remark reached Feldman, he had little choice but to wait, though he had no memory of saying any such thing. Still, Marilyn had made her move and they would have her signed before every agent in town started chasing her.

Two days later, Marilyn arrived at Fox to find an astonishing sight. A plump-cheeked, kinky-haired Lilliputian, wearing a dark business suit and a large, crimson bow tie, handed her a massive bouquet of flowers. Abe Lastfogel, president of William Morris, focused his bright blue eyes on her. He behaved as if it were every day that he came to the studio personally to gush over Marilyn. After Johnny Hyde's death, Lastfogel had ducked Marilyn's calls, refusing to do anything for her. Now, he pretended to be shocked when Marilyn mentioned her lawyer's letter. Insisting that he hadn't received it, he vowed that his being here had nothing to do with anything but her marvellous self.

Marilyn firmly stated that she really did plan to change agencies. And that, she assumed, was that.

That afternoon, Joe Schenck summoned her to his office. The agent had been in to see him, of course. After all the lies Lastfogel had just told her, Uncle Joe insisted he was "an honorable man" and criticized Marilyn's treatment of him. Reminding Marilyn that he always looked out for her interests, he declared that she was crazy to fire Lastfogel. She should stay with William Morris.

Marilyn left Schenck's office badly shaken—not so much because she believed him about Lastfogel, but because he had been adamant that she should not go to Famous Artists. Suddenly, she was completely unsure again. Marilyn was well aware that Schenck and Feldman were close friends; maybe she'd be a fool to trust Feldman if even his friend warned her not to. But if she couldn't yet bring herself to sign with Feldman, Marilyn still did have other, very immediate needs. And nervous as she was, she had at least figured out a way to satisfy them.

Marilyn placed another call to Gordean. Would he come to the studio again? Over cocktails, Marilyn described Lastfogel's visit, including the bouquet and the talk that followed. She told of being summoned by Joe Schenck and repeated all he said. Then, having conveyed the message that Lastfogel did not plan to give up easily, Marilyn reassured Gordean that she had every intention of signing—just not tonight. She sent him to a sneak preview of *Niagara* in Pasadena.

If Marilyn had intended to remind Gordean that it would be worth fighting to represent her, here was proof. The audience went wild when Marilyn, in a skin-tight red silk dress, sang "Kiss" in a low sultry voice, and when she lay naked, arms outstretched, beneath a white sheet. The theater erupted in cheers and wolf whistles in response to a prolonged shot of her walking in high heels, the camera focused lovingly on her rear.

Marilyn had told Gordean that they should talk when he got back to the studio. As promised, she was waiting for him. Aware that the audience's reaction to *Niagara* would be fresh in his mind, she proceeded to tell Gordean about her financial troubles. She only earned $750 a week, and half of that went to acting lessons with Natasha Lytess and Michael Chekhov, as well as dancing and singing lessons in preparation for *Gentlemen Prefer Blondes*. Barely enough was left to cover the rent on the suite she'd moved into at the Beverly Hills Hotel. She indicated that she had no idea how she could possibly survive.

When Gordean reported the whole saga to his boss, Feldman wasted no time in offering to lend Marilyn $3,500. Gordean delivered a check to Marilyn's hotel. She promised to come to his office later that day to sign the contracts, but she never showed up.

Feldman realized that he would have to try a new tack if he hoped to get Marilyn to make the move to Famous Artists. The loan hadn't done the trick, and he knew that time was of the essence. He would try a more personal gesture, something to show Marilyn how well he planned to treat her as his client. Charles Chaplin was due in Los Angeles for his first visit since being sent into political exile some years before. Feldman, who was giving a black-tie dinner in Chaplin's honor, decided to invite Marilyn. This would be the first time that she had been invited to a Feldman A-list dinner as a person in her own right. A great many people in town would have given almost anything for an invitation to the Chaplin evening. Marilyn, however, declined.

She was clearing the decks for *Gentlemen Prefer Blondes*. Being directed by Hawks in the role of Lorelei Lee was the sort of opportunity Johnny Hyde had longed to get for her. Now that she had acquired that opportunity entirely on her own, Marilyn did not want anything to go wrong. The challenges were enormous. She was always uneasy about her acting abilities, but *Gentlemen Prefer Blondes* would also require her to sing and dance in elaborate production numbers. Hawks, recognizing that she needed to concentrate, asked Zanuck to relieve her of all publicity assignments. There had once been a time when Marilyn had to beg the publicity department to send her out, but now it was they who constantly made demands on her. Zanuck, with much fanfare, suspended all of her publicity work for the duration of *Gentlemen Prefer Blondes*. He notified the press that Marilyn would be unavailable for interviews, personal appearances, or photographic sessions. The announcement, of course, was itself a publicity gesture; it signaled how important Twentieth believed this picture was going to be for Marilyn's career.

Marilyn, intent on proving herself, reported to the studio for wardrobe, makeup, and color tests on November 1. Hardly had she done so, however, when her focus was shattered by something that neither Zanuck, Hawks, nor anyone else could have prevented. There was a new crisis over her mother. Gladys had disappeared from Grace Goddard's house in September, then resurfaced in Florida at the house of her daughter Berniece. She alternated between violent rages and interludes of rigidity and muteness. One focus of Gladys's anger was the nude calendar scandal, the implication being that Marilyn's sinful behavior had again driven her mother insane. Grace, who had always made the important decisions about Gladys's care, advised that she should be put on a train and sent back to California. Marilyn, contacted on October 31, paid for the ticket. By the time Gladys arrived in Van Nuys, however, she was in no condition to be taken in. Grace was at home with her husband when she heard Gladys raving on the front porch. Once before, when Gladys was in this condition, she had attempted to stab Grace. Afraid of what Gladys might do this time, Grace called an ambulance. Marilyn was in pre-production when she learned that once again her mother had been committed to the state hospital.

The news revived all of Marilyn's worst fears about herself. Gladys was a paranoid schizophrenic. Would Marilyn go insane like her mother, her grandmother, and other members of her family? As is often the case in such families, there had always been much talk of an inherited taint. Certainly, much as she may have tried to conceal it from others, Marilyn had abundant evidence that something was very wrong with her. She experienced violent mood swings, veering between depression and intense bursts of energy. She had bouts of sleeplessness. She was often angry at herself. She had attempted to take her own life.

Even if Marilyn hadn't inherited a mood disorder, Gladys's actions would have been enough to drive her to the edge of madness. Marilyn had grown up being told that she was the embodiment of sin and evil. From childhood, she had had to live with the message that the very circumstances of her birth had driven her mother mad. Gladys had imposed on the child an insupportable burden of guilt. As if all that were not enough, once again Marilyn, as an adult, was being blamed for her mother's illness. Worse yet, it was happening at a moment when Marilyn had been hoping finally to prove that Gladys was wrong about her. From the first, Marilyn's powerful drive to be a movie star had been a means to establish her worth. Now it was as if Gladys, in choosing this of all moments to erupt, were actually trying to make it impossible for Marilyn to succeed. It was as if the mother who had once tried to snuff out her daughter's life was trying to do it all over again.

Determined not to let that happen, Marilyn pushed the nightmare of her mother as far back in her thoughts as possible. She turned her full attention to work. For hours she would stand without a word of a complaint as her costumes were fitted, then torn apart and refitted. Marilyn was to have a completely different look for this film. Though she would be playing a nightclub dancer and singer, Hawks wanted her to appear polished and sleek in a way that she had not in previous films. His personal taste in women—as evidenced by his former wife, Slim—ran to a much more sophisticated look than Marilyn currently possessed. Not that Hawks expected Marilyn to emulate his lanky racehorse of an ex-wife, but he did want to move her as far away as possible from the small-time pin-up girl she'd been. In *Gentlemen Prefer Blondes*, the keynote of Marilyn's costumes would be simplicity. Her dresses would be flashy enough, but only in terms of color and sparkle; otherwise the emphasis was on strong, simple, clean lines. Hawks also ordered a total makeover. Marilyn sat patiently as various makeups were tried out, her hair set and colored, until the director pronounced every element exactly right.

When she wasn't working on her new look, Marilyn practiced her dance numbers with Jane Russell and the choreographer Jack Cole. Marilyn, honest about her weakness as a dancer, drove herself to exhaustion. She insisted on going over every number countless times. Russell would finally reach a point where she was unable to continue, but Marilyn, unwilling to go home, would beg Cole to stay on for another few hours in order to work with her alone. She simply would not permit herself to be tired. She seemed to believe that, through an act of will, she could transcend her limitations.

Friday, November 14, was the last day of pre-production. When Marilyn finally went home from dance rehearsals late that night, her doorbell rang. It was Jack Gordean, making a last-ditch attempt to get the agency contracts signed. Precisely as Feldman had feared, the situation had recently become more complicated, another suitor having arrived on the scene in the form of Lew Wasserman, head of MCA. Marilyn took the papers from Gordean, promising to have them back after the weekend, but on Monday morning Marilyn called to say that preparations for the film had kept her from the contracts. She also dropped some hints about having been in touch with MCA.

That day, at the age of twenty-six, Marilyn began the film that would profoundly alter her life. That day, it immediately became apparent that, with Hawks's guidance, Marilyn had discovered her gift. She had a flair for comedy. She had a natural sense of timing. On *Bringing Up Baby*, Hawks had had enormous difficulty in getting Katharine Hepburn to adjust to the requirements of deadpan humor. Repeatedly, Hepburn would fire off a line, then wait for the laugh. Hawks had to show Hepburn that the whole point of this sort of comedy was to go right ahead as though she had no idea she was being funny. Only when Hepburn understood the principle intellectually was she able to deliver her finest comic performance. Marilyn, by contrast, didn't need Hawks to set her straight. Ignoring people's reactions, she raced from joke to joke. She radiated complete innocence of how wonderfully funny she was.

As usual, all this came at great cost to Marilyn. She would arrive at the studio hours early, only to hide in her dressing room long after the time had passed for Hawks to begin. Annoyed, he assumed that it was laziness, or perhaps a late night out, that made Marilyn unable to show up on time. The truth could hardly have been more different. Good as she was, Marilyn was simply terrified of going in front of the camera. Having come so close to success, she could not bear the thought of failure. It was Jane Russell who finally figured out what was going on. Every morning, Russell would stop at Marilyn's dressing room and personally lead her to the set. Once there, Marilyn worked at a snail's pace, which helped to make the shoot long and arduous. The more exhausted Marilyn became, the more pressure she put on herself to make her performance seem effortless. Despite her anxieties, the rushes confirmed that Hawks had been right to take her in this new direction. By February, even Marilyn had begun to accept that her hard work was paying off.

Again, the shadow of her mother fell across her hopes. Grace notified Marilyn that she could no longer be responsible for Gladys, and asked Marilyn to take over her mother's care at once. Grace pointed out that Marilyn was an adult now, after all. Marilyn's $750 weekly salary, though barely enough to pay her own expenses, was far more than Grace ever hoped to earn. Marilyn suddenly faced huge bills. Gladys would have to be moved to a private institution, since the unending press scrutiny of Marilyn's life made it unwise for her mother to remain in a public facility. On February 9, 1953, Marilyn arranged for Gladys to be transferred to Rockhaven Sanitarium. Marilyn had to face the fact that from that day on, to all intents and purposes she was the protector of a woman who, she believed, had tried to murder her as an infant. It was as though the mad mother refused to let go.

That morning, even as Gladys was being moved, Marilyn betrayed her own tortured feelings about her mother. She appeared at the Fox wardrobe department to select a dress for that evening's *Photoplay* Awards. The fan magazines were then very powerful and the annual *Photoplay* banquet was a major event, attended by important members of the film industry. Tonight, Marilyn was to be honored as Best Newcomer, which was why Twentieth had made an exception to its ban on her public appearances while *Gentlemen Prefer Blondes* was being shot. From the first it was evident that Marilyn knew precisely what she wanted: a skin-tight gold lamé dress she'd worn in *Gentlemen Prefer Blondes*. The costume designer, Billy Travilla, pointed out that this was impossible. The material was too thin to be worn in public; the gown had been designed with the camera and a careful lighting set-up in mind. If she tried to wear it to the dinner, the delicate dress might not survive. Besides, it would look like she had arrived naked, wearing only a coat of gold paint. Instead of deterring Marilyn, Travilla's warning seemed only to strengthen her determination.

Nor, later, would Marilyn listen to Natasha's protests that the costume was vulgar, all the more so as she intended to wear it without underwear. Her mother had accused her of being a slut; tonight, Marilyn seemed intent on going out in front of the world and behaving like one. After months of trying to save herself through hard work, suddenly she appeared hell-bent on self-destruction.

DiMaggio had refused to accompany her to the dinner, so Sidney Skolsky was drafted as Marilyn's escort. In addition to his syndicated newspaper column, he wrote articles for *Photoplay* under the heading "Sidney Skolsky Sounds Off, From a Stool at Schwab's." Two hours after the banquet began in the Crystal Room at the Beverly Hills Hotel, Skolsky was still waiting in the lobby for Marilyn. She was upstairs in her suite, where dressmakers sewed the tissue-thin fabric onto her body. It was nearly time for her name to be called when she finally emerged from the elevator. The low-cut, pleated gown fit so tightly around the hips and knees that Marilyn had to walk with short, dainty steps. Sidney gripped Marilyn's elbow, steering her inside. As she came through the door, Jerry Lewis, the master of ceremonies, spotted her from the stage. He jumped on a table and shrieked in his ear-splitting voice, "Whoooo!" That triggered the crowd. Laughter, whistles, cheers and jeers filled the Crystal Room. Marilyn wriggled up the aisle to the podium, her "derrière," as the columnist James Bacon would write, resembling "two puppies fighting under a silk sheet."

Flashbulbs popped on all sides, photographers shouting for her to turn this way and that. The few people who looked away from Marilyn's body to her eyes noticed that there was something very strange about them. She appeared to be drugged. The laughter she provoked was that of a group of men smoking cigars as they watched a dirty movie. No one was laughing in appreciation of Marilyn Monroe's comic skills; they were laughing at her.

By the time the banquet was over, it appeared that Marilyn might have succeeded in sabotaging her own career. Joan Crawford, of all people, led the attack. "It was like a burlesque show," the forty-eight-year-old actress told a reporter. "But those of us in the industry just shuddered. Sex plays a tremendously important part in every person's life. But they don't like to see it flaunted in their faces. She should be told that the public like provocative feminine personalities; but it also likes to know that underneath it all, the actresses are ladies." Far more alarmingly, Crawford warned that she anticipated protests against Marilyn's behavior by various women's clubs and that American women might boycott any film in which Marilyn appeared if she failed to clean up her act.

The next day, Sidney Skolsky helped Marilyn formulate a reply. "The thing that hit me the hardest about Miss Crawford's story was that it came from her," Marilyn declared. "I've always admired her for being such a wonderful mother—for taking four children and giving them a fine home. Who better than I know what it means to homeless little ones?" With that response, Marilyn did her best to repair some of the damage she herself had done. At the same time, she came perilously close to disclosing the real trigger of her rage that night; her entire performance had been directed at her mother.

Marilyn's press release was only partially effective. Just as Crawford had warned, letters of protest against Monroe's flagrant sexuality poured in from women's groups. Zanuck, nervous about a possible boycott, immediately sent word to Hawks that the costume Marilyn was to have worn for the number "Diamonds Are A Girl's Best Friend" was to be replaced by something more discreet. The nude leotard stitched with strategic "diamonds" was quickly replaced by a strapless, shocking-pink gown, carefully lined to ensure that it didn't cling too tightly. Marilyn agreed to whatever was suggested. She seemed to have regained control of herself, remembered who she really was—and most of all, what she wanted to be. All that she wanted now was to find the focus and the strength necessary to finish the picture.

But her troubles weren't over. As Marilyn tried to pull herself together in the week following the Photoplay debacle, Natasha decided to take advantage of her vulnerability. Declaring that Marilyn's vulgarity had damaged her own reputation, Natasha demanded a raise in compensation. If Marilyn refused to go to Zanuck, or to pay Natasha out of her own pocket if necessary, Natasha threatened to quit. She would stop coming to the set. She would stop spending nights in Marilyn's hotel suite, where they rehearsed on a green velvet sofa with the heavy blue curtains tightly shut. Natasha told Marilyn that she had active tuberculosis and that her doctor had advised her to stop working. She would be happy to have the opportunity to rest.

Marilyn panicked. She was convinced that she could not finish the film without Natasha, and she believed that if she did not finish it, her life would be ruined and not worth living. Still, there was no way she could go to Zanuck on Natasha's behalf. He would throw her out of his office. And with the expense of her mother's care, Marilyn had no money of her own. There was only one place to turn. On February 19, ten days after the *Photoplay* dinner, Marilyn drove to Charlie Feldman's house in Coldwater Canyon. In November, Marilyn had literally left his agent on her doorstep waiting for her to sign a contract. When Feldman himself had later called from New York, begging her at least to let him discuss her needs with Spyros Skouras and offering to fly back to Los Angeles at a moment's notice, he had offered to lend her money if she needed it.

Though Feldman had no idea why Marilyn had suddenly called now asking to see him, he was delighted to hear from her. Two years had passed since he had predicted that convincing her to sleep with him wouldn't be a problem. Almost the same amount of time had passed since he'd begun his first tentative attempts to sign her as a client.

Since she had last been at Feldman's house, with Kazan, he had begun to assemble a new art collection. Marilyn, standing among the rare African masks and statues, affected a quality that Joe Mankiewicz once described as her "pasted-on innocence." She was desperate, but also shrewd enough not to let Feldman see that. She began by coyly telling Feldman that just before Johnny died, he had advised her that Charlie ought to take over as her agent. She claimed Johnny had said that Charlie was someone she could trust if she ever needed anything. After that lead-in, Marilyn told Feldman about her troubles with Natasha.

If Feldman thought, as Marilyn had just set him up to do, that this meant Marilyn had come here to join Famous Artists at long last, he was mistaken. By the time Marilyn left that night, Feldman had given up pushing her to sign a contract. He would work for her without pay now simply in the hope that someday, in her own time, she would sign. Henceforth, Famous Artists referred to Marilyn Monroe as its client, though the agency had nothing in writing and no guarantee of receiving so much as a penny for its efforts. Marilyn left Feldman's house with his promise to take care of Natasha. He would go to Zanuck and somehow get Natasha more money—and he would do it for free.

Feldman welcomed this first opportunity to serve, however

unofficially, as Marilyn's agent. He conferred with Henry Hathaway, who confirmed Marilyn's dependence on Natasha. Next, Feldman met with Natasha, who stated her demands bluntly. As he told his staff later, she expected "a helluva lot of dough." Finally, he went to Zanuck and laid out the situation in the starkest terms. Marilyn was obviously becoming a valuable property for Fox. Natasha had made it clear that she intended to carry out her threat to quit. So if Zanuck expected Marilyn to finish the Hawks film, he would have to meet Natasha's demands. At that point, Natasha earned $175 a week. Feldman convinced Zanuck that, compared to the money Gentlemen Prefer Blondes was going to bring in at the box office, whatever Fox agreed to pay Natasha would be "peanuts." Zanuck agreed to offer her $500 a week. This time, however, Natasha was not as smart as she thought. She was too impatient and quickly grabbed the offer. In fact, Zanuck had been willing to go as high as $1000 a week to keep her—which would have been $250 more than Marilyn herself earned.

Emboldened by her success in extorting a raise, Natasha was soon going head to head with Hawks over his direction of Marilyn. That, as anyone could have told her, was a mistake. Hawks had a justifiably high opinion of his own merits as a director and brooked no interference. He was not amused when he saw Natasha signal Marilyn to demand retake after retake. Hawks informed Marilyn that when he shouted "Cut!", he expected her to look at him, not at Natasha. When Natasha's signals continued, Hawks banned her from the set. Zanuck backed Hawks fully.

Marilyn was convinced that she could not go on without Natasha, the one person on a film set whose opinion she trusted unequivocally. Directors, producers, actors, executives, all had their own agendas. Natasha's sole purpose was to make sure that every shot displayed Marilyn to advantage. For all of Natasha's willingness to exploit Marilyn's dependence, Marilyn continued to believe that she could rely on her coach to look out for her interests. Hawks, however, would not relent, and Marilyn had to finish with only off-the-set coaching.

On March 6, 1953, after four months of arduous work, Marilyn completed Gentlemen Prefer Blondes. Niagara had made her a major box-office star when it opened in January, grossing more than $6 million against a cost of $1.25 million. But that film had not maximized Marilyn's potential. Now, as the rough cut of Gentlemen Prefer Blondes was being assembled, the Fox executives could see that Marilyn had tapped into the qualities that were uniquely hers as a performer. She had taken Anita Loos's rather slight sketch of Lorelei Lee, and out of it she had created a rich, vivid, distinctive character that was entirely her own. In fact, it was less Lorelei Lee whom she portrayed in *Gentlemen Prefer Blondes* than an entirely new character named "Marilyn Monroe" or "the girl."

Bits and pieces of "the girl" may have emerged in previous films, but this was the first time Marilyn had put them all together. Thanks to Hawks, her look in the film was blonder, sleeker, cleaner-lined than in the past. Thanks to Hawks, her performance was supported by a beautifully-made film. But the essence of Marilyn's own creation was a perfect balance of sex and humor. In *Niagara*, Marilyn's over-the-top sexuality had been cast as deeply threatening. Rose Loomis confirmed the fears of a puritanical 1950s America that sex was perilous. In *Gentlemen Prefer Blondes*, Marilyn's self-deprecating humor and wonderful silvery giggle made sex seem innocent, safe, and, above all, fun. Far from minimizing the sex, a leavening of humor allowed Marilyn to use her sexuality more effectively than she had ever managed to do before. In an important twist, "the girl" has wit but—unlike the tougher, more knowing character Mae West once created—she doesn't use her wit as a weapon. The character Marilyn created is totally unthreatening to men. Also, unlike West, "the girl" seems completely unaware that she is being funny. That made the character difficult to play, but Marilyn brought it off to perfection.

Still, this was something considerably more than just a well-crafted and deftly performed character. Hawks's technical virtuosity—his masterful framing and editing, his impeccable comic timing—certainly helped Marilyn to create an enduring comic type, but in ways he probably didn't understand, her portrait of "the girl" was driven by her own life experience. For all of her intense sexuality, Marilyn communicated that on some level she, too, was as uncertain about sex, and as vulnerable to being hurt by it, as anyone else. The rantings of her mother and of the Bolenders—the Bible-pounding religious family with whom she'd spent her early childhood—had inculcated in her a core belief that sex was dirty and bad. Marilyn's discovery of "the girl" was fueled by her own need to contend with that past and all it had taught her. It allowed her to proclaim that, far from being the doomed sinner Gladys branded her as, she was actually a sweet, innocent, good girl whom everyone should love.

Audiences were thrilled and relieved to discover that it was all right to laugh at sex; but so, in her own, very touching way, was Marilyn. That personal element infused her performance with special power. In *Gentlemen Prefer Blondes*, Marilyn, drawing on her own private needs and conflicts, transformed herself into a star of the first magnitude.

✦   ✦   ✦

Even as Marilyn had been working out the character of "the girl" in *Gentlemen Prefer Blondes*, Arthur Miller's new play, featuring a character based in part on Marilyn, opened on Broadway. Two years after he met Marilyn, the play he had been trying to write out of his moral crisis finally came to fruition. Ironically, at a moment when Marilyn was poised to demonstrate to a repressive, puritanical America that sex could be innocent and carefree, Miller, in his new play, put out a counter-argument. In the troubles that befall John Proctor as a result of his infidelity, Miller warned that sex, far from being without consequences, is very dangerous indeed. Significantly, Miller set the drama in America's Puritan past, the source of so much of the country's enduring guilt and anguish about sex.

The Crucible was Miller's first original stage play since *Death of a Salesman*, and expectations on Broadway ran high. Instead of Elia Kazan, with whom Miller and Kermit Bloomgarden had broken, Jed Harris directed the production. (Kazan was then at work on Tennessee Williams's *Camino Real*, due to open in March.) As an indictment of HUAC and McCarthyism, *The Crucible* was a brave and timely political drama. But in a way that audiences had no means of gauging, the play's motor was deeply personal. Whatever its flaws, *The Crucible* drew power from the playwright's own guilt in the aftermath of his encounter with Marilyn.

The Crucible reworked the autobiographical play Miller had been sketching before he went to Salem. Like the character of Quentin in that earlier effort, John Proctor has had an extramarital affair but is intent on saving his marriage. Miller, in his notebook, described Proctor as paralyzed by guilt. Proctor has diverged from his own ideal of decent conduct. Respected as forthright and principled, he secretly thinks himself a fraud. Like Quentin's wife, Elizabeth Proctor is judgmental and unforgiving.

John complains that, though he ended his affair with Abby months ago, Elizabeth has turned their home into a courtroom. Elizabeth knows that her husband wants to make amends, yet she is forever accusing and condemning.

In short, the Proctor household in seventeenth-century Salem, Massachusetts, resembled the Miller household in Brooklyn, New York. At least, it resembled the household Miller had once described to Kazan. There was the same striving by the husband to repair the marriage, the same refusal by the wife to forgive or to believe in him. Abby, the dismissed servant girl, refuses to abandon hope of a more lasting relationship with Proctor. He in turn remains strongly attracted to Abby, yet he pointedly discourages her from waiting for him, much as Miller had warned Marilyn that he was not the man to make her life work out as she hoped. Still, Marilyn dreamed of supplanting the wife, and so does Abby.

In obvious ways Abby stands for Marilyn, but as Abby is the character who names names—that is, identifies people as witches—she also brings Kazan to mind. Given all that had happened, it is not surprising that Marilyn and Kazan would be inextricably tangled in Miller's thoughts. Both were important people in Miller's life, whom he had given up in order to sustain his sense of himself. He used the connection to link the personal subplot, the betrayal of one's wife through adultery, and the political main plot, the betrayal of one's friends and associates by naming names. The Crucible posed the question: If I have committed one form of betrayal, how can I feel morally superior to someone who commits another? Proctor didn't think he could. Like Proctor, Miller was trying to figure out how to persist as a voice of moral authority when he knew that, in private, he had violated his own ethical code. Could Miller really condemn Kazan when he, too, was guilty of betrayal?

Miller, in his notebook, dug more deeply into the sources of Proctor's guilt than he dared in the finished play. Early on, Miller contemplated allowing Proctor to realize that he actually wants his wife dead. It would appall a principled man to discover that about himself. Unfortunately, ideas like that did not find their way into The Crucible. If they had—if Miller had permitted John Proctor to be darker, edgier, and more complex—he might have written a better play.

As it is, Miller allows Proctor to emerge from his moral crisis too easily and, worse, undramatically. In Act Four, Proctor is absolved from his crippling guilt not by anything he does, but by something Elizabeth says. Proctor has just told Elizabeth there is no reason to refuse to save his own life by confessing he has consorted with the devil. He cannot mount the gibbet like a saint, he insists, for that would be a fraud. "Nothing's spoiled by giving them this lie that were not rotten long before." Elizabeth, aware that he is referring to his relationship with Abby, makes a confession of her own. She accepts responsibility for having driven him away. "I have sins of my own to count," Elizabeth declares. "It needs a cold wife to prompt lechery . . . John, I counted myself so plain, so poorly made, no honest love could come to me! Suspicion kissed you when I did . . . It were a cold house I kept!"

So, after two years of struggle with the moral questions provoked by desire and infidelity, Miller had concluded that it must have been the cold wife's fault after all. His reasoning was tortuous, to say the least. Ironically, in a play about forced confessions, Miller put the words in the wife's own mouth. Proctor, emboldened, defies his tormentors. He refuses to name names and dies a hero.

Reviews of *The Crucible* were mixed. Inevitably, the question arose whether it was a worthy successor to *Death of a Salesman*. "There is a terrible inertness about the play," said Eric Bentley in the *New Republic*. "The individual characters, like the individual lines, lack fluidity and grace. There is an O'Neill-like striving after a poetry and an eloquence which the author does not achieve. 'From Aeschylus to Arthur Miller,' say the textbooks. The world has made this author important before he has made himself great; perhaps the reversal of the natural order of things weighs heavily upon him."

Bentley raised a question that would gnaw at Miller for years to come: Would *The Crucible* have been a success had it been directed by Kazan? Had the triumph of *Death of a Salesman* been attributable, in part, to Kazan's collaboration? Indeed, on another occasion Bentley would go so far as to describe Kazan as "virtually co-author of *A Streetcar Named Desire* and *Death of a Salesman*." Not surprisingly, Miller blamed the failure of *The Crucible* on Jed Harris. In light of all this, one can understand Miller's persistent longing, so evident in the notebooks, to discover some way to justify working with Kazan again. And in a writer who valued his own work above all else, one can appreciate the strength required to stay away from Kazan for so long, when the cost to Miller's own career seemed evident. Despite his desire for another triumph on the scale of *Death of a Salesman*, and despite his and others' awareness of the price that was to be paid, he cut off his collaboration with Kazan in the belief that it was the right thing to do.

As *The Crucible* (and later work) made clear, Miller did not stop thinking about Kazan and the woman they had shared. The play's complex psychological dynamics attested to the enduring power of the Miller–Kazan–Monroe triangle in the playwright's consciousness. At the same time, *The Crucible* marked a shift in the nature of that configuration, as the triangle assumed a political as well as a sexual meaning. With *The Crucible*, Miller set himself up as Kazan's polar opposite, both politically and morally. More and more, the public would come to view Miller and Kazan as symbols of the conflict that ravaged America in the HUAC years. The vital role that Miller's feelings about Marilyn Monroe played in shaping *The Crucible* hinted that her participation in the triangle was by no means finished. In 1953, whatever Marilyn's current circumstances might be, *The Crucible* lent a certain inevitability to her future involvement in both men's lives.

+ FOUR +

In the beginning, Darryl Zanuck had questioned whether Marilyn would be able to handle the demands of her role in *Gentlemen Prefer Blondes*. Soon after the production began, however, he knew how wrong he had been to doubt her. And he knew how valuable a commodity she was about to become. Eager to make every penny he could, Zanuck decided to repeat the formula of *Gentlemen Prefer Blondes*. Marilyn played an adorable gold-digger in that picture, so that's exactly what she must do again. He assigned her to *How to Marry a Millionaire*, with a script by Nunnally Johnson. Zanuck overlooked one essential ingredient that made *Gentlemen Prefer Blondes* a success: Howard Hawks was one of the finest directors in the business. Jean Negulesco, who would be directing *How to Marry a Millionaire*, was mediocre at best. A gregarious Romanian with a bit of the con man about him, he was cultured and an art lover, but no artist. He had charmed his way into the movies, and Zanuck was one of his main supporters. Thus, though it seems not to have occurred to Zanuck, the question remained: Without a director of Hawks's calibre, would Marilyn be able to pull off a second miracle? Hawks's mastery of the formal elements of filmmaking contributed just as much to an actor's performance as anything the actor himself did. This was something Negulesco's direction lacked. At best, he could help with a line reading, but Negulesco's sense of framing, composition, camera movement and editing were as weak as Hawks's were strong.

Zanuck scheduled *How to Marry a Millionaire* to begin on March 11, four days after Marilyn completed *Gentlemen Prefer Blondes*. That raised a second big question, which Zanuck seems also not to have asked:

Was Marilyn in any condition to go into another picture immediately? Her eighteen weeks with Hawks had left her physically and psychologically drained. She had been consuming sleeping pills like candy in order to get even a few hours of rest after practicing her lines with Natasha late into the night. In the morning, she would take another pill to get through the day. By the time she was finished working with Hawks, she was thinner than she'd ever been in her life—and her nerves were raw. As if having a mere four days off between assignments was not bad enough, Spyros Skouras, alarmed by the damaging publicity that followed the *Photoplay* Awards, demanded that Marilyn use the time to fly to Boston to appear at a children's charity benefit.

Several times in the last days of filming Charlie Feldman had dropped by to watch, and he'd grown alarmed at how fragile Marilyn seemed whenever the camera was not on her. He'd observed her turmoil over Natasha, and realized that the toll taken by her work seemed to go beyond mere physical exhaustion. Having lent her money to pay for Gladys's care, he knew something of Marilyn's terror that she might one day end up like her mother. So Marilyn was much on his mind as he witnessed the emotional crisis of another actress; it struck him as a warning of what might lie in store for Marilyn.

When Vivien Leigh came to Los Angeles to shoot the interiors for William Dieterle's *Elephant Walk*, Feldman arranged a dinner party in her honor at the Beachcomber restaurant. Though the dinner took place as scheduled, before her arrival Vivien, who was a manic depressive, had suffered a nervous breakdown on location in Ceylon. During the seventy-two-hour flight to California, Vivien, raving and tearing at her clothes, had attempted to leap out of the plane. Her husband, Laurence Olivier, traced her condition to the miscarriage she had suffered in 1944, after which she alternated between periods of madness and normality.

On the Paramount lot, she had lucid moments, but there were numerous disturbing episodes. She drank, she hallucinated, she had screaming fits. Having previously played the tortured character Blanche Dubois in *A Streetcar Named Desire*, now she recited Tennessee Williams's lines as though they were her own thoughts. (She later said that doing Blanche on stage and screen had "tipped" her into madness.) When it became evident that Vivien was in no condition to finish *Elephant Walk*, the Los Angeles psychoanalyst Ralph Greenson was brought in. "I will have that woman working next week," Greenson promised, before Olivier, heeding the advice of a different psychiatrist, took his wife back to England for electroshock therapy. She was replaced in *Elephant Walk* by Elizabeth Taylor.

Henceforth, Feldman made concern for Marilyn's physical and mental health a priority. He didn't want her to end up like Vivien.

Nonetheless, Marilyn began *How to Marry a Millionaire* on schedule. Zanuck had by no means been alone in pushing the project for Marilyn. *How to Marry a Millionaire* was to be one of the first CinemaScope films, and the new wide-screen process was very much Spyros Skouras's baby. Skouras, intent on winning back that portion of the film audience that had defected to television, staked his reputation on CinemaScope's ability to "save the movies!" He, as much as his adversary Zanuck, wanted Marilyn in the film.

On Feldman's advice, Jean Negulesco did everything possible to make Marilyn feel happy and relaxed at their first meeting. He had been told to turn on the full voltage of his charm to calm the highly-strung young woman. Sensing that she longed to be taken seriously and loved to learn, he won her over by talking about art. He showed her his own paintings and drawings, teaching her about Chagall, Gauguin, Matisse, and Miró. He drew her portrait in brown ink. When she protested, as she sat for him, that she could not understand modern art, Negulesco replied that art is like sex; it isn't something one understands but something one feels.

When they began to shoot, Negulesco continued his campaign to put Marilyn at ease. He could be of little real help to her as a director, but he went out of his way to eliminate the usual sources of tension. On the set, Negulesco cheerfully accepted Natasha's hawk-eyed presence behind his director's chair. When Marilyn demanded another take, he didn't have to turn around to know that Natasha had shaken her head. He seemed less annoyed than amused. He smiled, shrugged, and did as Marilyn asked. Sometimes she demanded fifteen takes or more. Other actors, irritated, knew they had to be good in every take because there was no telling which one Negulesco would select.

Marilyn and the director, whom she affectionately called "Johnny," developed a rapport. But they had not been shooting long when Marilyn collapsed and had to be hospitalized with near bronchial pneumonia. She had gone directly from one film to another, and had been pushing herself relentlessly. Feldman, already nervous about her fragility, began to be really frightened.

The studio was mainly concerned about the cost of the lost days, and someone came up with the bright idea that maybe they could compensate for the expense with some extra publicity. The studio called Marilyn at Cedars of Lebanon Hospital to tell her that photographers were on their way over. It was a mark of how sick Marilyn was that she exploded with rage; usually, she would have done anything she could to accommodate them. Feldman warned the studio's executive manager, Lew Schreiber, that Twentieth was pushing Marilyn too hard. Now that she was everyone's investment, Feldman argued, they would all be wise to protect her. Marilyn came back to work in a few days, but though she put on a good show in public, it was months before she fully regained her strength.

It was not her physical condition, however, or even her constant fear of not being good enough that bothered Marilyn during this time. Her co-stars in How to Marry a Millionaire were Lauren Bacall and Betty Grable, who had been the leading box-office star during World War II as well as the U.S. military's favorite pin-up girl. For more than a decade, the peachy-skinned Grable remained on the top-ten list of box-office personalities. In her day, she'd earned some five million dollars yearly for Fox. Now, at thirty-six, she was considered by studio executives to be "used up," and it was no secret that How to Marry a Millionaire would probably be her last film under contract. She accepted her lot with dignity. "Honey, I've had it," Grable told Marilyn when Negulesco introduced them on the set. "Go get yours. It's your turn now." It was not long before the idea that Grable had passed the torch to her became a focus for Marilyn's anxieties.

At 1 a.m. on Thursday, July 25, Marilyn was woken by the phone as she slept beneath a satin comforter. She had a party line in the three-room garden apartment she had recently rented on North Doheny Drive, but the call was for her—a drawling voice saying "wonderful" over and over again. Feldman never called in the middle of the night, but he had just been to a screening of Gentlemen Prefer Blondes and could not wait to tell her.

Niagara had broken box-office records, but it was Gentlemen Prefer Blondes that introduced the funny, sexy, innocent, appealing Marilyn

Monroe that audiences around the world would fall in love with. Feldman was certain that after *Gentlemen Prefer Blondes*, the public was going to demand to see "the girl" again and again. He talked to Marilyn for a long time about what the Hawks film meant for her future. He assumed she'd be excited that they'd finally hit upon a crowd-pleasing, money-making formula, but Marilyn wasn't responding in quite the way Feldman had expected. Though she was pleased by his compliments and enthusiasm, at the same time she seemed confused, uncertain, almost wary.

Life had taught Marilyn to be suspicious. Now and then, some of her mother's and grandmother's clinical paranoia may also have kicked in. Marilyn was always on the alert for the moment when things would go wrong. It wasn't a question of worrying that she might be hurt or abandoned; she expected that to happen, it was only a matter of when. The experience of working with Betty Grable had set off alarm bells in Marilyn's head. She knew she had replaced Grable in *Gentlemen Prefer Blondes*. And she knew it was widely anticipated that from this point on she'd take over Grable's position at Twentieth. Filmgoers had evidently wearied of seeing Grable in the same sort of role. Even if they hadn't, Grable was too old to keep doing those roles.

So even before *Gentlemen Prefer Blondes* had been released, Marilyn was worried about losing all she'd won. Before she had actually tasted success, she was thinking about how to protect herself. Instinctively, she assumed a defensive posture. Accustomed to being used and abandoned, she was already seeking ways to avoid suffering that fate again. Marilyn was smart. She didn't want audiences to tire of her. She had been rushed into a second film where she had to repeat the character she'd just played in *Gentlemen Prefer Blondes*. And here was Charlie telling her that the idea was to have her do "the girl" many times more.

With an eye on the future when she would no longer be able to play "the girl," Marilyn was already preoccupied with convincing the studio to let her try different kinds of roles. At a moment when Twentieth seemed to be very happy with her indeed, she was already viewing the studio in adversarial terms. Whatever Zanuck might have in mind, she didn't want to re-enact the Betty Grable story: endlessly repeating the same tired formula until the studio decided that she was "used up." Betty Grable was thirty-six; what age would Marilyn Monroe be when Twentieth no longer wanted her?

Feldman, for his part, didn't seem to understand. He never really comprehended Marilyn's terror of being exploited. But there was one person who, however much he resented her work, was every bit as wary and suspicious as she. At a moment when Marilyn was particularly concerned with protecting herself against a host of potential users, Joe DiMaggio's role in her life became increasingly important.

+   +   +

A blue Cadillac with the license plate "JOE D" was often parked outside Marilyn's small white apartment house on Doheny, below the Sunset Strip. A high iron gate opened onto a courtyard. A fountain splashed blue-tinted water, but the sound was frequently drowned out by a television set in Apartment Four. Behind a screen door, then a black enameled door, a tiny hall led to the living room which contained a fireplace with a brick hearth, with mirrored walls on both sides. One mirror slid back to disclose the television set that DiMaggio, stretched out on a bright orange velvet sofa beneath several bookshelves, watched incessantly when he visited. Oversized crystal and ceramic ashtrays, filled with Joe's cigarette butts, littered the cocktail table and other surfaces.

Off the hall was a small, dark bedroom. A double bed was flanked by a folding snack tray with a brass lamp, and a wooden night-table with a black telephone. The portrait of Lincoln hung over the bed.

When the Cadillac was gone, the apartment quiet, baskets of velvety, long-stemmed roses arrived several times a day. The delivery boy left them in front of Miss Monroe's screen door. The attached card always bore the same message: "I love you, I love you."

To most observers, Joe, who had his own quarters at the Knickerbocker Hotel, remained a shadowy presence in Marilyn's life. Sometimes he was the subtext of Marilyn's conversation, as when she asked Jane Russell what it was like to be married to a professional athlete. (Russell's husband played NFL football.) Sometimes Marilyn talked openly about Joe, as when she told David Conover, the photographer who had discovered her in 1946, that DiMaggio had proposed on numerous occasions.

Did she love him? Conover asked.

"I don't know," Marilyn replied. "He's very sweet and kind. And very much a gentleman. But sometimes he's so boring I could scream. All he knows and talks about is baseball. That's why I'm not sure." She complained to Sidney Skolsky in a similar vein.

Though DiMaggio's refusal to escort Marilyn to industry events like the *Photoplay* Awards led people to speculate about the relationship, afterwards, more often than not, his blue Cadillac would be waiting for her outside. "You know Joe, he doesn't like crowds," Marilyn would apologize before they drove off together.

In contrast to those who merely glimpsed or heard about Joe, the few people who had dealings with Marilyn on a close daily basis, such as her new lawyer Loyd Wright and her agent Charlie Feldman, saw DiMaggio as a formidable presence, a strong if taciturn personality. Joe desperately wanted to marry Marilyn, but he was too stoical to allow other people to see his feelings. It was a point of honor to keep those feelings bottled up inside, leading him to suffer severe stomach-aches and ulcers.

He very much wanted Marilyn to give up acting, but as long as she planned to remain in the movies he did much to help and advise her. He wanted to protect her. He wanted to prevent all those phonies from taking advantage of her. He may also have wanted to show Marilyn that she could trust and depend on him. Whatever his motives, DiMaggio had an increasing influence on some of her most important decisions.

That May, just as she finished *How to Marry a Millionaire*, Marilyn's weekly salary escalated to $1,250. It was an insignificant sum in relation to the box-office success of *Niagara* and, soon, *Gentlemen Prefer Blondes*. There was no question that the terms of Marilyn's contract had to be completely renegotiated. In 1950, Johnny Hyde had made a deal on behalf of a starlet in whom he alone believed. By the summer of 1953, it was obvious that Marilyn was about to be a very major star. From the moment Feldman had seen the rushes of *Gentlemen Prefer Blondes* and heard the buzz about Marilyn at the studio, he'd known that the time to start talking about a new deal would be after the film went into release. If audiences and critics reacted as he expected they would, Marilyn would be in an excellent position to maximize her salary demands.

Meanwhile, Feldman had considered other ways to squeeze money out of the studio. A strategy he had used with other clients seemed appropriate here: Feldman urged Marilyn to buy the screen rights to a novel and to commission a screenwriter to tailor a script for her.

Famous Artists would then make it a condition of her new contract that Zanuck purchase the rights from Marilyn. He calculated that would earn her a profit in excess of $200,000. Marilyn, advised by her lawyer to go ahead, agreed. Feldman's office sent ten different books to Doheny, and Joe and Marilyn studied them carefully.

The sports pages were DiMaggio's typical reading matter, but in the end it was he who chose the novel *Horns of the Devil*. Marilyn, with $5,000 advanced by Feldman, bought the book strictly on Joe's say-so. Then she conferred with the screenwriter Alfred Hayes, whom she had met during *Clash by Night*. She paid him another few thousand dollars of Feldman's money to complete a script. The decision to buy *Horns of the Devil* would have a significant impact on the timing of the contract negotiations. For tax reasons, Marilyn had to hold on to the screen rights for at least six months after the date of purchase. Therefore, if the rights were to be used as a negotiating tool, she couldn't sign a new studio contract until six months had passed.

Even at this stage, Feldman was not being paid for his work on Marilyn's behalf. Johnny Hyde had negotiated her current contract, and the agency commission deducted from her paycheck still went to William Morris. As long as that contract remained in force, no matter who handled Marilyn's day-to-day interests, William Morris collected the commission. That situation would change when a new studio contract was signed. Then, Feldman would be entitled not only to the agent's commission but also to a cut of the proceeds from the sale of *Horns of The Devil*, if (and that "if" was beginning to be a source of embarrassment) Marilyn had finally signed an agency contract with Famous Artists. She had postponed so many times that Feldman had stopped raising the issue. Until she did sign, Feldman would not be entitled to a penny, no matter how many hours he and his staff devoted to her.

On July 15, 1953, *Gentlemen Prefer Blondes* was released. It was a spectacular critical and box-office success. This was the moment Marilyn had been working toward since she was a sad, lonely little girl in an orphanage. This was everything Grace and, later, Johnny Hyde had wanted for her. *Niagara* had excited audiences; but the impact of *Gentlemen Prefer Blondes* was entirely different. Suddenly, people felt they really knew "Marilyn Monroe." And it was immediately obvious that they couldn't get enough of her.

Zanuck expected to hear from Feldman with his demands for a new contract, but the agent, usually so aggressive, was mysteriously silent. What Zanuck didn't know was that the purchase of *Horns of the Devil* would not become final before August 5, 1953. Lest a deal be struck before the six months required by the tax law had safely passed, Feldman did not plan to renegotiate Marilyn's contract until February. The delay had several advantages. By that time, the box-office figures on both *Niagara* and *Gentlemen Prefer Blondes* would be in and *How to Marry a Millionaire* would have opened. Furthermore, six months would give Marilyn and her representatives plenty of time to work out exactly what they wanted from Twentieth.

At the moment, however, Marilyn was preoccupied with the more immediate issue of what assignments Zanuck planned under her current deal. A few weeks after the premiere, she was due to leave for Canada for her next film, *River of No Return*, with Otto Preminger directing. Marilyn was unhappy with her role as a frontier cabaret performer. Soon there was new cause for upset. Just before she left town, Zanuck announced that when she was finished with Preminger, he intended to put her in another musical. He didn't have a finished script for *The Girl in Pink Tights*, so he sent Marilyn a précis of the plot. That was enough to convince Marilyn that *Pink Tights* was, in her words, "another Betty Grable picture."

Marilyn's impulse was to refuse. She talked angrily to Feldman about wanting to protect her career from being destroyed by Zanuck. The agent, for his part, thought there might be another reason to turn down the assignment. He suggested that Marilyn should say no just to signal that she was aware of her new power at Twentieth. Feldman was thinking ahead to February; he didn't want Zanuck to imagine that Marilyn had waited to ask for a new deal because she or her agents were naïve or oblivious to the fact that she'd become "the most important personality on the lot." Feldman also thought that Marilyn would need a rest after she finished *River of No Return*. And he was worried that she risked over-exposure with so many films in release.

As Feldman and Marilyn talked, her personal history began to cloud her thinking. The idea of refusing an assignment seemed to make her exceedingly nervous. Marilyn said that if she turned down *Pink Tights*, Zanuck would put her on suspension. She had no savings. She lived from one paycheck to the next. How would she get along? Feldman promised to advance money to tide her over financially. Besides, he pointed out, she was too valuable for Zanuck to keep her off the payroll for long. Sooner or later, Zanuck would have to give in and put Marilyn in a project more to her liking. Still Marilyn wavered. One minute she planned to refuse *Pink Tights*; the next she said she would do it if Zanuck borrowed Gene Kelly as her co-star. It became evident that she was just trying to find a way to justify accepting a role she didn't want. In raising the issue of suspension, Marilyn had come perilously close to alluding to her lifelong fear. Constantly being passed from one foster home to another had taught her to dread being cast out and abandoned.

Finally, Feldman sent Marilyn off to Canada without a decision having been made. He reassured her that since there was still no script, nothing was definite. There was plenty of time to make up her mind if and when she was formally assigned to *Pink Tights*. Meanwhile, "Mr. Z."—as Marilyn called Zanuck—had made a number of unprecedented concessions to her on *River of No Return*, confirming Feldman's view that she was "in the driver's seat." In the past, Marilyn's sole request had been permission to have Natasha on the set. This time, she also asked for her choreographer from *Gentlemen Prefer Blondes*, Jack Cole, to help with the dance numbers. She asked permission to meet with Preminger to discuss script changes. And, newly concerned about the calibre of her leading men, she asked for Robert Mitchum, then under contract to RKO. Zanuck agreed to everything.

Preminger was considerably less accommodating. The trouble started in the train's dining car, where he took an instant dislike to Natasha. Preminger, born in Vienna, couldn't understand why Natasha insisted on pretending she was Russian. In Banff, dislike quickly turned to hate. Time and again Natasha wrecked line readings by encouraging Marilyn to enunciate each syllable. The result—mannered, artificial speech—was disastrous. According to Preminger, Marilyn's exaggerated lip movements were impossible to film. When Preminger tried to correct Marilyn, she ignored him. Refusing to speak in the distinctive "soft, slurred voice" that Preminger so admired, Marilyn seemed concerned only with what Natasha thought. Mitchum, for his part, agreed with the director.

"Now stop that nonsense!" Mitchum would say, slapping Marilyn's backside a second or two before Preminger started shooting. "Let's play it like human beings. Come on!"

Natasha was also a source of dissension in Marilyn's own camp. DiMaggio had unexpectedly decided to tag along on location, accompanied by the spectral George Solotaire. Joe's ostensible reason for making the trip was to do some fishing. Some company members, however, suspected that he was really there to keep an eye on Marilyn with Robert Mitchum. Nonetheless, to careful observers, it seemed to be Joe and Natasha, not Joe and Mitchum, who were at war. Natasha found DiMaggio sullen and vapid, and he treated her as though she were one of the very people in Hollywood against whom he needed to protect Marilyn. He hated users; he hated phonies; he hated sycophants.

Also appearing in the film was the child actor Tommy Rettig. One night as the company was eating dinner, Natasha approached little Tommy and warned him that without a coach's help most child stars lose their gift. "You must learn to use your instrument," said Natasha, wasting no time in applying for the job. Though Marilyn frequently forgot her lines, sometimes requiring twenty or more takes, the eleven-year-old's memory was impeccable. The next day, the boy, visibly agitated, forgot his dialogue. Unable to do as Preminger asked, he began to cry. Preminger summoned his mother, who disclosed what had happened at dinner.

When Preminger was angry or irritated, prominent blue veins bulged in his shiny, shaven head. Not for the first time, Natasha was banished. "You can be with Miss Monroe in her dressing room if she wants you there," said Preminger, "but you are not permitted on the set."

This time, however, there was a new twist. On Saturday, August 8, Marilyn decided to test her power, as DiMaggio had often done with the Yankees. Instead of dealing with Preminger on her own, pouting or calling in sick as she was known to do, Marilyn contacted her agent. She wanted the situation resolved before she saw Preminger again on Monday. Feldman talked to Zanuck, who, for the first time, backed Marilyn over a director in the matter of Natasha. It was a huge victory. Even Joe, who loathed Natasha, had reason to be exultant.

Tensions ran high on the set, where Preminger, humiliated, hoped to provoke his own firing. It was no secret that he preferred to work as an independent, and he had agreed to direct *River of No Return* only because he owed Twentieth one more picture on his contract. Preminger may have been ordered to reinstate Natasha, but that didn't mean he had to be nice to Marilyn. Deriding her talent as an actress and recalling Marilyn's days as one of Sam Spiegel's "house girls," he advised her to return to her "former profession."

Rainy weather added days to the schedule. The production was further stalled when Marilyn, wearing high green leather wading boots to protect her costume during rehearsals, slipped on a rock in the rushing river, tearing ligaments and tendons in her left leg. Twentieth flew in an orthopedic surgeon, who kept Marilyn off the set for several days.

On September 1, Marilyn flew to Los Angeles with Natasha, her leg in a cast. While she finished *River of No Return* at the studio, work proceeded on *The Girl in Pink Tights* under the supervision of the producer Sol Siegel. Not long after Marilyn's return, Famous Artists notified Siegel that Marilyn was not eager to do the film.

Meanwhile, Natasha had begun to pressure Marilyn not to risk suspension. When Hugh French of Famous Artists met with her, she spoke of little but Natasha's fears about what would happen to her own salary if Marilyn refused an assignment. Soon, Natasha went too far. She demanded $5,000 for a third mortgage on her house, but accepted the thousand Marilyn raised by selling a mink stole Johnny Hyde had given her. Afterward, in conversation with French, Marilyn characterized Natasha as an "extremely tricky woman." They had often taken up the cudgels against one another in private, but this was the first time Marilyn had anything bad to say about Natasha to anyone else. For those like DiMaggio and Feldman who tolerated Natasha because she seemed so important to Marilyn, it was an encouraging sign.

After finishing with Preminger, Marilyn accompanied DiMaggio to San Francisco on October 10. Her experience with Joe in San Francisco was dramatically different from what it had been in New York. A continent away from Table One, this was the city where he had roots. Though his background as the son of poor immigrants fueled the rage that later characterized him, Joe may never have known greater tranquility than when he was at home with his large, affectionate family.

That, no doubt, is why he wanted Marilyn to spend some time in the big, comfortable stone house in the Marina District that he'd bought for his parents during the Great Depression. It had wonderful views: In one direction, you could see the Golden Gate Bridge; in the other, Fisherman's Wharf, where Joe owned a family-run seafood restaurant. The house stood for everything Joe had fought for. Its stones had been a bulwark against hard times. In an era of national economic crisis, fans, disgusted with DiMaggio's salary demands, had booed him on the baseball field. They thought he was merely greedy. They failed to see that he only asked to be paid what he was worth. They failed to see that he was only trying to protect the people he loved.

His parents were dead, but the stone house retained its powerful emotional significance. Though Joe himself lived in lonely, nondescript hotel rooms, it was important that the old place on Beach Street remained in family hands. He might arrive there without notice, and his widowed sister Marie always had everything ready. Joe protected his family, but it is also true that Marie protected Joe. She and Marilyn spent many hours in the kitchen, cooking Italian food and discussing Joe.

Marilyn had to go to Los Angeles for the premiere of *How to Marry a Millionaire* on November 4, 1953. From the first, there had always been the possibility that without Hawks, Marilyn would be unable to repeat the miracle of *Gentlemen Prefer Blondes*. The Hawks film had been well-made in every way. The script, the production numbers, the editing—all had been perfection. On every possible level, *How to Marry a Millionaire* was inferior filmmaking. Negulesco was no match for Hawks. Yet, dull as it was, audiences loved it for Marilyn's performance. *How to Marry a Millionaire* demonstrated two things: that Marilyn could perform the "Marilyn Monroe" character brilliantly without the guidance of an expert director; and that people would flock to any film, no matter how bad, that had the character in it. Marilyn had done something more than create a character. She had launched a brand name.

While in Los Angeles, she completed some retakes for *River of No Return*. In deference to Marilyn, Zanuck assigned Negulesco to film the new footage, and he finished in time for her to spend Thanksgiving in San Francisco with the DiMaggios.

Though Joe professed disdain for her career, he could hardly remain oblivious to the box-office success of *How to Marry a Millionaire*. In 1953 alone, *Niagara*, *Gentlemen Prefer Blondes*, and *How to Marry a Millionaire* grossed in excess of $25 million; Marilyn earned more for her studio than any film star that year. The time had come for Joe to step in and ensure that Marilyn was paid what she was worth. His influence had already begun to shape Marilyn's thinking about certain key issues. Money had always meant little to her; what fueled her was a desire for respect. Joe made her see that money and respect might be linked. For Joe, money was a sign of respect. The more management was willing to pay, the more they respected an athlete. To Joe's mind, the same principle applied to a film studio and its stars. It was only a matter of time before Marilyn—vulnerable as she was to his approval—began to see things Joe's way.

When Joe returned to Los Angeles with Marilyn on November 29, he called her lawyer, Loyd Wright, to set up a meeting. It was evident from their talks that Joe had decided to take an active if behind-the-scenes role in Marilyn's contract negotiations. It was also evident that the people who said that DiMaggio was uncomfortable with any subject other than baseball were far from correct. Joe was a shrewd business strategist, and under the right circumstances he enjoyed making his views known.

DiMaggio indicated that he differed with Feldman on one crucial point. Though Feldman thought Marilyn should refuse *The Girl in Pink Tights*, he had reconciled himself to the fact that the prospect of suspension made her nervous and told her that it didn't really matter if she agreed to do the film after all. If Siegel sent her a decent script, or if he managed to borrow Gene Kelly, it was fine with Feldman if she decided to proceed. He saw no connection between that assignment and the upcoming contract negotiations. DiMaggio, however, had spotted a connection. Realizing that this would prevent the studio from accumulating a backlog of Marilyn Monroe pictures, he told Wright that they should not allow her to do *The Girl in Pink Tights* or any other film until her new deal was in place. If Twentieth had several pictures ready for release, Zanuck would be under no pressure to give her the deal she deserved. *River of No Return* had already been shot, and Joe didn't want Zanuck to have another film to put beside it on the shelf.

Toots Shor once asked DiMaggio what made him great. Joe replied that it was anticipation, the ability to figure out a play before it happens. That, as everybody in Marilyn's corner quickly realized, was what Joe had just done. He'd seen what the agents and lawyers had failed to see. He'd prevented them from making a tactical error. Wright communicated DiMaggio's views to Feldman, who was in Switzerland. As of December 1, the battle plan changed drastically. Marilyn assured her lawyer that she fully agreed with the new plan to refuse any and all assignments until after February, when a deal had been made.

On the morning of Saturday, December 5, when Joe was away, Marilyn received a call from Twentieth's casting director, Billy Gordon, asking her to report on Monday to begin rehearsals for *The Girl in Pink Tights*. The studio, unable to get Gene Kelly, had cast Frank Sinatra. Four days previously, Marilyn had seemed completely clear about what was at issue. This morning, with Gordon on the phone, she was sent into a panic at the prospect of actually refusing an assignment.

Marilyn managed to get off the phone without agreeing to anything. She called Hugh French, who could hear that she was very nervous. To buy time, French and Jack Gordean informed the casting director that Marilyn would not attend rehearsals until she'd been sent a script. Then, both agents rushed over to Doheny. Marilyn seemed to have forgotten Joe's plan completely. She wanted Famous Artists to see what could be done about getting her assigned to other pictures right away. In particular, she demanded to be tested for the role of Nefer the prostitute in *The Egyptian*. Marilyn did not want to be reminded that if she accepted a new picture she would lose significant leverage in the contract talks. She did not want to hear that Zanuck refused to consider her for *The Egyptian* because Bella Darvi, his mistress, coveted the role. She did not want to know that Feldman was in Switzerland because Jean Howard, his ex-wife, had had a serious operation. Marilyn, panicking about Monday and the decision it required, projected her anxieties onto Feldman. She resented his failure to be there precisely when she needed him most.

In his suite at the Lausanne Palace, Feldman stayed up past 2 a.m. typing drafts of a long, rambling letter to Marilyn. He was frantic and exhausted. Though divorced since 1946, he and his ex-wife remained close. He said that the past few weeks at her bedside had been the worst ordeal of his life. He couldn't possibly return until Jean had been discharged from the hospital, yet suddenly the entire Marilyn Monroe deal was threatening to explode in his absence. A telephone call from his staff reminded him that Marilyn was volatile. He had to be cautious about every word he wrote. He did not want her to misinterpret. He did not want to provoke her to seek advice from another agent. And he did not want to say anything that, if repeated, would damage his relationship with Zanuck. Marilyn was touchy, but so was Zanuck, especially on the subject of Bella Darvi.

Feldman reassured Marilyn that he had watched the rough cut of *River of No Return* with Zanuck and that both of them thought she was great. But nothing he could do right now, he promised, not even fly back to Hollywood to sit in front of Zanuck's door twenty-four hours a day for a month or more, would change Zanuck's mind about *The Egyptian*. As soon as his ex-wife was out of the hospital, Feldman planned to meet Skouras in Paris to discuss Marilyn's contract. He implored her to hold on until then.

+   +   +

It was said that when Darryl Zanuck entered his green and gold office on the Fox lot, his buck teeth preceded him by a second or two. Marlon Brando thought he looked like Bugs Bunny. Jean Negulesco called him "a swollen egoist with a smooth sneer." Ben Hecht recalled that at story conferences, Zanuck, plotting at the top of his lungs, resembled "a man hollering for help." Speaking, often shouting, in a distinctive Nebraska twang, he appeared to be intoxicated by the sound of his own voice. He swung a polo mallet at an imaginary ball as, marching to and fro, he dictated to three secretaries at a time. Souvenirs of African safaris adorned the office floor and walls.

Zanuck believed that a good story was more important to a film's success than stars. No script was made without his approval. Before a film went into production, Zanuck, who had once been a screenwriter, made copious marginal notes on the script. He didn't have to read the next draft; he knew that all his suggestions would be followed religiously. Zanuck refrained from interfering with the work of directors and actors on the set. He did, however, submit notes on the rushes. When a director finished a first cut, Zanuck rolled up his sleeves. Night after night, he would start after dinner, editing the footage himself until long past midnight. Zanuck, for better or worse, subscribed to the old Warner Bros. aesthetic. He liked films that were brisk and laconic; mercilessly he snipped out entire sequences. Zanuck was capable of working wonders in the editing room, of seeing the diamond in the dross. But he was also known to butcher a film, excising so much of the story that it no longer made sense. On *Niagara*, for instance, Zanuck had removed as many as six major sequences, leaving gaping holes in the narrative. Zanuck had the reputation of an egoist, yet when a film triumphed, he took no credit. "My boys did it!" he liked to say. When a film bombed, he blamed only himself.

On December 7, Zanuck called Jack Gordean to find out what the hell was going on. Marilyn had failed to report for rehearsals of *The Girl in Pink Tights*. DiMaggio was back and Marilyn had calmed down enough to remember their strategy and stay home. Gordean had already fielded calls from the casting director and the producer, to whom he reiterated that Marilyn couldn't come in before she received a script. Siegel, guessing that wasn't the real reason, asked whether Feldman planned to use *Pink Tights* as the basis for a new deal. Gordean reassured him that Marilyn merely wanted the courtesy of being permitted to read the script before she decided whether to accept the role.

Zanuck's call came half an hour later. He was famous for his temper, and his tirade went on and on. He insisted that Twentieth had made Marilyn a star, and that the studio was best equipped to select her material. He claimed that *Pink Tights* had been expressly designed as a vehicle for her. He cited the many people he'd hired specifically for the production. He reminded Gordean that Marilyn's contract did not give her script approval, and advised him to warn Marilyn that if she didn't come in right away he would have to resort to drastic measures. When Gordean, knowing there was not a chance Zanuck would agree, reported Marilyn's desire to be tested for *The Egyptian*, Zanuck, in a spluttering rage, declared that the role of Nefer had already been cast.

Elia Kazan once observed that Zanuck reached for his polo mallet the way other men light a cigarette. He did some of his best thinking strutting about like a rooster. Perceiving that it was in his best interest to talk to Marilyn face to face, Zanuck tried another tack. Instead of the threats and vitriol that came naturally, he would lure her in with a display of kindness and concern. Zanuck dictated a letter, ostensibly to Siegel and Henry Koster, the director of *The Girl in Pink Tights*, in which he gushed about how perfect it was for Marilyn. He said he was glad they'd decided not to let anyone read the script until it was ready. He loved the revisions they'd made so far, and raved about the new complexity of Marilyn's role. He was delighted that this picture called for Marilyn to do some real acting. Any actress would jump at a part like this, he said, but only Marilyn could do it properly. He suggested that Siegel and Koster set up a meeting with Marilyn later in the week to tell her the complete story.

A secretary announced that Mr. Gordean was on the line. Gordean reported that he had just been to see Marilyn. He had told her all Zanuck said, but she remained adamant. (Gordean did not disclose that, having conferred with Loyd Wright, he had strongly advised Marilyn to leave town.) Zanuck, instead of exploding, cheerfully asked the secretary to read Gordean the letter to Siegel and Koster, obviously expecting him to repeat its contents to Marilyn, who would have to wonder whether she was making a mistake. Afterward, Zanuck got back on the phone to suggest that Gordean arrange a time for Marilyn to talk to Siegel. Zanuck offered to attend, but only if Marilyn wanted him to.

On Tuesday morning, Zanuck didn't wait to hear from Gordean. He ordered Marilyn to appear later in the day to dub a song for *River of No Return*. As Marilyn saw, it was one thing to hold up a picture that had not yet gone into production, and quite another to refuse to do additional work on a film that had already been shot. She had to decide whether a song really needed to be dubbed. If this was just a trick to get her onto the lot to discuss *Pink Tights*, she feared she'd crumble under Zanuck's pressure. After consulting with Joe, Marilyn sent word that she couldn't come in.

Meanwhile, Zanuck attacked from another, unexpected direction. He visited Natasha on the Fox lot. That night she called Gordean to criticize Marilyn's attitude to the studio. Natasha, whom Marilyn trusted to take her side on every issue, angrily insisted that Marilyn report to work immediately. Before she had a chance to call Marilyn, Gordean got through first. Marilyn, hurt and enraged by Natasha's betrayal, refused to take her call. When the phone rang, Joe told Natasha that if she had anything to say, she should tell it to Marilyn's agent. That was the end of Marilyn's intense relationship with her dramatic coach. Though they would work together in the future, Marilyn never felt the same about her again.

When Zanuck learned that Joe was blocking the phone, he sent Roy Craft of the publicity department to the apartment on Doheny. Marilyn may have been one of Hollywood's biggest stars, but anyone could open the high iron gate, cross the courtyard to Apartment Four, open the screen door, and ring the bell. The black enameled door opened and there was Joe, six feet one inch tall. Marilyn hid somewhere in the apartment behind him. On the baseball field, DiMaggio had a reputation for being what players called a "Red Ass"—an extremely tough, menacing character. His whole body would tighten, the veins and muscles in his neck throbbing. DiMaggio wouldn't let Kraft in. Angry words were exchanged and the publicity man left.

On Wednesday morning, the phones at Famous Artists rang constantly with calls from Twentieth ordering Marilyn to report for retakes on *River of No Return*. Suddenly, three major sequences had to be reshot while Robert Mitchum and Tommy Rettig were available. The studio insisted that if Marilyn refused, the entire film would have to be shelved. Gordean, hoping to talk to Marilyn first, ducked Zanuck's calls for most of the day. But Marilyn, holed up with Joe, had decided to let the phone in her apartment ring endlessly. There was no getting through to her.

When Gordean finally returned his call, Zanuck was breathing fire and fury. He pointed out that this was the first time in his twenty-five years in the film industry that an artist had refused to complete an assignment. If Marilyn didn't report immediately he threatened to call Hedda Hopper, Louella Parsons, and other journalists. He promised to "assassinate" her. He insisted that he was prepared to "destroy an asset"—namely Marilyn Monroe—if that's what it took to punish her.

"This will be the godamnedest story I have broken in this goddamned town," Zanuck vowed. "It will be all over the whole damn industry."

Meanwhile, Frank Ferguson, the studio lawyer, had drawn up documents officially notifying Marilyn to report for retakes. A messenger delivered the papers to Doheny, pushing them partway under Marilyn's door. While he waited to see if she or DiMaggio retrieved the papers, the gate opened to admit Gordean and French. Since Marilyn refused to answer the phone, the only way to talk to her was in person. Gordean rang the bell, calling into the apartment to identify himself.

Joe and Marilyn didn't open the door in case someone from the studio was watching, but they came close enough to confer in whispers with the agents out in the courtyard. Gordean asked Marilyn to call him at the office right away. He couldn't say much more than that. On spotting the messenger, Gordean exchanged a few cordial words with him, saying he'd rung the bell without success and obviously nobody was in the apartment.

Joe and Marilyn waited until dark to sneak out. She called Gordean from a pay phone, instructing him to meet her in front of the Knickerbocker Hotel. There, Gordean reported his talks with Zanuck. He made sure that Joe agreed with everything being done. As things stood, Famous Artists believed the retakes were a ruse. So long as Marilyn was unreachable, the studio had no case.

Marilyn would be safe at Joe's house in San Francisco. They planned to drive up tonight. Gordean warned that the studio would do everything to find her. Soon, the press would be looking for her, too. Fortunately, Marie was an old hand at screening people her brother didn't want to hear from. Marilyn and her agents agreed on a code—"Mr. Robin is calling"—that would enable them to get through on the phone.

Zanuck, in the meantime, sent an angry telegram to Switzerland, warning Feldman that Marilyn's career would be over if she didn't show up. He declared that while he was perfectly willing to renegotiate Marilyn's salary, he would never consider giving her story approval. The next morning, Feldman had a frantic call from his office. Gordean had put out feelers at the studio; he discovered that additional footage for *River of No Return* really did need to be shot. Under the circumstances, Famous Artists agreed to bring Marilyn back from San Francisco. They would have to hope they could prevent Marilyn from accepting *Pink Tights* if Zanuck got to her on the lot.

Hugh French picked up Marilyn and Joe at the airport, and gave her script pages for the retakes. Marilyn dreaded a confrontation, and Feldman warned Zanuck that Marilyn would walk off the set if he pressured her about *Pink Tights*. There had been a time when she would have done anything to enter the production chief's office; now she'd do anything to stay away. As French drove her to Doheny, she asked him to accompany her to the studio and stay with her all day.

To Marilyn's relief, Zanuck was nowhere in sight as she arrived on the Fox lot on Friday, December 11. Nor did Zanuck show up during the day. He didn't have to. Aware that Marilyn trusted Jean Negulesco, Zanuck had arranged for the director to have a nice little chat with her. When French was out of earshot, Negulesco urged Marilyn to go right over to Zanuck's office and "straighten out the situation" on her own. Negulesco must have been very persuasive, because Marilyn was about to do just that when French managed to stop her.

That weekend, Feldman had two days of meetings with Skouras at the Plaza Athenée hotel in Paris. Skouras was on his way back to New York from Greece. They discussed Marilyn for six hours on Saturday. They had dinner together that night and another meeting on Sunday. They negotiated, as Skouras liked to say, "between men and friends."

Marilyn had three key demands. She wanted more money. DiMaggio had shown her that money was a sign of respect. She wanted to make fewer films. Feldman had convinced her that this would help make her more valuable. And she wanted to control the choice of script, director, and cameraman on all her films. That, for Marilyn, was the most important issue; she saw it as non-negotiable. She believed that she alone had made herself a star, but that too often she had had to do it by fighting and subterfuge. She believed she had earned the right openly to determine the direction of her career.

Feldman, determined to postpone the actual negotiations until February, saw the meetings with Skouras as preliminary. He was merely laying the groundwork for later talks with Zanuck. Careful not to make specific demands, Feldman pointed out general areas of concern. He spoke of Marilyn's salary. He spoke of the need for her to make fewer films. He said not one word about the issue of creative control.

The Old Greek, in the thick of negotiations, liked to play with yellow worry beads. He was known to grow oddly sentimental, suddenly bursting into tears. That, like his tendency to doze off, was probably just a trick. In the end, he agreed in principle that he wanted all the same things for Marilyn. Still, Skouras explained, "the Coast" bitterly resented anything that smacked of interference from New York. Zanuck liked to think he made all his own decisions. Skouras advised Feldman to get Zanuck to recommend a deal first. Once the Coast said yes, New York would enthusiastically concur, and then Skouras could take the matter to his board. Feldman sent word to Marilyn that she had a real friend in Skouras.

Marilyn finished the retakes two days before Christmas and went to San Francisco. The past few weeks had left her nerves in tatters. But the worst pressure was yet to come. The prospect of being officially notified to report for Pink Tights, and the likelihood of suspension if she refused, hung like the sword of Damocles over her head. Marilyn, having brought her career to this point, did not want to make a mistake.

DiMaggio was a rock through all of this, the one person Marilyn could always depend on. Because of the crisis, he now focused on Marilyn and her problems in a way he simply never had before. He didn't just talk about baseball. He talked about Marilyn's career, her salary, her troubles with the studio. He was in close contact with her agents and lawyers. In the past, Marilyn had complained that Joe was boring; now she listened eagerly to all he had to say because so much of it had to do with her. For many months, Joe had been asking Marilyn to marry him; finally, at Christmas 1953, she was seriously tempted.

On Christmas morning, Joe surprised Marilyn with a Maximilian mink coat, in a shade called black mist. Flinging the voluminous coat over her shoulders, Marilyn instinctively wore it "like a poncho" (as Mankiewicz says of Margo Channing in the screenplay of All About Eve). From then on, the mink became one of Marilyn's props.

Marilyn was starting to feel safe in the stone house on Beach Street when, just before New Year's Eve, Twentieth officially notified her that Pink Tights would begin filming on January 4, 1954. The carefully worded document, delivered to Feldman's office, could be used in a lawsuit. The studio wasn't talking about rehearsals; the cameras actually started to roll that day. On Joe's advice, Marilyn ignored the notice. She learned of her suspension from reporters who called for her reaction. Marie didn't put them through. Feldman had advised Marilyn to avoid journalists.

In New York, Feldman met with Skouras. There was nothing to be done so long as Marilyn refused to come in for Pink Tights. Due to return to Los Angeles, Feldman changed plans when he learned that Skouras was flying out as well. Feldman didn't want to find himself in a room with both Skouras and Zanuck. What if they insisted on renegotiating Marilyn's contract then and there? The minute they all sat down, things were likely to proceed quickly, and he had to delay until February. So on January 11, Feldman, lingering in New York, sent word to Marilyn that she faced a month or more of suspension. He urged her to try to hold on. That, as everybody knew, wasn't going to be easy.

The next day, at a family birthday party for DiMaggio's brother Tom, Joe yet again asked Marilyn to marry him. This time she said yes.

On Thursday, January 14, at 12:30 p.m., Marilyn called Harry Brand at the Fox publicity office. "I promised you that if I ever got married, I'd let you know, so I'm keeping my word." Meanwhile, Reno Barsocchini, the manager of Joe DiMaggio's Grotto on Fisherman's Wharf, called his friend Municipal Court Judge Charles Peery out of a Bar Association lunch. He asked the judge to come to City Hall right away to marry Joe and Marilyn.

When Marilyn emerged from Joe's Cadillac onto the pigeon-filled plaza outside City Hall, she was wearing a chocolate-brown broadcloth suit with a white ermine Peter Pan collar. She sported Bambi eyelashes and clutched a spray of three white orchids. Joe, in a dark blue suit, wore the same blue polka-dot tie as on their first date. He had a white carnation in his lapel. The wedding party included Mr. and Mrs. Barsocchini, Mr. and Mrs. Tom DiMaggio, and Mr. and Mrs. Lefty O'Doul. Lefty had been Joe's manager when he played in the Pacific Coast league.

A court clerk escorted them to the third floor, where, despite their efforts to keep the wedding quiet, a crowd of reporters and photographers waited in an outer office. Marilyn, pent-up after many days of avoiding the press, couldn't resist answering a few questions.

"I met him two years ago on a blind date in Los Angeles," she explained, "and a couple of days ago we started talking about this."

Joe, puffing on a fat cigar and sipping brandy from a paper cup, finally cut in. "All right, fellas, I don't want to rush you, but we've got to get on with the ceremony."

The single-ring ceremony in the judge's chambers took all of three minutes. One journalist, standing on a desk in the outer office, watched through a transom as the judge pronounced Joe and Marilyn man and wife. When the newlyweds came out, flashbulbs popped and reporters shouted more questions.

"We're very happy," said Marilyn.

Did they want children?

"We expect to have one," said Joe. "I can guarantee that."

"I'd like to have six," said Marilyn, holding Joe's arm and looking at him adoringly.

"We'll have at least one," said Joe.

Where did they plan to live?

"We'll probably be doing a lot of commuting," said Joe, "but San Francisco will be our headquarters."

Did Marilyn really plan to give up Hollywood to become a housewife?

"What difference does it make?" Marilyn grinned. "I'm suspended."

When Darryl Zanuck learned of the wedding, he had little choice but to lift Marilyn's suspension. If he hadn't, the press and public reaction would have been unforgiving. To allow the newlyweds time for a honeymoon, Zanuck notified Famous Artists that he expected Marilyn to report for work no later than January 25. Charlie Feldman, waiting until February to renegotiate Marilyn's contract and sell the rights to *Horns of the Devil*, could not have been happier.

+ FIVE +

The Cadillac with "JOE D" plates had been parked in front of the Clifton Motel in Pasa Robles since eight the previous night. At 1 p.m. on Friday, the door to room 15 opened and Marilyn appeared in the bright sunlight, bundled in a loose-fitting yellow polo coat. A red scarf concealed her cotton-candy hair. There was no sign of yesterday's false eyelashes. Her face scrubbed clean of makeup, she put on a pair of oversized dark glasses and climbed into the passenger seat. Joe settled the bill—$6.50 for the night—with Mr. Sharpe in the office. He had requested a room with a double bed and a television set—the latter, presumably, so that he could watch the news about the voting for the Baseball Hall of Fame in Cooperstown, New York. As it happened, Joe wouldn't be elected until the following year.

"We've got to put a lot of miles behind us," Joe was heard to say as he and Marilyn headed south. The destination was Loyd Wright's remote mountain cabin in Idyllwild, about fifty miles from Palm Springs. They planned to stay there for ten days, after which Joe was due in New York for a television commitment.

In all directions there was snow as far as the eye could see. The cabin had a billiard table but, to Marilyn's delight, no television set. The only other people on the property were a discreet caretaker and his wife. There were no ringing telephones. There were no legal papers being served. There were no agents or studio employees or reporters pounding on the door. The newlyweds took long walks in the snow. Joe taught his bride to play billiards. And they talked—so much so that Marilyn later told Sidney Skolsky that she and her husband were finally beginning to get to know each other.

105

They returned to Los Angeles on the 24th. It was the day before Marilyn was due back at Twentieth, though of course she had no intention of showing up. As she opened the high iron gate at Doheny, she saw a copy of the script for *The Girl in Pink Tights* wedged behind her screen door. Zanuck had sent it over as a courtesy, with another copy to Famous Artists.

Zanuck was by no means conceding that Marilyn had the right to approve scripts, and he certainly wasn't interested in her opinion. If, as seems likely, Zanuck thought that no harm could be done in giving Marilyn the script, he was wrong. Up to this point, Marilyn had insisted that she was refusing to report to work because she hadn't seen a script. Now, she was going to do something different. She was going to pass judgment. Worse, she was going to question Zanuck's judgment. She was going to imply that she knew better than the production chief whether a script was good.

The next day, when Marilyn failed to appear, her lawyer told reporters: "She read the script and does not care to do the picture." Twentieth wasted no time in suspending her again. Hours later, the press office released a hard-hitting statement: "Producer Sol C. Siegel, who made Miss Monroe's highly successful musical *Gentlemen Prefer Blondes*, has had a complete script and full musical score ready for the CinemaScope camera. In addition, Henry Koster, who directed the most successful picture in the industry's history, *The Robe*, was assigned to *Pink Tights* and other cast principals have been ready for filming to start. This has involved the studio in a tremendous investment. If Miss Monroe's failure to appear is based on her desire to approve scripts, the studio wishes to point out that the outstanding success of Miss Monroe's previous vehicles is evidence enough of the studio's ability to select stories for her."

Privately, Zanuck expressed rage that Marilyn would dare to criticize one of his productions in the press. He thought the idea of her having any input at all was ludicrous. As far as Zanuck was concerned, Marilyn was an idiot and didn't know the first thing about filmmaking.

Feldman was delighted to learn that as soon as DiMaggio returned from New York, he planned to take Marilyn to Japan for the start of the baseball season there. Lefty O'Doul, known as Mr. Baseball to Japanese fans, had invited Joe to participate in an exhibition tour, during which they would also give some workshops for Japanese players. Since Marilyn was suspended, Joe asked her to come along.

For Feldman, the timing could not have been better. He would begin the negotiations with Zanuck without having to worry that Marilyn, always a loose cannon, would somehow foul things up. Besides, there was talk of Marilyn's making a side trip to Korea to entertain the U.S. troops there, the Korean War having ended six months previously. From Feldman's point of view, the publicity would be a great advantage. Twentieth would have a hard time attacking Marilyn in the press at a moment when she was singing and dancing for American boys overseas.

Marilyn arrived in San Francisco on the night of January 28. Joe flew in from New York earlier in the day. Before they went to Honolulu, there was a mishap at home on Beach Street. Marilyn came up behind Joe and put her arms around him. Joe, sensitive about being touched, instinctively threw her right hand back with such force that the thumb had to be put in a splint.

"I just bumped it," Marilyn insisted, as she and Joe arrived at the airport on January 29. Reporters had noticed that she was trying to conceal her thumb in the folds of her mink coat. When they saw the splint, they wanted to know what had happened.

"I have a witness," Marilyn went on. "Joe was there. He heard it crack." Clutching Marilyn tightly, he stared immovably at her right hand.

Did she plan to make another film soon? someone inquired. "We're not concerned about that now," Joe interjected. "We're on our honeymoon."

When Pan American flight 831 touched down in Honolulu, thousands of fans rushed onto the airfield screaming "Marilyn! Marilyn!" An inadequate security force was powerless to hold them back. There was pandemonium. The crowd surrounded Marilyn, pawing at her hair and clothing. Some fans later claimed to have broken off strands of her hair. Finally, police formed a ring around the couple and forced a way through to an airport lounge.

Marilyn's reception in Tokyo was equally vociferous. At the airport, she had to be smuggled out through the luggage hatch. A large police contingent was waiting at the Imperial Hotel as Joe and Marilyn drove up in a black convertible. When the police closed the lobby doors, fans plunged through the plate-glass panels in an effort to reach Japan's number one foreign box-office star. Only after "the honorable buttocks-swinging madam," as Marilyn was called in the Japanese press, put in a brief appearance on a balcony did the crowd finally disperse.

That night, Marilyn, in a clinging red wool dress, held a press conference for seventy-five Japanese journalists at the hotel. She was assisted by Lefty O'Doul. "We are told you do not wear anything under your dress," shouted one reporter. "Is it true?" DiMaggio cut a poignant figure, lurking nearly unnoticed in the corner of the large room. That kind of question pained him. Neither was he thrilled when Marilyn announced that she did indeed plan to spend about four days entertaining the troops in Korea.

The side trip was exceedingly important to her. Marilyn had often talked to Feldman about her desire to go to Korea, since she believed that she owed a good deal of her success to the U.S. soldiers who collected her posters. It was said that there were more pictures of her pasted up in bunkers, military offices, and footlockers than of any other actress. More lonely soldiers wrote to Marilyn than to anyone else in Hollywood. The military newspaper *Stars and Stripes* featured so many photographs of Marilyn on its cover that it often had to run repeat shots.

On February 16, Marilyn flew to Seoul, accompanied by Lefty's wife. She wore a combat jacket over a man's army shirt and trousers, and combat boots. At the Seoul City Air Base, they transferred to a helicopter that took them to the cold, mountainous location, formerly a war zone, where the First Marine Division was stationed. In addition to the pilot, there were several other soldiers on board.

The sight of thousands of men waiting on the mountain where she was to perform thrilled Marilyn. She instructed the pilot to fly in a low circle so that she could wave to the troops. Then she threw open the sliding door. Shouting at the two soldiers to sit on her feet, Marilyn slid belly-down out of the helicopter. Laughing and blowing kisses, she dangled in mid-air over the shrieking, whistling, applauding Marines. The danger seemed only to enhance her euphoria. Four times she ordered the pilot to circle the mountain as the excitement below kept building.

By the time the helicopter landed, Marilyn had the crowd worked up to a frenzy. There was a makeshift platform with an upright piano and a microphone. Marilyn disappeared into a dressing area behind some burlap curtains that flapped in the icy wind, and changed into a skin-tight, embroidered sheath dress with plum-colored sequins. Despite the piercing cold, her shoulders were bare, the low-cut dress held up by fragile spaghetti straps. She wore rhinestone-covered hoop earrings, a pearl bracelet, and stiletto heels.

When Marilyn peeked through the burlap curtains, what she saw exhilarated her. Some thirteen thousand men, wearing heavy, hooded parkas and fur-lined hats, were all there for her. Marilyn loved the power she had over men. When she felt that power most strongly, all her insecurities dropped away. Marilyn had been known to hide in her dressing room in fear of facing a film camera. She had been known to vomit and to break out in spots. But at moments like this, she was transformed into a different person. She fed on the noise, the adoration, the sexual frenzy of the crowd.

Marilyn strutted out onstage to wild cheers. She caressed the microphone, holding it close to her moist red lips. She talked to the troops in a baby voice. Singing "Diamonds Are A Girl's Best Friend," "Do It Again," and other songs, Marilyn seemed oblivious to the piercing cold. It might have been the hottest day of the year.

That night, Marilyn was the guest of honor at a dinner attended by some fifty officers. The Signal Corps had hooked up a telephone connection to Joe, with the conversation to be broadcast on a public address system. As Marilyn spoke to her husband, she was still keyed up after the performance. "Do you still love me, Joe?" Marilyn purred for all to hear. "Do you miss me?" Though he said that he did, DiMaggio, who hated being made to look ridiculous, sounded tense, measured, subdued. He remained that way when Marilyn returned to Japan, exuberant about her experiences in Korea.

"Joe, you never heard such cheering," she told him.

"Yes, I have," DiMaggio answered ruefully.

Marilyn was running a fever, a prelude to the fully fledged pneumonia that would keep her in bed at the Imperial Hotel until it was time to go home.

After a few days of Marie's pampering in San Francisco, Joe went to New York on business. Marilyn, her voice still a bit raspy, flew to Los Angeles for the *Photoplay* Awards ceremony at the Beverly Hills Hotel. This year, she was to be honored as Hollywood's most popular actress.

"I can't even say I'm glad to be home, because home is with my husband and he isn't here," Marilyn told reporters at the airport on March 5, 1954. As she talked she waved her left hand, calling attention to a glittering diamond bracelet. "Joe's in New York and he'll be here in a few days. He's the head of our family and I'll live wherever he decides, but he doesn't know yet what city it will be."

As always, Marilyn came to the ceremony late. There was considerable awkwardness when she entered wearing a white satin dress with a wrapped top, her hair tinted a Harlow-esque platinum. This year, however, it wasn't Marilyn's costume that caused a stir, but her position on the dais four seats from Darryl Zanuck. As the date required by her tax situation had finally passed in her absence, Feldman had begun negotiating her contract in earnest. The talks were still in progress. Marilyn and Zanuck did their best to ignore each other, though he appeared to listen as she answered a reporter's question.

"I am still under suspension," said Marilyn, blowing away a strand of platinum hair that had fallen over her face. "I have no idea when the suspension may be lifted, and consequently can give no definite answer about my return to pictures."

Feldman waited until Joe arrived in Los Angeles to convey to Marilyn the details of his discussions with Twentieth. They met in his paneled office on March 15. Sitting under a Renoir painting, the agent reviewed all he had accomplished so far. At such moments Feldman tended to be self-effacing.

He had convinced Zanuck to abandon The Girl in Pink Tights. He had convinced him to pay Marilyn a lot more money. He had convinced him that she must be required to do no more than two films a year. And he had convinced him to buy Horns of the Devil for $225,000, whether or not Marilyn actually appeared in the film. On all these issues, the production chief had moved swiftly because, thanks to Joe, Twentieth had no backlog of unreleased Marilyn Monroe films beyond River of No Return.

On one issue, however, Feldman had been unable to budge Zanuck. He emphasized that from the start, he had repeatedly insisted on Marilyn's right to approve scripts, directors, and cameramen. But Lew Schreiber had been quick to point out that Twentieth would never consider such a request. Zanuck alone decided what scripts were made on the Fox lot and who made them. This was the hot-button issue for

Zanuck. Certainly, all his statements to the press had signaled that he had no intention of giving Marilyn a voice in such decisions.

Though he certainly never told her so, Feldman didn't believe Marilyn was equipped to have that kind of responsibility anyway. Her own agent was certain that if only Zanuck would make a small, symbolic concession in this area, she would forget all about creative control and focus on the one really important issue: money. But Feldman failed to understand that this was not just a whim of Marilyn's. It went to the very heart of what she wanted. Winning the right to these controls would confirm that Marilyn finally had the respect that, she believed, came with stardom. She needed a sign from Zanuck that her childhood dream really had come true.

Marilyn was upset, but Feldman minimized the problem. He assured her that he was still trying to persuade Zanuck to give her some form of creative control. But, he emphasized, Marilyn would have to compromise as well. By the time the conversation was finished, Feldman had persuaded her to scale back her demands drastically. In the end, she asked only for the right to approve her own choreographer and dramatic coach. It was very little, but at least it would be a sign that Zanuck acknowledged Marilyn had earned the right to a voice in the creative process. Marilyn was certain that Feldman understood how much this meant to her. Surely, after all she had done in the past year, no one would refuse such a tiny request.

Zanuck was especially eager to settle, Feldman believed, because he wanted to cast Marilyn in *There's No Business Like Show Business*, a backstage musical that featured the songs of Irving Berlin. It was scheduled to start in April, under the direction of Walter Lang. Feldman also mentioned the tantalizing possibility of using Marilyn in an independent production of his own. He had been talking to Billy Wilder about a film of the hit Broadway comedy *The Seven Year Itch*. Wilder and Feldman would produce together, with Wilder directing and George Axelrod writing the script. Though Feldman made no promises that Twentieth would permit him to shoot *The Seven Year Itch* there, if all went well he wanted Marilyn to star.

Marilyn may have been ambivalent about Feldman personally, but she respected his talents as a producer, especially his ability to choose prestigious projects. *The Seven Year Itch* would be Feldman's first independent production since *A Streetcar Named Desire*. The participation of Wilder, whose work Marilyn admired, made the project irresistible. This would be Marilyn's first opportunity since *Gentlemen Prefer Blondes* to work with a director of the first rank.

Joe and Marilyn returned to Feldman's office three days later. As he was close to a deal with Zanuck, Feldman advised Marilyn to start *There's No Business Like Show Business* even if she didn't have a signed contract yet. The musical promised to require a lengthy shoot, and Feldman wanted Marilyn to be finished by the time Wilder, currently at work on *Sabrina* with Audrey Hepburn, was free. Wilder and Axelrod planned to work on the script sometime during the summer. Though Marilyn disliked the idea of another musical, she agreed to the assignment strictly because she was eager to do *The Seven Year Itch*.

Feldman also urged Marilyn to accept the studio's proposal that if a contract hadn't been finalized in time, she begin the picture at her old weekly salary of $1,250. The moment a new salary and other terms had been agreed on and the papers were signed, Twentieth would retroactively pay the difference. That amount, Joe would be happy to hear, promised to be substantial. The studio was fast approaching Feldman's target price of $100,000 per picture.

In the days that followed, Marilyn was euphoric. All these months of listening to Joe and to Charlie finally appeared to have paid off. Excited about *The Seven Year Itch* and confident that her new deal at Twentieth was nearing completion, Marilyn swept into Famous Artists on March 31 and signed the papers officially making her their client. As soon as she signed her new studio contract, Feldman would finally begin to be paid.

+   +   +

As the door to Marilyn's luxurious, ground-floor dressing room in the two-story, beige stucco Star Building at Twentieth opened, the aroma of Chanel No. 5 perfume filled the air. The scent lingered when Marilyn was absent. Sunlight peeked through the edges of closed Venetian blinds. Marilyn had inherited dressing room M, said to be the best on the lot, from Betty Grable. An outer area was decorated with crimson-upholstered Queen Anne chairs and sofas. When the fluorescent lights were turned on, a spacious dressing table was visible inside, adorned with a small framed photograph of Joe—gray-streaked hair growing to a widow's peak—and littered with countless tiny prescription bottles from Schwab's. Mirrors large and small hung on all sides.

Twentieth lifted Marilyn's suspension on April 13 and she returned to the lot the next day. She hadn't set foot in her dressing room since December 23. Afterward, at the studio's request, she met with reporters in Sol Siegel's office. Asked about her contract, Marilyn declared that she and Twentieth were still "working out details" but that she anticipated signing very soon.

How was married life?

"As far as I'm concerned baseball players make good husbands," said Marilyn. "Joe and I want a lot of little DiMaggios."

The journalists applauded. The studio executives winced.

"Am I expecting now? Oh, no, but I wish I were. We want children as soon as possible."

Joe and Marilyn had rented a furnished, two-story, eight-room Tudor cottage on North Palm Drive in Beverly Hills. It faced directly onto the street, affording little privacy. A curved brick path, bordered by chrysanthemums and red roses, led to the front door. Behind were a large patio and a turquoise swimming pool. There were usually two Cadillacs on the driveway. By contrast with Joe's immaculate blue car, Marilyn's black convertible with black leather upholstery tended to be messy, the back seat cluttered with old clothes and unpaid traffic tickets.

On April 23, Marilyn, sipping a vodka on the patio, noticed an advance review of *River of No Return* in the *Hollywood Reporter*: "If *River* proves anything at all, it is that Marilyn Monroe should stick to musicals and the type of entertainment that made her such a box-office lure. If the film fails to bring in smash returns, Twentieth Century–Fox can attribute it to Marilyn's inability to handle a heavy acting role. Most of her genuine values are lost here. . . . If Twentieth persists in casting her in epics calling for emotional histrionics and dowdy costumes, revealing as they may be, it is going to affect her box-office pull."

Marilyn screamed. Crying, she raced upstairs to find the long, rambling letter Feldman had written from Switzerland back in December. Hadn't he told her that he'd watched a rough cut of *River of No Return* with Zanuck? Hadn't he assured her that they both thought she was great? If Zanuck and Feldman really knew what they were doing, how could they have been so mistaken?

For the past few weeks, Marilyn, looking forward to *The Seven Year Itch*, had been certain that she'd made the right decision in putting herself in Feldman's hands. She'd been grateful to Joe for devising the strategy that, apparently, had allowed her to beat the studio. But Friday's *Hollywood Reporter* changed everything. Marilyn began to worry that her career was in danger. All weekend, she was nervous, brooding, uncertain.

On Monday, things got worse. Feldman informed Marilyn that he wouldn't be making *The Seven Year Itch* at Twentieth after all, since Skouras had been unable to get a deal through his board. He apologized, but obviously he was going to have to make *The Seven Year Itch* without her. Marilyn reminded her agent that she had agreed to appear in *There's No Business Like Show Business*, preliminary work on which had already begun, solely because she wanted to work with Wilder on *The Seven Year Itch*. Feldman was anxious to keep Marilyn happy as the time to sign her studio contract approached, so he agreed to go back to Skouras about *The Seven Year Itch*.

Meanwhile, Feldman called Marilyn on May 5 to say that Twentieth had prepared the first draft of her new contract. He would send over a copy for her to review. When the papers arrived, Marilyn was shattered. In the draft, even the very minimal creative controls she had asked for were missing. At Feldman's urging, Marilyn had made significant concessions. She had abandoned her request to control scripts, directors, and cameramen. She had asked only to be permitted to approve her choreographer and dramatic coach. Even Zanuck had to have seen that her demands were merely symbolic. Yet he would concede nothing which acknowledged that Marilyn had had a hand in her own stardom.

Marilyn grew furious. As she saw it, the contract meant only one thing. Twentieth did not respect her. She had created a great character whom the world adored. She had filled the studio's coffers. She had accomplished everything she had set out to do, except in one important respect. From the beginning, Marilyn had always believed that if only she could become a star, the respect she longed for would be part of the package. But it hadn't turned out that way. To her utter bewilderment, the long, desperate struggle had been pointless. She'd worked. She'd studied. She'd fought. She'd pushed herself beyond the limits. She'd more than earned everything she wanted. Yet Zanuck and the others took credit for her success. They didn't take her seriously. They saw her as no more than the dumb blonde she portrayed on screen.

To make matters worse, to some extent both her agent and her husband fundamentally shared the studio's view. Feldman didn't see why Marilyn didn't just sign the papers and get on with her career. DiMaggio, to her horror, agreed. A contract that gave Marilyn enough money, as this one did, was good enough for Joe. Marilyn, furious and feeling betrayed, had to face the fact that, when it came to the most important issues, the people closest to her were not on her side.

Three days later, Feldman called with what he thought was great news. He had struck a deal with Zanuck; he was to make The Seven Year Itch at Twentieth after all. Feldman assumed that Marilyn would be delighted. Instead, she angrily told him that she suspected him of having sold out her interests to push through his own deal. Feldman laid out his entire deal with the studio for Joe and Marilyn. He certainly didn't want it said that he'd won concessions for himself at a client's expense. In fact, the offers he'd had to produce The Seven Year Itch at Warner Bros. and United Artists would have been better for him financially. He'd agreed to a less lucrative deal at Twentieth only because of Marilyn's eagerness to work with Wilder.

On May 20, Feldman's attorney informed him that Marilyn seemed happy again. This may have been true, but it was not because of anything Feldman said or did. That month an important new player had quietly entered the fray. Feldman didn't know about him. Neither did DiMaggio. Yet Milton Greene, a thirty-two-year-old fashion and portrait photographer, had begun to exert considerable influence on Marilyn. Though successful in New York, Greene was desperate to break into the movies. Not as a cameraman, however. His dream was to produce.

Richard Avedon called Greene "the greatest photographer of women" he'd ever encountered. Before meeting Marilyn in September 1953 on assignment for Look magazine, Greene had produced memorable images of Judy Garland, Grace Kelly, Marlene Dietrich, and other movie stars. His pictures appeared in Life, Look, Harper's Bazaar, and Vogue. Among publicists and magazine editors, he had a reputation for being particularly effective with "needy" women. He knew how to handle the divas.

Greene was said to resemble a slim Peter Lorre. He dressed in black from head to foot, with a red kerchief round his neck. Like Marilyn, he was a nail-biter. Careful never to raise his voice, he came across as shy, sensitive, idealistic, and sympathetic. His speech was laced with Brooklynese. He had a disarming smile, boyish and seductive. He made a star feel calm, comfortable, and secure. He showered her with admiration and respect. He made her feel she was the center of the universe. He made her want to pour out her troubles to him.

Greene turned up in Los Angeles in May 1954 at a moment when Marilyn was feeling intensely isolated and confused after the debacle of the contract. It was their third encounter, Greene having brought his wife, Amy, to meet Marilyn in October. Feeling comfortable in the warmth of his company, Marilyn complained bitterly about her studio, about her inability to control the kinds of pictures she made, about the roles that Zanuck insisted she play. She didn't understand why stardom had failed to give her what she wanted, nor did she understand why neither her agent nor her husband seemed to hear what she was saying.

Greene's response was to take pictures. It was Sunday and the studio lot was empty. In the wardrobe department, Greene dressed Marilyn in Jennifer Jones's costume from Song of Bernadette—a close-fitting jacket, a full skirt, heavy black stockings, and black wooden shoes. Then he steered her to the French village set for What Price Glory?, where she posed as a peasant girl in a series of dramatically lit, richly textured images that resembled paintings.

Marilyn was delighted. Greene had photographed her as one might have photographed Greta Garbo. He had provided Marilyn with an image of herself as she longed to be seen. He didn't confuse her with the dumb blonde she'd created on screen. He perceived something in Marilyn that all the others did not. He seemed to understand where her dream had gone wrong. He helped clarify matters: Perhaps stardom wasn't the problem, so much as the particular kind of stardom she had attained.

Marilyn had been drawn to Hollywood outsiders before. Arthur Miller had been an outsider. So had DiMaggio, until he became so entangled with her agents and lawyers that, much as he despised the film industry, his perspective seemed little different from theirs. Besides, DiMaggio never thought that Marilyn had any acting talent; the husband's principal concern, like that of her agents and lawyers, was to maximize her income.

Milton Greene was the first man since Johnny Hyde who appeared to believe in Marilyn unreservedly. The others were interested in money. Greene was interested in her being allowed to develop her talent. He told Marilyn what she wanted to hear. At a moment when Twentieth was refusing to give her any control over the films she made, Greene insisted that creative control was precisely what Marilyn must have. Feeding off each other's enthusiasm, they were eager to take their collaboration a step further. Before Greene returned to New York, they made plans. In the naïve belief that still photographs would be accepted as proof that she could play different kinds of parts, Greene and Marilyn talked about doing a picture book that showed her in a variety of character roles. And they talked about making movies together.

Meanwhile, attorneys for Twentieth Century–Fox and Famous Artists met at Loyd Wright's office to go over the first draft of Marilyn's contract. Marilyn, furious at Zanuck's refusal to give her even the most minor approvals, had insisted that all her original demands be revived. Wright sent Frank Ferguson back to Twentieth with Marilyn's demand for a clause permitting her to approve scripts, directors, and cameramen.

Marilyn began filming *There's No Business Like Show Business* on May 28. By that time, returning to Twentieth without a signed contract seemed much less good an idea than it had in March. She had only agreed because she'd been assured that her basic demands had been met. With Marilyn back on the lot, the pressure was off Twentieth to keep her happy.

Convinced that Zanuck wouldn't budge, Marilyn's agents urged her to compromise again. At first, Marilyn was adamant that she would not. Then she called Hugh French late at night to say that she was willing to discuss giving up approval of her cameraman and director. On two points, however, she remained firm. She would never sign a contract that failed to give her the right to approve her choreographer and her dramatic coach. If Zanuck insisted on controlling the films she appeared in, so be it. At the very least, Marilyn expected to control the details of her own performances. That meant having Jack Cole and Natasha Lytess. Marilyn wanted her agents to understand that, though she certainly hadn't forgiven Natasha, she continued to require a coach. Until she found someone better, Natasha would have to do.

On June 15, French went to Lew Schreiber. Despite Marilyn's willingness to compromise, the studio general manager wasn't in a conciliatory mood. Schreiber, known as Zanuck's right hand, said that Twentieth would never give Marilyn any creative approvals whatsoever. Afterward, Gordean and French visited dressing room M. Marilyn, livid, refused to back down. Finally, Gordean proposed that their only hope was to go around Schreiber. Skouras was due in Los Angeles at the end of the week. He'd always had a soft spot for Marilyn. Gordean advised her to present her demands to Skouras personally.

The night before Skouras flew out to the coast, Feldman conferred with him in New York. That way Marilyn could work her magic without having to explain exactly what she wanted. Skouras arrived in Los Angeles on Friday morning, June 18. He saw Marilyn that evening. As arranged, Hugh French came in as the meeting was about to break up. By that time, Marilyn certainly appeared to have brought the old man around. Skouras made no commitments, however. Obviously, New York had to clear matters with the Coast. Skouras asked Marilyn to visit him at the Beverly Hills Hotel on Sunday afternoon to continue their discussions.

By Sunday, Skouras, presumably having talked to Schreiber, was singing a different tune. Marilyn knew something was wrong the minute she walked in. The indulgent father had metamorphosed into a stern father. He insisted that Twentieth had given her all it could. When Marilyn made a scene, Skouras panicked. He called Feldman in New York. But Feldman couldn't be found and Marilyn stormed out before anything could be settled.

The following week, Marilyn collapsed on the set. After she was rushed home, a studio spokesman announced that Marilyn had been in poor health since her bout with pneumonia in Japan. Reached by telephone, Marilyn herself denied reports that she was pregnant.

"I'm not expecting a little baseball player yet, but that doesn't mean that Joe and I don't want one."

Skouras sensed that her remarks were directed at him. Marilyn seemed to be saying that if he failed to give in, she could always get pregnant and stay away for the duration. Skouras called Loyd Wright with a new offer. Marilyn and the studio would share the right to approve her choreographer and dramatic coach; in the event of a disagreement, however, Twentieth would have the final say.

Marilyn's lawyer and agent concurred that she should sign. Marilyn disagreed. She vowed that if she didn't get what she wanted, after completing *There's No Business Like Show Business* she'd "sit out" the remaining four years of her studio contract. She mysteriously alluded to other plans that would permit her to "come out smelling like a rose." What other plans, Charlie Feldman wanted to know. He was in New York building the entire production of *The Seven Year Itch*—basically a two-character piece—around Marilyn. If matters weren't settled soon, his picture might be without a star. Darryl Zanuck was in Paris at the moment. Feldman intended to fly there immediately to appeal to him to give Marilyn all she was asking for. When Hugh French told Marilyn about the trip, he added that Feldman was not optimistic.

"In that case, I'll see you in four years!" she gleefully replied.

Feldman was en route when Gordean and French went to dressing room M with his suggestion for a compromise. His idea was for Marilyn to prepare a list of coaches and choreographers she'd like to work with. Marilyn cut the agents off. She wasn't interested in any of this right now. To Gordean's astonishment, she said that she couldn't sign a contract before Zanuck came back from Europe. Upon his return, she needed to see Zanuck alone to discuss several confidential matters. When Gordean asked what those might be, Marilyn refused to say. The agent was taken aback. Didn't Marilyn realize that Feldman was about to meet with Zanuck? If she had a proposal of her own, they had to know. Marilyn snapped that if Feldman couldn't wait until she had seen Zanuck, that was just too bad.

Gordean lost patience. He told her that her demands were imprac-tical. After Marilyn signed her contract, if she didn't like a coach or a choreographer, all she had to do was refuse to appear. Marilyn retorted that she didn't want to refuse pictures anymore, because the publicity hurt her career. She was tired of having to fight the studio. Gordean replied that no matter how many points were spelled out in Marilyn's contract, she'd always have to fight. And she could always rely on her agents to fight for her. Marilyn wasn't so sure. Still, no sooner did the agents leave than she called Loyd Wright. She said she'd sign the contract if Twentieth would promise to let her have the last word in the event of a dispute. The studio didn't have to put it in writing; all she sought was an oral agree-ment. Wright and Gordean, eager to settle, went to Schreiber.

As everyone knew, Zanuck had to say yes before the number two man gave a final answer. Feldman worked on him in Paris, and Zanuck agreed in time for a July 8 meeting between both sides at the studio. Across a conference table, Schreiber assured Wright that Marilyn would have the approvals she wanted. Wright called Marilyn, who promised to come to his office the next day to sign. The lawyers on both sides, the studio executives, and the agents breathed a sigh of relief.

To everyone's horror, Marilyn failed to show up at her lawyer's office. When Wright finally reached her by phone, she said she needed a few more days. Marilyn stalled until Monday, July 19, when a call from her persuaded Wright that he'd have her signature by the end of the week.

Meanwhile, Milton Greene had wired Sidney Skolsky to set up a telephone conversation with Marilyn on July 20. When Marilyn cryptically spoke about other plans, she meant her ongoing discussions with Greene. When she declared that she was tired of fighting the studio, the subtext was Greene's proposal to set up an independent production company. More likely than not, their first film would be the life story of Jean Harlow that Skolsky hoped to produce—thus his willingness to act as a go-between. But Greene needed time to put some money together. The moment Marilyn signed her new studio contract, his dreams would be short-circuited.

Frantic to keep her from settling with Twentieth, Greene obviously couldn't call Marilyn at home. DiMaggio, as was his nature, would be deeply suspicious of what Greene wanted. Joe, satisfied with the $100,000 per picture fee and the $225,000 price tag for *Horns of the Devil*, had been ready for Marilyn to sign in March. So long as Marilyn intended to remain in motion pictures—and DiMaggio would have preferred that she didn't—at least she'd be making decent money. He had steered clear of all the back-and-forth over creative approvals that had preoccupied Marilyn in the intervening months.

Two days after her conversation with Greene, Marilyn arrived at Wright's office in a rage. Suddenly, she was suspicious again about Feldman's deal at Twentieth. Marilyn remained eager to make *The Seven Year Itch*, but insisted that she didn't owe the studio "a damned thing" and would sign the contract when she was good and ready. She instructed the attorney to arrange for her to meet Zanuck, with no one from Famous Artists present.

Feldman, in New York, decided that the time had come to bring DiMaggio back into the picture. He was due to return to Los Angeles on July 28, and he invited Joe and Marilyn to dine with him at home that evening, along with Loyd Wright. Marilyn refused.

On July 30, as Feldman approached dressing room M in the Star Building at Twentieth, he could smell the faint aroma of Chanel No. 5. Based on what he'd heard from various agents, lawyers, and studio executives, he hardly knew what sort of reception to expect. Lately, Marilyn had had some pretty bad things to say about her agent. But when Feldman entered the fluorescent-lit rear room, Marilyn, at her dressing table, turned and greeted him warmly. Reflections on all sides suggested a funhouse hall of mirrors. Marilyn acted as though nothing were wrong. She smiled as though she adored him. When Feldman perceived that Marilyn wasn't going to say a word about her contract, he happily did the same. The contract could wait, *The Seven Year Itch* could not. He had to know whether he could count on her to appear in the film, which was scheduled to start in September. When Marilyn spoke excitedly about the week of location work in New York, Feldman was relieved.

As the actress and the agent had done two years previously after she failed to sign with Famous Artists, they tacitly agreed to stop talking about the issue at stake. They tacitly agreed not to mention the contract, or the money and other terms Feldman had negotiated. Marilyn would get none of those things so long as the new contract remained unsigned, and Feldman would continue to receive not a penny for all his work on her behalf. She remained at her old salary scale; the studio would simply pick up her option under the original contract. Feldman assumed Marilyn was being her usual mercurial self. He didn't suspect that she was leaving things open because Greene was waiting in the wings. Nor did he realize that when Marilyn told him about the project she really wanted to do next, his ability to set that up for her would determine his future as her agent—as well as a great deal else of significance in her life.

Suddenly, Marilyn was desperate to be cast in *Guys and Dolls*. Marlon Brando, who'd been filming *Désirée* on the Fox lot, had visited Marilyn on the set of *There's No Business Like Show Business*. He told her he'd agreed to star in Joe Mankiewicz's film version of the Broadway musical.

"Maybe I'll do it too," Marilyn suggested. "Wouldn't that be wonderful?"

"Be nice," said Brando.

So Marilyn urged Feldman to persuade Samuel Goldwyn to request her on a loanout from Twentieth. Feldman perceived, and Marilyn appeared to understand, that if Goldwyn did ask for her, she'd have to sign with Twentieth before Darryl Zanuck even considered loaning her out. He promptly arranged for Marilyn to talk to Goldwyn on the phone about *Guys and Dolls*.

"I'd rather do it than breathe!" she told Goldwyn.

+   +   +

On September 8, 1954, a loud television set could be heard throughout the cottage where Joe and Marilyn lived. Upstairs, in the master bedroom, two assistants were preparing Marilyn for a 9 p.m. flight. They'd been at it for hours. A limousine was coming in a few minutes. Hugh French was supposed to meet her at the airport.

Her bags were already packed with clothing which Twentieth had lent her for New York. Marilyn's own closets were surprisingly bare. Her personal wardrobe consisted of little besides some snug sweaters and numerous pairs of tight, tapered Jax slacks with ankle-baring cuffs and a rear zipper—and, of course, the mink coat Joe had given her for Christmas. The other clothes Marilyn wore in public were largely borrowed from the studio.

Much of the day, a Wednesday, had been devoted to clothing. Marilyn had rushed through last-minute costume fittings for *The Seven Year Itch*. At the moment, she was being outfitted in a travel costume that was supposed to cling to her like a second skin. It consisted of a sheer wool beige dress, the top wrapped snugly around her chest and tied in a bow. It was exceedingly uncomfortable.

After hours of nips and tucks the effect was nearly perfect. No ordinary person would possibly wear such an outfit on a cross-country flight. Marilyn intended to undress as soon as she had run the gauntlet of photographers to the privacy of her sleeper. Before the plane landed, assistants would dress her and do her hair and makeup all over again.

Finally, Marilyn slipped into a matching beige coat with a beige fur collar and trim. Then she rushed downstairs in high heels, having neglected to put on stockings, telling herself that since she'd probably remove her stockings on the plane anyway, there was no reason to wear them in the first place. She approached the dark, noisy room where Joe and a friend were staring into the dull gray glow of a TV set. The sight was painfully familiar to her by now. Next to Joe's chair was the small, wooden folding tray on which he liked to eat dinner.

After eight months, this is what her marriage had come to. Joe watched TV. He played golf. He went to the track. He played poker. He complained to Jimmy Cannon that life in Los Angeles was dull. Soon after they were married, he'd asked Marilyn to abandon her career and move with him to San Francisco. She promised to think about it. Meanwhile, he was unhappy that she had turned their home into a sort of Grand Central Station. The phone and doorbell rang at all hours. His ulcer acted up. Filled with resentment, he'd retreat behind a wall of silence. Sometimes he didn't utter a word to Marilyn for days at a time. He grew particularly upset when studio personnel invaded the house.

Marilyn lingered in the doorway. When Joe didn't say anything, she asked how she looked.

"Nice," Joe snapped.

Tension hovered in the smoky air. Marilyn's assistants had just gone home in anticipation of joining her at the airport, and Joe often made a scene after her visitors left. This evening, to make matters worse, Marilyn had asked Joe to accompany her in the limousine. Marilyn wanted him to put in an appearance at the airport to counter rumors that her marriage was disintegrating.

Joe and Marilyn were almost never seen in public together. Joe, who despised Hollywood publicity, refused to attend industry events. Off the baseball field, he didn't like to be photographed; he preferred not to be observed. On the rare occasions when the couple dined out, they ate in grim silence. Marilyn might as well have been George Solotaire.

Several days previously, an attempt to permit photographers to get an affectionate shot of Joe and Marilyn together had backfired. As it had been noted in the press that Joe never visited the set of *There's No Business Like Show Business*, Marilyn invited him to watch her shoot the big musical number "Heat Wave." A sullen, sweaty DiMaggio, in a dark blue suit, watched from the shadows as his wife strutted about in a plumed headdress and a tight, skimpy two-piece outfit that left her midriff exposed. As she sang and danced, Marilyn's eyes darted nervously in Joe's direction. Sensing his disapproval and disgust, Marilyn stumbled and fell. Afterward, photographers asked Joe to pose with his wife. He refused, insisting he wasn't dressed properly. Marilyn tried to conceal her hurt when Joe later agreed to be photographed with Ethel Merman.

Marilyn was relieved that Joe had agreed to ride with her to the airport, though she worried how he'd react to the news that they were to stop at Hedda Hopper's house. The gossip columnist was so powerful that Twentieth could hardly refuse her an interview with Marilyn before she left for New York. Joe declined to go inside. "I'll knock on the door when it's time to go," he said, obviously brooding about the fact that he was to be the principal topic of conversation.

Indeed, hardly was Marilyn through the door when Hedda Hopper asked, "What's this about you and Joe not getting on?"

At the airport, Joe, eager to put the question to rest, was photographed giving Marilyn a farewell kiss. As Hugh French escorted Marilyn onto the plane, much in her life remained unsettled. Marilyn was playing Feldman and Greene against one another. She was waiting to see what each could do for her. One man had to lose, but either way Marilyn won.

In the past few days, she'd talked a lot to Feldman about *Guys and Dolls*. Marilyn had even mentioned it to Hedda Hopper, at the risk of being embarrassed later if she didn't get the part. At Marilyn's behest, Feldman had dined with Goldwyn. He'd called six times to reiterate Marilyn's interest. Finally, he'd arranged for her to meet Goldwyn after work one evening. Just before she went to New York, Feldman had reported that Goldwyn was one hundred per cent enthusiastic. But she also needed the director's approval. While Marilyn was in the east, she hoped to plead her case to Mankiewicz. She had not seen him since *All About Eve* and she wanted to show him how much she had changed in four years. If, as Feldman anticipated, Goldwyn made an offer, Marilyn would have no choice but to sign her new contract at Twentieth immediately. That would put Greene out of the running before he'd even started.

While Marilyn waited to be cast in *Guys and Dolls*, she was secretly talking to Greene to see what he came up with. In New York, she expected to hear from him about his progress. *Guys and Dolls* was

Marilyn's priority; but if Goldwyn failed to make an offer, as soon as Marilyn completed *The Seven Year Itch* she hoped to jump ship—both from Twentieth and from Famous Artists. In other words, though no one but Marilyn knew it yet, everybody's fate depended on whether Feldman could get her *Guys and Dolls*.

In New York, more than sixty photographers and cameramen, tipped off by the studio, were waiting at Idlewild Airport when Marilyn emerged from the plane. She posed on the ramp for nearly forty-five minutes as airport employees whistled and cheered. When fans broke through the gray wooden barricades, police ushered Marilyn into the terminal building.

Her arrival made headlines. "MARILYN WIGGLES IN," declared the front page of the *New York World Telegram*. Crowds gathered outside the St. Regis Hotel on Fifth Avenue, where more police barricades had been set up. In an eleventh-floor suite, Marilyn sipped tea laced with vodka. Excited by her reception, she pressed Hugh French to set up a meeting with Mankiewicz. When she discovered that the director had flown to Los Angeles for a few days, Marilyn insisted on calling him there.

"You see, I've become a star," Marilyn proudly told Mankiewicz.

The director was unimpressed. He talked to her, she thought, as though she were a piece of trash. "Put on some more clothes, Marilyn, and stop moving your ass so much," he replied.

Despite the insult, Marilyn struggled to win him over. Finally, Mankiewicz cut off the conversation with the news that the part of Miss Adelaide had already been cast. Refusing to give up, Marilyn instructed Feldman to keep after Goldwyn and get her the role.

Mankiewicz's unkind words were a brutal reminder of why Marilyn hated Hollywood. By contrast, Milton Greene saw Marilyn as she wished to be seen. On Friday, September 10, at his cavernous studio on Lexington Avenue, he photographed her as a ballerina. Sensing Marilyn's discomfort, he loosened her up with Dom Perignon. When her snowy white Anne Klein costume didn't fit, he refused to panic, telling her simply to hold it up against herself. In a series of images that brilliantly captured the conflict in Marilyn's personality between the innocent and the lurid, she posed on a wicker chair before a vast black backdrop, a partly-naked ballerina with incongruous red lipstick and toenail polish.

On Sunday morning, the day before Marilyn was to begin *The Seven Year Itch*, the phone rang in Greene's converted barn in Weston, Connecticut. It was DiMaggio. He had flown to New York and wanted the photographer and his wife to have dinner with him. Marilyn, after all, was considering turning over the responsibility for her business and professional dealings to a man she hardly knew. Any husband, not least one as innately distrustful as Joe, would want to check the guy out.

That night, as many as a thousand fans waited on East 55th Street. When Marilyn left the hotel, she was wearing a fitted, black wool suit with a large fabric rose stuffed into the plunging neckline, presumably in deference to her husband. The crowd on the sidewalk was huge, and Joe seemed to be wondering how he was going to get from the top of the steps to the car. A great many people wanted something from Marilyn—an autograph, a photo, whatever. That's why Joe felt compelled to protect her. And that's why he and Greene spent an ostensibly innocuous social evening together in the back room at El Morocco. Joe needed to see exactly what he was dealing with.

When Joe married Marilyn, a bookie at Toots Shor's laid eight-to-five odds that they'd separate before their first anniversary. No one dared mention that to Joe, yet the crowd at Shor's seemed to be watching and waiting. The marriage simply did not seem meant to last. One evening, the DiMaggios were to have to dinner at Shor's with Sam Shaw and his wife. But when Marilyn arrived from the set, Joe became enraged at the very sight of her. It was obvious that she wasn't wearing panties beneath her form-fitting skirt. Joe was fiercely determined to put a stop to this habit of hers, so Marilyn was sent off to the ladies room with Ann Shaw. At length, a pair of panties was delivered and Marilyn dutifully put them on before rejoining Joe and Sam at the table.

Shaw had become friendly with Joe when he and Jimmy Cannon collaborated on a DiMaggio documentary. Currently, he was doing the still photographs for *The Seven Year Itch*. Knowledgeable, well-read, up on all the latest cultural phenomena, he had a reputation as a man with good ideas. When he talked, Feldman, Skouras, and many others in Hollywood listened intently. When Shaw first read the script of *The Seven Year Itch*, Feldman's ears had perked up at something he said. In 1941, Shaw had photographed some sailors with their girls at the Steeplechase in Coney Island for *Friday* magazine; the cover showed one of the girls, her skirt caught in a gust of wind. Shaw suggested replicating the image in *The Seven Year Itch*. No one could have suspected that the picture of Marilyn cooling herself over a subway grating would become famous long before the movie opened. Even less could they have suspected that filming it would trigger the breakup of her marriage.

Joe was at Shor's with George Solotaire and Jimmy Cannon when the columnist Walter Winchell came up to Table One and announced that he was going over to Lexington Avenue to watch Billy Wilder shoot. Tongue in cheek, Winchell said he'd heard there was this girl named Marilyn Monroe in the picture. Did Joe want to tag along?

Pictures and stories about Marilyn had dominated the New York papers for days. On Monday, midtown traffic had been held up for hours as the actress, wearing a scanty slip, filmed a street scene at an East 61st Street townhouse. The *Daily News* dubbed her "a roadblock named Marilyn Monroe." The *Journal-American* announced that Marilyn would be filming late on Wednesday night outside the Trans-Lux, 52nd Street Theater: "There won't be any admission charge when Marilyn appears for the shooting of street sequences for her new film *The Seven Year Itch*. Miss Monroe's costume is expected to be more revealing than the one she wore yesterday to stop the traffic."

About fifteen hundred fans filled klieg-lit Lexington Avenue at an hour when it was usually deserted. Others watched from rooftops. There were police barricades everywhere. DiMaggio, unable to see his wife, was about to turn back, but Winchell insisted on asking a policeman for help. No sooner did the cop spot DiMaggio than a contingent of police cleared a path for the baseball god. "Higher! Higher!" the crowd roared. The cops led DiMaggio to the front, where flashbulbs popped incessantly as photographers took stills of Marilyn. She wore a sheer white, billowy, sleeveless, backless dress and stood over a grating. The actor Tom Ewell was nearby.

"Roll 'em!" called Billy Wilder. As a train passed beneath—actually a wind-blowing machine manned by special effects people—Marilyn's skirts flew up to her shoulders. She wore no stockings. A dark patch of pubic hair was visible through two pairs of sheer white nylon panties. "More, more, Marilyn!" onlookers shouted. "Let's see more!" There was oddly little pretense of keeping people quiet. On the contrary, the numerous takes seemed calculated to work up the crowd and to guarantee that magazines and newspapers would print a great many pictures of Marilyn in her panties. The entire evening was a spectacular publicity stunt. At length, the sequence would be reshot in the studio.

For DiMaggio, the night was intensely real. He'd never expected anything like this. The gift of anticipation, apparently, had abandoned him. He saw Marilyn's skirt fly up again and again. He listened to men hoot and whistle at his wife. He watched the camera seem to focus on her crotch. He heard one wag exclaim that he thought she was a real blonde. Finally Dead Pan Joe could hide his feelings no more. Turbulent emotions overcame his ever-present fear of embarrassing himself. "I've had it!" Joe hollered as he turned on his heel and walked off. Winchell followed.

Marilyn, no doubt anticipating a terrible scene later, was frantic. She confronted Wilder. "I hope all these extra takes are not for your Hollywood friends to enjoy at a private party."

The filming went on for five hours.

Jimmy Cannon once observed that Toots Shor always seemed to be a customer in his own store; he guzzled more booze, had more laughs, and stayed up later than any regular. Toots was still there when DiMaggio came in. The gargantuan proprietor trudged across the saloon to Table One and ordered a round. His voice was loud and obnoxious. Unfortunately, when Joe disclosed what had happened, Toots said exactly the wrong thing. "Aww, Joe," he growled affectionately. "What can you expect when you marry a whore?"

That remark ended the close friendship of Joe DiMaggio and Toots Shor. Joe, seething, marched back to the St. Regis. In the pre-dawn hours, angry shouts issued from Suite 1105–1106. Other guests on the floor were prevented from sleeping. Marilyn knew that her marriage had ended that night.

Scheduled to return to the studio on Friday, Marilyn flew home with Joe immediately. Dressed in black, her hair tousled, she slept most of the way. At Los Angeles International Airport, she refused photographers' requests to remove her sunglasses. Marilyn put up a good front in public, but when she and Joe reached the cottage, she exiled him from the upstairs bedroom. Joe sheepishly took up residence on the ground floor.

Hardly was Marilyn back when the telephone rang. Feldman was desperate to talk to her before she saw a news item announcing that Mankiewicz had cast Vivian Blaine in *Guys and Dolls*; Blaine had played

Miss Adelaide on Broadway. Feldman assured Marilyn he'd done everything to get her the part. He promised there would be other terrific roles. He'd heard great things from Billy Wilder and knew *The Seven Year Itch* was going to be a triumph for her.

Marilyn wasn't really listening anymore. The conversation had spelled Feldman's doom. The moment he said he'd lost *Guys and Dolls*, he was finished. Marilyn was ready to clean house. As far as she was concerned, Feldman, like DiMaggio, was on his way out of her life. The only difference was that Marilyn needed to maintain the semblance of a cordial relationship with Feldman, who, after all, was the producer of her current film.

Eleven days later, Joe was due back in New York for the World Series. He didn't want to lose Marilyn. Struggling to patch things up, he admitted he was wrong to be the way he was. "I regret it but I cannot help it," said Joe, stiffly. He was devastated when Marilyn told him she wanted a divorce. She had made up her mind and that was that. She planned to see a lawyer while he was away.

In New York, Joe stayed with George Solotaire at the Hotel Madison. Covering the World Series, he gave no hint that he was in turmoil. Now and then an associate would ask about the missus, and Joe matter-of-factly indicated that she was fine. He was no more curt or taciturn than usual. Jimmy Cannon did, however, notice that when the Series moved to Cleveland, Joe seemed in a hurry to get home. Frantic to talk to Marilyn, he caught the first flight out.

As DiMaggio came up the driveway on the morning of October 2, only the messy black Cadillac convertible was outside. But when he let himself in, he discovered little Sidney Skolsky having breakfast with Marilyn in the dining room. The hypochondriacal newspaper columnist, who claimed to know every doctor in town, shared her passion for pills. At Schwab's, Marilyn was notorious for the number of doctors who, apparently unaware of each other, signed her prescriptions. At the moment, however, endometriosis was causing her pain so severe that no quantity of pills seemed to help.

Both Marilyn and Sidney were surprised. Joe wasn't expected until the following day. Sidney was famous in Hollywood for having spanked Shirley Temple after she damaged his new hat, and for having bitten Louella Parsons on the arm during a professional dispute at Chasen's restaurant. But he was terrified of DiMaggio, especially of being given a good going-over with those big hands.

Joe greeted him. Instead of asking to be left alone with his wife, Joe inquired if he could do anything to change her mind about the divorce. Skolsky, eager to stay out of the dispute, said no. Jerry Giesler, a Hollywood attorney known for his ability to grab headlines, was scheduled to come to the house the next day. It was probably no accident that the media-savvy attorney waited until after the World Series—when baseball was off the front pages—to announce the divorce.

Marilyn, in constant pain, closed herself in the master bedroom. Joe was prohibited from going upstairs. At one point that evening, he did enter the room. In contrast to his violent mood in New York, he was penitential. He promised to change if only Marilyn would take him back.

On Monday, November 4, Giesler, accompanied by the Fox publicity director, Harry Brand, met about one hundred reporters on the lawn outside the cottage. Marilyn remained in the upstairs bedroom, Joe in the living room.

"The divorce action will be filed Tuesday in Santa Monica Superior Court," said Giesler. "The charges will be gentle—just mental cruelty."

"Marilyn still has a lot of work to finish on her picture," Brand chimed in. "She's due at the studio in the morning. I don't know if she'll make it."

"Is there any chance of reconciliation?" a reporter shouted.

"I discussed reconciliation," said Giesler. "None is possible."

The next day, Giesler served the divorce papers to DiMaggio, still in residence on the ground floor. Then he went upstairs to rehearse Marilyn and Sidney for Wednesday. It was said of Giesler that he worked like a movie director, meticulously rehearsing and choreographing his clients. Marilyn's first meeting with the reporters camped outside her house had to be carefully stage managed. DiMaggio remained immensely popular. His reputation was stately. The very qualities that had made him the man to be seen with at the time of the nude calendar scandal made him hard to get rid of now without making Marilyn appear unsympathetic. She, after all, was divorcing him. She had publicly humiliated him in New York; his upset over the skirt-blowing scene had been widely reported. America's sympathies were likely to be with Joe. Nobody wanted to see the Big Guy get hurt.

Giesler detailed the scene he expected Marilyn to play the following day. Though Marilyn had initiated the divorce, she must appear to be as devastated as Joe. There was to be no trace of her steely determination to get rid of him. Giesler instructed Marilyn to hold his arm for support. Suddenly, she was to stumble on the winding brick path. That was Sidney's cue. He was to break out of the crowd and rush to Marilyn. Giesler, however, would ignore Sidney. The huge attorney would grip Marilyn and steer her to the car. Throughout, she was to appear as if she were being torn apart.

On the morning of October 6, Marilyn, in the upstairs bedroom, prepared to meet the press. An assistant did her makeup. Marilyn slipped into a clinging black jersey dress, fastened by a wide leather belt with a rhinestone buckle. She decided whether to wear a pair of short white gloves or to hold them in one hand. Meanwhile, downstairs, Reno Barsocchini slung a bag of gold-plated golf clubs over his shoulder, picked up a pair of leather suitcases and walked outside. He was still loading the trunk of DiMaggio's car when the cottage door opened again. "Hello, fellas," said Joe.

He wore a gray suit, a white shirt, and a tie. His lips curled into a tense smile. He walked briskly, snapping "No comment" as reporters shouted questions all at once. His bearing called to mind Toots Shor's remark that DiMaggio even looked good striking out. Joe faltered only once, putting out a massive hand to steady himself as he brushed past Marilyn's black convertible.

"Where are you going?" someone called.

"I'm going to San Francisco," said Joe, about to enter the passenger seat of his own car.

"Are you coming back home?"

"San Francisco's my home. It's always been my home." He closed the door, Reno started the engine, and the blue Cadillac with "JOE D" plates rolled down the driveway.

Fifty minutes later the cottage door opened again. Marilyn seemed disoriented as flashbulbs exploded en masse. She appeared to feel faint. She clutched Jerry Giesler's arm.

"I'm sorry, I can't say anything, I'm sorry," Marilyn whispered as microphones were thrust in front of her face.

She gripped the white gloves in one hand, wiping her eyes with the handkerchief clutched in the other. She chewed her lower lip, and kept her head down. She seemed on the verge of collapse. When a reporter asked what DiMaggio had done to her, Marilyn burst into tears.

"Miss Monroe will have nothing to say this morning," said Giesler. "As her attorney I am speaking for her and can only say that the conflict of careers has brought about this regretable necessity."

Marilyn stumbled on the brick path. Sidney Skolsky broke out of the crowd to assist her. Giesler, ignoring him, held Marilyn tightly and steered her to his car.

Joe had until Friday, October 15. If he did not contest the divorce complaint, Giesler would move for a default hearing. Meanwhile, the only person to speak out was Natasha Lytess, who relished the opportunity to vent her wrath at Joe: "The marriage was a big mistake for Marilyn and I feel she has known it for a long time." Natasha had never forgiven Joe for the night he refused to put her through on the phone. She blamed him for Marilyn's subsequent coolness toward her, refusing to come to terms with the fact that, in Marilyn's eyes, the dramatic coach had betrayed her. She seemed to believe that without Joe, things would return to what they had been. "Now this is all behind her," Natasha exulted.

Hours before the deadline, DiMaggio arrived in Los Angeles and checked into his former quarters at the Knickerbocker Hotel. Asked why he was in town, Joe said cryptically: "To take care of what I have to take care of." In the end, however, he did not contest the divorce complaint. He didn't even hire his own lawyer. Instead, he chose to permit Giesler to handle everything. Marilyn was granted a divorce on October 27, 1954. It would be final a year later.

Soon afterward, Sidney Skolsky was shocked to learn that DiMaggio wanted to reach him. Full of trepidation, he called the Knickerbocker. Joe summoned him to his room the following day, ominously declining a suggestion that they meet in a restaurant. He needed to see Sidney alone.

Sidney arrived fearing the worst. Following Joe's instructions, he sat on the edge of the bed. Joe pulled up a chair. The two men were so physically dissimilar that they might have come from different planets.

rilyn, then known as Norma Jeane Baker, led a sad, lonely childhood in a
es of foster homes.

Norma Jeane's modeling career began by chance when an Army photographer spotted her working on a factory assembly line during World War II.

Joe Schenck, one of richest men in Hollywo took Marilyn under wing soon after dropped her contra

...rilyn poses for publicity shots at Twentieth Century–Fox, where she signed her studio contract in 1946.

Elia Kazan was completing post-production on the film of *A Streetcar Named Desire* when he began an affair with Marilyn in 1951.

Marilyn with her dramatic coach, Natasha Lytess.

Marilyn arrives at RKO in the fall of 1951 to begin *Clash by Night*, the first picture on which she had star billing.

Marilyn with Joe DiMaggio. She began seeing Joe in 1952, at the time of the nude calendar scandal.

Twentieth Century–Fox production chief Darryl Zanuck threatened to "destroy" Marilyn when she demanded a new contract which would give her a voice in the kind of films she made.

With Walter Winchell and Joe Schenck at Ciro's in 1953 shortly after she finished *Gentlemen Prefer Blondes*, the film which made the whole world fall in love with the character she had created.

Marilyn and Betty Grable report for *How to Marry a Millionaire*. Marilyn was terrified that Darryl Zanuck planned to use her up and discard her as he was about to do with Grable.

Marilyn and Joe DiMaggio married in San Francisco in January 1954, at the height of Marilyn's contract battle.

ntertaining U.S. troops in Korea. Marilyn fed on the noise, the adoration, the sexual
enzy of the crowd.

The image of Marilyn cooling herself over a subway grating, shot in New York in September 1954, became famous long before *The Seven Year Itch* opened. It also triggered the end of her marriage to Joe DiMaggio.

Marilyn and attorney Jerry Giesler face the press in October 1954, after DiMaggio was served with divorce papers.

The brief marriage to DiMaggio was over after only nine months.

In New York early in 1955, after Marilyn stunned Hollywood by announcing that she no longer considered her studio contract to be valid. Behind her is her business partner Milton Greene.

Lee Strasberg, the head of the Actors Studio, articulated a whole new set of dreams for Marilyn in 1955.

Under Strasberg's tutelage, Marilyn studied to be a serious actress.

With Truman Capote at El Morocco. Through friends like Capote, Carson McCullers, and Tennessee Williams, Marilyn was taken up in Manhattan as she simply had never been in Los Angeles.

A blowup of the skirt-blowing scene was put up in front of Loew's State Theater for the premiere of *The Seven Year Itch* in June 1955.

Joe DiMaggio escorted Marilyn to the premiere, though she was secretly seeing Arthur Miller.

Arthur Miller, the author of *Death of a Salesman*, seemed never to have been more in love with anyone than he was with Marilyn. Marilyn met Miller briefly in Hollywood in 1951. In 1955 they began a serious love affair in New York.

One was small and flabby, the other huge and muscular. Sidney had no idea why he was here.

DiMaggio's voice, usually so sharp and strident, was gentle: "You know everything. There's one thing I must know. Is there another man? Why did Marilyn divorce me?"

One can only imagine what it cost DiMaggio, intensely proud and reserved as he was, to ask another man that question. That he did so proved, if proof were needed, how much he loved Marilyn, and how devastated he had been by the divorce.

+ SIX +

On the evening of Saturday, November 6, 1954, Marilyn pulled into a Hollywood gas station. She had completed principal photography on The Seven Year Itch two days previously. She wore long, glittering rhinestone earrings and a rhinestone bracelet on her left wrist. She had borrowed a strapless red chiffon gown with a low-cut back from the studio wardrobe department. Her neck and shoulders were bare. She appeared to be high. Marilyn's escort, Sam Shaw, had a mustache and a mop of dark hair. He wore a hired tuxedo with sewn pockets and over-sized patent leather shoes from Western Costume.

At that moment, Sam and Marilyn were out of gas, broke, and an hour late. She cajoled the attendant to fill the tank for free. They proceeded to Romanoff's, the glamorous Beverly Hills restaurant where the doorman always greeted you with a sunny "Welcome home!"

Down three steps from the bar was the dining room. Within, about eighty members of the Hollywood aristocracy attended a candlelit, private dinner party. A dance band played. The men wore black tie. Many faces in the room were instantly recognizable. Marilyn later said that it had been like stepping into a dream. Among those who feasted on steak and champagne she saw Clark Gable, Claudette Colbert, Humphrey Bogart, Susan Hayward, Gary Cooper, Loretta Young, James Stewart, and George Burns. On each round table, the centerpiece was a cardboard cutout of Marilyn in the skirt-blowing scene from The Seven Year Itch.

Sidney Skolsky rushed up to greet The Monroe. Tonight seemed like the culmination of all they had worked for. There could be no doubt that *The Seven Year Itch* marked a watershed in her career. *Gentlemen Prefer Blondes* and *How to Marry a Millionaire* had introduced audiences to an enchanting creature known as "the girl," who did much to dispel America's fears about sex. But in those two films, there had still been one false note in her character: She had played a gold-digger, so unavoidably there had been a lingering sense of threat. *The Seven Year Itch* took "the girl" to a new level. She isn't a gold-digger. Indeed, she doesn't seem to want anything from the man at all, except a chance to cool off in his air-conditioned apartment. As played by Tom Ewell, the male character embodies the particular pressures of 1950s' puritanism. He's terrified of sex, yet thinks of little else. "The girl," humorous and carefree, shows him there's absolutely nothing to worry about. She takes the peril out of sex, but leaves in the pleasure. The emblem of her innocent sexuality is the skirt-blowing scene, in which Ewell peeks under Marilyn's skirt—but without consequence to either of them. The image, provided by Sam Shaw, was so powerful because it perfectly articulated the fantasies of a buttoned-up era, and the immense relief when those fantasies, far from destroying us, prove to be utterly harmless. In *The Seven Year Itch*, Marilyn had finally embodied precisely the right character to appeal to the American psyche. With this film, she became a vivid cultural symbol.

Charlie Feldman saw *The Seven Year Itch* as only the start of a long and mutually profitable association. Tonight, he and Billy Wilder were hosting a dinner in Marilyn's honor. Feldman had assembled the film industry elite to salute her on the eve of a brilliant new beginning. "I feel like Cinderella," Marilyn whispered in Sidney's ear. "I didn't think they'd all show up. Honest."

George Axelrod came over to tell Marilyn he'd loved the seven reels he'd seen so far. "It's because of Billy," said Marilyn. "He's a wonderful director. I want him to direct me again. But he's doing *The Lindbergh Story* next, and he won't let me play Lindbergh."

Wilder did offer one important piece of advice. He was appalled by an item in the *Hollywood Reporter* about Marilyn's desire to portray Grushenka in *The Brothers Karamazov*. "Marilyn, don't play that part," he warned. "Everybody's making jokes about it. You have created a great character. Stay with the character you've created. You'll be an actress and a star like Mae West. Eighty years old, you'll be playing lead parts with the character you created."

Wilder asked her to dance. Impressed by the director's swoops and glides, Marilyn inquired where he had learned to dance, and he told her that he had been a gigolo in Berlin. She danced with Clark Gable. She danced with Darryl Zanuck. She danced with Charlie Feldman. It was, said Sam Shaw, "the night of her life."

How different this all was from the isolation Marilyn had known with Joe. As far as most people were concerned, he was out of the picture. She had moved to an apartment on De Longpre Avenue in West Hollywood. As well as a celebration of present and future success, tonight was also supposed to be a kind of coming-out party for Marilyn.

Nevertheless, as would soon be apparent, Joe, for better or worse, remained a powerful presence in Marilyn's life. Determined to find out if she was involved with another man, DiMaggio had hired a private detective to follow her. For all she knew, Barney Ruditsky or one of his assistants might be lurking outside Romanoff's. For all she knew, Joe, the veins and muscles in his neck bulging, might suddenly storm in and embarrass her as he done the previous Friday night as she dined with friends.

Marilyn had spent much of November 5 at the studio recording a song for *There's No Business Like Show Business* with her singing coach, Hal Schaefer. The twenty-nine-year-old Schaefer, an associate of Jack Cole, had attempted suicide during the shooting period, by swallowing typewriter cleaning fluid and about one hundred pills. While he was in the hospital, Marilyn secured permission to delay one last bit of recording until after she completed *The Seven Year Itch*, in order to give Schaefer time to recuperate. That evening, Marilyn and Schaefer dined with another of his pupils in her apartment on Waring Avenue in West Hollywood. DiMaggio, tipped off by Ruditsky, rushed to the building, accompanied by his friend Frank Sinatra. There could be no mistaking Marilyn's messy black Cadillac convertible parked outside, but Ruditsky and another detective burst into the wrong apartment. Alerted by the noise, Marilyn and Schaefer slipped out without running into DiMaggio or Sinatra.

For all that, Marilyn remained ambivalent. Joe may have been volatile and possessive, but he was also loving. He had caused a scene the night before her party at Romanoff's, but the day after the party he drove Marilyn to Cedars of Lebanon Hospital where she was to undergo surgery for endometriosis. He waited until Marilyn was admitted and put to bed. Then he stayed for half an hour talking to her until a nurse ordered him to go.

On Monday morning, a "No Visitors" sign was posted outside Marilyn's fifth-floor room. But when nurses brought her upstairs following surgery, Joe was waiting. He spent the rest of the day with her. He ate dinner with her. He talked to her and held her hand until late at night. Finally, a nurse came in to say there was a crowd of reporters in the lobby. Marilyn, still groggy, asked Joe to talk to them. "She's looking wonderful, but I guess she's having kind of a rough time," DiMaggio told them.

Did his presence mean that Joe and Marilyn were reconciling, everybody wanted to know.

"I'd rather you didn't ask me about that."

Joe's kindness did not change Marilyn's mind about the divorce. Nor did a party at Romanoff's weaken her resolve to leave Famous Artists and Twentieth Century–Fox. Marilyn had known that she would fire Feldman since September 16, when he failed to get her the role of Miss Adelaide in *Guys and Dolls*.

Why was Marilyn so angry at Feldman? What had he done to become the focus of her resentment? He had, after all, offered her the opportunity to appear in *The Seven Year Itch*. He had made it possible for her to give the best performance of her career so far. Marilyn did not doubt that he had other strong projects in mind for her. If she wanted to continue to make good films, Feldman was uniquely equipped to make that happen. But more importantly, Marilyn understood that Feldman didn't respect her as she wanted to be respected. He had never connected with her dreams. His attitude toward her had never really been different from Zanuck's. When Marilyn realized that he wanted her to sign a studio contract that offered her no creative control, Feldman's fate was sealed.

Feldman, for his part, had no idea that anything was wrong. When she visited his office on the afternoon of November 22, Marilyn behaved as if she had every intention of staying with him. It might seem odd that she put on a performance for Feldman at this point, but she admired his literary taste. She eagerly listened to his ideas for new projects; she shamelessly picked his brain.

Feldman gave Marilyn a copy of Terence Rattigan's light comedy

The Sleeping Prince. Vivien Leigh and Laurence Olivier had performed it on the London stage when Vivien was recovering from her nervous breakdown. Feldman had been putting out feelers about buying the property for Marilyn since February, when she was in Japan; his idea was for Marilyn to portray the chorus girl opposite Richard Burton as the prince. But there was no rush. Feldman, thrilled with her performance in *The Seven Year Itch*, was eager to protect his investment. He wanted Marilyn to have a long rest.

A week later, Marilyn appeared without warning in Frank Ferguson's office at Fox, requesting copies of all her old contracts. She said that her papers had been placed in storage following the divorce, and asked many oddly detailed questions about the contracts. When Ferguson inquired why she didn't talk to her own lawyer or her agent, Marilyn replied cryptically that Wright and Feldman didn't know much about what was going on.

Suspicious, Ferguson contacted Loyd Wright. Wright waited to see if Marilyn would call to say what this was all about. When she didn't, he alerted Feldman. By that time, however, Marilyn had already sent the copies to New York. Milton Greene wanted to show them to his lawyer, Frank Delaney.

Delaney pored over the documents, and concluded that several months previously Twentieth had failed to pick up Marilyn's option in time. Following a suspension, it was customary for film studios to add the missed time onto a performer's contract. According to Delaney, Twentieth had miscalculated the number of days they could wait before renewing her contract. The technicality, he argued, rendered her 1951 contract null and void. Thus, Marilyn had begun *The Seven Year Itch* without a valid contract. Now that it was finished, she was free to do as she wished.

The lawyer drew up papers establishing Marilyn Monroe Productions, and Milton Greene flew to Los Angeles to deliver them. There was also an undated letter for Marilyn to sign, informing Feldman that Famous Artists was no longer authorized to act for her. Greene's people would fill in the date later when they agreed precisely when it ought to be sent. Marilyn and Greene decided to go full steam ahead with *Harlow*.

Like Marilyn, Sidney Skolsky had spent the past few months playing Feldman and Greene against each other. Encouraged by her, Sidney had conferred with both men about the film he hoped to produce. Strictly to please Marilyn, Feldman had agreed to talk up *Harlow* to Zanuck, and promised to represent Sidney if a deal was made. Though Greene seemed more enthusiastic, Sidney was happier with Feldman. There was no question that a powerful agent and producer was more likely to be able to put a deal together. Still, *Harlow* was Greene's only project, while Feldman of course had much else on his plate. But what did Sidney's preferences matter anyway? He knew that whether they went with Feldman or Greene was for Marilyn to choose.

Marilyn wanted to buy Harlow's life story immediately. The screen rights were held by Sam Briskin and two other partners. Skolsky was uneasy, recalling Feldman's insistence that for tax reasons Skolsky, not Marilyn, must own the rights. At the moment, however, Marilyn was intent on running her own show. She was in no mood to be reminded of anything Feldman might have said about money matters. Sidney, hoping to protect her, made up his mind to contact Feldman in New York.

When Feldman learned that Marilyn was about to buy the rights to Harlow's story, he was appalled. It wasn't that he suspected Marilyn's plans to set up her own production company; he simply assumed that she was nervous about taking a rest and impatient to know where her career was headed. To that impatience he also attributed her having asked Ferguson for copies of her contracts. He warned Sidney that under no circumstances must Marilyn be permitted to buy another story. She still owned *Horns of the Devil*, since the transfer to Twentieth had been held up when she failed to sign the new contract. The acquisition of a second story would wreck the tax advantage that Feldman had so carefully structured. If Skolsky doubted any of this, Feldman urged him at least to have Marilyn call a lawyer to go over it with her independently.

Eager to please Marilyn, Feldman decided to make *Harlow* happen. That's what she seemed to want, and that's what she was going to get. He pitched *Harlow* to Zanuck, who was passing through New York on his way back from London, and he agreed to meet Skolsky on December 8, his first day back at the studio. Feldman invited Marilyn to lunch at his home on December 11, when he would be able to report on that meeting.

Skolsky canceled the appointment, saying he was sick. When Feldman heard, he called from New York to say he'd be back two days later and would personally accompany Sidney to Zanuck's office. Again, Skolsky mysteriously canceled at the last minute, claiming he couldn't get out of bed. With her plans finally about to come out in the open— plans that involved *Harlow*—Marilyn did not want Sidney to make a deal with Zanuck.

On Saturday, Marilyn kept her lunch date with Feldman. Though Skolsky had yet to meet with Zanuck, the agent had much else to discuss. He also had many new treasures to exhibit. That year he had acquired a rare K'ang Hsi' Chinese screen. In Pietrasanta, Italy, he had picked up a white marble statue of Venus, the ancient goddess of love and beauty, and a statue of Bacchus, the god of wine. In Florence, he had bought a large, oval, antique mahogany table. In New York, he had discovered two small, exquisite wood carvings of African women. When Feldman displayed his new toys, he always made a mental note of who loved what. If you expressed particular enthusiasm about a painting or an *objet d'art*, you might find that Charlie had left it to you in his will. Existence, he liked to think, "is to be in the minds and hearts of friends."

Marilyn lingered over lunch for three hours. She was perfectly charming throughout. For once, Charlie didn't have to listen to complaints or accusations. She laughed and smiled. They talked of the past. They planned for the future. She seemed sincerely appreciative of his efforts.

For his part, he was very complimentary about her performance in *There's No Business Like Show Business*. He reiterated his high hopes for *The Seven Year Itch*. He expressed confidence that he'd be able to sell *Harlow*. He inquired about Sidney Skolsky and looked forward to rescheduling that meeting with Zanuck. He wondered if Marilyn had had a chance to read *The Sleeping Prince*. Had she liked it at all? If so, he wanted to acquire the rights from Terence Rattigan at once.

Feldman was satisfied that the meeting had gone well when Marilyn happily agreed to have lunch with him again on Tuesday the 13th. (She later canceled, of course.) He hoped that by then he would have something to report on Sidney's meeting with Zanuck. She knew that by then Feldman would have received the letter firing him. She had it dated December 11. Perhaps he would realize that even as they had been enjoying a leisurely meal together, Marilyn had been putting a knife in his back.

Fireworks exploded throughout Los Angeles that week. Marilyn dismissed her agent and her lawyer. She notified Twentieth that until fur-ther instruction the studio was to do business directly with her or with Frank Delaney, her new attorney. She also indicated that she might no longer be bound to the studio. This was the outcome of the terrible moment seven months previously when, reading her new contract, Marilyn fully grasped what the men at the studio thought of her.

+ + +

Once before, at a time like this, Marilyn had been advised to get out of town. That's what she did now. Traveling as "Zelda Zonk," she flew to New York with Greene. His wife picked them up at the airport. By then, word of the unexplained firings had reached the press. Exactly what Marilyn planned to do next was anyone's guess.

Reporters gathered outside Greene's midtown Manhattan photog-raphy studio. Others watched the entrance to the apartment house on Sutton Place South where he had a pied-à-terre. Still others waited at the foot of the driveway to his country house in Connecticut. Disappointingly, when the car returned from the airport, only Mr. and Mrs. Greene were visible. Marilyn was hiding in the dark, cold trunk.

Greene's guest room was done up in purple. It had its own bath-room, and there Marilyn liked to soak in a bubble bath, her hair in a top-knot, the room filled with steam. She had little concrete idea of what faced her. Suddenly, she was financially dependent on Greene. She couldn't cash her weekly paycheck from Twentieth, because she mustn't appear to accept the terms of her old contract. Delaney was going to argue that Marilyn had made *The Seven Year Itch* on a one-picture-only basis at the $100,000 fee Feldman had previously negotiated.

Marilyn relied on Greene for everything. She ate with the family. He advanced her money for whatever she needed. He wasn't worried; she could pay him back later. He felt certain that as soon as people knew what they were doing, investors would beat a path to his door. Twentieth would be des-perate to make a deal and Marilyn could return in a matter of weeks. He and she would be filming *Harlow* on the Fox lot—and on their own terms—in no time. Now that Marilyn had asserted her independence, the first step was a press conference to announce Marilyn Monroe Productions.

Before Greene could do that, however, Frank Ferguson sent Marilyn a telegram ordering her to report for work at Fox in five days. Neither she nor Greene had anticipated that. She knew the studio had the right to demand retakes for *The Seven Year Itch*, and she certainly did not want to jeopardize a film she loved. At the same time, Greene, like Feldman before him, worried about her mercurial nature. He was determined to keep her from going back before she had publicly committed herself to Marilyn Monroe Productions.

Delaney wired back that Marilyn was ill and could not possibly return. In response, Lew Schreiber, reminding Marilyn that Twentieth always tried to cooperate, postponed the retakes until January 3. Delaney countered that while Marilyn's health did appear to be improving, she needed until the 10th to recover. Schreiber growled that he expected to see her at 10 a.m. The people at Twentieth, of course, still had no idea of what Marilyn's plans were.

They had to wait until Friday, January 7, 1955, to find out. That evening, reporters and photographers crowded into Frank Delaney's house on East 64th Street for what Greene had touted as the unveiling of "the new Monroe." Marilyn had not been observed in public for three weeks, and there was considerable curiosity about exactly what Greene meant. Unfortunately, Greene himself wasn't sure. The purpose of the gathering was to announce Marilyn's break with Twentieth and the formation of her own production company. In that case, "the new Monroe" signified an independent woman determined to take control of her own business and artistic affairs. The whole point was to attract investors to Marilyn's exciting new venture. But somewhere along the way, Greene lost track of all that. When all was said and done, he remained a glamour photographer at heart. Instead of preparing an effective presentation, he and Marilyn devoted themselves to trying to come up with her "new look." By the time Marilyn was ready to face the press, she seemed to think that "the new Monroe" referred simply to the costume and hair color Greene had helped her devise for the occasion. From first to last, the calamitous evening revealed just how confused Marilyn still was about what she wanted and where she was headed, and how utterly ill-equipped Greene was to clarify things for her.

Marlene Dietrich, all in black, put in an appearance. So did Elsa Maxwell, Sidney Kingsley, and Richard Rogers. Cocktails were served for about an hour as guests awaited a "new and different" Marilyn. Shortly after six, the front door opened and Marilyn blew in like a snowdrift. She was dressed from head to toe in white. A fluttery white mink coat covered a white satin sheath with flimsy, loose spaghetti straps. She wore satin high heels and white stockings. Her long, sparkling diamond earrings were on loan from Van Cleef & Arpels.

Marilyn seemed disappointed when people asked what was new about her. "But I have changed my hair!" she protested. Her wind-tossed hair did seem a shade or two lighter. Asked to describe the new color, Marilyn replied in a child's voice, "Subdued platinum." Greene's intention was that people would instantly think of Jean Harlow, that the costume would identify Marilyn with the tragic figure whom Louella Parsons called "Hollywood's first platinum blonde." Instead, the crowd received Marilyn with good-natured amusement. They responded as though she were one of her comical, ditzy blonde film characters.

A reporter, perhaps thinking of *How to Marry a Millionaire*, asked if Marilyn actually owned the white mink.

"It's mine for the night," a wide-eyed Marilyn shot back.

If Marilyn hoped to be taken seriously, her entrance set the wrong tone. She sat for a press conference, Delaney at her side.

"I have formed my own corporation so I can play the kinds of roles I want," Marilyn announced. Delaney interjected that his client was referring to Marilyn Monroe Productions, Inc. From now on, the new firm would "see to it she plays only what she wants to play." She was leaving Twentieth. She planned to get into television. She wanted to produce as well as act.

"I don't like some of my pictures," Marilyn explained. Pressed to say which ones, she named *River of No Return* and *There's No Business Like Show Business*. She declared herself "tired of sex roles" and vowed to do no more. "People have scope, you know," said Marilyn. "They really do." Somebody called out that Fox appeared to think Marilyn was under contract. What did she have to say to that? Delaney and his associate Irving Stein insisted that the studio was mistaken and that Marilyn was "a free agent."

Following some questions about her personal life—"We are very good friends, Joe and I, we always shall be"—Marilyn thanked everybody and got up. As reporters left to file their stories, Marilyn had a twinkle in her eye. She believed she'd done it. She'd broken her contract. She'd announced her new production company. Everything was happening exactly as Greene had promised. Greene, for his part, didn't yet have a clue that the evening had gone wildly wrong.

Meanwhile, people were rushing up to talk to Marilyn. She and the Greenes were deluged with dinner invitations. Marlene Dietrich invited her to stop by for a drink later that night. Amy Greene wanted to see Sinatra at the Copacabana, but feared it was too late to get in.

Soon, Marilyn was leading the Greenes past the bar at the Copa. Instead of stopping her, a bouncer excitedly rushed ahead to announce her presence. If he'd had any rose petals, he might have tossed them in her path. Sinatra, in the middle of a number, was playing to a full house. There was a stir in the smoky nightclub as Marilyn made her entrance, high heels click-clicking. Sinatra, annoyed, stopped the orchestra. He wanted to know what the hell was going on. When he saw Marilyn in an ankle-length white mink coat, he knew. A ringside table with three chairs materialized. For the rest of the evening, as far as the audience was concerned, Marilyn, bare-shouldered in glistening white satin, was part of the show.

Afterward, Sinatra took the trio to dinner at "21." By the time Marilyn and the Greenes arrived at Marlene Dietrich's Park Avenue apartment, Marilyn was tipsy. As Dietrich welcomed her guests, she noticed a trace of scarlet lipstick on the collar of Marilyn's white fur. She later reported to a friend that she found the sight maddeningly erotic.

Marilyn went to bed that morning convinced she owned New York. Milton Greene shared her confidence. When Saturday's papers arrived, Marilyn felt humiliated. Instead of being taken seriously by the press, she was treated as a joke. "The new her didn't show up" and "She looked just the same as before" were typical remarks. Photographs of Marilyn's "new look," with captions like "Different?" and "Pretty Much the Same," invited readers to judge for themselves. There was nothing mean-spirited in any of this, but it was hardly the respectful coverage she had anticipated. And it certainly wasn't the image she'd hoped to put across. Greene's idea of costuming Marilyn to look like Jean Harlow had led the reporters to focus on all the wrong things.

The Los Angeles Times ran a humorous story with the headline "New Marilyn Same as the Old—and That's Plenty." At Twentieth,

Zanuck was no less upset than Marilyn, though for very different reasons. This was the first he had heard of Marilyn's plan to form her own corporation. Though neither she nor Greene could have known it, they had selected the worst possible time to try to break her contract. Zanuck was quietly engaged in a tense, bitter, emotionally-charged conflict with Elia Kazan over virtually the same issue. As chance would have it, both Marilyn and Kazan had opened fire on Twentieth in the very same week in December, 1954. Hardly had Twentieth received word that Marilyn's studio contract was "abandoned and terminated," when Zanuck read Kazan's letter of December 16 asking to be let out of his own six-picture deal.

Zanuck admitted to being bowled over. He regarded Kazan not just as a business associate but a close friend. In Zanuck's view, Kazan's actions were capricious, and the letter was little better than a betrayal. On December 22, in a long letter by turns passionate and cold, Zanuck urged Kazan to reconsider. He insisted they were both men of character; otherwise, said Zanuck, they wouldn't be friends. He recalled all he had done to persuade his board to offer Kazan the largest salary Twentieth had ever paid a director.

Zanuck specifically compared Kazan to Marilyn. He could no more call off Kazan's contract than he could hers. That Marilyn might have a better offer did not alter the fact that she already had a long-term commitment. Zanuck, citing his own responsibilities to stockholders, made it clear that he had no intention of allowing either Marilyn Monroe or Elia Kazan to walk away.

By January 1955, Kazan at least seemed to accept that he still had a contract with Twentieth. He said so in a letter, quickly adding that he wasn't happy about it. Zanuck saw that from this point on the negotiations would be delicate, and pleaded with Skouras to steer clear. Accustomed to speaking his mind, Zanuck tried to be diplomatic. He mustn't insult or offend Kazan. He proceeded gingerly.

It did not come naturally to Zanuck to check himself. Once before, when Marilyn had challenged his authority, Zanuck had threatened to "assassinate" her in the press. He had declared himself ready to "destroy an asset" if that was what it took to punish her. Marilyn's press conference came in the middle of Zanuck's ticklish negotiations with Kazan. His pent-up rage instantly found an outlet. He went berserk.

Marilyn had no idea what action Zanuck would take, when she and the Greenes flew to Los Angeles the day before she was due back at Twentieth. But she knew he would be furious with her. She spent Sunday night at her apartment and arrived on the studio lot at 10 a.m. without having looked at Monday's papers. Greene rode shotgun. Yet at first, it appeared that she did not need a protector. To Marilyn's relief, her fears seemed to have been groundless. Everyone was cordial. There was no sign of Zanuck. After a pleasant interview with the columnist Dick Williams, she reported to Billy Wilder to do retakes for a single scene.

Most people that day avoided mention of the events of the past few weeks. After Wilder finished shooting, however, Roy Craft of the publicity department approached Marilyn on the sound stage. Asked about her remarks at the press conference, Marilyn denied having said that she had severed her connections with Twentieth.

She was told to return the next day to complete some advertising artwork in the portrait gallery. That was fine with Greene, as it had to do with The Seven Year Itch. Another request dismayed him, however. Marilyn was asked to report for a costume fitting for How to Be Very, Very Popular. Nunnally Johnson, hoping to repeat the success of How to Marry a Millionaire, had written the script as a vehicle for Marilyn; he also planned to produce. Marilyn liked Johnson and was inclined to listen to what he had to say. But to report as ordered would undermine Delaney's argument that her commitment to Twentieth ended with The Seven Year Itch.

Marilyn left the studio lot in a terrific mood, exceedingly pleased with the way the day had gone. Perhaps this wasn't going to be so difficult after all. On her way home, she saw the Los Angeles papers. Over the weekend, Twentieth had contacted them all. In forty-eight hours, the light-hearted laughter had turned to ugly derision.

"Marilyn Monroe is a stupid girl and is being fed some stupid advice," declared the "Trade Views" column on page one of the Hollywood Reporter. The author, Billy Wilkerson, was the publisher of the influential trade paper. In a most unusual move, Twentieth had disclosed details of the new $100,000 per picture deal that Marilyn had refused to sign. "Marilyn Monroe is the most publicized individual in the world," Wilkerson continued. "Unquestionably, she is a big box-office draw, a top money attraction. Much of this has been due to her handling by

Twentieth, and the pictures she has been given, the talent she has been surrounded with to bring her up to the spot she now occupies. For her to ignore this, taking her case to the nation's press, is a stupid move, based on stupid advice, and we rather think she will gain nothing from it because when the public is told that her new deal would have brought her better than a quarter of a million a year there will be no sympathetic reaction and some of her attractiveness will have been lost."

The studio announced plans to hold Marilyn to the letter of her old contract. If she resisted, Zanuck vowed to prevent Marilyn from making another picture until August 8, 1958.

So much for Greene's ability to handle the press. Obviously, the opportunity to put her message across in New York had been badly mishandled. Far from being taken seriously, Marilyn heard herself called "stupid" and "foolish." She was devastated. So much for Greene's confidence that the studio would be desperate to make a deal. Twentieth treated Greene as if he had no idea what he was doing—and the fact was, he didn't. He was a fine photographer but an inept businessman. His intentions may have been decent, but he was out of his element in Hollywood. Marilyn had fired Feldman and Wright, so she could hardly turn to them for advice. That night, she agreed to have dinner with DiMaggio. For a man who hated her career, he got a lot of mileage out of advising Marilyn during her professional crises.

The next morning, following Greene's instructions, she avoided the costume fitting by having her maid call Billy Gordon, the casting director, to say she was ill. After a talk with the studio attorney, Gordon reached Marilyn by phone late in the afternoon. Pointedly avoiding the subject of How to Be Very, Very Popular, he asked Marilyn how she was feeling.

"A little better."

"We would like you to come in tomorrow and do the stills on Seven Year Itch."

"Fine. I would like to start as early as possible."

On Wednesday, Marilyn worked in the portrait gallery until 4 p.m. and agreed to finish up the next day. She was about to go home when a casting assistant handed her a brown envelope. Inside was a notice to report for a costume fitting at 10:30 the following morning.

Marilyn didn't know what to do. If she went, she would seem

tacitly to accept the studio's right to put her in another picture. That might destroy her chance to have her own production company. If she failed to report, something considerably worse might happen: She might wreck her career. That might well be the result if Zanuck made good on his threat to keep her off screen for more than three years. Could Marilyn afford to ignore the chorus—including the *Hollywood Reporter*, Louella Parsons, and Hedda Hopper—all warning that she had been given bad advice? Joe, too, was wary. In the past few days, Greene hadn't exactly proven himself a competent business partner.

Marilyn didn't want to do the costume fitting, but she didn't want to refuse either. She arrived at the studio on Thursday morning, but went directly to her dressing room. The framed photograph of Joe still decorated her dressing table. Assistants did her hair and makeup in anticipation of a 1 p.m. appointment in the portrait gallery. They were nearly finished when the phone rang. Marilyn instructed a helper to tell Billy Gordon that she had stepped out and would return soon. Promising to meet her assistants at the portrait gallery in two hours, Marilyn disappeared.

She never showed up. In tears, Marilyn called the stills department to say she was ill and had to go home. When someone checked her parking space outside the Star Building, the black Cadillac was gone.

Afraid that she was about to flee with Greene, Twentieth ordered Marilyn to report to Nunnally Johnson on Saturday for pre-production work. Zanuck was concerned that if they waited until Monday, Marilyn might be gone; it would be harder to exert pressure on her in New York.

When the studio suspended her for failing to show up on Saturday morning, Marilyn did go to New York. DiMaggio followed soon afterward, taking up residence again with George Solotaire. On January 19, he helped Marilyn move her things to the Gladstone Hotel on East 52nd Street off Park Avenue. Sam Shaw, who knew the owner, had arranged for her to stay there. From the time Marilyn arrived, the small, stuffy apartment hotel, crammed with red velvet furniture, was under siege. Photographers gathered outside the revolving front door. Sometimes they were permitted to photograph Marilyn in a gloomy little room off the lobby.

At the time, the Gladstone was also the temporary home of Carson McCullers. Known as "Choppers" because her cheeks resembled a pair of lamb chops, McCullers was the author of *The Heart is a Lonely Hunter*, *The Member of the Wedding*, and other books. She was physically demonstrative, always hugging and kissing friends and acquaintances, despite a stroke which had left one hand curled up like a hook. She carried a walking stick that she waved tipsily in the air by way of greeting. McCullers drank heavily and gobbled "pinkie tablets," as she and Tennessee Williams called Seconal. She had attempted suicide and had spent time at the Payne–Whitney psychiatric clinic. Williams once said that McCullers had known so much tragedy that it scared people—himself included—into a kind of indifference toward her. It was, Williams said, as if McCullers were "hopelessly damned" and one could not afford to think about it.

From the first, McCullers and Marilyn adored each other. There was "a sort of natural sympathy" between the skinny, tomboyish, slightly stooped novelist and the voluptuous movie star.

Though living in Victorian splendor, Marilyn was broke. For several weeks, she had been forbidden to cash her paychecks; now there were no checks at all. Greene doled out forty dollars a week in spending money, as well as paying her rent and other expenses, including her mother's fees at the mental institution. Soon, a letter came demanding a promissory note for the nearly $20,000 that Feldman had advanced. Feldman's attorney seemed to enjoy declaring that he understood Marilyn was in no position to pay back the money at this time.

The funds Greene had predicted would pour in after they announced Marilyn Monroe Productions never materialized. Threats of a lawsuit scared off investors. Greene did have one lead, however— Henry Rosenfeld, a dress manufacturer from the Bronx. That month Rosenfeld happened to be out of town on business. Rather than wait, Greene asked Marilyn to accompany him to Boston, where she could charm the wealthy businessman. It was a throwback to the days when she had to sing for her supper. It was a reminder of all that she had hoped to put behind her.

When Marilyn told Joe about the trip, he insisted on coming along. On January 23, he drove her to Boston. Greene traveled separately. The last thing Greene needed was DiMaggio in the middle of his business, but Joe left no choice. Joe's brother Dom and his wife lived in Wellesley, a Boston suburb. The night before the meeting, the two couples dined in town. A reporter approached their table in the private back room of a restaurant.

"Is this a reconciliation?" he asked Joe, who turned hopefully to Marilyn.

"Is it, honey?"

"No, just call it a visit."

Rosenfeld was very taken with Marilyn, but he simply was not the major investor Greene desperately needed. He declined to bankroll Marilyn Monroe Productions. At length, all Greene managed to wheedle out of Rosenfeld was some cash to help pay her hotel bills. In the end, Greene had asked Marilyn to flash her thousand-watt personality for nothing more than rent money. Afterward, she and Joe drove back to New York. Greene returned to Connecticut in defeat.

That evening, Joe carried Marilyn's bags into the Gladstone. He was a happy man, having just learned of his election to the Baseball Hall of Fame. A reporter asked Marilyn if she and DiMaggio were getting back together. This time, to Joe's delight, Marilyn pointedly avoided saying no. "It's not immediate."

For obvious reasons, Marilyn grew disenchanted with Greene. Joe, for his part, urged her to return to California. Greene worried about holding onto Marilyn, particularly when she expressed doubts about his lawyers, and asked Sam Shaw to reassure her. Informing Greene that Feldman was his friend, Shaw refused to intercede, and in fact told Marilyn that from a business perspective, she had been better off with Feldman. He also offered an important piece of advice. In light of the past few weeks, he recommended that Marilyn stay out of the press until The Seven Year Itch was released. Otherwise, the public might get bored with her. Marilyn instantly saw Sam's point. Greene disagreed, unwilling to give up the spotlight. On Monday, January 31, she and Greene had an argument in the car on the way from Connecticut to the city.

By this time, Marilyn had very nearly given up. The dream that had sustained her for so many years was almost dead. She'd managed to become a movie star, yet she had utterly failed to win the respect she was after. Greene had by no means clarified matters; his efforts had ended in embarrassment and fiasco. Perhaps Joe was right. Perhaps she ought to go back to Los Angeles. Perhaps it was time to accept that she was never going to get what she wanted.

Everything seemed to point to Marilyn's imminent departure when, on the evening of Tuesday, February 1, Sam Shaw escorted her to a dinner party given by Paul Bigelow. Greene invited himself along. Known in theatrical circles as "the fabulous Bigelow," their host was the devoted companion of Carson McCullers's cousin Jordan Massee. Tennessee Williams called Bigelow a "fantastic and rare character." Bigelow called himself a "professional catalyst." He liked to put people together, to make exciting things happen.

That night, Marilyn was seated opposite McCullers's great friend, Cheryl Crawford. Slim and erect, she had short auburn hair and a strong, forbidding face with thin lips and a tense forehead. She wore a dark, tailored wool suit, with a bit of silk scarf exposed at the throat. She wore sensible, low-heeled shoes. Her voice was deep, rich, and masculine.

Miss Crawford was one of Broadway's most important producers. Bigelow was her assistant. She had launched the Group Theater with Harold Clurman and Lee Strasberg. Later, she had founded the Actors Studio with Elia Kazan and Robert Lewis. She radiated courage and authority. Clifford Odets called her "a mariner steering for the pole star." In a business populated by temperamental personalities, she seldom grew angry—"about once every two or three years."

Tonight, apparently, was such an occasion. Crawford, in a flat Midwestern accent, announced that Marilyn had behaved despicably with a very good friend of hers. She passionately defended Charlie Feldman as a man of tremendous integrity. That, perhaps, was the last name one would have expected to hear in this context, yet Crawford insisted that Marilyn had treated him unfairly. Feldman had had Marilyn in mind when he purchased the film rights to Edward Chodorov's *Oh, Men! Oh, Women!*, which Crawford had produced in 1953. She told Marilyn that the material would have been perfect for her.

Marilyn tried to tell her side of the story. Milton Greene jumped in. The conversation became so heated that, at one point, Crawford turned to Sam Shaw and said that Greene was "evil and just no good." When Crawford was dismayed, two long, dark lines at the ends of her mouth curled sharply downward—an emotional Geiger counter.

Marilyn persisted and Crawford listened. She explained why she had left Famous Artists. She argued that Feldman, unwilling to jeopardize his position at Twentieth, hadn't fought for her hard enough. Her objections were limited to Feldman as an agent; she insisted she had all the respect in the world for him as a producer. She said that Feldman had more taste than anyone in Hollywood and could always be counted on to hire the best directors, writers, and other talent.

.   Crawford was won over. At such moments, her face would soften dramatically, the dark creases seeming to disappear. She had a warm smile and a merry laugh. After that, the women enjoyed a long, lively conversation about acting. Crawford, fascinated and impressed, invited Marilyn to accompany her to the Actors Studio. She and Kazan and Bobby Lewis had opened the Studio in 1947 as a private workshop where professional actors and actresses could "stretch their capabilities" and "tackle their limitations." It was neither a school nor a theater. It was off-limits to the public, and off-limits to anyone casting a show. The point was to be permitted to develop one's craft in an atmosphere free of commercial pressures. The point was to be encouraged to try things one hadn't done before. The point was to be allowed to fall flat on one's face. The Studio was an oasis, a refuge, a sanctuary. Kazan called it "the purest place in the world to work."

Marilyn accepted and they set a date. In the past month, her dream of reinventing herself had become a cruel and humiliating nightmare. Cheryl Crawford offered Marilyn a whole new chance. In one extraordinary and unexpected moment, everything seemed to have turned around for her again.

PART TWO

+ S E V E N +

As Cheryl Crawford ate breakfast in her East 54th Street apartment, she would watch the barges float past on the murky East River. This was probably the last peaceful time of her day. As a Broadway producer, she maintained a frantic schedule. She prepared budgets. She interviewed actors. She attended rehearsals. She had drinks with agents and investors. She strove to be, as Elia Kazan called her, a "helper of talent."

Seated at a nineteenth-century French desk that had been on stage during *Oh, Men! Oh, Women!*, she crafted letters to her authors. She did not flinch from sharply criticizing new work by friends like Carson McCullers and Tennessee Williams. Though firm in her own opinions, she recognized that she was not infallible. She struggled to avoid huge mistakes, such as she had made in turning down Arthur Miller's *Death of a Salesman*. When offered the play by Kazan in 1948, Crawford, to her eternal regret, decided that no one would want to see a drama about an unhappy traveling salesman. Willy Loman struck Crawford as pathetic rather than tragic.

A good portion of Cheryl Crawford's day was devoted to administrative duties at the Actors Studio. More than once, her financial acumen had been responsible for keeping the institution afloat. She raised funds. She pored over the books. She inspected real estate. She haggled with landlords. She resisted Paula Strasberg's ceaseless demands of a pay raise for her husband Lee. By and large, Crawford left the creative decisions to her partners.

Crawford took pride in her tranquility in moments of crisis. She liked to say that at the Group Theater she had played the "WASP shiksa" to Harold Clurman's and Lee Strasberg's fiery "Old Testament prophets." She performed a similar function with Kazan and Bobby Lewis, later with Kazan and Strasberg, at the Studio. She was the cool head, the mediator in moments of passionate dissension.

It was a short walk from Crawford's apartment to the Gladstone Hotel, off Park Avenue. On Friday, February 4, 1955, she arrived there early. Marilyn simply could not be late to observe her first session at the Actors Studio. The women took a cab crosstown to the Malin Studios on West 46th Street.

Marilyn, wearing her dark mink, black sunglasses, and a black kerchief, took her place in the roomful of intense, mainly young, casually dressed actors. They smoked cigarettes and drank coffee from paper containers. Marilyn, in a corner, slouched in her seat, trying to make herself invisible.

In front, several members of the twice-weekly workshop waited to perform a twenty-minute scene. A canvas film director's chair facing the makeshift stage remained notably empty. Obviously, no one dared sit there. In front of the vacant chair was a low table, and on it an assistant put a glass of steaming hot tea and two white index cards.

As if on cue, the moderator entered. The hush that fell over the room, the air of expectation, could hardly be attributed to his appearance or manner. He was squat, pale, partly bald, and hook-nosed. He had a crepe neck and a double chin. He took off a black raincoat, flinging it over the back of the canvas chair with thick, pasty-white hands. He wore large spectacles and dark, loose-fitting, priestly clothes. His body was rigid and unmuscled. He sat straight-backed, mouth clenched. A patch of gray fur sprouted on the back of his neck.

He clicked open a gold travel clock and put it on the table. Every now and again, he emitted a peculiar snort that some observers attributed to suppressed rage, others to a chronic sinus condition. He glanced at one of the index cards. In a low-pitched voice, he crisply identified the first of two scenes to be performed.

It was said that the master teacher Lee Strasberg could open inner doors that one scarcely knew existed. Some admirers called him the Rabbi. Some compared him to a psychiatrist or a harshly judgmental Jewish father. Harold Clurman insisted that no one in the world knew more about acting. Strasberg scrutinized a performance, said Clurman, with the intense concentration of a jeweler studying the inner mechanism of a watch. After the room lights shot on following a workshop performance, he analyzed, criticized, clowned, pontificated, and attacked. He struck poses and gazed into the air for inspiration. Someone compared him to a revivalist preacher. His speech was swift and argumentative.

Strasberg was often unabashedly rude. He was notorious for passing acolytes on the street or in the hall without so much as a nod or a hello. Was he being sadistic, or was he merely shy? He tended to look right through people as if they did not exist.

He was a spellbinding lecturer, who revelled in displays of his own vast learning. His words often failed to make literal sense. "Darling," he would say, "nothing here can be understood." Partisans insisted that Strasberg could speak clearly when he wanted to. They claimed he was trying to do something considerably more difficult: communicate with the unconscious mind. He asked oddly personal, often intrusive questions, leading one disgruntled Studio member to groan that Sigmund Freud wasn't as nosy as Lee Strasberg. Unlike other acting teachers who stressed language and text, Strasberg focused on psychology. He ran his workshops as though they were group therapy sessions.

He taught actors to draw on personal experience. He instructed them to turn inward. He challenged them to probe their own psyches. He pushed them to feel more intensely. He encouraged them to "take a minute," retrieving a powerful emotional experience related to the scene they were about to perform. "You pick a situation three to five minutes before the actual height of the experience," said Strasberg. "And you try to remember not what you experienced, not what you felt, but what you saw, what you heard, what you touched, what you tasted, what you smelled, what you experienced kinetically. You try to see the person. You try to hear the voice. You try to touch the fabric. You try to feel the heat."

Often the experiences summoned up from memory were painful, troubling, explosive. Students were known to rush to the door in tears. Elia Kazan worried that Strasberg's approach came perilously close to self-hypnosis, and frowned on what he saw as a good deal of "glassy-eyed psychological posturing." Other critics argued that Strasberg taught actors to present their own response to a dramatic incident rather than the character's.

He quoted Goethe: "The actor's career develops in public, but his art develops in private." He talked of "possibilities of progress" and of "talent in flux." He railed against commercialism. He warned students not to go Hollywood. He spoke of never having outgrown his youthful idealism. He recalled certain incandescent performances of the 1920s, evoking Jacob ben Ami, John Barrymore, Jeanne Eagels, and Eleonora Duse.

On her first visit to the Studio, Marilyn was in awe—both of the workshop, with its air of unrestrained emotionalism, and of Strasberg himself. After the session, Kazan came over to talk to her. He'd rarely seen her in the three years since his HUAC testimony. Still, they had remained friendly. As recently as three months ago, he'd sent her his love through Sidney Skolsky. At the moment, Kazan was set to begin rehearsals for Tennessee Williams's Cat on a Hot Tin Roof in five days. After that, he planned finally to direct Williams's Baby Doll (then titled "Mississippi Woman") at Warner Bros. He was still negotiating with Darryl Zanuck about the picture he owed Twentieth.

Kazan took Marilyn over to meet Strasberg.

By the time Marilyn left the Studio, she was bubbling with excitement. This was a world she had heard a great deal about from Kazan. But it had always been a mystery, existing somewhere "out there." At last, she had seen the place for herself and it was everything she'd imagined—and more. Above all, Marilyn was enthusiastic about Strasberg. He had mentioned that he also taught acting classes to groups of approximately thirty students, in which he concentrated on basic training in technique. The fee was thirty dollars a month, and Marilyn would be most welcome to join. The possibility intrigued her, but the prospect of working with him in front of others seemed utterly terrifying.

Afterward, Marilyn could not stop thinking about all she had seen and heard at the Studio. She decided that before she returned to California, she needed desperately to talk to Strasberg. She had Milton Greene call to ask if Strasberg might be willing to see her privately. A meeting was arranged at Strasberg's home on West 86th Street.

One entered the Belnord, a fortress-like apartment house, through a large courtyard. Marilyn knocked on Strasberg's door for the first time with trepidation. Strasberg's teenaged son noted that she "tiptoed" in. Kazan had warned her that he could be frightening. Fresh from the experience of directing *East of Eden*, Kazan was perhaps thinking of James Dean's trembling response to Strasberg when Dean was at the Studio. But Marilyn, deeply suspicious, wondered whether Kazan simply wanted to keep her away.

The first thing one noticed in the deep, narrow apartment was Strasberg's vast library. Books were everywhere, cluttering the floors, lining the walls, pouring out of closets and cabinets. There were piles in the bathroom and in the kitchen. It was said that to walk from the front door to the living room could be dangerous. Strasberg took pride in having assembled one of the world's best private theater collections.

For all the disorder, Strasberg, like Karl Marx, claimed to know the location of every book he owned. He never stopped buying. He adored the rare and the arcane. His quest for hard-to-find titles never ceased. He was constantly in touch with dealers, and new volumes were delivered almost daily. He spent money he didn't have. Once, when a large package appeared, Paula said ruefully that that was her insurance policy and her fur coat. She lamented that Lee's obsessive collecting would cause her and their two children to starve. He responded to her moods by dashing out to acquire more rare texts.

He would cut open a book's pages with a fish knife. He enlisted students to translate from Chinese, Japanese, Russian, and other languages. He wasn't merely a fetishistic collector; he read and savored his books. He cherished the knowledge they contained. A typical moment found Strasberg bent over some esoteric volume like a cabalist, music from his gigantic collection of classical recordings thundering in the background.

Mozart played on the phonograph that first day as Marilyn told Strasberg about herself. Without makeup, Marilyn looked considerably younger than twenty-eight—like a "pubescent virgin," said Truman Capote. She sat on a sofa that had appeared on stage in Tennessee Williams's *The Rose Tattoo*. Unseen in the hallway beyond, the dumpy, ample-bosomed Paula, redolent of Jungle Gardenia perfume, eavesdropped on the conversation.

Marilyn realized that Strasberg was exactly the person she'd been looking for. He was kind and wise. He listened with immense interest to all she had to say. Better yet, he seemed to have the answer to her problems. He knew precisely what she'd done wrong. Since that terrible day nearly a year ago when Charlie Feldman had handed her a new contract which seemed to deny her any credit for all that she'd achieved, Marilyn had lived in a state of perplexity. Unsure why Hollywood stardom had not brought respect, Marilyn had turned to Milton Greene. By now, however, she was well aware that Greene did not have the answer. Marilyn had come to her first session at the Actors Studio convinced that life would probably never be different.

As Marilyn related her story, Strasberg showed her that he sympathized and understood. He outlined a plan for her. He explained that being a Hollywood star would never bring her the dignity she craved. She would only be able to achieve that in one way: if she studied to be a serious actress. She must perform the great roles. To Marilyn's astonishment and delight, Strasberg seemed sincerely to believe in her ability to become such an actress. And he expressed a willingness to help her get there. According to Strasberg, there had been nothing wrong or unrealistic about Marilyn's goal; the only problem had been the particular means she had chosen to attain it.

Strasberg insisted that Marilyn reminded him of Laurette Taylor and Jeanne Eagels. He marveled at her "sensitivity." He declared that he wanted to "study her problems." He claimed to have glimpsed her "underlying personality." It was just beneath the surface, waiting to be released. He compared Marilyn to a buried treasure. He knew he was the man to unearth it.

"Strasberg exaggerated beyond the pale what her potentials were," said the director Frank Corsaro, who befriended Marilyn at the Studio. At the same time, Strasberg offered Marilyn "a sense of self." He assumed the role of "spiritual father." "He articulated her ambitions, her spirit, her needs," said Corsaro, "in a way that was very touching in itself but profoundly out of joint with her situation." Marilyn took comfort in the fact that suddenly she wasn't alone anymore; she had found someone who could tell her what she must do. Strasberg's dogmatism was very attractive, and she quickly permitted him to exert an enormous influence over her, precisely because she had come to feel such panic with Milton Greene. She had never really recovered from being laughed at following the press conference in New York. Strasberg, so firm in his convictions, seemed to offer an antidote to Greene's incompetence.

For all his authoritarianism, Strasberg was prepared, even eager, to accommodate Marilyn's special needs. As a rule, he did not offer individual instruction. Strasberg always said that an actor must learn to use his talent in front of others. But when Marilyn suggested that she would be too frightened to perform in front of a group, he invited her to come to the apartment several days a week to study with him privately. Soon, Marilyn would be confident enough to attend Strasberg's regular classes, in addition to observing at the Studio.

There was one other thing he wanted her to do. Strasberg often advised actors to enter psychoanalysis in order to put them in touch with emotionally-charged material they could use in their work. "To the actor," said Strasberg, "something that is a problem for somebody else becomes a creative force for him. It serves as the material that he transmits, that he transmutes, that he somehow shares." Strasberg told Marilyn that if she planned to study with him, she should find a psychoanalyst with whom to work simultaneously.

Given Marilyn's experience with men, she had been pleased that Strasberg had asked to see her at his home with his family present. After they had talked together a while, Lee took Marilyn to the kitchen, where his wife had begun to prepare dinner. Paula, every bit as warm and friendly as Lee, invited Marilyn to eat with them. The invitation sealed Marilyn's fantasy. Not only had she encountered a father figure tonight, but she'd been welcomed into his family. At a moment when Marilyn had been particularly disoriented and confused, the Strasberg household offered a sense of comfort, stability, and well-being.

After dinner, Marilyn left the Belnord determined to remain in New York. As a result of her meeting with Strasberg, she abandoned all thought of returning to Los Angeles in defeat. The reason for this change of direction wasn't just that she'd found Lee brilliant, or that she'd been enthralled by his work at the Studio. Had that been all that had occurred, Marilyn still would have faced the dilemma of what to do about her life and career. Tonight, something truly amazing had happened: Lee had provided a solution to Marilyn's problems. He had explained where she'd gone wrong and reassured her there was a way to make things right. He had shown Marilyn that she didn't have to give up hope.

Unsettled as everything in her life still was, Marilyn no longer appeared to care. Thanks to Strasberg, she had hope again. Her goal remained the same: She still wanted to change how people viewed her. Only the means to that end changed. She realized that she had to start over. She would have to work as feverishly to transform herself into a serious actress as she'd once done to become a star.

Suddenly, Marilyn was full of plans. Several things needed to be done right away. She had to find a psychiatrist. She had to set up a schedule for her private lessons with Lee. She had to find a more permanent place to live. She planned to remain in New York not as a negotiating ploy with Fox, nor because of her partnership with Milton Greene. She would stay because Lee Strasberg had provided her with a brand-new dream and promised to help her achieve it.

Within days of seeing Strasberg, Marilyn's life altered entirely. Suddenly, her daily schedule was nearly as busy as Cheryl Crawford's. Marilyn wasn't floating anymore; she had a direction again. She wanted to devote every waking moment to her goal. First, Marilyn asked Milton Greene to put her in touch with an analyst. She began to see Dr. Margaret Hohenberg, a Hungarian analyst who had previously treated Greene. Two mornings and three afternoons a week, Marilyn went to Dr. Hohenberg's office on East 93rd Street. These sessions were scheduled around Marilyn's work with Strasberg. On Tuesday and Friday mornings, she took a cab to the Malin Studios to sit in on Lee's workshop. Three nights a week, she studied independently with Strasberg at his apartment, often staying for dinner with the family. Before long, she joined one of Lee's private classes. They met four hours weekly; two hours were devoted to sense memory exercises, two to scene work.

Hardly had Marilyn begun at the Actors Studio when she was asked to participate in a fundraising benefit on March 9, 1955. The Studio was desperately in need of permanent quarters and the benefit, a preview of Kazan's *East of Eden* at the Astor Theater, was to raise money for the purchase of a deconsecrated Greek Revival-style church as its new home. Marilyn considered the invitation a huge honor, interpreting it as a sign that she'd been accepted into the fold. In fact, the Studio was eager to have Marilyn on view because of the publicity her presence guaranteed.

The night was a magical experience for Marilyn. Arriving in a limousine which Cheryl Crawford had sent to collect her at the Gladstone, she wore a strapless white silk brocade sheath dress with tightly fitted hips. Around her shoulders she had a matching brocade shawl edged with fox fur. She spent much of the evening on the arm of Marlon Brando, the two of them serving as "celebrity ushers." Marilyn was thrilled to be paired with Brando, who represented everything she aspired to as an actor. After the film, Marilyn went on to a reception across the street at the Astor Hotel. At the party, she was surrounded by Studio members and devotees eager to meet Strasberg's newest convert. Almost everyone seemed as friendly and welcoming as the Strasbergs had been. Overnight, Marilyn appeared to have discovered a whole new set of friends and, in Lee and Paula, even a new family.

Soon, Marilyn's wonderful new life in New York extended well beyond the confines of the Actors Studio. Through friends like Carson McCullers, Tennessee Williams, and Truman Capote, Marilyn was taken up in Manhattan as she simply had never been in Los Angeles. There she had been a star among stars; here she was a novelty, something entirely unique and different. In New York, everyone was curious about Marilyn. Everyone wanted to meet her. She turned up at the Colony and the Plaza Oak Room with Capote, who was then preparing to write *Breakfast at Tiffany's*. She joined Carson McCullers and Tennessee Williams's mother, Miss Edwina, as the latter received one hundred guests for cocktails in the St. Regis Hotel library to celebrate the premiere of *Cat on a Hot Tin Roof*. She was on view at Constance Collier's lunch parties, where the regular guests included Greta Garbo and Katharine Hepburn.

Capote had first taken Marilyn to Collier's dark studio apartment on West 57th Street. Nearly blind, with scant feeling in her hands and feet, the ailing seventy-seven-year-old English actress supplemented her income by working as a dramatic coach. When Marilyn learned that Hepburn was one of Collier's students, she became very excited. In Hollywood, Hepburn was treated with the kind of respect that had always eluded Marilyn. As if Marilyn were not already busy enough at the Studio, soon she, too, was taking voice and diction lessons with Collier. Strasberg had shown Marilyn the way, and she was relentless in her determination to reinvent herself as an actress. Everything else seemed unimportant by comparison.

A few weeks previously, Marilyn had hinted that she might be ready to take DiMaggio back. But as each day passed, she seemed to have less and less time for poor Joe. When Marilyn wasn't taking lessons or seeing her analyst, she preferred to sip coffee in the luncheonettes where the kids from the Studio hung out. And for the moment anyway, she had a new man in her life. Marlon Brando had called her at the Gladstone after the Studio benefit. He was due in Los Angeles at the end of March to attend the Oscars and begin a new film, but before he left town, he embarked on a brief love affair with Marilyn.

Joe told Sam Shaw that he was shocked by the change in Marilyn. It wasn't just Brando, but Marilyn's whole new focus. DiMaggio, unsure of quite what he was dealing with, fought to hold onto her. He struggled to make himself useful. He kept his nose in her business. He monitored Milton Greene and his lawyers. He was bewildered by the fact that suddenly Marilyn was in no hurry to return to Hollywood. "If I close my eyes and picture L.A.," she said, "all I see is one big varicose vein."

Marilyn knew that she had to reach some settlement with Twentieth about her contract, but her real interest lay elsewhere now. Milton Greene was still very much a presence in Marilyn's day-to-day existence; he was bankrolling her stay in New York, after all. But she was no longer here to be with him. She remained in New York for one reason only: to become a serious actress under Lee Strasberg's tutelage. In ways that DiMaggio failed to comprehend, once Strasberg came into Marilyn's life she felt differently about almost everything that just days before had mattered tremendously to her.

On March 14, five days after the Actors Studio benefit, Twentieth had sent three checks to Greene's lawyers, covering the weeks prior to Marilyn's suspension. The lawyers, still disputing that Marilyn had a valid contract, sent them back. After that, Twentieth refused to deal with Frank Delaney anymore, and announced plans to postpone the release of The Seven Year Itch until sometime in 1956. The decision suggested that Zanuck was prepared to wait out Marilyn in the negotiations.

In fact, there were no negotiations. Greene's lawyers could hardly do much so long as Twentieth wouldn't see or speak to them. Charlie Feldman, aware of Marilyn's predicament, decided to try one more time. He sent one of his agents to approach Marilyn in New York, ostensibly to discover whether she would be interested in appearing with Richard Burton in The Sleeping Prince, should Feldman acquire the rights. Marilyn said yes but showed no inclination to go back to Famous Artists. She appointed MCA, Feldman's rival, to represent her in talks with Twentieth.

The appointment was significant, suggesting as it did the difference a few weeks had made in Marilyn's attitude. Strasberg's attentions, and the life she had quickly made for herself in New York, had given her new confidence. In January, she had been ready to go back to Twentieth on the studio's terms, having finally despaired of ever persuading Zanuck to give her any degree of creative control. Now, less than two months later, Marilyn changed tack. If Twentieth would not give Marilyn what she'd earned, she was prepared to fight for it. At the same time, she knew that Milton Greene could never wage that war for her on his own. Marilyn's decision to bring in the powerhouse MCA put Zanuck on notice that she intended to win.

In another significant gesture, Marilyn moved out of the Gladstone Hotel in April. Shortly after Brando left town, she sub-leased Suite 2728 at the Waldorf Towers from the actress Leonora Corbett. Greene paid the rent, requiring him to mortgage his house and borrow from friends. The Towers apartment, though small, boasted a city view that was especially dramatic at night. The three rooms were decorated in blue and gold, with white accents.

Marilyn, who had few possessions, added touches of her own. On a table in the tiny living room she placed a spare, elegant drawing of her by Zero Mostel, a neighbor of the Strasbergs. She often chatted with the rotund actor in the Belnord courtyard. On another table she stacked some books about acting and the theater. She rarely ended a private session with Strasberg without borrowing at least one book. On the refrigerator top she stored a great many vari-colored jars of skin ointment and other beauty preparations. She hung the print of Abraham Lincoln above the bed. "I've never had a home," Marilyn said at the time. "Not a real one with all my own furniture. But if I ever get married again, and make a lot of money, I'm going to hire a couple of trucks and ride down Third Avenue buying every damn crazy kind of thing."

Not long after Marilyn had moved into the Towers, two new friends from the Studio, Eli Wallach and Anne Jackson, invited her to accompany them to a party. It was there that Marilyn encountered Arthur Miller for the first time since her arrival in New York.

One did not ordinarily find Miller at parties. He was a loner, especially now that he didn't hang out with Kazan anymore. He disliked loud, crowded rooms. When he talked, he preferred a background of silence.

Marilyn, all in white, was sipping a cocktail when she spotted him. He had, William Styron once said, "a gentleman farmer's rumpledness." Six feet two and a half inches tall, he towered over most people in the room. Marilyn realized that he was coming toward her.

She hadn't seen him since January 27, 1951. The day after Charlie Feldman's party in Miller's honor, Marilyn and Kazan had taken him to the airport. At the time, Marilyn thought Arthur was going home to work on The Hook and assumed he'd be right back. She had no idea that he'd left because he feared what was about to happen between them. She had no idea that four years would pass before they encountered one another again.

Marilyn was hardly the person she'd been four years previously. Back then, she had been an obscure starlet who barely knew whether she had the talent or the strength to go on. Today, she was a world-famous movie star, one of the most valuable properties in Hollywood. Back then, she'd been desperate for publicity of any sort. Today, Marilyn could barely go outside without the press documenting every step. And, of course, in the interim Marilyn had married for a second time and divorced.

Miller, at thirty-nine, seemed barely to have changed at all. He was still obsessed with the need to match the success he'd had with Death of a Salesman. The Crucible certainly hadn't done that for him, and he was about to try again with a new one-act play, A View from the Bridge, which was due to open on Broadway in the fall with another one-act play he'd completed. Martin Ritt was to direct, Kermit Bloomgarden and Robert Whitehead to produce. Casting was already under way.

There was another constant in his life. Though Miller had come to the party alone, he was still very much married. For all the talk of leaving his wife, he and Mary had bought a nineteenth-century house on Willow Street in Brooklyn Heights. With his own hands, he had put down a cork floor, redone the kitchen, and carried out other renovations as though he planned to stay for a long time.

Yet there could be no denying that the connection between Marilyn and Arthur remained strong. She reacted to him with the same fascination she'd felt during their strange interlude in Los Angeles. As far as she could see, he was powerfully drawn to her as well. Nonetheless, when the evening ended, he left without asking for her telephone number. Eli Wallach and Anne Jackson took her back to the Waldorf. Marilyn, terribly disappointed, had no idea whether she'd ever see Arthur again.

Days passed, and when Marilyn heard nothing from him she decided to engineer a meeting. She called Sam Shaw to suggest they spend the day taking pictures in Brooklyn Heights. The fact that the weather was rainy didn't seem to concern Marilyn. Her real reason for going out to Brooklyn was the chance that she and Sam might run into Arthur on the street.

The downpour made it impossible for them to work outside at all, and finally Sam suggested they drop in at a friend's apartment. It wasn't entirely by chance that the particular friend he took Marilyn to see was Norman Rosten; Sam had figured out why Marilyn wanted to spend the day in Brooklyn in the first place. Rosten, a poet and playwright, was Miller's best friend. They had been at the University of Michigan together, and their wives, Hedda and Mary, had been roommates there. The Millers and the Rostens, who lived around the corner from one another, were very much a foursome.

Norman and Hedda didn't immediately recognize Sam's "model." By the time they realized who she was, Marilyn had thoroughly charmed them both. The day had turned out better than she'd hoped; even if she hadn't managed to run into Arthur, she'd found a way into his life. When Norman suggested they all go to a neighborhood party afterward, Marilyn eagerly agreed. Undoubtedly, she hoped Arthur might turn up at the gathering. Though he didn't, Marilyn went home that night determined to cultivate a friendship with the Rostens. Sooner or later that friendship was bound to lead her back to Arthur.

As it happened, Arthur made his move first. After two weeks of silence, he called Paula Strasberg at home. If a man planned to cheat on his wife, Paula was the last person on earth he'd want to know. Paula, an inveterate gossip, had nearly broken up the Kazans' marriage when she notified Molly of his affair with Constance Dowling. She thought wives ought to stick together, and believed in eliminating the younger woman. In choosing her to call for Marilyn's number, Arthur was virtually ensuring that Mary would find out.

Finally, Marilyn received the call she'd almost given up waiting for. This time, Arthur did not fail to show up for their appointment, as he had done in August 1951. Soon, he and Marilyn were meeting regularly at her apartment whenever they could steal a few hours together. As far as Marilyn was concerned, her reception by Lee Strasberg had been wonderful enough, but Miller's reappearance in her life made New York feel like paradise.

Part of the intense appeal of the Actors Studio had been the degree to which it connected with Marilyn's long-ago fantasy of New York based on her encounters with Miller and Kazan. Arthur made all the elements of that fantasy click into place. With Strasberg, Marilyn had regained hope that she could change the way others saw her. Miller did something considerably more: If a man such as he could love her, perhaps she might actually learn to love herself. That was something she had never even dared to hope could happen. Marilyn, electric with life, was determined not to let him go again.

+   +   +

When Marilyn arrived, usually late, at the Actors Studio, she would take a seat beside Frank Corsaro. Marilyn's radar told her that Corsaro was probably closer to Strasberg than anyone else in the room. She would slip off her pitch-black glasses to show a face bare of makeup. She was usually, said Corsaro, "somewhat rumpled and not quite all put together," and called to mind "an unmade bed." He wondered whether this wasn't somehow deliberate, as though Marilyn wanted to distinguish herself from her glamorous Hollywood persona.

Corsaro often found himself staring at Marilyn's hands. "For a beautiful woman, she had the dirtiest fingernails I've ever seen," he recalled. Meanwhile, Marilyn, her eyes half-closed, listened to Strasberg. She almost never asked questions in class, and he wisely avoided singling her out.

Harold Clurman once remarked that "Lee could talk for three hours in one sentence." Strasberg tended to hide behind jargon, and no doubt many people in the room had a good deal of difficulty understanding him. Inevitably, Marilyn leaned over to Corsaro.

"What's he talking about?" she murmured.

As Strasberg talked on, Corsaro provided simultaneous translation. Her education continued at various Broadway hangouts afterward. Corsaro frequently escorted her to a little Greek diner. When the others explicated Strasberg's lectures, Marilyn, cradling a coffee cup in her hands, hung on every word.

Marilyn's reverence for Strasberg prevented her from seeing what was evident to many others. She had arrived on the scene at a moment of enormous crisis in Strasberg's professional life, when his authority and dominance at the Studio were very much in question. Far from being sincerely concerned with Marilyn's needs, Strasberg had instantly perceived in the great movie star an opportunity for his own salvation.

The source of the crisis was Elia Kazan. The two men had a long and troubled history dating back to the Group Theater, where Strasberg had publicly humiliated Kazan, who was then employed as his stage manager. When some bit of stage claptrap didn't work properly, Strasberg chastised Kazan before the entire company; the younger man was driven to tears. It was not in Kazan's nature to forgive or forget. He appeared to take malicious pleasure when, years later, his own theater and film commitments left him little time to teach, and Strasberg was an old failure thrilled to be offered a teaching post at the Actors Studio. Kazan's remarks about Strasberg were loaded with subtext. When Strasberg's name first came up as a possible replacement for Bobby Lewis, Kazan snidely declared that Lee would certainly be able to put in the time. When he praised Strasberg as "one of those people that are by very nature teachers," Kazan subtly reminded everyone that Strasberg had failed as a director.

The great stage productions Strasberg dreamed of directing had never materialized. He had failed in Hollywood as well. For three years a director of screen tests at Twentieth Century–Fox, he was fired by the studio on May 26, 1947. Strasberg remained bitter that the world had not properly recognized or rewarded his gifts. In private, he was known to grow so angry about his circumstances that blood poured from his nostrils. Clifford Odets predicted that Lee's arteries would "crack" prematurely. Cheryl Crawford observed that her colleague appeared to suffer some "ulcerating pain." Frank Corsaro noted that "Strasberg's fury and anger never abated."

Strasberg was appointed Artistic Director in 1951, but the Actors Studio was then still very much Kazan's domain. If the Studio was known outside theatrical circles, it was for Kazan's plays and films. A *Streetcar Named Desire* had opened on Broadway two months after the Studio was founded. Kazan's direction and Brando's acting quickly came to represent the Studio's bold new performance style. Kazan was a hero to the kids, as he fondly called the young actors and actresses at the Studio. Many desperately hoped that he would cast them in his next production. Though casting directors were barred from the workshop, it was no secret that Kazan used the Studio as, in Corsaro's words, a "pool of talent for his own enterprises."

In an unexpected twist of fate, Strasberg's life had changed dramatically after Kazan's HUAC testimony. Kazan's position at the Studio, as elsewhere in the arts, was suddenly very different. As Irene Selznick pointed out, of all those who named names Kazan was the one who was least forgiven, "because he had been the epitome of courage and strength." Quite simply, people expected better of Kazan. They thought he was tougher, and resented his efforts to justify what he had done. They accused him of having succumbed to "the rat race of success."

There was a perception that Kazan, of all people, had been in a position to break the blacklist—or at least to try. There was a feeling that he was "too important to be ignored." He would have inspired many others by doing the right thing himself. And no matter what his fate in Hollywood, he would have been able to work on Broadway where the blacklist had virtually no power. Had he refused to name names, Kazan, unlike those who could work only in Hollywood, would have continued to enjoy a good income in New York as well as the opportunity for artistic expression.

Instead, Kazan allowed himself to become the very figure of the informer in American culture. Zero Mostel dubbed him "Looselips." Others called Kazan a "stool pigeon." Arthur Miller and Kermit Bloomgarden snubbed him. People would cross the street to avoid having to decide whether to acknowledge him. Wherever Kazan went, he kept his antennae up to know what sort of greeting to expect. Kazan even had to be on guard at the Studio, where he fell out of favor with the kids. Some withdrew from the workshop because of his participation. Others vowed never to work with "that sonofabitch" again. The situation became so intense that a meeting had to be called, and a number of members urged the Studio publicly to condemn Kazan's actions. In the end, however, a decision was made to take no position.

Though Kazan maintained a gruff exterior, he was acutely sensitive to the fact that many people at the Studio had turned on him. He confessed to Cheryl Crawford that there were moments when he actually considered withdrawing altogether. He steered clear of the Studio for a while, and in his absence Strasberg became the new father figure. Strasberg greatly relished his new status. For the first time, he didn't have to live under Kazan's shadow. For the first time, he wasn't constantly reminded that Kazan, not he, had the important career. To all intents and purposes, the Actors Studio became Strasberg's kingdom.

Strasberg's domination was short-lived. To his fury, in 1953 Kazan made his first conscious effort to find a way back. Eager to reclaim the Studio, Kazan cast Studio actors in Tennessee Williams's *Camino Real* when, as he recognized, others would have been more appropriate. Thus did Kazan flaunt his power. Lee Strasberg might have charisma, but he wasn't a working director. He couldn't offer the kids roles in Broadway shows. Kazan tempted the kids with the very success for which some accused him of having sold out.

The triumphant release of *On The Waterfront* in July 1954 consolidated Kazan's position at the Studio; Marlon Brando's bravura performance made Kazan a hero there once more. Strasberg's worst nightmare had come true. After *On the Waterfront*, there could be no doubt that once again he played second fiddle to Kazan. *East of Eden*, another film that the public tended to associate with the Studio, exacerbated Strasberg's predicament. Rather pathetically, he attempted to share in the credit for both Brando and James Dean, though Brando had actually been trained by Strasberg's enemy Stella Adler, and Dean had fled in terror after only a brief stay at the Studio, when Strasberg sharply criticized his workshop efforts.

From Strasberg's point of view, Marilyn could hardly have arrived at a more opportune moment. She provided him with a weapon in his struggle for authority at the Studio. Marilyn Monroe would be Strasberg's movie star, as Brando and Dean had been Kazan's. Her miraculous transformation would be a testament to Strasberg's own gifts as a director. Though he led Marilyn to believe that he had confidence in her talent, in fact the only one he really had confidence in was himself. As far as Strasberg was concerned, when Marilyn finally gave a great performance, it would be his accomplishment, not hers.

From the first, though Marilyn did not suspect it, she was back in a similar situation to the one she'd been in with Darryl Zanuck. For all the work Marilyn had done to become a star, in the end Zanuck had claimed the credit for her success. He had insisted that Twentieth Century–Fox—not Marilyn herself— had made her what she was today. Strasberg intended to do much the same thing: He planned to take credit for his protégée's achievements. He wanted to be something more than Marilyn's instructor; when she was ready—and there was no telling when that might occur—he hoped to direct her as well. In short, Strasberg saw Marilyn as a vehicle to the success that had long and stubbornly eluded him. Marilyn would make it possible for Strasberg to direct the great productions of his dreams.

Blind as Marilyn was to Strasberg's self-serving motives, she failed to understand what he was really up to when he insisted that she would never win respect as a movie star. Of course, it was precisely Marilyn's stardom that made her so useful to Strasberg. At the same time, without significant professional credits of his own, he needed to adjust the balance of power in their relationship. Strasberg had to convince Marilyn that she had not accomplished anything on her own. He had to invalidate her hard-earned achievements in Hollywood. He had to reduce her to point zero. He had to make her accept that, despite all she had done in her career to date, she had come to him with nothing.

In the past, Marilyn had almost never failed with interviewers. She needed only to flash her "Marilyn" persona, and most press people were charmed. But something unprecedented happened on April 8. When Edward R. Murrow interviewed her at Milton Greene's barn for the television program *Person to Person*, Marilyn was bland and colorless. Determined to be thought of as a serious actress—whatever that might mean, and at times she didn't seem sure—Marilyn was unwilling to play the character she had always used to such great effect. In the absence of that character, Marilyn lacked a distinctive voice; evidently, she hadn't yet found a substitute for "the girl." Billy Wilder once remarked that when Marilyn appeared on screen, you simply couldn't take your eyes off her. That was by no means the case on the Murrow show. The Greenes, particularly Mrs. Greene, occupied center stage, while Marilyn seemed to disappear into the woodwork.

In Los Angeles, Darryl Zanuck wondered whether she had lost her mind. He was convinced that she'd made an idiot of herself on *Person to Person*. If she kept up this sort of thing, he believed, *The Seven Year Itch* would be a hard sell by the time it was released in 1956. Zanuck conferred with Spyros Skouras and Al Lichtman, the head of the sales department, and they agreed to release the picture immediately, before Marilyn could do any more damage. Zanuck selected June 1, 1955, Marilyn's twenty-ninth birthday, for the New York premiere. He wanted her to attend; but she was on suspension and he refused to invite her officially. Instead, he had some tickets sent to her through Sam Shaw.

Obviously, Marilyn couldn't attend the opening with Arthur Miller. She turned up at the Loew's State Theater with Joe DiMaggio. The fifteen hundred guests included Tyrone Power, Grace Kelly, Henry Fonda, and Judy Holliday. Thousands of fans crowded Broadway in the hope of catching a glimpse of Marilyn. There was a pained smile on Joe's face as he escorted her past a huge blow-up photograph of the skirt-blowing scene. By the time they entered, the film had started.

The excitement in the theater was palpable. Several times in the course of the evening the audience erupted in applause. They laughed at all the right moments and there was a standing ovation at the end. Hedda Hopper called The Seven Year Itch Marilyn's "first great picture." Under ordinary circumstances, Charlie Feldman and Darryl Zanuck would have fêted Marilyn afterward. As it was, DiMaggio took her to Toots Shor's. When Joe and Marilyn came around the large, circular bar, Toots led the crowd in shouting "Happy birthday!" Joe, eager to please, had arranged a surprise party.

But Marilyn couldn't enjoy herself. Despite Joe's efforts, the evening seemed to tear her up inside. It was obvious that everyone had adored her in the picture, and Marilyn knew that Billy Wilder had helped her to give her best performance to date. But she could take no pleasure in her achievement. Her encounters with Strasberg had caused her to turn violently on all that she had accomplished in Hollywood—including The Seven Year Itch. Anyone might have expected Marilyn to be proud of herself tonight, but the premiere had very much the opposite effect. The success of the "Marilyn Monroe" character—a character the whole world seemed to have fallen in love with—brought her only self-loathing and disgust.

Before the evening was over, she had an argument with Joe, who seemed hardly to comprehend what was going on, and walked out of her own party. Sam Shaw saw her home.

On several occasions after that, DiMaggio was observed in the shadows outside the Waldorf Towers, hiding in dark doorways. He stood apart from the fans and photographers, but he, too, watched and waited. "He loved her beyond anybody's comprehension," said Sam Shaw. Ann Shaw worked very hard to get Joe and Marilyn back together. Marilyn asked Ann to stop, insisting that she liked things the way they were.

Finally, DiMaggio appeared to have had enough. When Sam went to France to document circus life, Joe followed. At night, he would dine with the Shaws and a *Paris-Match* crew. He wanted to go to Italy to visit the places where his parents had been born. He gave the impression that he hoped somehow "to find himself." He never spoke of Marilyn, or discussed what he was going through. "He felt, but he didn't talk," Shaw recalled.

At this point, few people knew that Marilyn was seeing Arthur Miller. Because photographers followed her everywhere, she and Arthur spent most of their time together in her apartment. Arthur, then at work on the production of *A View from the Bridge*, would stop off to see Marilyn on his way home. When Truman Capote, Miller's neighbor in Brooklyn Heights, guessed the identity of Marilyn's "masked marvel," she jestingly threatened to have Capote bumped off if he told anyone. Arthur was married with two children. He had a reputation as a man of conscience. He had to be discreet.

At a moment when Miller was preparing to stage a public indictment of the betrayer, he secretly betrayed his wife. His meditations on the topic of infidelity in his notebooks and in *The Crucible* suggest that it cannot have been easy. His joy with Marilyn, combined with fears for his marriage, left him unable to focus on casting and other production matters. For the moment, he seemed to live most intensely on the twenty-seventh floor at the Waldorf Towers.

Miller was confused, conflicted. He told himself he didn't want his union with Mary to end. He valued stability and routine. The anchor of a home life permitted him to write. He adored his children. Yet he couldn't bear to give up Marilyn. Eventually, Arthur's older brother sensed that he was weighing something. Kermit Miller, concerned but by no means judgmental, finally reached out. But Arthur didn't want to talk about his affair. At the same time, Arthur did appear to want Kermit and other family members to know. Why else would he drive out to Kermit's house in Marilyn's car?

There was no question that Arthur seemed different. He had a face that might have been chiseled on Mount Rushmore. Marilyn loosened him up. She made him grin. He seemed suddenly more tender-eyed and accessible. He seemed never to have been more in love with anyone. Arthur, it would be said in the Miller family, had had his train wreck rather late in life.

Miller did not think much of Lee Strasberg, but he shared and sometimes outdid the latter's high hopes for Marilyn. He gushed (uncharacteristically) about her talent as much as DiMaggio had minimized it. He told Kermit Bloomgarden that when Marilyn finally appeared on stage she would devastate audiences. He predicted she would be one of the theater's great stars. Marilyn, to her immense delight, found herself with two saviors: Strasberg and Miller, the great teacher and the great author. She called them the smartest men on earth. She spoke of each as though he were the Wizard of Oz, capable of making her wish come true. In both cases, she failed to perceive the needy, imperfect human being behind the curtain.

Miller had one other thing in common with Strasberg. At the moment, both men were strongly affected by Kazan. Miller, like Strasberg, had been propelled into a state of crisis by On the Waterfront. Indeed, Kazan's triumph may have been even harder for Miller to swallow than it was for Strasberg. In 1951, Miller had gone to Hollywood with Kazan in search of the success that On the Waterfront eventually brought; the film was received as precisely the kind of major breakthrough in the art of cinema that Miller had aimed to achieve in The Hook. To make matters worse, On the Waterfront, in both theme and atmosphere, bore an unmistakable resemblance to Arthur Miller's waterfront screenplay. It was as though Kazan had extracted the essence of that earlier, unrealized work and made it his own.

On the Waterfront was linked to Miller in another significant way. On the day Kazan had told Miller of his intention to name names, Miller, in turn, had disclosed his own plan to research the Salem witch trials. Kazan and his wife had instantly perceived that Miller planned to write a parable of the HUAC hearings. On the Waterfront, with a script by Budd Schulberg, was Kazan's answer to The Crucible. It was the story of an ex-prizefighter who finds the courage to testify in court against the mob. The world may call him a stool pigeon, but in his heart he knows he's done the right thing. "I'm glad what I done—you hear me—glad what I done!" he shouts at the end, echoing what Kazan claimed were his own feelings about having testified.

While Kazan was preparing *On the Waterfront*, he had been warned by Miller's lawyer John Wharton that if he went forward, he'd never direct another Miller play again. At length, when Kazan collected his Oscar as Best Director for *On the Waterfront*, he found himself thinking of that lawyer, and of Miller himself. Kazan had never forgiven Miller for snubbing him with Kermit Bloomgarden. The night *On the Waterfront* received eight Oscars, including the awards for Best Picture and Best Screenplay, was Kazan's revenge.

As chance would have it, Marilyn had turned up in New York at a moment when *The Hook*—the screenplay Miller had been trying to sell when he met her—was again very much on Arthur's mind. Thrown back to that time four years previously when he had abandoned both his script and Marilyn, Miller proceeded to rewrite history in two important ways. In February, he wrote a stage play that reclaimed the waterfront atmosphere of *The Hook* as his own. Soon after, Miller picked up where he had left off with Marilyn—except that this time he was not about to walk away.

A View from the Bridge was Miller's answer to Kazan's defense of the informer in *On the Waterfront*. In Miller's play, a man's decision to name names leads inevitably to his destruction. Miller longed for a world where, he said, "actions had consequences again." It's not hard to see why he would have felt that way. On Broadway, *The Crucible* had been a critical and commercial failure. Miller, in speaking out against the HUAC witch-hunt, had reaffirmed his credentials as a man of conscience. He had acted bravely at a time when it was dangerous to speak one's mind. He had gone on record against the prevailing insanity, a gesture that seems all the more impressive when one considers that Miller was innately cautious. Miller, unlike Kazan, had done the right thing. But as a playwright, he had disappointed. Meanwhile, with *On the Waterfront*, Kazan had climbed back to the top. No wonder Miller was drawn to what he called the "inexorability" of his story. At least in art, if not in life, the rat paid a price for his actions.

In *A View from the Bridge*, Miller returned to a play, "An Italian Tragedy," that he had tried to write following his first encounter with

Marilyn in Los Angeles. In 1951, Miller, troubled by his own feelings for Marilyn, had been attracted to the wayward husband's tale. Filled with guilt, he could identify with the betrayer. And at a moment when, in Miller's absence, his friend Kazan was sleeping with Marilyn, the playwright had been naturally drawn to the idea of a sexual triangle. Then there was the protagonist's decision to inform on the illegal immigrant, an element that would have held little personal interest at the time unless Miller fantasized (unconsciously?) about destroying his rival in love.

In 1955, however, there can be no doubt that the informer theme was of prime concern to Miller. Add the author's wish to see betrayal punished, and one can see why the play jelled as it had not in 1951, when Kazan's HUAC testimony had yet to come between them. In one significant way, Miller, in A View from the Bridge, altered the anecdote he had heard long ago on the Brooklyn waterfront; he added an accusation that Rodolpho, the illegal immigrant, is secretly a homosexual. Eddie, the longshoreman, makes much of the fact that Rodolpho is a singer, a curious detail as Miller himself once aspired to sing professionally. As a teenager, Miller had practiced at home, crooning in a tenor-baritone voice with a lamp for a microphone.

Whereas in 1951 Miller would have identified with Eddie, four years later Kazan was, literally, the informer. Thus, in the later version, Miller and Kazan exchanged places in the triangle. Miller, always cautious and a bit fearful with women, appears to have glimpsed some aspect of himself in Rodolpho. That, no doubt, was part of the story's appeal: working with emotionally-charged material Miller did not fully comprehend. In the play's most disturbing scene, Eddie kisses his niece. Then he forcibly kisses Rodolpho on the mouth to show that that's what the young man really wants. Was Miller trying to make sense of his own powerful emotional connection to Kazan? Was he trying to understand why, the first time around, he had chosen to leave Marilyn?

A View from the Bridge was not the only Miller work that seems to have been created in reaction to On the Waterfront. Not long after Kazan's film dominated the Academy Awards, Miller, in New York, began work on a new screenplay, his first since The Hook. Significantly, Miller and Kazan, in cooperation with Kermit Bloomgarden, had once hoped to set up an independent film production company on the east coast. On the

Waterfront had been shot independently in the east, and that was Miller's plan for his own screenplay-in-progress, "Bridge to a Savage World."

In an echo of Kazan's treatment of alienated youth in *East of Eden*, Miller's script dealt with the gangs of violent, rebellious teenagers that terrorized American cities in the mid-1950s. They "rumbled" with rival gangs; they fought with chains, zip guns, switchblade knives, and broken bottles. Combined Artists, a small independent production company, had commissioned Miller to write a feature film. It would be made with an "important" cast in association with the New York City Youth Board. In exchange for 5 per cent of the profits, the municipal agency would give the filmmakers access to police and social workers.

For several weeks, Miller interviewed gang members in the Bay Ridge section of Brooklyn. He saw the boys as savages. He compared them to "the hordes that roamed the virgin forests." He wrote: "These are children who have never known life excepting as a worthless thing. They have been told from birth that they are nothing, that their parents are nothing, and that their hopes are nothing."

Their fight for self-respect reminded Miller of Marilyn. The script, as it evolved, focused on a Youth Board worker who tries to get through to one of the boys. "To save one of these," said Miller, "is obviously a great piece of work." By his own account, Miller saw himself as engaged in an effort to "save" Marilyn. Thus, as so often with Miller, in his own feelings about Marilyn he discovered the emotional connection he needed to write.

By July, Miller had completed an outline and the Youth Board had approved it. Before the project went forward, however, it had to be approved by the city government. Suddenly, Miller found himself caught in a political firestorm. Since *The Crucible*, it had been inevitable that the political right would come after Miller in revenge for what Eric Bentley called "Broadway's principal challenge to McCarthyism."

In 1954, Miller had had the first hint of what was to come, when he was denied a U.S. passport to attend a Belgian production of *The Crucible*. The right had put him on notice that they intended to punish him. One year later, the attempt to enlist the Youth Board's help for the gang film provided Miller's enemies with a pretext to go after him again. On July 22, 1955, the *New York World Telegram and Sun*, a prominent right-wing newspaper, ran an article headlined "Youth Board Filmster

Has a Pink Record: Miller Hit Kazan for Telling All." The article questioned whether a city agency ought to underwrite Miller, "a veteran backer of Communist causes."

As proof of Miller's Communist sympathies, the newspaper offered his attitude to Kazan: "But three years ago, he broke up a long, deep-rooted and profitable friendship with Elia Kazan, after the latter testified before the House Un-American Activities Committee. The playwright, the *World Telegram and Sun* disclosed at the time, would not tolerate Mr. Kazan's identification of Communists in the party unit to which he once belonged. He expressed strong disapproval of the testimony to Broadway intimates and cut all communication with his theatrical teammate, asserting he no longer wanted the director to profit from his writings."

HUAC planned four days of entertainment business hearings in New York in August. The committee, sensing that there were no more big names to go after in Hollywood, decided to set up shop temporarily on Broadway. The theatrical figures they pursued, however, were largely obscure and unsuccessful. A notable exception was Arthur Miller. One of the committee's tactics of harassment was to suggest unofficially that certain individuals might soon be called; Dolores Scotti, a HUAC investigator, notified city officials that Miller was about to be subpoenaed. The merest suspicion of subversive activity was often enough to infect one's ability earn a living.

Miller's prestige made him a particularly desirable target for a committee that found itself increasingly starved of the publicity that was its lifeblood. The political climate in the United States was quite different from what it had been when Kazan testified in 1952. A number of factors had contributed to a lessening of public interest in the hunt for Communists, including the end of the Korean War and the 1954 Senate vote to "condemn" Senator Joseph McCarthy. HUAC in 1955 was like a great wounded bear, all the more threatening and dangerous in its weakened condition.

Mrs. Scotti warned that Miller was likely to be an unfriendly witness and that that would embarrass the Youth Board. She noted that Miller had a "heavy front" record. She declared that he had participated in various "Communist-dominated and -controlled organizations." She mentioned his ties to the National Council of American–Soviet

Friendship and the Committee of the Arts and Sciences and Professions. She pointed out that his dossier was already one and a half inches thick.

The city government deferred its decision until after Miller had appeared before HUAC. Initially, it was anticipated that he would be called in mid-August. Almost as soon as the Board had decided to postpone the decision, Mrs. Scotti announced the launch of a full-scale investigation of Miller in hopes of finding someone to "place him in the Party." They would not call Miller in August after all. The new plan was to delay the subpoena until November. Mrs. Scotti said it was a shame they had to wait so long, but if Miller were called individually the liberals would complain that HUAC was persecuting him. HUAC planned to round up some other people and throw Miller in with the group.

With this political cloud over his future, Miller began rehearsals for *A View from the Bridge* in August. Each day, as he entered the New Amsterdam roof theater—the same theater where Miller and Kazan had once prepared *Death of a Salesman*—Miller walked past a life-sized cutout of Marilyn, her skirt flying up in the air, advertising *The Seven Year Itch*. Her image was everywhere in Manhattan. The whole city, indeed much of the nation, seemed to be fantasizing unrepentantly about Marilyn. But it was Miller alone who had actually realized the fantasy of the male character in *The Seven Year Itch*. He was having an affair with Marilyn while his wife and children were away in the country. The author of a famous play, set in a Puritan colony, about the perils of sex had fallen in love with "the girl." That summer, no one seemed more eager to believe he'd been wrong about sex than he.

Interestingly, even as Miller was working to bring to life his version of the Miller–Kazan–Monroe triangle, elsewhere in the city that triangle seemed to be on Kazan's mind as well. Marilyn's love affair was no longer entirely a secret; during weekends on Fire Island with the Strasbergs, she poured out her heart to Paula, who could hardly resist the temptation to spread the news. Kazan also had reason to think of Miller when his own name came up in the newspaper coverage of Miller's political problems. And of course, by this time the script of *A View from the Bridge* was in circulation among theater people in New York. So it comes as no surprise that, whether consciously or not, Kazan's feelings about the triangle would surface in a project of his own.

That summer, Tennessee Williams, in Rome, had been sending off bits and pieces of his *Baby Doll* screenplay for Kazan to work on. Marilyn was Williams's first choice for Baby Doll Meighan as the playwright then conceived her: a witless, fat, sexy, languid, thumb-sucking woman who sleeps in a crib. In late July, at almost the precise moment that the Miller story broke in the *New York World Telegram and Sun*, Williams sent Kazan his ideas for the third act. The letter elicited a curious response; Kazan, admitting that his own concept was quite weird, asked Williams to consider the very different third act he had in mind. Though at length Williams rejected the proposal in every detail, it provides a fascinating glimpse into Kazan's mind.

The men in Baby Doll's life are her foolish husband, Archie Lee, and his smarmy, manipulative business rival, Silva. Silva manages to seduce Baby Doll, whose marriage has not yet been consummated. In the end, as Kazan saw it, a snake bites Archie Lee's heel. Silva, on his knees, cuts a slit in the other man's skin with a pocket knife. Then, in an act of brotherhood, he puts his lips to the wound and sucks the venom. It's an image more charged even than the kiss in *A View from the Bridge*.

A feeling of comradeship develops between Silva and Archie Lee. Spitting out a mouthful of poison, Silva exclaims that he certainly never thought he'd be doing this. Afterward, the shaken, exhausted men, once rivals, go off together for a drink, leaving Baby Doll alone. It is striking that, like Miller, Kazan described a heterosexual triangle with homosexual overtones. He, too, seemed to be stalking the emotionally loaded topic of the men's relationship with each other. Miller and Kazan were not on speaking terms, but they communicated through their work; they communicated through their views of Marilyn.

At the end of August, Miller went on the road with *A View from the Bridge* and its minor companion piece, *A Memory of Two Mondays*. The first tryout took place on August 22 at the summer theater in Falmouth, Massachusetts. In Boston, Miller ran into trouble with the city censor after the press described the show as containing "some of the strongest Anglo-Saxon words heard on Boston stages in years." At the last minute, words and phrases had to be blue-penciled, but even then there were problems. Several ladies fled a matinée after the actor Van Heflin kissed Richard Davalos on the lips. Nonetheless, the show proved to be popular and advance ticket sales in New York were substantial. And for Miller, in the midst of his political troubles, there was the consolation of a visit from Marilyn. Incognito, with a white knitted cap that covered her brow, Marilyn spent a carefree day with him in Boston. Unusually for her, at the moment Marilyn was the one who seemed to believe everything was going to be all right.

On September 29, Marilyn attended the Broadway premiere of *A View from the Bridge* at the Coronet Theater. She sat on the left side of the orchestra, so that she would not run into Arthur or his wife. She did, however, meet Arthur's parents, Isadore and Augusta Miller, when Augusta rushed up to the movie star and introduced herself as the playwright's mother.

"I admire Mr. Miller's plays," Marilyn replied cautiously. "I'm a first-nighter at all of them."

When the first reviews came in, it was immediately evident that once again the success Miller so desperately sought to recapture had eluded him. The New York critics, though respectful, tended to be unenthusiastic. Part of the problem was that both plays were slight. There was considerable embarrassment about the rather grand treatment they had been given. "Such was the hubris of the time," said Brooks Atkinson years afterward, that the two one-act plays "were produced solemnly like major works of art, as if Mr. Miller were already a classic author."

Worse, Miller no longer seemed to trust his audience. In *Death of a Salesman*, Miller, as Thomas Mann once observed, didn't tell playgoers what to think. Willy Loman had been wonderfully lifelike and full of ambiguity. The characters in *The Crucible* and the 1955 version of *A View from the Bridge* were something entirely different. They weren't real and complex; they were good or bad, positive or negative, illustrations rather than living, breathing people. *The Crucible* and, now, the one-act *View* failed dramatically because, as Kenneth Tynan said privately of *The Crucible*, Miller refused to "give the other side its due." There was no authentic conflict, no battle of equals. *A View from the Bridge* was a condemnation of the informer, not a dramatic analysis. It was preaching, not playwriting.

Eric Bentley wrote a trenchant joint review of *On the Waterfront* and *A View from the Bridge*. "It will surprise no one that, in Mr. Kazan's movie, the act of informing is virtuous, whereas, in Mr. Miller's new play, it is evil. What is surprising, or at any rate appalling, is that both stories seem to have been created in the first place largely to point up this virtue and that evil, respectively. Now it is easy enough to end by winning the game if you begin by stacking the cards, only you then have to concede that the game loses all its interest as a game."

Faced with another failure, Miller tried to be philosophical. He told himself that a writer who has enjoyed success early on must avoid being caught up in the struggle for continuing recognition. He insisted he wasn't after just another cheap Broadway hit. He saw himself as a serious artist in a land of comic-book writers. He told himself that, if he cared to, he could churn out works which, however well-received, would leave him feeling ashamed. Yet the fact remained that Miller's effort to reclaim his material from Kazan had been unsuccessful. It was Kazan who had had the huge triumph with his waterfront film, while Miller's play had been a disappointment. But at least Miller still had Marilyn—or did he?

As October began, Marilyn took an incredible step. When the Actors Studio reopened that fall, she returned as an observer; but this year, she had a specific purpose in mind. Marilyn wanted the female lead in Kazan's new film which, with a script by Tennessee Williams, was an especially prestigious project to an actress who had rejected Hollywood in favor of the intellectual superiority of New York. Like everyone else at the Studio, Marilyn knew that Kazan was about to cast Baby Doll. Marlon Brando was Kazan's first choice for Silva—his alter ego. Though Brando had rejected an earlier version of the screenplay, Kazan hoped that Williams's final draft would change his mind.

As for the role of Baby Doll, Kazan had decided that Marilyn would no longer be appropriate. Williams had changed the character to a child bride of nineteen, whose father married her off on the condition that Archie Lee not sleep with her until her twentieth birthday. Though Williams continued to see Marilyn as Baby Doll, Kazan insisted that, at twenty-nine, she was too old. The director had been searching for another actress since August 20. Marilyn, with the single-minded determination that had made her a star, decided to campaign actively for the role, whatever that might mean for Miller and Strasberg.

Since that fateful first night at the Belnord with Strasberg, Marilyn had been waiting for a chance to prove herself as an actress. Lee had given her a new dream. In Baby Doll, Marilyn saw an opportunity to realize that dream. What could be more perfect than a package that included Tennessee Williams, Elia Kazan, and Marlon Brando? (As it happened, the role of Silva later went to Eli Wallach.)

With the instinct for survival that had kept her going all her life, Marilyn put on blinders and focused only on what she needed. No matter that Miller and Kazan were at odds, or that Williams was Miller's only true rival in the American theater. No matter that Strasberg was locked in a struggle of his own with Kazan, or that Marilyn herself was to have been Lee's weapon in that struggle. Either she didn't see any of these things, or she didn't care. In her mind, Baby Doll was the one role that could transform her career and give it a whole new direction. Williams was right; Marilyn probably would have been brilliant in the film.

Marilyn went to Kazan. When he told her she was wrong for the part, she begged to test. She dispensed with her pride. She put aside the fact that she was a famous movie star. She would test, and test again, if that was what he needed to believe in her. But he refused.

She wouldn't give up. When Kazan turned his attention to the young actress Carroll Baker, Marilyn persisted in campaigning for the role. And Williams persisted in wanting to cast her. In the end, Kazan had his way. Perhaps he really did think Marilyn was too old. Perhaps he didn't think she was up to the part; though Kazan thought that Marilyn was a talented light comedienne, he did not share Miller's and Strasberg's estimate of her potential. Or perhaps he simply enjoyed rejecting a woman whom both Miller and Strasberg so desperately wanted and needed for their own purposes. Whatever Kazan's reasons, he turned Marilyn down. She was bitterly disappointed.

It is tempting to speculate about what would have happened to Marilyn had Kazan cast her in Baby Doll. Almost certainly, her life would have been different in a number of significant ways. Had she been directed by Kazan at that stage in her career, she probably would not have become as dependent on the Strasbergs as she later did. What need would there have been for Lee if it had been Kazan who enabled Marilyn to do her first important dramatic role? What need would there have been for Paula? Had Marilyn done well in a film written by Tennessee Williams, quite possibly she would have been treated differently by the public, and even by the industry. And who can say what would have happened to Marilyn's relationship with Arthur Miller had she gone to Mississippi in November to shoot Baby Doll with Kazan?

All that can be known for sure is that after Marilyn lost Baby Doll, she was determined to find another great role that would allow her to show the world that she had become a serious actress. She was convinced that somewhere out there was a magical script that would change everything for her. From that point on, she would not rest until she found it.

+ EIGHT +

By the time Marilyn lost *Baby Doll* in October 1955, Twentieth and MCA had almost come to terms on her new contract. When she signed, she would be paid an additional $142,500 for *There's No Business Like Show Business* and *The Seven Year Itch*. Marilyn, it will be recalled, had started *There's No Business Like Show Business* at Charlie Feldman's urging with the understanding that once she had a signed contract, she would collect the difference between her new per-picture fee and her old salary. Furthermore, she was to receive $225,000 in four installments for the screen rights to *Horns of the Devil*, the novel Joe DiMaggio had advised Marilyn to buy as an investment. She had done so with Feldman's money and had yet to repay him.

That October, Marilyn borrowed something else from Feldman: the idea for her first independent production. One other important matter to be settled in Marilyn's new contract was the right to make outside pictures. With the money from Twentieth, she intended to buy Terence Rattigan's *The Sleeping Prince*, the play Feldman had offered to acquire for her in 1954 and again the previous spring. Since Laurence Olivier's stage production in 1953, no one had bought the film rights. Before Feldman had even considered *The Sleeping Prince*, Rattigan had written to Darryl Zanuck about the possibility of casting Marilyn. He sang her praises, comparing her to Vivien Leigh and professing bafflement at the critics' refusal to give her her due. Zanuck didn't rule out buying *The Sleeping Prince* for Marilyn, but he didn't make an offer either.

In the fall of 1955, though no papers were signed, Rattigan gave permission to the producers Hugh "Binkie" Beaumont and Anatole de

Grunwald to try to put together a film. Hardly had Rattigan's agent given his approval when he thought of another possibility: Why not try William Wyler, Olivier's close friend and favorite Hollywood director? Wyler immediately expressed interest, especially if Olivier were to play the prince. In an ill-considered move, Rattigan approached Wyler without a word to Beaumont or de Grunwald, who thought they were the only ones offering the play around. In early November 1955, Rattigan flew to the United States to confer with Wyler in California. To keep the producers from guessing the real reason for his trip, Rattigan made up a story about a sudden urge to attend the Ryder Cup golf tournament in Palm Springs.

Through Wyler's friend Jean Negulesco, Marilyn heard that Rattigan was en route to California. By this time, in her mind *The Sleeping Prince* had replaced *Baby Doll* as the film that would change the direction of her career. As far as Marilyn was concerned, this was the magical property that would allow her to prove herself as an actress. She had decided that *The Sleeping Prince* must be hers, and she took immediate action to get it before Wyler did. Rattigan's plane touched down in New York, where he was to have a ten-hour layover before boarding a flight to California. At the airport, a message from Marilyn awaited, asking Rattigan to meet her that afternoon at 4:30 at the Barberry Room in Manhattan.

The Barberry Room was empty when Rattigan arrived. He ordered a martini. Then he had a second and a third. By the time Marilyn arrived, an hour had passed. She bought him another drink. She mentioned lots of money, and said she wanted to come to terms right away. She was prepared to draw up a contract on a cocktail napkin. She took off her smoked glasses and cooed, "Do you think there's any chance that Sir Larry would do it with me?"

Marilyn knew that Wyler had been offered the rights. Rattigan couldn't use the story about the golf tournament on her. But he could—and did—fail to mention that the property was being shopped around in Europe by Beaumont and de Grunwald. It was obvious that Rattigan desperately wanted to accept Marilyn's offer on the spot. Still, he had no choice but to go forward with Wyler. He promised to let her know what happened.

Not long after Rattigan returned to London, Wyler decided against doing the film after all. Rattigan, delighted, sent a message to Marilyn. The rights were hers if she still wanted them. Marilyn was ecstatic. She believed that she finally had in her hands the important role she longed for. The Sleeping Prince was certainly the sort of thing Marilyn did well. Yet from the first, she seems to have had a basic misperception of the nature of the material. Perhaps it was the aura of Laurence Olivier, or that Vivien Leigh—whom Marilyn associated with Kazan—had preceded her in the role. Perhaps it was simply the fact that The Sleeping Prince would be a costume picture that led Marilyn to mistake the property for something it was not. In any case, her expectations were a prescription for disappointment.

In contrast to Baby Doll, The Sleeping Prince did not contain the transforming role Marilyn had set out to find. A piece of fluff, it was not qualitatively different from other light comedies she had done. But Marilyn did not realize that until much later. For the moment, she remained utterly convinced that once she had appeared with Olivier, people would never be able to treat her the same way again.

This seemed particularly important at a moment when Marilyn was being satirized nightly on Broadway. A new play, Will Success Spoil Rock Hunter?, offered a painful reminder that many people saw her as a joke. On October 13, Marilyn had attended the premiere of George Axelrod's comedy about a dumb, self-absorbed film star "whose golden curls and fantastic behind have endeared her to moviegoers the world over." Played by Monroe-lookalike Jayne Mansfield, the character insists she's a serious actress; she complains of being thought of as a sex symbol; she even starts her own production company.

Other characters included a suave, globetrotting agent, a foreign-born movie mogul who speaks fractured English and tends to burst into tears, the star's inept business partner who first met her when he was on assignment for a popular magazine, and her estranged husband, a brutish, temperamental athlete. Axelrod, who had written The Seven Year Itch, may have given Marilyn her best script to date, but he had also had an opportunity to observe her closely on the set. He had put many of her characteristics, her hopes and dreams, and even some of her lines in the play. On opening night, Marilyn conducted herself with immense dignity. The fact that she was then hard at work to change her image seems to have given her the strength to hold her head high.

That month, in New York, Marilyn signed the papers to finalize her divorce from Joe DiMaggio. Her lawyer, Jerry Giesler, then filed the papers at the court in California. On October 31, 1955, Los Angeles Superior Court Judge Elmer D. Doyle granted the final decree. Her marriage to DiMaggio was legally at an end. Marilyn was free to marry again.

Marilyn's relationship with Arthur changed when his wife found out about the love affair. Soon after his fortieth birthday on October 17, Mary threw Arthur out of their house in Brooklyn and he moved to temporary quarters at the Chelsea Hotel on West 23rd Street. Though his romance with Marilyn was still officially a secret, more and more they began to see each other in the presence of friends. Chief among these were Norman and Hedda Rosten.

Marilyn had strategically cultivated the Rostens' friendship in the months since she had met them with Sam Shaw. The situation was particularly awkward and painful for Hedda, who did not wish to betray her friendship with Mary Miller. But Hedda was by nature warm, nurturing, and motherly. She and Norman tended to adopt people with problems, which was why someone once dubbed their household The Broken Wing Society. Inevitably, they soon adopted Marilyn.

Apart from his marital problems, Miller's life had become extremely complicated on account of his political situation. The threatened HUAC summons did not materialize in November, but before the Youth Board allowed him to proceed with "Bridge to a Savage World," he was asked to "clear" himself by disavowing Communism. He declined as a matter of principle. He believed no American should be required to pass a political means test. Much as he wanted the screenwriting assignment, he refused to compromise his conscience and his sense of himself.

The Board found itself under tremendous pressure from the American Legion and the Catholic War Veterans to have nothing to do with Miller, whose patriotism they questioned. On December 7, there was a vote, and the board officially decided not to contract with the film company that had hired Miller. The next day the newspapers were full of the decision. With all hope of the film dead, Miller focused on negotiations to take A View from the Bridge to London.

The nature of his future with Marilyn remained undecided. Both of their lives were changing so rapidly that it was extremely difficult to make plans. Marilyn insisted she didn't want to put any kind of pressure on him—but as anyone could see, a permanent commitment from him was precisely what she wanted. Increasingly, marriage to the great writer and a chance to prove herself as an actress were the two halves of Marilyn's dream.

Hardly had she had an opportunity to become excited about *The Sleeping Prince* when she received disturbing news from London. Anatole de Grunwald, who had known nothing of Rattigan's negotiations with Wyler or Monroe, had meanwhile made arrangements of his own with John Huston. The deal had been made in good faith, and Huston expected the producer to go through with it no matter what Rattigan might have been up to in America. Rattigan had no choice but to tell Marilyn what had happened. Avid to hold on to Monroe and Olivier for his film, he hoped to persuade Huston to accept them both.

For weeks, there was no decision on any of this as Huston resisted the idea of casting Marilyn. Angry at what he perceived to be Rattigan's double-dealing, Huston insisted that he wanted Jean Simmons in the part. The uncertainty lingered throughout December, while Marilyn remained every bit as determined to make *The Sleeping Prince* hers as Huston was to hold onto the property for himself.

Meanwhile, a far longer-running battle seemed about to end that month as Twentieth prepared a preliminary draft of Marilyn's new contract. The moment of decision was finally at hand. The battle had begun two and a half years ago, following the release of *Gentlemen Prefer Blondes*. A full year had passed since Marilyn left the studio with the claim that she was no longer legally under contract. The battle had heated up considerably in the last six months, after Zanuck decided to bring forward the release of *The Seven Year Itch*. That left Twentieth with no Marilyn Monroe films stockpiled for future release, and, as DiMaggio had long ago predicted, the moment that occurred the studio had to make a deal. The huge box-office and critical success of *The Seven Year Itch* put even more pressure on Zanuck to get Marilyn back in front of the cameras. As matters stood, it would be months before Twentieth had another Monroe film ready for release.

For tax reasons, both Twentieth and MCA wanted to make sure the deal was in place before the end of the year. Yet down to the very last day, Zanuck and a number of his closest associates remained profoundly uncomfortable with Marilyn's requirements. To Zanuck's irritation, Marilyn had increased her demands considerably since 1954, when she'd reluctantly accepted that the issue of director approval wasn't even on the table. On this latest round, Marilyn, aware of her power, insisted on the right to approve directors and cameramen on all her films. Zanuck regarded that demand as a fundamental challenge to the way he made pictures. He took Marilyn's rebellion personally. Were Marilyn to win, her victory would be a public humiliation for him. To the very end, the Zanuck faction argued that the studio should call Marilyn's "bluff" and refuse her demands. Frank Ferguson insisted that Marilyn's old contract was still in effect and that Twentieth's "unconditional surrender" would be a tactical error.

Skouras did not see things the same way. Once again, the conflict between Skouras and Zanuck worked to Marilyn's advantage. Skouras was first and last a businessman. His ego was not caught up in the studio's dealings with Marilyn. As far as he was concerned, nothing mattered besides the fact that Marilyn was an extremely valuable property. That she demanded a degree of creative control concerned him not at all. As the year drew to a close, Skouras did everything in his power to push Marilyn's deal through.

Finally, there was nothing Zanuck could do to stop the new contract. Marilyn's representatives made clear that she would give not an inch on the matter of director approval. At last, in an effort to save face, Zanuck insisted that Marilyn could have cameraman approval only on the first and fourth pictures she did at the studio, not on the second and third. This petty, even pathetic gesture suggested the massive blow to Zanuck's ego that Marilyn's victory represented.

"We made the stars, but they've forgotten that," Zanuck complained on another occasion. "Now they think they're entitled to run the business. Faces, that's all they are, just faces. But in today's market it's only faces that count, not brains. I'll tell you one thing: they'll never run my business, because I won't be here." The following year, Zanuck stepped down as production chief, signing a deal with Fox under which the studio would release the films he produced independently. Skouras, needless to say, was not sorry to see his old adversary go.

On December 29, 1955, at 4 p.m., the Board of Directors of Twentieth Century–Fox held their regularly scheduled meeting in New York. On the table in front of each board member was a typed agenda. The third order of business was consideration of a new agreement with Marilyn Monroe Productions. Skouras, who presided over the meeting, urged the board to approve the contract. There was some dissent, but Skouras pushed the deal through. His support of Marilyn was not a sentimental act of friendship, as some people seemed to think. It was just good business sense. For the studio's sake, Skouras wanted Marilyn back at work as soon as possible. Indeed, Twentieth already had a new film lined up for her—William Inge's *Bus Stop*. The sooner the contract was signed, the sooner production could begin.

The terms Marilyn had won were considerable. MCA had held onto the $100,000 per picture fee Feldman negotiated. Under the new contract, however, instead of owing the studio fourteen films in seven years, Marilyn would be required to do only four. In addition, Marilyn had the right to make outside pictures. When the board approved that, Marilyn Monroe Productions finally became possible. But the most important part of the contract, as far as Marilyn was concerned, was not even mentioned in Skouras's presentation. Marilyn had the right to approve the director on all of her films at Twentieth, and the right to select her cameraman on two. That was precisely the sign of respect she believed she had earned, and that Zanuck had persisted in denying her.

For Marilyn, the battle had never been about money. It had been about dignity. It had been about being taken seriously. It had been about getting credit for her own achievements. In the end, Marilyn had accomplished something that few people in Hollywood had expected her to do. She had brought Darryl Zanuck to his knees.

On December 31, 1955, the new contract was signed. That night, as Marilyn sipped champagne, she had something truly remarkable to celebrate. She had won revenge for the terrible insult a year and a half previously, when Twentieth refused the contract terms she knew she had earned. Had the studio given Marilyn what she wanted then, all they would have had to concede were a few tokens of creative control. As it turned out, Zanuck's stubbornness had resulted in a contract that gave Marilyn much, much more than she had originally asked for.

On January 4, 1956, the *New York Morning Telegraph* made the first public announcement of Marilyn's breathtaking victory—and Twentieth's humiliation. The next day, other newspapers chimed in. "BATTLE WITH STUDIO WON BY MARILYN" and "ACTRESS WINS ALL DEMANDS," the headlines declared. Exactly one year before, these same newspapers had called Marilyn "stupid" and "foolish" for insisting on contract provisions far less advantageous than those she had just negotiated.

In the middle of all this, Marilyn received a cable from Rattigan. Huston, blaming Rattigan for a "double-cross," had withdrawn from the project in disgust. The rights to *The Sleeping Prince* were Marilyn's. Better yet, Olivier wanted to do the picture with her. A private screening of *The Seven Year Itch* had only made him more eager to come to New York to meet her personally.

On February 5, Olivier, Rattigan, and Olivier's manager, Cecil Tennant, flew into New York. Not long afterward, in a heavy rain, the trio arrived at the building on Sutton Place South where Milton Greene had an apartment. Greene had run short of cash and when Marilyn's Waldorf Towers sublet ended, he had installed her in his own riverside apartment until some money began to come in from Twentieth. When Greene needed to stay in town, he slept at his photography studio.

By this time, Marilyn not only wanted Olivier to co-star in her first independent production; she hoped he would direct as well. Olivier's most recent film, *Richard III*, acclaimed in England, was about to be released in America. Kenneth Tynan had recently called Olivier "the greatest actor alive." So Marilyn had set her sights as high as possible. Yet now that Olivier had finally arrived for their first meeting, she was terror-stricken. As Milton Greene served the guests drinks and entertained them in the living room, Marilyn hid in the bedroom. For more than two hours, Olivier's commanding tenor filled the three small rooms of the apartment. The guests were becoming tipsy, yet there was still no sign of Marilyn. Finally, Olivier took matters in hand. He went to the bedroom door and called to her, begging her to come out and end the suspense. The door inched open and Olivier and Monroe—the Knight and the Garter, as they came to be known—glimpsed each other for the first time in six years.

Did Olivier remember their previous encounter? Marilyn certainly did. It was August 1950, and Johnny Hyde had taken her to Danny Kaye's party to welcome Vivien Leigh to Hollywood for *A Streetcar Named Desire*. Vivien, radiant in an olive-green dress, had been Kazan's dinner partner; they had come out on the train together from New York. Olivier had arrived soon afterward to film *Carrie* with William Wyler, and the couple were borrowing Charlie Feldman's house for three months. At the dinner, Larry and Vivien charmed everyone with a joint speech in verse. But there was trouble below the surface.

Olivier, for his part, was ambivalent about Kazan. When Olivier directed his wife in A Streetcar Named Desire in London in 1949, he had been overwhelmed by the precedent of Kazan's sensational staging on Broadway. Again and again he found himself peeking at Kazan's prompt book. He had written to Tennessee Williams that he didn't like finding himself in the position of merely reheating someone else's dish. He told the American producer Irene Selznick, in London to look out for the playwright's interests, that he felt "like just a stage manager." Determined not to echo Kazan, Olivier ignored stage directions and cut the text mercilessly. He blamed his own pride, and justified himself to Williams by warning him that without new readings a play cannot live. He was intent on reshaping A Streetcar Named Desire in his own image, and was determined to control his wife's interpretation of Blanche Dubois.

Olivier had not originally wanted to direct Streetcar. He had only agreed because Vivien loved the play and strongly identified with Blanche. Eager to emerge from her husband's shadow, she longed to be accepted in "the big tragic roles." Like Marilyn, she wanted to be taken seriously. In his staging of Streetcar, Olivier made all that possible—but at what expense to the play? After the run-through, Irene Selznick, appalled, concluded that this was no longer a Tennessee Williams play. It had turned into a struggle between Laurence Olivier and Elia Kazan.

The struggle continued in Hollywood. Under Olivier's direction in England, Vivien had finally proven, to herself as much as others, her worth as an actress. She promptly let Kazan know that she preferred to do things Larry's way. It was the first day on the set and other cast members were watching. Kazan courteously reminded Leigh that Olivier was not directing the film—he was. Vivien resisted at first. At home each night, an irate Olivier fought to prevent Kazan's interpretation from taking over. He despised the Actors Studio and the Method. But increasingly, Vivien discarded Olivier's instructions and did as Kazan asked. Before long, she discovered that she loved Kazan's direction. It was a crushing defeat for Olivier, one he would never forget.

Marlon Brando was another thorn in Olivier's side. When Olivier directed A Streetcar Named Desire, Brando's precedent irked, haunted, and overwhelmed him as much as, perhaps more than, Kazan's. Brando, though he was being touted as potentially "an American Olivier," incarnated a new acting style with which Olivier himself felt excruciatingly uncomfortable. Brando made Olivier feel old-fashioned. In correspondence with Williams, Olivier was defensive about his decision to cast an actor who would play Stanley Kowalski as Olivier himself, not Marlon Brando, might have done. Olivier made much ado of not wanting a bruiser type in the role. Though he had not seen Brando's stage performance, Olivier insisted he was after something subtler and less ape-like.

Olivier's passionate resentment of Kazan, Brando, and the Actors Studio, dating back to A Streetcar Named Desire, was to form the subtext of his painful dealings with Marilyn during the filming of The Sleeping Prince. But as he led her to the living room to see Cecil Tennant and Terence Rattigan on a rainy February night in 1956, Olivier did not yet associate Marilyn with any of that.

Olivier saw in Marilyn, in his son's words, "the prospect of glamor and money." Preoccupied with his rapidly approaching fiftieth birthday, Olivier saw a chance to feel young again. He saw a challenge and an opportunity to reinvent himself. After the glory of his recent Stratford season, especially Peter Brook's staging of Titus Andronicus, Olivier was eager to display versatility.

"I'm sorry, I just didn't know what to wear," Marilyn was saying, her voice a low murmur from the back of her throat. She wore a simple, dark dress and a touch of makeup. "Should I be casual or formal? I went through my entire wardrobe twice, but everything I tried on wasn't kinda right."

She believed she had been dressing for one of the most important encounters of her life. She wanted Olivier to take her seriously—that's what this was all about for Marilyn—yet at the same time, years of experience told her that if she played "the girl," few men could resist. There was no way that Marilyn could be sure of the right image to project.

By the time she had spoken, however, Olivier and the others were at her feet. He found her adorable and amusing, more physically attractive than anyone he could possibly imagine. Olivier had such a wonderful time, talking, laughing, and drinking, that he neglected to mention business. So did his associates. The visitors were about to head back to their hotel when Marilyn stopped them.

"Just a minute," Marilyn said softly. Olivier noted that she used a small voice to good effect. "Shouldn't someone say something about an agreement?"

The next day, Olivier met with Marilyn to discuss the specifics of *The Sleeping Prince*. She had agreed to a price of $125,000 for the film rights, plus an additional $50,000 for Rattigan to write the script. It was far more than Rattigan would have gotten elsewhere, but Marilyn seemed only to care about being certain that the property was hers. That afternoon, Olivier agreed to direct and co-star in the film. His company would co-produce.

Olivier had decided to work with Marilyn despite his wife's objections. He told himself—and seemed rather to relish the idea—that Vivien was jealous. The Oliviers had performed *The Sleeping Prince* in London three years previously, while Vivien was recuperating after her collapse on *Elephant Walk*. She had a relapse during the 1955 Stratford season and doctors believed her condition was incurable.

In good times, Vivien slept four hours a night at best. When she entered the manic phase, she slept hardly at all, leaving Olivier to perform *Titus Andronicus* in a state of sheer physical exhaustion. To make matters worse, Vivien had humiliated her husband by resuming a love affair with Peter Finch. At the time Olivier went to New York to meet Marilyn Monroe, Vivien was planning to co-star with Finch in Noël Coward's play *South Sea Bubble*.

Why, one might ask, did the Oliviers stay together? It was said that they had once signed a deal with the devil, who agreed to make Larry and Vivien king and queen of the stage on one condition—they must remain married forever. Put another way, they were, said Noël Coward, "trapped by public acclaim." People loved the very idea of them as a couple. But it wasn't just a matter of how others saw them; it was how they saw themselves.

Both Oliviers strongly identified with, and constantly strove to live up to, their image as passionate lovers. When on one occasion Larry privately declared, "There's nothing to touch your Majesty's cunt," before he and Vivien made their entrance in a play, she wasted no time afterward repeating the endearment in a letter to her friend Ruth Gordon. As a romantic couple the Oliviers had very much lived and loved in public. But now, all that seemed to be coming to an end. They were losing more than each other; they were losing a sense of themselves.

Though it would be difficult to imagine a woman more different from Vivien, over lunch at "21" it seemed as if Olivier might be about to recapture some of that intensity with Marilyn Monroe. He didn't just want to go to bed with Marilyn or to have an affair. He wanted, as he said, "to fall most shatteringly in love." That's what had happened when he met Vivien. Evidently, he desperately wanted to repeat the experience. He even fantasized about divorcing Vivien in order to marry Marilyn as he had once left Jill Esmond. Jill had been pregnant at the time he went off with Vivien. Olivier, stung by Vivien's affair with Finch, imagined people saying "poor Vivien" as once they had said "poor Jill."

And what did Marilyn want? A press conference would do. A year after the newspapers had mocked her efforts to become a new Marilyn, Olivier's desire to collaborate with her would force people to take her aspirations seriously. Besides, she wanted everybody to know that "the greatest actor alive" was working for her now.

That Marilyn feared she might not really be worthy of the respect she longed for is suggested by something that happened on Wednesday, February 8. It was the day before she and Olivier were to meet the press at the Plaza Hotel. When Marilyn left her daily psychiatric session on East 93rd Street, she always did the same thing. The choreography never varied. She would come out the front door, pause, put her hand over her mouth and cough. Only then did Marilyn look up, apparently having pushed back inside whatever emotionally-charged material she had disclosed to Dr. Hohenberg. Today, as she emerged from the doctor's office, Marilyn carried a manila envelope containing contact sheets from a recent photo shoot with Milton Greene.

In these black-and-white photographs, taken at the so-called Black Sitting, Marilyn posed in black lacy undergarments and torn fishnet stockings. She was drunk, having imbibed large quantities of champagne. There was nothing innocent or little-girlish about this woman, nothing of the self-mocking bewilderment that, in The Seven Year Itch and other films, lent fun, charm, and lightness to Marilyn's sexuality. Gone was the "beautiful child" who spouted double entendres as though she had no idea what they meant. Marilyn's half-closed eyes were glassy, her tipsy smile rather sad. She looked as if she knew perfectly well what the tawdry poses implied. She looked beat, tired, used up. Meant as test shots for Bus Stop, a number of the pictures simply went too far.

Whether or not Marilyn actually showed the contact sheets to Dr. Hohenberg, to bring them to her psychiatrist's office the day before her press conference was, perhaps, to voice her own feelings of unworthiness. It was to disclose her deepest fears and self-doubt at the very moment she was claiming her right to be respected.

On Thursday morning, some two hundred journalists waited in the Terrace Room at the Plaza Hotel. One wag remarked that the announcement of the press conference had produced "more commotion than an offer of free beer on the Bowery." Olivier, in a dark brown suit, waited on a settee outside Marilyn's dressing room as she put on a low-cut, skin-tight black velvet dress with thin straps, and dangling pearl earrings. She was accompanied by the photographer Eve Arnold, who complimented her on her outfit.

"Just watch me," said Marilyn, mischievously winking at her in the dressing-table mirror. All trace of the tormented, divided woman who had clutched the contact sheets only the day before had vanished.

Moments later, Olivier, Rattigan, and Greene escorted Marilyn onto a vine-encrusted balcony overlooking the crowd. A photographer called out for Olivier to put his arm around her.

"You'll have to see the picture!" Marilyn demurred.

Olivier, a grave expression on his face, clutched Marilyn's arm, slowly helping her down the white marble stairs. Seated at a table, they announced their plans to make a movie together. Olivier chain-smoked.

"Miss Monroe has an extremely . . . uh . . . an extraordinarily . . . uh . . . cunning gift of being able to suggest one minute that she is the naughtiest little thing alive and the next that she is beautifully dumb and innocent," said Olivier. "The audience leaves not knowing quite what she is."

Did Marilyn intend to continue studying at the Actors Studio?

"Oh, yes," said Marilyn, inhaling deeply. "I'd like to continue my growth in every way possible."

Suddenly, her right strap popped, apparently as planned. She gasped and the crowd went wild. By the time a woman reporter came forward with a safety pin, it was evident that Marilyn's stunt had guaranteed front-page coverage for the news conference.

When the commotion died down, somebody asked Marilyn to name her favorite actors.

"Sir Laurence," said Marilyn, glancing at Olivier. "And Marlon Brando. He, too, is an actor-artist."

The press, unnerved by Marilyn's newly intellectual tone, turned ugly. Was it true, a reporter asked skeptically, that she wanted to do *The Brothers Karamazov*? And if it was, which role did she intend to play?

"I want to play Grushenka," Marilyn said over the laughter that filled the room. "She's a girl."

One journalist asked if she could spell "Grushenka," a question that seemed to underscore the fact that even the presence of "the greatest actor alive" would not persuade certain people to treat Marilyn as anything but a joke.

But that day, even the nastiest questions could not diminish Marilyn's victory. As far as she was concerned, she finally seemed to have everything necessary to change the direction of her career. She was due in Los Angeles at the end of the month to start the first of four pictures for Twentieth. The studio had purchased the rights to *Bus Stop* expressly as a vehicle for Marilyn. Joshua Logan, one of the sixteen approved directors on her list, was set to direct. In *Bus Stop*, Marilyn would have a chance to demonstrate how much she had improved as an actress. After that, she would go on to England to make *The Sleeping Prince* with Olivier and establish once and for all her credentials as an actress.

Olivier went home completely smitten with Marilyn. He was eager to encounter this strange and dazzling creature again. At this point, Arthur Miller played no part in Olivier's calculations about a possible future with her. But Miller had plans of his own. *A View from the Bridge* was due to open in London; and with Marilyn due in England for her film, a decision of some sort would have to be made.

Soon after Olivier left, Arthur took Marilyn out to Brooklyn to meet his parents officially. Though rumors had appeared in the press, Miller was still publicly denying a romance with Marilyn; he did, however, admit that he was going to seek a divorce. But there was no question of keeping the truth from his parents. Once his divorce was final, he intended to make Marilyn his wife.

Isadore and Augusta Miller lived on East 3rd Street at Avenue M in Flatbush. Arthur had long had an uncertain relationship with his illiterate father. Isadore—a tall, striking figure with tremendous physical authority, piercing blue eyes and a large square head—was said to resemble an Irish cop. From the first, he had disapproved of Arthur's desire to write. In fact, he simply didn't understand it. Kermit Miller, who often stood up for his younger brother, tried to explain what Arthur hoped to do, but Isadore persisted in regarding the very idea of being a writer as somehow "unmanly."

Isadore appeared to see things very differently, however, when Arthur introduced Marilyn as the girl he planned to marry. At last, his father seemed to understand him.

"Such a charming girl, Arthur," he said as Marilyn finished her second bowl of matzoh-ball soup. She wore a simple gray skirt, a black silk blouse, and no makeup.

When the guest declined another refill, Isadore grew alarmed. "You mean, you don't like our matzoh-ball soup?"

"Oh, I just love it," said Marilyn. "But gee, isn't there any other part of a matzoh you can eat?"

From their first meeting, Marilyn and her future father-in-law adored each other. Once Arthur had disclosed his plans to his parents, Marilyn found herself on the verge of realizing every aspect of what, only months before, had seemed an almost impossible fantasy. That February of 1956, it certainly looked as if she were about to have everything she wanted.

Only one hurdle remained before Marilyn felt ready to return in triumph to Hollywood. She needed to prove herself in front of the Actors Studio. By this time, she was aware that there was considerable cynicism among Studio members about the movie star in their midst. What had Marilyn been doing there all this time, just sitting and watching? Why hadn't she been required to audition like everybody else? Why hadn't she done a scene and been subjected to the judgment of others? Why did Strasberg appear to coddle her? Sometimes they even arrived by cab together. It was said that, in Marilyn's company, Strasberg resembled the foolish, besotted professor in Josef von Sternberg's *The Blue Angel*. Not that anyone suspected Lee might be sleeping with Marilyn. Someone laughed that were Strasberg to find himself in bed with her, he would probably have a stroke.

By and large, the resentment wasn't against Marilyn herself—she had the reputation of being "a good egg"—so much as against Strasberg. Hadn't he warned his disciples against going Hollywood? Didn't he often rail against the perils of commercialism? Marilyn represented everything to which Strasberg claimed to stand in flaming opposition. So what was she doing here? Why did he insist on transforming the Studio into some kind of "circus act"? Some malcontents saw Marilyn's presence as an indication of Strasberg's desperate hunger for success. Was Marilyn his ticket to the recognition he had never been able to achieve on his own?

Technically, an individual who passed the Actors Studio audition had no responsibility to do a scene. Participation was strictly voluntary, and one was not required to seek or to accept Strasberg's advice. One didn't even have to attend the workshops. Indeed, there was no pressure to do anything at all. But Marilyn's case was different. No matter how low in her seat she slouched, her notoriety made it impossible for her to be treated like everybody else. Before she left to film *Bus Stop*, she simply had to perform a work-in-progress. She had to prove she belonged here. She had to demonstrate that Strasberg wasn't crazy.

Though Strasberg usually let members decide when, if ever, they were ready, finally he had little choice but to urge Marilyn to do a scene. Usually he encouraged actors to select their own material, but in this case he picked Noël Coward's *Fallen Angels*. He assigned Marilyn to work with Maureen Stapleton, who had a reputation for being "always good."

The women rehearsed two, sometimes three times a week. Before long, Stapleton told Marilyn she was having a terrible time with Coward and suggested they look for another play. Marilyn assumed she had failed somehow. Nothing Stapleton said convinced Marilyn it wasn't her fault. Finally, they shifted to the bar scene in Eugene O'Neill's *Anna Christie*, a scene famous for being the first time Greta Garbo talked in the movies. Marilyn took the role of Anna while Stapleton played Marthy, an old prostitute. The actresses clicked with the new material and Stapleton, relieved, asked Marilyn whether she noticed a difference.

"Nope," said Marilyn. "I don't think I was very good in either one."

At home, Marilyn worked on the play with Arthur. They read aloud together, Miller playing the role of old Chris. At first, Marilyn's voice was so soft that Miller could barely hear her. It struck him that Marilyn sounded as if she were praying rather than acting. She laughed and said she couldn't believe she was doing this. Yet she persisted. The rehearsals with Stapleton continued for about eight weeks. Marilyn worried she'd be awful. She feared she couldn't make herself heard. She dreaded forgetting her lines. She knew she was on trial and that some people would be happy to see her fail.

Several times Marilyn had set a date for the performance. Several times she had canceled. On one occasion, Marilyn, seated on a bench in Central Park, performed her scene for Sam Shaw. That day she found the key to what she wanted to do. Marilyn imagined that she was speaking her lines in the rain. Finally, a notice appeared on the Actors Studio bulletin board. As was customary, no names were posted. But everyone knew this was to be Marilyn's workshop debut. It was one week after she faced the press with Olivier.

Since October 1955, classes had met at the Studio's new home, the deconsecrated white brick church on a grimy stretch of West 44th Street, off Ninth Avenue. Sandstone steps led to a double door, but members knew to enter through the basement. Inside, the walls were adorned with colorful theatrical posters and photographs of Duse and Stanislavsky. Up some steps was a high-ceilinged performance area, formerly the main area of worship.

Every seat was taken, except the canvas director's chair in front. A number of members had to stand. Paula Strasberg, who owned a huge collection of exotic fans from around the world, fanned herself nervously. She wore a black, knee-length shawl and a long gold chain heavy with trinkets. She said she hoped people intended to give Marilyn a chance and claimed to be so anxious that she thought she might have a heart attack before the session was over.

Marilyn had arrived early. She adjusted the baby spotlights. She arranged some bottles and other props from her apartment. Wobbly on stiletto heels, she looked as though she were about to pass out. Stapleton advised her to leave a script on the table in case she forgot her lines. But Marilyn declined. An office assistant, alarmed by Marilyn's pallor, handed her a shot of Scotch.

Finally, Lee Strasberg, looking as grave as Olivier at the press conference, took his place. In a crisp voice, he announced the scene to be performed and the room lights faded.

"Gimme a whisky," commanded Marilyn. "Ginger ale on the side. And don't be stingy, baby."

One wasn't supposed to applaud a workshop presentation, but

when Marilyn finished, the audience violated tradition. Maureen Stapleton said she had done beautifully. Susan Strasberg, Lee and Paula's daughter, found her real and poignant. Cheryl Crawford called the performance "luminous with exciting gradations of feeling." Not everyone thought Marilyn brilliant, however. Some applauded her talent, others merely her bravery. Kim Stanley was one of several actresses who rushed up to apologize for having harbored doubts. "I really admire you so much because that's so hard to do," she told Marilyn. "It's hard for all of us to work in front of each other."

Paula Strasberg just thanked God the ordeal was over. Lee, immensely relieved, insisted he hadn't been nervous. Of course, just because Marilyn had done a single scene didn't prove she could handle an entire play. Nor did it necessarily mean she would be able to repeat her success outside of class. Marilyn, for her part, was certain she had failed. She lamented that she had let her teacher down. At Strasberg's new ten-room apartment on Central Park West afterward, she was tearful.

"The whole thing was bad. I could feel it."

Paula disagreed. "Darling, you were good up there on that stage. And you were not just good. You were very good. You have taken the beginning steps as an actress and you did us all proud."

+ N I N E +

On the morning of February 25, 1956, a limousine pulled away from 2 Sutton Place South. Marilyn, a dark mink coat slung over her shoulders, was on her way to the airport. She was due in Hollywood in two days for pre-production on her first film for Twentieth under her new contract. Joshua Logan planned to start filming *Bus Stop* on location in Phoenix, Arizona, on March 15; he wanted to take advantage of the yearly rodeo there, using the thousands of spectators as extras.

While Marilyn shot *Bus Stop*, Arthur would go to Nevada for six weeks to establish residency in order to file for divorce. The plan was for Miller to be free to marry before they went to England in July. He was to stay in one of two isolated cabins near the Paiute Indian reservation at Pyramid Lake, forty miles from Reno; the other cabin was occupied by Saul Bellow, then at work on *Henderson the Rain King*. Bellow, too, was there to divorce. Though Miller was legally required to remain in Nevada for forty-two consecutive days, he intended to sneak out at intervals to meet Marilyn in Los Angeles. In addition to his divorce, before Arthur could leave for England with Marilyn he would have to get a passport, something which might prove difficult. In 1954, Miller's request for a passport to travel to Brussels for a production of *The Crucible* had been denied. There was every chance that he might have trouble again.

Marilyn was delighted to be doing *Bus Stop*. It had been a hit play in New York. Its author, William Inge, was widely considered to be one of the period's finest playwrights, though a notch or two below Williams and Miller. It was a prestigious project, and her appearance in it would give Marilyn stature in the New York society she now held in such respect:

Kim Stanley, a leading light at the Actors Studio, who had starred in *Bus Stop* on Broadway, had lost out to Marilyn for the film version.

So now it was finally happening. Everything Marilyn had done for many months had led to this moment. This is what all the fighting had been about. This is what all the preparation had been for. She was returning to Los Angeles in triumph. She had taken on the Hollywood studio system and she had won. She was eager to collaborate with an important director who would treat her with dignity and respect.

Marilyn's hard-won victory also brought immense new pressures. She had forced the studio to accept her right to make career decisions. She had insisted that she must be listened to in the future. In the weeks that followed, Marilyn would have to prove that she was worthy of all she had won. If she failed in her first film back at Twentieth, she would look like precisely the dumb blonde Darryl Zanuck insisted she was. Marilyn was intensely aware of how much was at stake as she prepared to step in front of a movie camera for the first time since the retakes for *The Seven Year Itch* in 1955.

It wasn't just her new contract that Marilyn had to live up to. In Hollywood, there had been countless jokes about her decision to study at the Actors Studio. On *Bus Stop*, she would have to demonstrate that she had actually learned something in New York. It would not be enough for her to be good. She had to show that she was better. She had to convince people that she was somehow different. *Bus Stop* was the first project Marilyn had approved, so it had to be a success. She had always gone in front of the camera as if it were a matter of life and death. From the first, so much had been at stake in Marilyn's film work that it had taken an almost unbearable toll on her. But there had never been more at stake than there was right now.

"Will acting spoil Marilyn Monroe?" many people were asking in Los Angeles, where newspaper, magazine, and newsreel cameramen packed the American Airlines terminal in anticipation of her return. She was the last passenger off the plane. Marilyn may have had difficulty remembering script lines, but she greeted a number of photographers by name, instantly endearing herself to the crowd. After hugging Roy Craft of the studio publicity department, she took questions in an airport waiting room. Marilyn's quicksilver laughter mingled with grinding newsreel cameras and the pop-pop of flashbulbs.

Yes, she was "a bit tired." No, she wasn't in love at the moment, "but I haven't given up yet." No, Milton H. Greene, looming nearby, was not making all of her decisions as rumored. She was the president of Marilyn Monroe Productions, Greene the vice-president.

No, the Greenes were not running the show. No, she wouldn't tell reporters what Greene's middle initial stood for; they'd have to ask him. Marilyn was not going to be drawn back into the ridicule she had endured one year previously when she arrived with Greene for retakes on *The Seven Year Itch*. She was smart enough to know—especially with *Will Success Spoil Rock Hunter?* on Broadway making a nightly joke of their partnership—that her business dealings with him made her an easy target. She had been burned once, at the time of the "new Marilyn." She was not about to let it happen again.

Marilyn deftly changed the subject. She preferred to talk about how much her life had altered since she fled several months ago.

"I like to think I've grown up a little," said Marilyn, "and I know I'm much happier than when I left." Indeed, as she arrived in Los Angeles that day it was evident that she was different. At the time of her disastrous appearance on *Person to Person*, Marilyn had not yet found a voice to replace the one she had rejected. In the intervening months in New York, however, she appeared to have discovered a winning substitute. Suddenly, she really was a new Marilyn. She seemed calmer and altogether more dignified. As she spoke about her hopes and dreams, a kind of shyness peeped through that was utterly irresistible.

Marilyn charmed the Hollywood press corps. But would she do the same with Joshua Logan? Logan was the first director Marilyn had actually chosen under her new contract, so they had better get along. Before accepting the assignment, the mercurial director of such hit stage musicals as *Mister Roberts*, *South Pacific*, and *Picnic* had asked a number of colleagues about Marilyn. Logan had also directed the highly successful film version of *Picnic*. He only considered doing *Bus Stop* because his, and Marilyn's, agent Lew Wasserman at MCA suggested that it might be a way for Logan to get Twentieth to back off from a lawsuit they were about to file against him.

Maureen Stapleton told Logan that Marilyn was great. But it was Lee Strasberg who made up Logan's mind. "I have worked with hundreds and hundreds of actors and actresses, both in class and in the Studio,"

Strasberg attested, "and there are only two that stand out way above the rest. Number one is Marlon Brando and the second is Marilyn Monroe."

Tall, heavy, and rumpled, Logan had a homely, weatherbeaten face that he himself despised. His enormous hands were hyperactive; a friend compared him to a "many-armed Hindu god." When he wasn't twisting the skin on his face as though it were putty, he was noisily playing with the coins in his trouser pockets. He scratched himself lustily. He picked at his shirt buttons and belt loops. He fiddled with his necktie. He fingered his mustache as though searching for fleas.

He was a catalogue of nervous tics and gestures. He paced back and forth. He took off and put on his wrinkled suit coat. He struck poses and emitted peculiar sounds. He was constantly muttering into a tape recorder. He had violent mood swings, alternating between blinky-eyed enthusiasm and a lusterless, detached stare. A manic depressive, he had spent time in mental institutions and received electric shock treatment. He was self-loathing and excruciatingly conscious of how he appeared to others. At the same time, as Elia Kazan once told Tennessee Williams, Logan possessed the sort of shamelessness that all artists must have.

Logan had met Marilyn at a dinner party arranged by Milton Greene in Connecticut. As the meal came to an end without Marilyn's having put in an appearance, Logan grew irritated and demanded to know where Marilyn was. Greene explained that she was dressing for dinner.

Finally, Marilyn came downstairs. Slightly disheveled, she seemed the image of the hillbilly singer in *Bus Stop*. Cherie, who sings in a nightclub until the wee hours, is never outside during the day. Thus the dead white effect, which Greene helped Marilyn to achieve with baby powder. She took a seat on the floor and talked about her concept of the role. Marilyn may have been silent during her many months at the Actors Studio, but she had picked up a frame of reference, a way of speaking about what an actor does.

Logan was enchanted. He promised himself never to grow upset about Marilyn's chronic lateness. And he promised never to raise his voice, Milton Greene having solemnly warned Logan that if he frightened Marilyn, he'd lose her. Whether the notoriously anxious and temperamental director would be able to live up to his vow was another matter.

This was by no means the only problem Logan faced in dealing with Marilyn on *Bus Stop*. As Marilyn began her first film since enlisting as Lee Strasberg's most famous disciple, there was the complication of just what Strasberg's role would be. Strasberg had devised a plan to assure that Marilyn remained his, even a continent away. Since that first night at the Belnord, his influence had grown to monstrous proportions. Marilyn believed herself totally dependent on him, and he seemed intent on keeping things that way. Of course, there could be no question of Strasberg himself turning up on the set as Marilyn's coach; that would be beneath his dignity. Strasberg's name did appear on Marilyn's list of six-teen approved directors, despite the fact that he had never actually directed a film, but in light of his inexperience no one at Twentieth had even remotely considered asking him to direct *Bus Stop*. Still, though Strasberg would not deign to be merely Marilyn's coach, nor was he pre-pared to put her in Joshua Logan's hands alone.

Lee sent his wife Paula to function as his "surrogate Method-ist." It was, pure and simple, a gesture to assert his continued control. Paula had long ago retired from a failed career as an actress. She had no real creden-tials as a teacher. Nor did she share her husband's considerable knowledge of theater history. But, as Frank Corsaro pointed out, she had "picked up all the asterisks of the Method." Marilyn accepted Paula—indeed, yearned for her presence—as Lee's surrogate. To almost everyone else, Paula was a joke, if a rather painful one. She seemed omnipresent in her enormous tortoiseshell spectacles, her hair pulled back tightly in a bun. Aching feet, too small and delicate for her heft, forced her to wear floppy velvet bedroom slippers much of the time. She carried an oversized purse loaded with snacks, pills, and smelling salts—the latter in case she fainted.

In contrast to Marilyn's fantasy of her, Paula was a bleak soul who tended to hover in her bedroom, disappointed, depressed, and suicidal. She regretted the past, and worried about the future. She claimed to be clairvoyant, reading tarot cards and drawing astrology charts. She kept a gun as protection against a former husband, and lamented her present husband's selfishness. Lee had never directed Paula on the stage. He had not made love to her in more than a decade. She complained about her swollen feet. She fretted about her weight. She was always hot, and fanned herself incessantly. She threatened by turns to join a convent in Connecticut or to jump out the window.

Arthur Miller thought Paula a comical character out of Molière. But the $1,500 weekly salary Lee had demanded for his wife's services was no laughing matter. Joshua Logan made clear that while Paula was free to work with Marilyn at home and in her dressing room, she was never to show her face on the set. Logan liked Paula personally, but he had no intention of permitting a situation that would enable her—or, by implication, Lee Strasberg—to challenge his own directorial authority.

The debate about Paula was reminiscent of the battles over Natasha Lytess. Natasha would often angrily claim in private that the real credit for the creation of "Marilyn Monroe" should be hers. Lee Strasberg was intent that, in due course, all credit for Marilyn's acting would be his. The Strasbergs' arrival on the scene meant that there was no longer any place for Natasha in Marilyn's life.

Indeed, apart from a desire to economize, one reason Marilyn had agreed to share a rented house with the Greenes and their small son, as well as Milton's assistant and two servants, was that she claimed to be afraid of Natasha. In Marilyn's absence, Twentieth, confused about Natasha's status, had kept her on the payroll. Though Marilyn never answered her pleading letters, Natasha had expected to return to her old post as soon as the contract dispute was settled. When she learned that Marilyn was due back for *Bus Stop*, Natasha expected to be summoned directly. Instead, she received a call from the studio firing her. A furious Natasha, who had learned that she had been replaced by Paula Strasberg, repeatedly phoned the house on North Beverly Glen Boulevard, but Marilyn either wasn't there or refused to take her calls.

Finally, Natasha appeared in person, pounding on the door and demanding to see Marilyn. She expected better treatment, she said, since after all she had once saved Marilyn's life. Lest that be forgotten, Natasha was wearing the antique cameo brooch which Marilyn had given her following the 1950 suicide attempt. As far as Natasha was concerned, Marilyn had only to snap her fingers and Twentieth would keep her on its payroll for years to come. It was the least Marilyn could do.

Marilyn's MCA agent was at the house when Natasha appeared. He answered the door, and while Natasha waxed indignant about all she had done to "create" Marilyn, he remained unimpressed. He refused to let Natasha in. "Your engagement with the studio is none of Miss Monroe's concern," he said, turning her away. That the agent was only following orders was suggested by the fact that Marilyn watched the painful encounter from a window. Natasha spotted her there and slunk off.

Soon afterward, Natasha poured her heart out to the press. "She needed me like a dead man needs a casket. I have letters in my drawer saying she needs me more than her life. She'll never be a star to me. She's Marilyn . . ." Natasha, consumed by bitterness, never saw Marilyn again. The star depended on others now.

A studio limousine arrived at the house at 7 a.m. to take Marilyn and Greene to the Fox lot for a meeting with Joshua Logan. Paula took a cab from the Chateau Marmont, where she preferred to stay; she would not even consider the idea of sharing a house with the others. Together, Milton and Paula made a comical sight. One was slim, the other fat. Both favored black. Both danced attendance on Marilyn. Both flitted about protectively, Greene chewing his fingernails, Paula clenching her jaw. Milton and Paula were supposed to be a team, yet they resented and largely ignored each other. At the moment, Greene had the advantage, Logan having confined Paula to Marilyn's dressing room.

Marilyn and Greene went over the sketches for her costumes with Logan and the designer. Glassy-eyed, the director seemed lost in a world of his own, so there was no gauging his response to the awful costume designs. They were clothes a glamorous Hollywood star would wear, not a sad, down-and-out showgirl like Cherie. Marilyn pretended to be delighted, and instructed the designer to put the costumes in production. But she was only testing Logan. She wanted to see whether he knew what he was doing. After the designer left, Logan, having promised to treat Marilyn with kid gloves, gently asked if she had really liked the sketches. With a wicked glint in her eye, Marilyn declared that she hated them. Logan, immensely relieved, emitted a magnificent belly laugh.

Soon, Marilyn and her director, who was built like a football player, were feverishly rummaging through the racks at the wardrobe department. They pulled out the most disintegrated and threadbare outfits they could find. The *pièce de résistance* was a decrepit, green-gold lamé coat, to which Marilyn proposed that they add a bit of moth-eaten rabbit fur. It was to be Cherie's touching and pathetic idea of glamor.

From then on, Marilyn and Joshua Logan were united in their determination not to permit Twentieth to turn *Bus Stop* into just another star vehicle. Marilyn's insistence on clownish, pearly white makeup and ratty, decidedly unglamorous clothes made clear that she intended to function as an actress, not just as a movie star.

Logan planned to defend Marilyn to the hilt. He went ahead to Arizona to set up the first day of filming, the massive parade in downtown Phoenix on Thursday, March 15, the day before the rodeo. There would be cowboys and Indians, scout troops and marching bands. Each year, some twenty-five thousand spectators looked on from bleachers on both sides of the avenue. *Bus Stop* was to be shot in CinemaScope, so colorful backgrounds were important.

Logan was said to have "a toy theater in the back of his head" where he staged the action of his plays and films. His powers of concentration were prodigious. He visualized every element, planned every detail, pictured himself in every role. He fussed and fretted about everything. Eruptions of the famous Logan temper were commonplace. Informed that Marilyn had missed her flight by twenty minutes, the director despaired. His vow to remain calm notwithstanding, Logan, much as he adored Marilyn, was temperamentally ill-equipped to cope with her own anxiety-driven behavior.

Throughout her career, the pressure to shine had often made Marilyn late. It was up to her to create a persona. It was up to her to turn on for the camera. It was up to her to create magic. It was up to her to make a film or an event a success. That had been hard enough in the past, but things were considerably more complicated now. It was no longer simply a matter of working herself up to be photographed. Coached by Paula Strasberg, Marilyn was intent on using all of the lessons she had learned from Lee in New York.

Paula extracted Cherie's dialogue from the screenplay and had it reproduced in a little brown book so that Marilyn wouldn't be distracted by the other characters' lines. Before each scene, Marilyn was going to have to "take a minute." She was going to have to search for a memory of her own that permitted her to connect with the material. If she had been nervous to the point of paralysis in the past, what must she have been going through now?

Press interest in *Bus Stop* was immense and Phoenix swarmed with reporters. When Marilyn arrived with her entourage, Greene forbade her to be interviewed or photographed. This caused considerable ill will when some photographers spotted Greene snapping pictures of his own.

To make amends, the Fox publicity department hired a stripper named Stormy Lee Scott to entertain the disgruntled journalists. But it was Marilyn they were all there for, and she was being kept under wraps. During the next five days, when Marilyn wasn't filming, she and Paula tended to remain incommunicado in the penthouse at the Sahara Hotel.

From the outset, there was tension between Marilyn and her leading man. Don Murray played Bo, the gauche cowboy who falls desperately in love with Cherie. Moments before the opening-day parade began, Logan discovered that it was to be led by all the contestants in the Junior Chamber of Commerce Rodeo. The procession, known as the Grand Entry, introduced the various cowboys, who rode out in pairs. Logan had been planning a very different sort of shot, but he abruptly changed course and asked Murray if he minded saddling up. The rangy actor said he didn't, but there was one problem. He had never been on a horse before.

Marilyn, already tightly strung on her own account, wasn't amused. "Well, why don't you do it anyway?" she jeered.

He mounted a horse and did remarkably well for a beginner. Logan arranged for him to have lessons immediately. But the fact remained that the co-stars had gotten off to a rocky start. The second assistant director, alarmed, warned Logan not to allow Marilyn to get to him.

The very next day, Marilyn nearly wrecked a complicated sequence which Logan had been setting up for hours. In flight from Bo, Cherie, carrying a suitcase, was to dash through the city streets to the bus terminal. There were liver-colored mountains in the distance and neon-lit bars and pizza joints along the way. To catch the moment before the sky shaded into black, the cinematographer Milton Krasner planned to shoot at precisely 6:30 p.m., the so-called magic hour. The underexposure from the dying light would give the effect of a rich, velvety blue.

At 2:30, Marilyn went to her trailer to fix her hair and redo her makeup. Most importantly, she wanted to review the scene with Paula. Meanwhile, Logan feverishly went over the scene numerous times with the cameraman, Marilyn's stand-in, and five extras. Three hours and thirty-five minutes passed.

"Where's Marilyn?" Logan was heard to say.

By that time, there were fifteen minutes left. He sent an assistant to her trailer. The assistant did not return. The cameraman's eyes were darting between his wristwatch and his light meter.

"Where's Marilyn?" Logan repeated.

His blood pressure rose as the orange sun descended. Finally, the cameraman announced they had only four minutes. If Marilyn failed to appear, the company would have to remain in Phoenix for an additional day, driving up the budget by as much as $50,000.

Logan propelled his massive, hulking frame in the direction of Marilyn's trailer, some five hundred yards away. He found her gazing dreamily into a mirror while Paula, madly fanning herself, hovered nearby. Logan's temper flared. He clutched Marilyn's wrist and dragged her outside, a man possessed. Tallulah Bankhead once said that "if there were an Oscar for best acting by a director, Josh Logan would wrap it up."

"I was coming," Marilyn pleaded. "I was coming."

By the time Logan had dragged Marilyn to her starting spot and shouted "Roll 'em!", he had just about killed her dream of being treated with dignity and respect. Would he have done that to Bette Davis? Would he have done it to Katharine Hepburn? Logan bore Marilyn no ill will, yet to her his actions were humiliating.

The real crisis was still to come. On March 17, they shot a sequence in which Cherie, attempting to escape from Bo, panics and heads in the wrong direction. Instead of running away, she darts past as he bulldogs a steer in the center of the arena, the crowd cheering on both sides. Bo's hands are occupied holding down the steer, so he is unable to stop Cherie.

Logan was allowed to shoot at the rodeo as long as he was careful not to interrupt the actual events. For this sequence, he chose a ten-minute intermission. Marilyn and the others rehearsed in the morning. When it was time to shoot, Logan, on the public-address system, asked the audience to behave as though they were witnessing a real event.

"Action!" he cried.

As Murray pretended to pin down the steer, Marilyn ran past. Then something happened that was not in the script. Marilyn, running to the exit, felt her shoe fly off. Immediately, she realized that the accident had been fortunate. Instead of wrecking the shot, the lost shoe made it more dramatic. But as she prepared to turn back, she perceived that her director wasn't so quick. To her horror, she sensed that Logan was about to yell "Cut!" Fortunately, the crowd stopped him. The sight of thousands of spectators roaring with delight persuaded Logan to let the cameras run. Marilyn returned to the center of the arena, collected her shoe and disappeared through the gate. By the time the cameras stopped, her disillusionment was complete. Marilyn had seen Logan hesitate and her faith was shattered. He was the one with the impressive list of directing credits, but he knew less about film than she. Instead of feeling better about herself, Marilyn panicked. How could she trust Logan after that? How could she put her performance in his hands?

Her initial thought was to have Lee Strasberg flown to the location immediately. But Greene wouldn't hear of it, insisting that Marilyn Monroe Productions could not afford the ticket. Marilyn had Sunday off. For hours, she and Paula conferred with Lee by telephone and listened to tapes of his lectures.

On Monday, Marilyn was still upset when she returned to the arena. Logan was filming in the bleachers. In this shot, thousands of spectators cheer a rodeo event, while the camera pans down to disclose Cherie asleep in the sun—a night person, she isn't used to being awake in the afternoon. The scene was charming and funny, in distinct contrast to Marilyn's mood at the time it was filmed. Between takes, she leaned over the side of the bleachers to vomit, sick with nerves.

Marilyn struggled to regain her confidence in Logan. When the company moved on to snowy Sun Valley, Idaho, she barraged him with questions about Stanislavsky. As a student, he had spent eight months with the Russian director, whose theories loosely formed the basis of Lee Strasberg's teachings. Logan warmed to the subject now, scarcely suspecting that Marilyn was trying to shore up her faith in him.

Nor did he guess that it was Marilyn's crisis of confidence that led Paula suddenly to turn up during filming as she had never dared to do before. Logan was shooting a scene in which Cherie, freezing cold in a skimpy coat, is delighted by Bo's offer of his warm, fleece-lined jacket. They completed one take, but the director wasn't satisfied. It seemed to Logan that Marilyn had put on Bo's jacket too quickly. He urged her to savor the experience more. He advised Marilyn to imagine that she was stepping into a bubble bath.

Logan heard Paula behind him. "That's a good image," she confirmed. "You're enjoying a bubble bath."

It was the first time Paula put her two cents in while Marilyn was working with a director. It would by no means be the last.

While Marilyn was in Sun Valley, Arthur went to Washington, D.C. to confer with the attorney Joseph Rauh, Jr. about his passport problems. Besides accompanying Marilyn to England for *The Sleeping Prince*, Miller wanted to be present when *A View from the Bridge* was staged there. Binkie Beaumont, the modern English theater's most successful impresario, had originally planned to open *View* in mid-March, but when British Equity prohibited most of the Broadway cast from appearing in the West End run he postponed it until October. Miller had agreed to expand the play to two acts.

On March 27, Rauh went over Miller's options. He was careful to point out the consequences of each. The major danger was that a passport application might trigger the long-threatened HUAC subpoena. Miller was well aware that Mrs. Scotti, the HUAC investigator, had been building a case against him. Rauh emphasized that in the end Miller must make up his own mind about which course to follow and that the decision would be difficult.

One alternative was simply to apply for a passport as if he had not had any trouble with the passport office before. Perhaps he would be lucky this time. It seemed to Rauh that, at the moment, the government's passport policy was more liberal than it had been in 1954. There was a chance Miller would slip through without being asked about his association with the Communist Party. Still, if he was going to be questioned, it might be strategic to raise the issue himself before the government did.

Miller's second alternative, the one Rauh clearly favored, was to submit an affidavit with his passport application. The lawyer advised Miller to declare that he was not a Communist Party member and had not been politically active for some years. He was to volunteer the information that, during a period of three months in 1947, he had indeed been present at three or four meetings of Communist writers. He was to attest that he had never had a Party card and that, as far as he could recall, he had never paid dues. But this raised the problem that the State Department might leak the affidavit to HUAC, triggering a subpoena.

Back in New York, Miller, in consultation with the attorney Lloyd Garrison, settled on a plan. He would write a short statement along the lines Rauh had suggested. Before he left for Reno, Rauh and Garrison would go over the statement and put it into final shape. About five weeks before he and Marilyn were due in England, he would apply for a passport like anyone else and hope for the best. If, however, the passport was held up, Miller would sign the affidavit and go with Rauh to submit it. Miller decided that, if necessary, he would take his chances on a leak.

By the time the cast and crew of Bus Stop returned to Los Angeles, Marilyn was ill. Part of it was due to nerves, part to the long hours working in the cold at Sun Valley wearing only light clothes. Her notes to Miller in New York suggested that she was feeling harassed. Miller, remembering the eagerness with which she had gone off to work with Logan, was mystified by his own inability to cheer her up.

Back on the Fox lot, Marilyn faced what she considered the most important scene in the film, indeed in her entire career thus far. For Marilyn, the most difficult part of filmmaking had always been dialogue. She was notorious at Twentieth for her inability to remember lines. Her nerves only made the situation worse. But during the past year in New York, Marilyn, influenced by Arthur, had come to believe that the key test of whether she had become a real actress was whether she could handle long blocks of complex dialogue.

As far as Marilyn was concerned, she was about to confront the scene that would gauge whether she had really "improved" in New York. Cherie, on the bus, talks at length about her past. She speaks of the men in her life. She speaks of her hopes and dreams. She speaks of the kind of man she longs to meet. Marilyn had never done a scene requiring this much dialogue before.

Even with less challenging material, Marilyn always had a good deal of trouble propelling herself into a scene. She would do almost anything to put off the moment when she had to turn herself on. She dreaded the responsibility of having to make it all happen. With the scene on the bus looming, Marilyn called in sick day after day. Logan did his best to shoot around her. Then on April 11, Lew Schreiber received word that Marilyn had checked into a hospital with acute bronchitis. Miller called her room everyday. They never talked for less than half an hour. There was concern at Twentieth that if Marilyn stayed out too long, she might go to England before completing Bus Stop.

On April 24, after missing twelve days of a forty-five-day

schedule, Marilyn finally came back to work. Logan, realizing that she was terrified of the next scene, had devised a plan to get her through the complicated speech. He faced two problems: Marilyn's poor memory, and the time she required to work herself up for each take. It would take forever to complete her speech if it was shot in a normal fashion. He had to find a way to relieve Marilyn of the psychological pressure of repeatedly having to turn herself on, while knowing there was no way she could get through the scene in a single take.

Logan had noticed that as long as the camera rolled, Marilyn remained "on," even if she had already made a mistake or forgotten her lines. The moment he called "Cut!" and the camera stopped, she was back at point zero again. So he filmed the scene without calling "Cut!" Each time Marilyn ruined a take, Logan kept the camera rolling. As he had expected, Marilyn was able to start the next take without her usual collapse—and the time it took to juice herself up again. When they were finished, Logan would piece her speech together out of all the tiny bits which had worked.

They shot like this for two days. They worked until 9:25 one night, 11:30 the next. Logan's tactic was very expensive, since he had to print ten times as much film as he would have otherwise. But in the end, he probably cut days from the schedule. And he had enough flashes of Marilyn's brilliance to assemble the deeply moving scene he was after. When Marilyn saw the rushes, she was thrilled. In her view, it was as if nothing she had done on screen before mattered. She had brought off a long, complicated speech at last. She could not wait to show the finished scene to Arthur. He perceived that Marilyn's attitude to Logan had improved.

Miller had arrived in Reno on May 1 to establish residency for his divorce. In anticipation of his weekend visits to Los Angeles, Marilyn rented quarters at the Chateau Marmont, next door to Paula. She assigned Greene's chauffeur to stock the hotel refrigerator with cheese and champagne, and to pick up Miller at the airport. Logan was no longer shooting on Saturdays, so Marilyn had weekends free.

Mostly she and Arthur were alone. Now and then Paula barged in. There were calls from Lee. On one occasion while Miller was there, Paula insisted on playing a tape recording of Strasberg's lecture on Duse. Marilyn and Paula listened solemnly for about twenty minutes. Arthur found the lecture absurd but held his tongue.

Following the weekend of May 12–13, Miller returned to Reno, intending to file his passport application at the end of the week. Contrary to plan, he had not yet completed the affidavit. A man in love, Miller considered proclaiming his "romantic motive" for wanting to go to England. Rauh and Garrison, however, discouraged Miller from alluding to his relationship with Marilyn Monroe. Garrison was particularly concerned that there would be a great deal of publicity should the affidavit leak to the public, while Rauh felt that he himself could always mention the romance later in an effort to show how silly the government would look if a passport were denied.

Even with Miller in worshipful attendance, Marilyn became increasingly annoyed by Don Murray's evident lack of interest in her. He had eyes only for the actress Hope Lange, whom he'd known in New York and later married. But this was more than just a case of a bruised ego. Marilyn hadn't made a film in a while. She was getting older. There was concern at Twentieth that her deliberately tattered image in *Bus Stop* might drive away her audience. Though she and Logan stuck to their concept of Cherie, there was always a chance that Marilyn could be making a terrible mistake. Her determination to signal the audience that she was a serious actress was a major risk, and Marilyn knew that. Her tense relations with her poor, unsuspecting co-star seem to have been a way of acting out her fear of failure. If Murray did not respond to Marilyn, was the audience about to do the same?

Murray, for his part, treated Marilyn good-naturedly. But things came to a boil on May 21, as they worked on Stage 14. In this scene, Cherie flees Bo in the Blue Dragon Cafe. He grabs at her, tearing off the sequined train of her gown. As Marilyn understood the action, Bo, in his anger, humiliates Cherie.

When Logan actually filmed the scene, it seemed to Marilyn that Murray tugged at the train gently rather than nastily, as if he feared the audience might not approve. Marilyn needed to feel his anger in order to react with anything like an authentic emotion of her own. Enraged that the scene had gone poorly, she grabbed the train and lashed her co-star across the face, cutting him near the eye.

Murray walked off the set, vowing not to return until Marilyn apologized. Logan, exasperated, chastised her for being vulgar. Marilyn was convinced the director hated her, and Greene refused to stand up to

Logan on her behalf. She told herself they were all simply afraid of women. Though at first Marilyn agreed to apologize, later she changed her mind.

By evening, she was despondent. It was sometime after eleven that night when Arthur Miller, asleep in his cabin at Pyramid Lake, heard someone at the door. The only immediate neighbor was Saul Bellow. For six weeks, one reached Miller by writing care of Bellow, Sutcliffe Star Route, Reno, Nevada, or calling a pay phone that stood next to a desolate, rarely traveled highway. The owner of a defunct motel nearby had to answer the phone, then drive out to the cabins in a pickup truck. By prior arrangement, when Marilyn called, which she did almost every day, she gave her name as Mrs. Leslie. It was a rare occasion, however, when Mrs. Leslie called late at night.

The road to the phone booth was dusty and bumpy. The desert air was cold, the sky thick with stars. There was a patch of soupy quicksand from which Indians had stolen the U.S. Government "Danger" signs. Several unsuspecting fishermen were rumored to have been swallowed up; their corpses were said to rise to the lake's gray surface every few years.

Three days previously, Miller had submitted his passport application, so now there could be no turning back. For a man in his position, this step was every bit as momentous and, potentially, life-changing as coming to Nevada to seek a divorce had been. It could only be hoped that the passport application would not trigger a HUAC subpoena. Clearly, Miller was nervous. In a letter to Lloyd Garrison, he declared that he was weary of holding his breath. He jestingly pointed out that the clerk had been nice and had not attempted to arrest him. Miller looked forward to a calm year—perhaps the year after next, or the year after that.

Standing in a chilly, unlit phone booth in the middle of nowhere, Miller could barely hear Marilyn. Her voice was frightened, desperate. "Oh, Papa," she was saying. "I can't do it."

She insisted that she couldn't work this way. She complained about Logan and the others. She recounted the collision on the set that day. She spoke bitterly of the director's having called her vulgar. She couldn't fight for herself anymore. She just wanted to live quietly with Arthur. She was on the verge of tears. To Miller, it sounded almost as if she were addressing herself. He had never heard such terror in her voice. He had never guessed the degree of her dependency on him. It had not previously occurred to him that he was all she had.

Though he had met Marilyn shortly after the 1950 suicide attempt, until this moment some six years later, Miller had not grasped that she might be capable of taking her own life. As he listened to her on the phone, all at once her suicide flashed before him. As her voice grew softer, he imagined that she was sinking beyond his grasp. He felt a responsibility to save her. But she was far away and he couldn't think of anyone in Los Angeles to call for help.

Suddenly, his breathing became irregular. He felt unsteady. His stork-like legs gave way. He dropped the receiver and blacked out. When Miller regained consciousness seconds later, he found himself on the ground. Marilyn's frantic monologue continued to pour from the receiver above. Rambling, she had apparently failed to realize that no one was listening anymore.

He reassured her. He did his best to calm her. By the time Marilyn hung up, she seemed better. She would try just to do her work tomorrow and not get so upset. Only one week of filming remained. Miller, walking home under the stars, told himself that he loved Marilyn and that her agony was his. At the same time, as so often with Miller, the world seemed to exist primarily to be part of his work. On the night he realized that Marilyn was suicidal, Miller, as he had not in months, perhaps years, felt the urge to write.

Marilyn finished shooting on May 29. She flew home on the night of June 1, her thirtieth birthday. The next day when she stepped off a plane in New York, reporters ambushed her with questions about Arthur Miller. Reporters had tracked him down at Pyramid Lake. He'd been overheard on a pay phone calling someone "darling." A handyman at the motel had tipped off the press about frequent calls from the breathy-voiced Mrs. Leslie. Miller was said to talk to Mrs. Leslie for as long as two hours at a time.

Did Marilyn intend to meet the playwright in New York? Did she and Miller plan to marry?

"I possibly will see him," Marilyn teased. "We're very good friends."

And how did Marilyn feel about turning thirty?

"Kinsey says a woman doesn't even get started till she's thirty," she replied. "That's good news."

Marilyn, noticeably pale and heavy-lidded, smiled and waved goodbye as her limousine drove off. Though it was a warm spring day, she was bundled in her dark mink coat.

Marilyn had returned full of hope. She would not know for some time if she had managed to bring off the picture. She would just have to wait and see. On the evidence of a rough cut of her long scene on the bus, however, Marilyn sensed that she had indeed accomplished what she had set out to do. No matter what happened to the rest of the film, she believed she had proven her worth in that one complex speech. But it remained to be seen how people would react. Nothing would be certain until the audience, and the critics, had pronounced.

While Marilyn waited for Arthur to complete his required stay in Nevada, she planned to shut herself away in her apartment and rest. Arthur was scheduled to remain at Pyramid Lake until June 11. On that day he would become a Nevada resident and get a divorce. Afterward, he was to join Marilyn in New York. By the time they went to England together, they would be man and wife. Three days before Arthur completed his residency, however, he was served with a HUAC subpoena. It was Friday, June 8. He was ordered to appear in Washington, D.C., the following Thursday.

As chance would have it, the timing of Miller's passport application had been unfortunate. Five days after he applied, HUAC had opened public hearings on "the fraudulent procurement and misuse of American passports by persons in the service of the Communist conspiracy." In some cases, it was asserted, Communist agents who applied for passports had "deliberately withheld" the purpose of the trip. Thus, Arthur Miller, author of the anti-HUAC dramas *The Crucible* and *A View from the Bridge*, was being called in to answer questions about his real reasons for wanting to go to England.

If Miller were to testify on the 14th, he would have to go to Washington immediately to confer with Joe Rauh. One didn't just casually show up at a HUAC hearing; there was too much at stake. As it was, Miller hardly had time to prepare. But if he left Nevada before June 11, he would be ineligible to file for divorce. He would have spent nearly six weeks in isolation for nothing. He and Marilyn would not be married in time to go to England on July 13—if he was permitted to go at all.

There was a good chance he would be denied a passport. There was also a good chance that if the committee was dissatisfied with his testimony, he could be held in contempt and jailed. Marilyn had a great deal invested, financially and psychologically, in *The Sleeping Prince*, but under the circumstances how could she bring herself to leave without him? From the moment Miller received the subpoena, his and Marilyn's lives were thrown into chaos.

✦ T E N ✦

During the early weeks of Arthur Miller's stay in Nevada, he had noticed a curious habit of Saul Bellow's. The novelist would head out to a spot behind a hill near his book-filled cabin and there, for some thirty minutes, he would scream into the vast mountainous silence.

That silence was shattered in the last days of Miller's stay as reporters descended on Pyramid Lake. On one occasion, a truck with a camera crew and an interviewer pulled up in front of Miller's remote quarters. Many other press people followed. Everybody wanted to know one thing: Did the playwright plan to marry Marilyn Monroe? Miller refused to say.

After Miller was served with the HUAC subpoena, Lloyd Garrison promptly asked for a postponement. Rather than say that Miller had not been given time to prepare—which was, of course, very much an issue—Garrison pointed out that his client needed to remain in Nevada another few days in order to be eligible to file for divorce. HUAC agreed to delay until Thursday, June 21. That gave Miller an additional week.

In later years, Miller was to argue that HUAC would never have "bothered" him if it hadn't been for his marriage to Marilyn Monroe. Since HUAC's inception in 1938, publicity for the politician-inquisitors had been the hearings' *raison d'être*. But it is also true that the committee had intended to call Miller before anyone knew about his relationship with a movie star. As Miller and his lawyers were aware, there had been plans to call him at the entertainment industry hearings in New York in the summer of 1955. In *The Crucible* Miller had spoken out against naming names, the very thing HUAC required people to do. Is it any wonder they went after him? Marilyn's presence in his life provided a most welcome publicity bonus, but she wasn't the reason he was summoned.

Miller's divorce hearing on June 11 took five minutes. Though it was he who had embarked on a relationship with another woman, he charged his wife, the former Mary Grace Slattery, with "extreme cruelty, entirely mental in nature." The divorce was uncontested. As he left court, the press lay in wait.

There were more journalists waiting the next morning as Miller stepped off an airplane in New York. That, apparently, was the way it was going to be from now on. How was this intensely private man, a natural loner who prized quiet and solitude, possibly going to live and work in the incessant media swirl that engulfed anything having to do with Marilyn Monroe? As in Nevada, Miller's having been called by HUAC seemed a mere footnote to the issue of his marriage plans. When Miller snapped that he had no comment, the reporters begged him at least to reveal whether he planned to see Marilyn now that he was back in New York.

"Oh, that may happen one of these days."

Did Miller intend to write a play for Marilyn?

"I don't know how to write a play for somebody," Miller insisted. "I'd be delighted if there were a part for her in one of my plays."

Miller went directly to Sutton Place South. Marilyn, eager to avoid saying anything that might complicate Arthur's situation with HUAC or prevent him from getting a passport, had gone into hiding. Nobody knew better than she how dangerous the press could be. Clearly the best approach was to steer clear of reporters at least until he arrived. Though they gathered outside the building every morning around eight, she refused to talk to them.

Marilyn had six weeks before she was to join Laurence Olivier in England. In that time, a thousand tiny details needed to be taken care of. Her publicist, Arthur Jacobs, was scheduled to go to London that very week. She had demanded complete control and now she had it, along with the responsibility that went with being in charge. Everything was complicated by the fact that her company's first independent production was being shot in another country, not in Hollywood where at least she knew how things were done. To make matters worse, with the exception of having held Marilyn's hand during Bus Stop, Milton Greene lacked film production experience. He, even more than she, was finding his way.

Marilyn didn't want to blunder in front of Jack Warner, who had agreed to finance and distribute *The Sleeping Prince*. Ironically, it was Warner who, in 1947, had first mentioned Arthur Miller to HUAC, suggesting that he and Elia Kazan were Broadway subversives. She wanted Warner to back future projects of Marilyn Monroe Productions.

In the best of circumstances, getting married right now would have been a huge pressure. Marilyn, having failed as a wife twice, was desperate to make this marriage work. She worshipped and idealized Arthur Miller. The fact that he actually wanted to marry her was a fantasy come true. That in itself, perhaps, was a prescription for disappointment.

She and Miller had had little time together in anything approaching what one might call normal circumstances. He had been married during most of their courtship, so more often than not they had seen each other with no one else present. A few stolen weekends at the Chateau Marmont, with Paula Strasberg barging in now and then, hardly provided an idea of what a life together was going to be like.

Something that happened the morning of Arthur's return, however, did suggest all they faced in the next few days. At 10 a.m., the actor and singer Paul Robeson appeared in the caucus room of the House Office Building in Washington, D.C. In a little more than a week, Miller would be doing the same thing. On stage Robeson had played Jim Harris, the African-American attorney who marries a white woman in Eugene O'Neill's *All God's Chillun Got Wings*, and Brutus Jones in a 1925 revival of O'Neill's *The Emperor Jones*. He had triumphed as Othello in 1943. But Robeson's passionate, angry, sarcastic, vituperative, intensely theatrical HUAC testimony now became one of his most famous performances. In the tradition of John Howard Lawson, Dalton Trumbo, Lionel Stander, and other fiercely unfriendly witnesses, Robeson declined to answer whether he was a Communist Party member. His contemptuous words and demeanor would leave no doubt about his opinion of HUAC and all it represented. There followed a unanimous vote to cite Paul Robeson for contempt of the Congress.

The precedent of that vote hung over Arthur Miller and Marilyn Monroe during the tumultuous nine days that preceded his own testimony. There was a chance that he, too, might face a contempt citation.

Marilyn was terrified that Arthur might be sent to jail for a year. They both could be dead in that time, she exclaimed.

Miller's case was very different from Robeson's. He had once supported left-wing causes, and he had attended some Communist meetings. But like a great many middle-aged people, he no longer agreed with certain of the political positions he had taken in youth. He thought of himself as someone who believed in democracy and loved his country as much as any man. He certainly didn't share Robeson's adoration of the Soviet Union. Unlike Robeson, Miller was willing to be questioned about his political beliefs. He was willing to talk about his past association with various Communist front groups. He was willing to discuss his attendance at three or four meetings of Communist writers in 1947. Under no circumstances, however, would he identify others who had been present.

Miller's lawyers reviewed the alternatives. He could rely on the Fifth Amendment when questioned about himself, then do the same when asked about others. Though there was a certain stigma attached, witnesses who invoked the Fifth Amendment were considered legally "safe."

A second, if unethical, course was to testify about himself, then pretend to forget others' names. One might also choose to identify persons already known to the committee through prior testimony. In telling the government what it already knew, one established credibility as a patriot without involving anyone who hadn't already been named. It wasn't the information that was important, so much as the act of self-degradation in cooperating with HUAC. Miller saw this as a "kind of mystical transference in which you gave them your soul." It wasn't for him.

The third course was to disclose everything about himself, then to inform the committee that as a matter of conscience he was unable to name names. Miller chose this last position, though it was by no means safe. As Joe Rauh had once pointedly warned Lillian Hellman, by telling HUAC everything about oneself and nothing about others one risked going to jail. Hellman, having talked the matter over with Dashiell Hammett, insisted she was not the type of person who could face jail and decided to take the Fifth. She hadn't been willing to run the risk; Miller was.

Something else Rauh had told Hellman bore strongly on the

Miller case. Before Hellman testified in 1952, the lawyer had indicated that their success would be measured not in the hearing room but in the next day's headlines. Would the headlines declare "Lillian Hellman Stands on Conscience, Won't Name Other People"? Or would they announce "Lillian Hellman Pleads Fifth Amendment"? As it happened, the former proved to be the case, making Hellman the clear victor in the publicity war. To read the notes Joe Rauh made in anticipation of Miller's hearing is to grasp his sense that the key moment would come when Miller was asked to name others present at the 1947 Communist writers' meetings. In response, Miller was to emphasize his own willingness to answer all questions about himself. He was to stress that his conscience would not permit him to name names. And, significantly, he was to insert a subtle yet unambiguous reference to Marilyn Monroe.

After weeks of ducking reporters' questions, Miller would use his HUAC testimony as the context in which to tell the world he planned to marry. That was what everybody had been waiting to hear. If Miller had wanted to separate the personal from the political, he could have made his announcement at any time before the congressional hearing. The story would have run separately; and by the time Miller testified, his connection to Marilyn would have been yesterday's news. Instead, for better or worse, a good deal of the coverage of Miller's testimony would focus on his wedding plans.

Miller was uncomfortable that his refusal to name names linked him to the artistic failures who, in his view, constituted the literary left. According to popular wisdom, these were the people who, having nothing to lose, refused to name names. They could afford to stand on principle. There were exceptions, certainly. But by and large it was thought that life's winners, figures like Elia Kazan and Clifford Odets, tended to cooperate with HUAC rather than give up the spoils of success. Though Miller planned to be an unfriendly witness, perhaps his connection with Marilyn would make him look like a winner, too.

Miller worked in the New York theater, where the blacklist had virtually no power. Besides, as an artist Miller was then very much in decline. Conceivably, a courageous moral stand in Washington would bolster Miller's reputation with the predominantly liberal Broadway audience. It would make his life as important as his work. Strange to say, his testimony might actually help, rather than hinder, his faltering stage career. For Marilyn, on the contrary, even to be associated with Miller at this point was to risk serious professional harm. He knew that. There was the possibility of picket lines, box-office boycotts, and other retaliation from patriotic groups, "Yahoos" as Miller called them. The film audience, whom Miller liked to call "the great unwashed," might turn on her.

Paula Strasberg, for her part, urged caution. Paula knew first-hand the power of the blacklist. She knew what it was to be unable to work. She told Marilyn about friends and associates whose lives HUAC had wantonly destroyed. Marilyn was on the brink of what looked to be the best years of her life as an actress. Paula asked her to consider whether she really wanted to risk all that, pointing out that Miller's troubles really had nothing to do with her. Perhaps she ought to let him take care of things on his own.

Twentieth Century–Fox representatives who phoned that week warned Marilyn against committing professional suicide. Another urgent call announced Spyros Skouras's imminent arrival from the Coast. He wanted to see Marilyn as soon as he reached New York. But Marilyn was determined to stand by Arthur. She vowed not to let the bastards hurt him. She wanted Miller to tell HUAC to go fuck itself, though of course—she said— the playwright would use better language.

The night before Miller was to go to Washington, Spyros Skouras turned up at Sutton Place South. Marilyn asked Arthur not to decline to see him. Charlie Feldman had once told Marilyn that she had a real friend in Skouras. Miller, who had met Skouras several years previously with Kazan, had contempt for the Fox president, laughing at his English in private and calling him "the Spiral Staircase." Skouras, though lampooned in *Will Success Spoil Rock Hunter?*, was by no means entirely comical. Elia Kazan's HUAC testimony in 1952 had been a vivid, and overt, testament to Skouras's power.

When Miller opened the door of Marilyn's apartment to let Skouras in, he saw a sleepy, scarcely threatening old man. Skouras seemed as though he might have had a bit too much to drink. His greeting and handshake were listless. But his innocuous appearance was deceptive. Those accustomed to dealing with Skouras, as Miller was not, knew that he often pretended to be weary. Seated on a sofa in Marilyn's living room, Skouras repeatedly slipped off the cushion.

After some small talk, Skouras got to the point. Not by accident had he arrived on the eve of Miller's departure. He urged the playwright to avoid making a mistake in Washington. Suddenly the sandpaper-voiced Skouras didn't look tired anymore. He pointed out that the committee members were his personal friends, and reasonable men. He offered to arrange for Miller to testify privately. If only Miller would agree to name names, HUAC's "usher" (as Miller later called Skouras) would arrange for the ritual humiliation to occur behind closed doors in executive session.

Skouras addressed his comments to Miller, but it was really Marilyn he came to see. Except for Miller's connection to Marilyn, Skouras couldn't have cared less about him. As was often the case, Skouras's meaning went beyond anything he actually said. The visit could only be interpreted as an implicit threat about the devastating impact Miller's testimony might have on Marilyn's film career. The Old Greek clearly hoped she would see things his way and convince Miller to cooperate with the committee. If Miller insisted on being an unfriendly witness, Marilyn's name must never be linked with his.

Marilyn had a great deal to lose, indeed every bit as much as Kazan when he backed down four years previously. She finally had her own production company. She finally had the studio contract she wanted. She finally had delivered the calibre of performance she'd worked for years to achieve. Presumably, Cherie in *Bus Stop* was to be only the first of many such roles. Yet Marilyn was willing to risk all that for Arthur. Elia Kazan, the tough guy, had crumbled, but Marilyn Monroe was determined to remain strong. She wanted to accompany Arthur to the hearing.

"Why shouldn't I go?" Marilyn said. "I mean, I'm not going to be influencing anybody. I just think I have such contempt for these people and I want to be there."

But when Arthur left with Lloyd Garrison, he told Marilyn he'd rather she stay in New York. "She's worried," he told Garrison on the plane. "She hopes I don't get slaughtered."

No sooner had Miller gone than Marilyn summoned her own lawyer to the apartment. Arthur was worried about his finances. *The Crucible* and *A View from the Bridge* had failed at the box office. He paid alimony and child support. Now all of a sudden, massive legal bills were about to be added to his burden. If he was cited for contempt and an appeal had to be mounted, he could find himself deeply in debt. Marilyn ordered Irving Stein to prepare a new will. With the exception of some money to be put aside for her mother's care, she left everything to Arthur. She refused to consider having a prenuptial agreement drawn up, and asked Stein to look into the possibility that Marilyn Monroe Productions might acquire the film rights to Arthur Miller's works. Clearly, she wanted to do everything in her power to put his mind at rest.

In the House Office Building, a circular marble staircase with a brass handrail led to the caucus room. Shortly before ten on the first day of summer, Miller was greeted by photographers' popping flashbulbs. Deeply tanned after several weeks in Nevada, he wore a navy blue suit, a white shirt, and a patterned silk tie. His dark, thinning hair was brushed straight back. There were shadows under his high cheekbones. He gnawed at an unlit pipe.

The strapping, crinkly-faced man at Miller's side was Joe Rauh. Rauh was in awe of Arthur Miller as he had not been of Lillian Hellman. He admired Miller's willingness to go to jail for his convictions. He admired Miller as a playwright and a liberal-intellectual. And he admired him as the lover of Marilyn Monroe. Rauh had yet to meet Marilyn. Ironically, Rauh's high regard may have worked against Miller's interests. Rauh had repeatedly sent Lillian Hellman back to rewrite, to refine points, to make certain that she used the national spotlight of a HUAC hearing to put her message across. With Miller, Rauh went over some general talking points, but he hesitated to push, prod, edit, criticize, and correct—all the things he had felt quite comfortable doing with his female client.

Thus, where Lillian Hellman had been pithy and to the point— the result of painstaking preparation—Miller entered the caucus room woefully ill-prepared and ill-rehearsed. Time, though in short supply, had not been the only problem. There was Miller's characteristic prolixity and Rauh's reluctance to tamper with Miller's language. And, perhaps, there was also Miller's arrogance. Where Lillian Hellman and Elia Kazan had controlled the proceedings by reading aloud a carefully crafted letter, Miller preferred to wing it.

Lawyer and client were tall, but both instantly seemed tiny as they entered the caucus room. With soaring ceilings, huge classical columns, and sparkling chandeliers, the room appeared to be the size of an athletic field. The setting was stark, theatrical, Kafkaesque. There were three levels. Chairman Francis E. Walter and a subcommittee consisting of Representatives Edwin Willis, Bernard Kearney, and Gordon Scherer sat under a furled American flag on an elevated platform, Miller at a table below. Miller may have privately looked down on his interrogators, but he would be required to look up as he testified. At the lowest level, behind the witness table, were tables and chairs for more than one hundred reporters who, as in a dream, scribbled incessantly on butter-colored pads.

With recalcitrant witnesses, Richard Arens, the HUAC counsel, was known to rant and pound. Today, apparently, was going to be quite different. The fiery Paul Robeson had insisted on interrogating the interrogator, but Miller, from the first, was calm, decorous, and respectful. He did everything to be cooperative. He was neither showy nor provocative. He seemed willing to be led through Arens's carefully prepared list of questions. He was ready to answer all questions frankly and forthrightly—except one.

The polite, initially bland exchanges masked the sharply adversarial nature of the encounter. Arens's plan was slowly and methodically to lead up to The Crucible, first laying out in painstaking detail Miller's long record of association with Communist and Communist-front groups and causes. By the time Arens was ready to draw him into a discussion of his anti-HUAC drama, anything Miller might have to say about the Communist witch-hunts would be invalidated, the writer's Marxist sympathies having been indisputably established. By then, no one could doubt that The Crucible, far from being a serious, objective political statement, had been Communist-inspired and served Communist ends; it would come as no surprise that The Crucible had been hailed in the Communist press. That's when Arens would order the witness to name names.

For all the meticulous planning, Arens appeared to lose control early in the testimony as he questioned Miller about his passport troubles. To Arens's dismay, Miller started to talk at length about The Crucible before, not after, his Communist credentials had been established. In recounting the incident in 1954, when he had been denied a passport to attend the Belgian premiere of The Crucible, Miller had a golden opportunity to talk about the play's witch-hunt theme. He had an opportunity to explain why the U.S. government hadn't wanted him to go to Belgium; indeed, why HUAC was interrogating him right now. He had a chance to state, clearly and succinctly, why he was opposed to HUAC. The moment called for high drama. It called for a memorable phrase, such as Lillian Hellman's, that, printed in tomorrow's newspapers, would convey Miller's message to the American public.

Instead, Miller began to talk in circles about airline schedules and other trivia. He droned on about his aborted trip. He missed his chance to seize control of the hearing before Arens had made a case against him. Arens wasted no time moving on to other matters. A succession of documents was produced, linking Miller to Communist or Communist-dominated causes. Miller pointed out that he had supported a number of things in the past which he would not do now. In the course of his testimony, Miller emphasized that his cooperation with various Communist-front organizations had been unfortunate and a mistake. He stressed his own patriotism and portrayed himself as a changed man who regretted his errors. Then he emulated the actor John Garfield, who, in his 1951 testimony, had depicted himself as a political innocent. "I know really very little about anything except my work and my field, and it seemed to me that the then prevalent, rather ceaseless, investigating of artists was creating a pall of apprehension and fear among all kinds of people." It was an exceedingly odd position for a prominent intellectual such as Miller to take.

At length, Arens reached the topic of Miller's passport application—presumably why they were all here in the first place. Miller confirmed that he wanted to travel to England.

"What is the objective?" Arens asked.

"The objective is double," said Miller. "I have a production which is in the talking stage in England of A *View from the Bridge*, and I will be there to be with the woman who will then be my wife."

That occasioned a good deal of scribbling in the reporters' section. Miller would have more to say on the subject a little later.

Now came the inevitable moment when Miller would be asked to name names. This was the moment he had discussed with Rauh. This was the one point at which Miller would politely refuse to cooperate. He spoke of a Marxist study course he had taken in a Brooklyn storefront in 1939 or 1940. He spoke of the Communist writers' meetings he had attended in 1947. He detailed his life at the time and the circumstances that had led him to attend.

"Can you tell us who was there when you walked into the room?" Arens asked pointedly.

"Mr. Chairman," Miller addressed Francis Walter. The witness was courteous and reasonable, his demeanor in marked contrast to Paul Robeson's obstreperousness. "I understand the philosophy behind this question and I want you to understand mine. When I say this I want you to understand that I am not protecting the Communists or the Communist Party. I am trying to and I will protect my sense of myself."

Miller's next words echoed those of Lillian Hellman. "I could not use the name of another person and bring trouble on him. These were writers, poets, as far as I could see, and the life of a writer, despite what it sometimes seems, is pretty tough. I wouldn't make it any tougher for anybody. I ask you not to ask me that question. I will tell you anything about myself, as I have."

"These were Communist Party meetings, were they not?" asked Arens.

"I will be perfectly frank with you in anything relating to my activities," said Miller. "I will take the responsibility for everything I have ever done, but I cannot take responsibility for another human being."

After repeatedly declining to name names, he went on to lecture the committee on his belief in democracy and his rejection of Communism. "I think it would be a disaster and a calamity if the Communist Party ever took over this country," said Miller. "That is an opinion that has come to me not out of the blue sky but out of long thought."

Walter noted that it was "very unfortunate" that Miller, for all his concern about political injustice, had failed to speak up for the victims of Communist tyranny.

"I think it is not only unfortunate," said Miller. "It was a great error."

That last phrase struck a chord. How could a witness who made such a remark be characterized as unfriendly? Walter was clearly impressed by Miller's willingness to admit the error of his ways. Miller had publicly abased himself. Wasn't that in large part what these hearings were about? For a moment, the chairman seemed almost to forget Miller's refusal to name names. Walter, who had lauded Kazan at the close of his testimony, now praised Miller. Joe Rauh was euphoric.

It was 12:30 p.m. Outside the caucus room, Miller, smoking a cigarette, announced that he would marry Marilyn Monroe "within a day or two." The ceremony would occur either in New York or Connecticut, where "I have a hideaway cabin." Having renounced past errors, he now hoped to be issued a passport so he could accompany Marilyn to England.

What if the application was denied?

"Whether I get a passport or not," Miller confidently declared, "we will get married. When Marilyn goes to London, she'll go as Mrs. Arthur Miller."

Francis Walter, in a separate encounter with reporters, called Arthur Miller "a frustrated idealist." As chairman of HUAC, he saw no need to hold Miller in contempt of Congress.

It was a sweltering day in New York. Reporters on Sutton Place South relied on an air-conditioner repairman who'd been working in Marilyn's eighth-floor apartment to confirm that she was upstairs. Marilyn, in tight beige toreador pants, heard the news of Miller's wedding announcement and later called Norman and Hedda Rosten in Brooklyn Heights.

"He announced it before the whole world!" Marilyn exulted. "He told the whole world he was marrying Marilyn Monroe. Me! Can you believe it?"

The Rostens, for their part, wondered whether Arthur wasn't simply using Marilyn "to get off the hook." But to voice their suspicions would have hurt Marilyn very much, and they certainly did not want to do that.

"You've got to come down right away, both of you," Marilyn implored. "I need moral support. I mean, help! I'm surrounded here, locked in my apartment. There are newspapermen trying to get in, crawling all over the place, in the foyer, in the halls. I told the elevator men to let you through."

Unknown to Marilyn, Norman Rosten's name had come up at the hearing. Unlike Kazan, he had not renounced his Communist past, and their continuing friendship had been cited by Arens in his attempt to discredit Miller. She had no idea of the danger of parading him in front of reporters just now.

After the hearing, Miller called to say he was done and would tell her everything when he returned. He planned to take a train to New York late Thursday night. When the phone rang soon afterward, Marilyn may have assumed it was Arthur again. Instead, to her horror, it was Hedda Hopper calling from Los Angeles.

Hopper was the first reporter to get through on Marilyn's private line. Marilyn could not afford to alienate the powerful journalist, but she didn't want to say anything that could hurt Miller either. Hopper was an aggressive interviewer who wouldn't stop until she had what she needed. Marilyn, caught off guard, was desperate to collect her thoughts.

Hopper asked how Marilyn was.

"I . . . well . . . I am . . . you know . . . I'm very happy about my forthcoming marriage. I'm marrying between now and July 13. I don't know where and I don't know the exact date. We've been making plans. But nothing definite about the time or the place."

"Will Arthur go to England with you?"

"Well, I hope he is able to."

"He is in Washington today, isn't he? Why didn't you go with him?"

"He said he'd rather have me stay here."

"Have you heard from him since he was on the stand? How did he say it went?"

"He said that he had finished for now and would tell me about it when he got back."

"Is he en route to New York?"

"I'm not sure what time he'll leave. I know he has other business to take care of in Washington."

Marilyn feared saying the wrong thing about Miller and HUAC. Anything Marilyn said might find its way into Hedda's next column. Hopper was out for a scoop. A fervent anti-Communist, she was known to castigate those who failed to cooperate with HUAC and laud those who did. Hopper was quite capable of devoting a column to a diatribe against Miller. Now was Marilyn's chance to prevent that from happening; she didn't want to botch the opportunity.

"I have to go now," Marilyn lied. "I'll call back. I have a call from London coming through. I promise I'll call back."

Marilyn hung up.

By the time Marilyn called back a few minutes later, she had an absolutely brilliant strategy.

"Sorry we were interrupted," said Marilyn.

"Was it London calling?" Hopper demanded. "What did they want?"

"No, I was speaking to Mr. Spyros Skouras. He would like to know if we would like to be married in his home."

Of course, it wasn't true. Skouras had made his feelings perfectly clear the other night. But in saying that Skouras had called immediately after the hearing, Marilyn implied that she and Arthur had his support. It was as if Twentieth's president wanted to shore Marilyn up on this most difficult of days; it was as if he wanted to show that the studio was behind Miller all the way. Why else would he have offered his home for the wedding? The Old Greek was a Hollywood power player, his every gesture carefully monitored, deciphered, and interpreted. At once, Marilyn had changed the subject from HUAC and subtly conveyed the position ·Hopper ought to take on Miller's testimony. The message was clear: The studio is going to back Arthur; this is where the power lies; you'd better support him, too.

It was a nervy move. Marilyn had not said in so many words that Skouras approved of Miller, only that he had offered his home for the wedding. Knowing Skouras as she did, she could be confident he would not deny the story; to do so would make him look bad. Marilyn also would have known that this was a scoop Hopper couldn't turn down; almost certainly the item would run immediately. Marilyn's priority was to protect Arthur. On the other hand, she didn't want Hopper to emerge with pie on her face when Marilyn failed to be married chez Skouras. Marilyn knew she'd need Hopper again. So she gave them both an out.

"He said he'd be happy to have us marry in his home," Marilyn continued. "I think it is lovely of him. I'd have to talk it over with Art."

"Art?"

"Yes, I always call him Art."

So, when the wedding took place elsewhere, Hopper could always attribute it to Arthur Miller's having turned down Skouras's invitation—a possibility Marilyn had carefully set up.

"How long have you known him?" Hopper inquired.

"First met in 1951 briefly," Marilyn replied. "It was on a set in Hollywood. I was making As Young As You Feel."

"Did you go out with him at that time?"

"No, not really. Not like on a date or anything," Marilyn explained. Then perhaps the day's events led her to think about the great friendship that had ended in the intervening years. For a moment, Marilyn sounded wistful. "He was Feldman's house guest and so was Gadg Kazan at the time. They were staying at the house. So that was how it was."

+   +   +

Friday, June 22, started badly. Arthur had arrived from Washington late the previous night. Marilyn, who had an appointment with her psychiatrist, avoided reporters by sneaking out a service entrance. She looked bedraggled. The usual black sunglasses concealed little. Her puffy face, devoid of makeup, suggested that she hadn't slept well or at all. Her straw-yellow hair was tangled and unwashed. Clearly, she hadn't bathed. The city was already uncomfortably hot.

The headlines showed that HUAC had won the publicity war. "Arthur Miller Admits Helping Communist-Front Groups in '40's" declared that morning's New York Times. "Miller Admits Aiding Reds, Risks Contempt" proclaimed the New York Daily News. The Chicago Tribune's headline was "Marilyn's Fiancé Admits Aiding Reds." The message wasn't that Miller had bravely refused to name names; it was that he had a Communist past. Evidently, he had done himself no favors by preparing so little and talking so much.

Miller came across as long-winded and not very likable. At best he'd been boring, at worst pompous ("I would be lying to you if I said that I didn't think the artist was, to a certain degree, in a special class") and self-absorbed ("I tell you quite frankly this suited the mood that I was in"). All the talk about Miller's moods and state of mind irritated people. There was consternation about his claim that he had failed to investigate many of the causes to which he lent his name. It was as if he took himself too seriously or not seriously enough. What sympathetic coverage there was concerned Miller's plan to marry Marilyn Monroe sometime before the 13th. Hedda Hopper revealed that the ceremony might take place at the home of Spyros Skouras.

That something had gone very wrong yesterday became clear when Marilyn returned from Dr. Hohenberg's. Photographers accosted her as she tried to slip in the service entrance.

"Leave me alone, boys, I'm a mess," Marilyn pleaded.

Under ordinary circumstances, especially with a star as well-liked and cooperative as Marilyn, the photographers almost certainly would have backed off. But not today. Ignoring Marilyn's protests—at one point she put a hand up in front of her face—the men snapped away. Shocked and upset, she rushed inside and went up in a service elevator.

The incident had been a frightening reminder of what could happen to Marilyn's image if her association with Arthur caused the press to turn on her. Wasn't that exactly what Spyros Skouras had come to warn her about? The next day's papers were sure to run the unflattering pictures. Marilyn, always sensitive to the power of publicity, decided to give them something else to print besides. Clearly, Arthur had made a mess in Washington. Marilyn decided to put her own spin on things right away. She called a press conference to be held on the sidewalk outside her apartment building at 4:30 p.m.

Meanwhile, Francis Walter changed his mind about Miller.

"I am quite certain the committee will discuss the advisability of citing him for contempt very shortly," Walter told reporters. "I am speaking only for myself but I don't see how we can consistently not cite him because he very obviously is in contempt. I don't know that there is anybody on our committee—certainly not the chairman—who would be disposed to interfere with any of the legitimate activities of Cupid, but despite June and Cupid this man will be dealt with just as everybody else who appears before this committee."

What did that mean for Miller's passport application? Did HUAC really plan to interfere with his honeymoon?

"I don't suppose there are too many places in this country where he wouldn't enjoy a honeymoon with Marilyn Monroe," Walter declared.

"Without his passport?" asked a reporter.

"Without his passport," the chairman pointedly replied.

That afternoon, reporters, photographers, and television and newsreel crews from around the world assembled on Sutton Place South. The heat was oppressive. Ordinarily, there would have been few people on the street at this hour other than some maids walking dogs or pushing baby carriages. Today, so many people turned up that twelve policemen were required to maintain order. A yellow ice-cream wagon at the foot of East 57th Street did a brisk business. By the time Marilyn was scheduled to appear, neighbors were hanging out of windows on both sides of the street. She kept everybody waiting another hour and fifteen minutes.

Finally, Marilyn Monroe and Arthur Miller emerged hand-in-hand in from the apartment-house lobby. She looked adorable, yet properly subdued for the occasion. Since being photographed that morning, she'd bathed and had her hair and makeup done. She wore a man-tailored, open-necked, cream-colored blouse. She had shiny gold cufflinks, a snug, belted black skirt, and black patent leather pumps. She clutched a pair of gloves as she had on the day she went outside with Jerry Giesler to announce that she was divorcing Joe.

"I've never been happier in my life," said Marilyn, nuzzling Miller for the cameras. He looked sweaty in a dark suit and tie.

As the couple stepped out onto the sidewalk, Marilyn leaned very hard on Arthur as if to emphasize that she depended on his protection, though in fact it was very much she who was going to protect him today. It wasn't enough to give a brilliant performance; she had to be a director, too. She had to coax a sympathetic performance out of him. She had to show people an Arthur Miller they had never seen before. She had to counter the impact of yesterday's testimony and get people actually to like the guy. It was a tall order.

"You better stop that," Miller whispered to Marilyn. "If you lean too hard, I'm going to fall over."

Marilyn, all smiles and giggles, responded by closing her eyes and kissing Arthur's weathered cheek.

"Do that again, Marilyn!" the photographers cheered.

She did—numerous times.

"It's a good thing that we'll only be getting married once," Miller remarked to reporters. "That's all I can tell you."

Marilyn whispered something in Arthur's ear that caused him to hold her very tightly, burrowing his nose in her forehead. He was the image of a man deeply in love, a man who certainly deserved to be permitted to go on his honeymoon.

Someone mentioned Francis Walter's statement that there weren't too many places in America where Miller would fail to enjoy a honeymoon with Marilyn Monroe.

"It would be rather difficult to honeymoon here," Miller declared, "since Miss Monroe is going to England."

"I won't be in the U.S.," Marilyn chimed in. "I've got to go whether he can or not." She paused to tilt her head back and gaze lovingly into Arthur's eyes. "I hope he'll go with me."

By the time these pictures appeared in Saturday's papers, Marilyn had adroitly shifted everyone's attention from the particulars of Arthur's testimony, which had not played well in the press, to the question of when and where the wedding was to take place. On Saturday morning, a rumor spread among reporters outside the apartment house that Marilyn was to be married that night. Marilyn didn't see her psychiatrist on weekends, so she remained out of sight all day. Eager to keep the press on her side, she sent down an assistant to field questions. The assistant denied the rumors, then, at the reporters' urging, called upstairs on the doorman's house phone to double-check with Miller.

Around noon, Miller, alone, roared off in Marilyn's black Thunderbird convertible. He returned two hours later. At 5:15 p.m., newsmen spotted him peeking at the crowd from an eighth-floor window. All heads looked up and Miller ducked. Clearly, he and Marilyn were going to have no privacy and no peace so long as they remained in town.

On Sunday night, Miller's station wagon, loaded with suitcases, appeared mysteriously. Soon afterward, Miller issued from the lobby and drove off alone. He went only so far as grim, cobblestoned York Avenue in the shadow of the clattering Queensboro Bridge. He parked on the east side of the street. Moments later, Marilyn, carrying a small, striped leather train case in one hand, a straw picnic basket in the other, darted out of 2 Sutton Place South. A yellow Checker cab took her four blocks uptown, stopping on the west side of York Avenue. Marilyn, on spike heels, ducked advancing cars with blazing headlights. No sooner had she reached the station wagon than she felt a hand on her shoulder roughly spin her around. Marilyn was hurled against the vehicle with such force that she nearly fell. The photographer was about to snap her picture when Miller emerged and, without so much as a glance at the fellow, helped her in.

In those days, there were no interstate highway connections between New York and Roxbury. The trip took three hours. Litchfield County was sparsely-populated dairy country with stone walls, eighteenth-century white clapboard farmhouses, and vivid red barns and silos. Arthur called the rolling terrain "my fields." It would have been hard to see much in the velvety darkness, but the air was perfumed with sweet rocket and trailing arbutus. There were black, red and white oak trees for the headlights to pick out.

In the winter of 1947, Miller, then married to his first wife, had come here in a borrowed truck looking for a certain house that was for sale. The narrow, twisty dirt roads, precarious in any conditions, were snow-covered and slippery. Snow was piled high on both sides. Miller lost control, sliding into a parked car. As chance would have it, the charming, seven-room, white frame house with shuttered windows and a painted chimney was the available property. It stood at the intersection of Old Tophet and Gold Mine Roads. It had forty-four acres and a clay tennis court. When Miller moved there, he and his cousin Morty, who had a house nearby, were said to be the first Jews in Roxbury. The area around Old Tophet came to be known as "the hill where all the Jews are."

Marilyn had never spent time at close quarters with Arthur's family before. Tonight, Isadore and Augusta had come up from Brooklyn. His children, Jane, eleven, and Robert, nine, were also present in anticipation of going off to summer camp in Massachusetts the following week. His ex-wife was nowhere in sight, of course, but this was still very much Mary's house. In back was the ten-by-twelve-foot shack where Arthur had written "the great American play" in six weeks. He liked to say that *Death of a Salesman*, originally titled "The Inside of His Head," had taken shape in his thoughts as he built the studio.

Roxbury was the sort of place where you awakened to discover cows studying you from the other side of a stone wall. You could walk for hours without seeing more than one or two cars. Few outsiders found their way into the tangle of gritty back roads which had long, hilly views. But when Marilyn awakened on the morning of Monday, June 25, she could hear the clamor outside. Voices in several languages drifted through the open windows. The grinding of newsreel cameras drowned out the small, tremulous sounds of barn swallows. She and Arthur had not eluded the press after all. It was Sutton Place South all over again. Only the yellow ice-cream wagon was missing.

Here, Marilyn couldn't hide on the eighth floor with the air-conditioner blasting and a doorman and other apartment-house staff to run interference. A great many reporters loomed on the other side of the fragrant green hedge that partly obscured the property. A helicopter could be heard just overhead as a news photographer shot an aerial view. In these conditions, how was Miller possibly going to get any work done on the expanded version of A View from the Bridge he had promised to deliver to Binkie Beaumont? He had never been the sort of writer to tolerate distractions.

This morning, he had to drive to Manhattan to confer with Lloyd Garrison. Before he left, however, he and Marilyn had little choice but to give reporters a photo opportunity. Marilyn knew that the press, always fickle, must be kept on their side. America's sympathy was every bit as important to getting that passport as anything Arthur's lawyers could say or do. Whatever serious matters he had to attend to later in the day, right now it was essential that Miller play the cuddly, nervous bridegroom.

Marilyn put on a pair of blue jeans, a sleeveless, button-front, white blouse, and moccasins. Miller wore dark trousers and a white shirt open at the collar. As they emerged into the bright sunlight, Marilyn, wearing dark glasses, threw her arms around Arthur's waist. Without high heels, Marilyn stood five feet five and a half inches; the top of her head reached Miller's shoulder. He had to crane his long, leathery neck to nuzzle her tousled hair.

"It won't be for several days at least," Marilyn told the adoring crowd before she went back inside.

"There'll be no wedding this week," Miller added as he prepared to drive off. "I can't say yet when."

Rather than face more questions, Marilyn remained in an upstairs bedroom. While the children played outside, Augusta Miller announced that Marilyn was "badly run down" and needed rest. Meanwhile, several reporters found their way to Hodge's general store in Roxbury center. Residents picked up their mail there, sipped coffee, and chewed the fat. They were said to be the kind of people who looked at an outsider twice before saying hello. The strangers didn't exactly get a warm welcome. There was a good deal of upset about the invasion.

One Hodge's regular who failed to show up on Monday was old Ed Dillingham. The crusty ninety-four-year-old asked a neighbor to pick up his mail, declaring, "I'm saving all my strength for Marilyn!"

Miller had a great deal to do that afternoon at the Madison Avenue office of Paul, Weiss, Rifkind, Wharton, & Garrison. Joe Rauh, in Washington, had been greatly disturbed by false press reports that

Miller was withholding an affidavit stating that he was not then and never had been a Communist Party member. The State Department would not consider issuing a passport without the affidavit.

Rauh had prepared a draft over the weekend and gotten it off to Lloyd Garrison for Miller to review and sign. He asked Miller to draft a supplementary affidavit consisting of passages from his literary work and interviews that indicated a belief in democracy. Rauh was especially eager for the State Department to see a 1954 interview with the Icelandic newspaper *Morgungladid*, in which Miller protested against "the tyrannical suppressions of liberty in Russia." In the light of Francis Walter's alarming statements on Friday, Rauh also wanted to move quickly to avert the possibility of Miller's being cited for contempt of Congress. HUAC had shied away from recommending a contempt citation against Paul Robeson; the committee feared he'd use contempt proceedings as a platform for more spotlight-grabbing histrionics. But the polite, soft-spoken, intellectual Arthur Miller was another story.

Garrison had written a letter to Chairman Walter requesting ten days to prepare a memorandum on precedents for not citing Arthur Miller for contempt. Miller reviewed the letter. His lawyers wanted to be sure that Walter received it before HUAC met in executive session on Wednesday morning. Otherwise, the committee might very well recommend a contempt citation. If the House voted to proceed, the Justice Department would launch an investigation with an eye to indicting Miller. So there was a good deal of nervousness in Miller's camp in anticipation of the moment when Walter read Garrison's letter.

And there was anxiety about Miller's four-family party line in rural Connecticut. When Walter reacted, Rauh and Garrison wanted to be able to confer with their client immediately without fear that others might be listening in. The presence of all those journalists in Roxbury meant that the details of the lawyers' telephone conversations could find their way into the next day's newspapers. The last thing Miller needed on Wednesday was a bunch of sharp-eared reporters hanging out at Hodge's general store.

On Tuesday, on discovering the press still camped out at Gold Mine and Old Tophet, Miller emerged from the house to propose a deal. Doctors had ordered Marilyn to get some rest. She needed to be able to sun herself without fear of being photographed through the hedges.

Obviously the reporters hesitated to budge lest they miss the wedding. Miller promised that the ceremony would not take place before Saturday. If they all returned to the city and left Marilyn alone, he vowed to "bare all"—whatever that might mean—at a press conference on Friday afternoon.

"I have always kept my word," the playwright declared, "and I will in this instance."

An hour later the reporters had dispersed. Though they may have assumed that Marilyn was lazily sunning herself, in fact the household was bursting with tension as she, Miller, and his parents awaited the news from Washington. If the committee recommended a contempt citation, the State Department was most unlikely to give Miller a passport. For many months to come, he might be required to devote time, energy, and money to his defense. Marilyn would have to go to England alone.

While the committee deliberated, Arthur's cousin Morty showed up at the house and collected two vials of blood, which would have to be tested before they could apply for a marriage license. They were to be married on Sunday, July 1 at the home of Miller's agent, Kay Brown, in South Salem, New York, just over the state border. Rabbi Robert Goldberg of New Haven, a prominent civil libertarian, agreed to perform the ceremony.

The result of the HUAC executive session on Wednesday was not what anyone in Miller's camp had anticipated. Initially, the news seemed to be good. HUAC had voted unanimously to wait ten days before deciding on a contempt citation, as Garrison had requested. But the reason they gave was not to allow Garrison to research precedents for not holding Miller in contempt. Instead, Miller was allowed ten days in which to change his mind about naming names. He had until July 7, six days before the scheduled departure for England.

As Arthur and Marilyn drove down to South Salem for a marriage license on Friday morning, they were under a good deal of pressure. By the time they returned, the dusty intersection of Old Tophet and Gold Mine was already clogged with parked cars. Reporters had begun to assemble in anticipation of the statement Miller had promised to make this afternoon. There were many new faces. Meanwhile, Morty and his wife, Florence, invited Marilyn, Arthur, his parents and children to lunch. In their absence, as many as four hundred journalists gathered outside Miller's farmhouse in the rapidly escalating heat.

Mara Scherbatoff, New York bureau chief for *Paris-Match*, arrived with a photographer named Paul Slade. His eighteen-year-old brother Ira had driven them up from the city. When there was no sign of Marilyn Monroe at the house, Scherbatoff made some inquiries and decided to drive to Morty's house. Paul Slade remained to set up his equipment on the grass with other photographers. The sunlight was punishing. The journalists' clothes grew damp.

Morty Miller's house was about a mile and a half away. Ira Slade and Scherbatoff parked outside and waited. Shortly before 1 p.m., Marilyn, Arthur and his cousin left in a station wagon. Morty drove quickly; he knew the winding dirt road well. The New York teenager took off after them. Gold Mine was badly rutted and the ride was a bumpy one. About three quarters of a mile from the crossroads, Slade took a sharp, difficult turn. Residents knew to slow down, but the kid proceeded at top speed. He lost control and the car flew off the shoulder into an oak tree. The reporters at Arthur's house, including Slade's brother, were startled by the sound of the impact.

Morty hit the brakes. He, Arthur, and Marilyn raced back on foot. The sight was horrifying. Both Scherbatoff and Slade were still inside the gnarled wreckage. The boy was crumpled behind the steering wheel. Scherbatoff, in the passenger's seat, had been hurled partway through the windshield. Her face was sliced open from the middle of her lip to her forehead. Teeth were missing. Her chest was crushed, her legs broken. Blood gushed from a severed artery in her throat. She was crying softly.

Marilyn helped to dislodge Scherbatoff, placing her on the ground beside the open car door. Arthur pulled the boy out. His injuries were considerably less serious. Meanwhile, Paul Slade had rushed to the scene. He hovered over Scherbatoff, stemming the flow of blood by pressing a finger on the exposed artery.

Marilyn and the Millers sped to Arthur's. Arthur, the first out of the car, dashed into the house. Morty, thin and bald with sunglasses and black sneakers, followed with Marilyn. She appeared to be traumatized, her white blouse flecked with blood.

"There's been a very bad accident up there," she was saying. "A girl has been terribly hurt. It's awful." Morty added that Arthur was calling the hospital right now.

The nearest hospital was in New Milford. Miller, told there wouldn't be an ambulance for two hours, grew frenzied. He notified the operator that the girl on the road was Marilyn Monroe and that the story would be front-page news tomorrow. That sped things up.

Marilyn, on automatic pilot, went upstairs to prepare for the press conference. It seems never to have occurred to her to cancel. She changed into a mustard green blouse and a black linen skirt. Despite the heat, Miller pulled a navy V-neck sweater over his white shirt. He puffed on a cigarette. He clenched his jaw.

Thirty minutes later, Marilyn was ready. After a lifetime of playing the happy girl, she was expert at masking her emotions. But in this instance, the disjunction seemed weird and disturbing. Suddenly, she was all smiles and laughter. There was not a trace of the very real upset people had witnessed only half an hour ago. Milton Greene, who had driven over from Weston, introduced the couple. As Marilyn and Arthur took their places under a maple tree behind the house, an ambulance siren could be heard in the distance.

Greene notified the photographers that they had twenty minutes to get what they needed. Marilyn, as though in a trance, hugged and cuddled Miller for the cameras. She kissed his forehead. She held his waist. She rubbed up against his back. Miller, clearly, was barely going through the motions. During the question-and-answer period, he was testy with reporters for the first time since appearing before HUAC.

"I'm not going to tell you where and when we're going to get married," he said. "If the press do not leave me alone, we will leave here for parts unknown."

After the reporters left, word came from New Milford Hospital that Scherbatoff had died on the operating table. Marilyn, distraught, had to be convinced that the woman's death was not somehow her fault. Paula Strasberg, in New York, called the accident a bad omen.

Miller had had enough. Eager "to stop all the publicity," he decided to get married immediately. It was a way of seizing control, the situation having gotten monstrously out of hand. Apparently in the belief that once the ceremony was over the media circus would end, he arranged for them to be married that evening at the Westchester County Court House in White Plains, New York. Judge Seymour Robinowitz promised to tell no one, not even his wife. Miller had ordered a ring from

Cartier's but it wasn't ready, so he borrowed Augusta's wedding band for the ceremony. Marilyn changed into a short-sleeved sweater. Arthur wore a blue blazer over his V-neck sweater and white shirt.

Judge Robinowitz pronounced Arthur Miller and Marilyn Monroe man and wife at 7:21 p.m. A bottle of champagne was produced, the exhausted couple toasting each other in front of a shelf of law books in the judge's chambers. Marilyn looked particularly wan.

"I'm glad it's over," said Miller. "Now the world can go back to what it was doing."

Later, one of Marilyn's publicists heard about Arthur's comment and said wryly, "He doesn't realize that this is only the beginning."

News of the civil ceremony meant that the press were caught off guard when Arthur and Marilyn went ahead with their plans for a religious ceremony. On the afternoon of Sunday, July 1, family and friends waited on the flagstone terrace at Kay Brown's white farmhouse while the bride and groom drove down from Roxbury. There were Arthur's parents and children. There were his brother Kermit, sister Joan, cousin Morty and their spouses. There were the Lee Strasbergs, the Milton Greenes, and the Norman Rostens. Because of the intense heat, the men removed their jackets. Long tables with white cloths and folding chairs had been set up beneath a large picture window. As usual, Marilyn was late.

Finally, the bride and groom arrived. Marilyn, in blue jeans, was rushed to a tiny bedroom upstairs, where the matron of honor, Hedda Rosten, helped her change into a beige chiffon wedding dress. (Hedda had been enlisted to accompany Marilyn to England as her personal assistant.) Meanwhile, Rabbi Goldberg and the guests assembled near the living-room fireplace.

Milton Greene led Marilyn out of the bedroom and presented her arm to Lee Strasberg, never a man who touched or allowed himself to be touched with ease. It meant everything to Marilyn that Strasberg had agreed to act as her surrogate father today; he gave the bride away. Paula, suicidal and half-mad, was, as Miller recognized, a mother figure to Marilyn.

The ceremony took ten minutes. Marilyn lifted her gossamer veil to sip red wine. She said "I do" in a soft, tremulous voice. Miller crushed the glass underfoot and the room erupted with cries of "Mazel tov!"

If there had ever been a moment of real happiness in Marilyn's life, this was it. Never as a child had Marilyn dared to imagine that she could feel about herself as she felt that warm June day as she danced in the sunlight with her new husband. In Arthur, Marilyn seemed at last to have found a voice strong enough to counter the lifelong echoes of Gladys telling her she was not worthy to go on living. As Marilyn snuggled in Arthur's arms in front of the wedding guests, she appeared to accept his verdict that she deserved to be loved.

For all of her happiness, Marilyn remained sick at heart about Mara Scherbatoff's death. She was desperately worried about Arthur's problems with HUAC and the State Department, and she grew feverish as July 13, her departure date, approached. But with Miller and Strasberg in her corner, it seemed as if Marilyn was going to be all right.

The day after he gave the bride away, Lee Strasberg appeared unexpectedly at Milton Greene's office. Greene, at work on last-minute production details, was scheduled to leave on the 10th. Strasberg announced that if Greene wanted the film to proceed, he had to pay Paula $2,500 a week excluding expenses. The salary was more than anyone but Marilyn Monroe and Laurence Olivier were to receive. As an alternative, Strasberg proposed that Marilyn Monroe Productions give him a percentage of the film in exchange for Paula's services.

From first to last, Strasberg was chillingly mercenary. For many years, he had failed to earn the kind of money that he and Paula believed he was worth. Paula never tired of haggling with Cheryl Crawford over Lee's Actors Studio salary. She never tired of pushing Lee. "If not for her," Clifford Odets once remarked, "Lee would be one of the little old scholars who shuffle around the streets with books under their arms." In Marilyn Monroe, Lee and Paula saw the solution to their financial woes.

Lee insisted that unless his demands were met, he'd refuse to let Paula go to England. That, of course, may very well have been Paula speaking through him. She played the good cop to her husband's bad cop. Pointing out that Marilyn was emotionally fragile, Lee predicted she would be unable to do the picture without Paula. That Strasberg was exploiting Marilyn's vulnerability—that she was already under huge pressure, and that his last-minute threat might precipitate a crisis—seems not to have bothered him at all.

Strasberg also got in a few gibes at the director. He insisted that

Laurence Olivier, who despised the Method and the Actors Studio, and had a particularly low opinion of Strasberg himself, was all wrong for Marilyn. Strasberg urged that George Cukor be hired instead. Cukor, it should be pointed out, was unlikely to have accepted. The Oliviers' friendship was one of Cukor's prized possessions, and he would never have done anything to jeopardize it. Strasberg has to have known that, at this point, there was little likelihood of Olivier's being replaced by anyone. Rather, Strasberg's objective seems to have been to sabotage Marilyn's confidence in Olivier before she reached England.

Why would Strasberg want to undermine Olivier? What interest would he have in setting up Marilyn's working relationship with Olivier to fail? Strasberg seems to have been afraid that if Marilyn gave a fine performance in The Sleeping Prince, Olivier, not Strasberg himself, would get the credit for her transformation. And from the moment Strasberg started working with Marilyn, that transformation was to have been his miracle, his brilliant achievement. Strasberg was prepared to destroy a film that meant everything to Marilyn if that would prevent Olivier from getting the credit Strasberg wanted for himself.

Strasberg, acutely sensitive to Marilyn's psychology, may have calculated that she didn't dare see his betrayal for what it was. By now, Strasberg, like Miller, was integral to Marilyn's sense of herself. On a film set, Paula was her lifeline to him. Milton Greene regarded Strasberg as a blackmailer. Marilyn, refusing to talk about the matter, insisted on giving Strasberg his money.

Paula's presence in England was now guaranteed. But what about Arthur? The clock was ticking. He had five days to change his mind about naming names. After that, HUAC was sure to recommend a contempt citation.

The very first line of the sixteen-page memo Garrison planned to submit on Friday, July 6, was a strong, clear statement of Miller's unwillingness to identify others who had attended the Communist writers' meetings in 1947. It wasn't a negotiable issue. This time there would be no ambiguity. Whatever the risk, Miller insisted on acting according to his conscience. No matter how diplomatic Garrison might be in the pages that followed, that opening sentence was like waving a red rag in front of a bull. Some committee members might not even bother to read further.

Miller's best hope for being permitted to accompany Marilyn to

England was somehow to extract a passport before Garrison sent off the memo. At the last minute, Rauh struck a deal with the State Department. If Miller signed an affidavit promising to return in the event of a contempt trial, he would be issued a passport good for six months. That was wonderful news.

As it happened, the affidavit reached the State Department the same day Francis Walter received Garrison's carefully worded memo. "If that's his answer to the opportunity offered by the committee to avoid contempt," Walter said of Miller, "then it seems to me he's inviting it." On Tuesday, July 10, HUAC voted to recommend that the House of Representatives cite Miller for contempt. Miller was due to leave the country on Friday the 13th. That meant the vote in Congress would take place while he and Marilyn were in London.

Miller's lawyers had one card left. They decided to use Marilyn. At Twentieth Century–Fox, she remained a very valuable property. A debate on the floor of Congress was the sort of publicity that could hurt even a beloved star. Rauh seemed convinced that if Spyros Skouras could be persuaded it was in his interest to intervene, a contempt citation might still be averted. Skouras had boasted that the committee members were his personal friends. Miller's camp wanted Skouras to influence Donald Jackson of California to ease up on Miller. The lawyers considered Jackson to be Miller's chief enemy. The Old Greek wouldn't be doing it for Miller; he'd be doing it, Rauh emphasized, to keep the tarnish off Marilyn.

Skouras, however, refused to help. Rauh, for his part, was mystified. Did that mean the studio was cutting Marilyn loose? Did it mean that Skouras regarded the destruction of her marketability as a foregone conclusion? Or was he merely waiting to see whether a box-office boycott actually materialized? Did he want to see how the fans reacted to her husband's political problems? Skouras's silence and the questions about Marilyn's future that it raised was one more thing that would weigh heavily on her in the weeks and months to come.

+ ELEVEN +

There was a pounding rain on the morning of Saturday, July 14, as the plane carrying Marilyn Monroe and Arthur Miller touched down outside London. They were rushed through customs, and shortly before noon Marilyn appeared in sight of a shouting mob of reporters, her right hand tightly clutched in Arthur's. On her other hand, she wore a simple gold band inscribed, "A. to M., June 1956. Now is Forever." A brief press conference had been scheduled in the snackbar of the airport hotel, where Laurence Olivier and Vivien Leigh waited.

Rumpled from the long flight, Marilyn was radiant nonetheless. She looked as if this were the proudest moment of her life. Indeed, in some sense it was. Marilyn had just stepped off the plane with her heroic new husband to be greeted by the world's finest classical actor, with whom she was about to co-star in her own film production. The moment was a reminder of how very far Marilyn had come from being the sad little orphan girl whom no one wanted.

Her pride in Arthur was evident. Unable to take her eyes off of him, she seemed to be making sure that Olivier noted exactly who her husband was. His presence beside her provided the validation she had always longed for. For his part, Miller looked every bit as proud to be with Marilyn. He obviously enjoyed being the envy of most other men. Certainly, at that moment, Marilyn must have believed that she really had finally found happiness—and that, as the inscription on her ring suggested, it would last forever.

Olivier was friendly, but far more reserved than he had been when Marilyn saw him last. Gone entirely were the teasing, the flirtatious joking. This should not have been surprising to Marilyn. Not only did he have his wife at his side, but Marilyn and Arthur were very much the honeymoon couple; the tone Olivier had taken in New York would have been entirely out of place. Marilyn, absorbed by Arthur though she was, seemed a bit taken aback by Olivier's crisply professional, rather distant manner.

The two couples posed for photographs, most of which caught Marilyn looking adoringly at Arthur rather than at her co-star. Vivien Leigh, for her part, seemed less than thrilled to have to pose next to a woman twelve years younger than herself. Dark-haired and petite, and considered by many to be "the most beautiful woman in the world," she was all too aware that the camera would only magnify their age difference.

An Austin Princess limousine transported the Millers to Surrey. Milton Greene and Arthur Jacobs came along, and four policemen on roaring motorcycles provided an escort. The Oliviers followed in a chauffeured Bentley. At Englefield Green, security guards unlocked a pair of white gates. The motorbikes led the way up a long gravel drive to Parkside House, the grand Georgian manor which had been rented for Marilyn and Arthur. Parkside was located just next to the Queen's own Windsor Great Park, and there was even an entrance from it to the Royal Gardens. Marilyn was daunted by the house's size and splendor, and though he did a better job of appearing unfazed, Arthur was clearly unsettled as well. Still, there was no doubt that Parkside was tangible evidence of Marilyn's success. Although a press conference had been scheduled for the next afternoon in London, Marilyn would not let Olivier go before the photographers at the gate were permitted to come up to the house for a few more pictures.

Arthur chose the music room as his work space. It was another world from the shack where he wrote in Connecticut, with a piano, an elegant desk, and French doors overlooking an expanse of green lawn. Here he would set up a typewriter on which to revise and expand A View from the Bridge. He also took notes by hand in three or four slender, brown, spiral-bound composition books.

There were eleven bedrooms. For the master bedroom, which was to be Marilyn's nest, Greene had insisted they find a large white bed and have the walls painted white as well. Heavy blackout curtains had been installed in order to help Marilyn sleep—always a source of anxiety, especially when she knew that she had to be up first thing in the morning looking fresh for the cameras.

That night, the Millers were both exhausted and more than a little disoriented by the unfamiliar setting in which they had been dropped. It wasn't just the house or the staff of servants that made them uncomfortable. They were still not completely at ease with each other. This was all very different from a few stolen hours at a hotel or even a weekend in Los Angeles. They had had only the chaotic past few weeks in which to get used to actually living together for the first time.

Still, Marilyn believed she had reached a safe haven with her new husband. Nervous as she was about Olivier, she was thrilled to have Miller, the great playwright, as her protector. Going in front of the cameras had always terrified Marilyn, a fact with which Arthur was only beginning to come to terms. But at least this time she had not arrived alone. That made an immense difference. During the long battle over her studio contract, Marilyn had clung to DiMaggio for comfort and advice. But he had always refused to have anything publicly to do with her work. Arthur, by contrast, seemed ready, even eager, to be there for Marilyn when she needed him.

The following day, Arthur was at Marilyn's side when, despite her promise to Olivier, she turned up an hour late for the press conference in the Lancaster Room at the Savoy Hotel. The press conference had been designed to placate the press, since Olivier intended to work on a closed set while filming. In Marilyn's absence, it had fallen on him to entertain the press alone, and he was in a foul humor when she arrived. Her eyes were hidden behind sunglasses, and her voice was scarcely audible. She seemed to be somewhat hung over. Nonetheless, Olivier was impressed by her ability to charm the audience. Any irritation about her having kept everybody waiting was quickly dispelled. They worked well together. Ostensibly so that all might hear, Olivier repeated each one of the reporters' questions in order to give Marilyn a few extra seconds to respond. Despite this, his manner, unchanged from the previous day, made Marilyn anxious. Insecure as she was, she took Olivier's remoteness for dislike, though in fact it was merely his way of dealing with their drastically altered circumstances.

A great deal had changed in the five months since Olivier

returned from his business meetings with Marilyn. Back then, anyone might have guessed that his marriage was coming apart. Some people guessed that Olivier tolerated his wife's passionate love affair with Peter Finch in order to prevent the mad, sleepless Vivien from undermining his ability to work; indeed, Finch had lived for a time at Notley Abbey, Olivier's home. Disenchanted with his marriage, Olivier had planned to fall "most shatteringly in love" with Marilyn Monroe. But Vivien, confronted with a very real threat to her marriage, acted quickly. Apparently at her instigation, Olivier confronted Finch, who withdrew from *South Sea Bubble*. And, at the age of forty-two, Vivien became pregnant. Indeed, only the day before Marilyn's arrival, news of the pregnancy had appeared in the press.

On the one hand, the pregnancy seemed like an attempt to repair the marriage. Olivier traced the origin of Vivien's manic depression to her miscarriage in 1944. The illness, said Olivier, caused Vivien to hate the person she loved most—namely, her husband. Twelve years later, the fact that she was pregnant again suggested the possibility of a whole new start. Olivier appeared to be elated. "Proves there's life in the old boy yet!" he told friends.

On the other hand, there could be no escaping the couple's personal history. Olivier's first wife, Jill Esmond, had been pregnant when he left her. However unconsciously, was Olivier setting himself up to repeat the past? Far from marking the rebirth of his second marriage, did the pregnancy put Vivien Leigh in the position that Jill Esmond had once occupied? Delighted as Vivien undoubtedly was, the pregnancy was no guarantee that Larry would stay. When he had left the pregnant Jill, he had run off with an actress who, it was generally agreed, had revivified his image on screen. Now, approaching fifty, did he hope that Marilyn Monroe would have something of the same effect on his image that Vivien Leigh had once had?

It's possible that Olivier himself might not have been able to answer some or any of these questions. All one can know for certain is that he had been very taken with Marilyn and that someone (Vivien perhaps) tipped off the press about the pregnancy shortly before Marilyn arrived. Vivien was in good mental and physical health, and the marriage was better than it had been in a long time. She didn't want anything or anyone to jeopardize that.

Something else had changed dramatically since January. Olivier certainly hadn't planned on Marilyn's being married to Arthur Miller. He had to wonder how a husband's presence would affect the production. Would Miller help or hinder? Milton Greene, on whom Olivier had been counting to handle Marilyn, seemed not to like Miller—a bad sign. Olivier, for his part, did not hold Miller in high regard. In conversation with Colin Clark, a young assistant on the film, Olivier dismissed the playwright as a "pseudo-intellectual." He found Miller smug and overly combative. Miller's passport troubles had caused Olivier to worry that Marilyn might not show up at all.

The changes on both sides made the outlook for Monroe's collaboration with Olivier considerably different from what it had been in January. But if Marilyn seemed oblivious to all this, Olivier was determined to find a way to cope.

Before the Millers headed back to Parkside after the press conference, Olivier politely asked Miller what plays he wanted to see. Miller selected John Osborne's Look Back in Anger at the Royal Court. The play had generated enormous excitement when it opened in May. "I doubt if I could love anyone who did not wish to see Look Back in Anger," declared Kenneth Tynan in his review. "It's the best young play of its decade." Dismayed by the number of English plays concerned with upper- and upper-middle-class life, Tynan saw Look Back in Anger as something new and vital, which gave voice to a "sophisticated, articulate lower class." Olivier had disliked the play, and urged Miller to choose something else. When Miller insisted, Olivier promised to have tickets for him at the next performance. Marilyn wanted to rest, so Miller went alone.

Miller was surprised to find Olivier at the theater. Despite his initial dislike of the play, Olivier would not permit himself to take the risk that Miller might be on to something that he himself had failed to perceive. This fiercely competitive streak, which drove him to keep growing as an artist, was part of what made Olivier great; he was intent on remaining open to new things. Olivier's determination never to seem old-fashioned or set in his theatrical ways makes understandable his immense frustration at the time of A Streetcar Named Desire, when he failed to connect with Tennessee Williams's work as Elia Kazan and Marlon Brando had done.

During the intermission, Olivier asked Miller's opinion. Miller was most enthusiastic. And Miller remained enthusiastic after the play when Olivier questioned him again. Later, Miller and Olivier met the author backstage. "God, I wish you'd write a play for me one day," Olivier told Osborne.

Olivier had scheduled three days of wardrobe and makeup tests that week, so Marilyn and Arthur had plenty of time alone together. They seemed blissfully happy. Among the servants at Parkside House, there was much giggling and speculation as the honeymooners spent many hours upstairs in their bedroom "playing trains," as it was thought. This reason was immediately suggested by Marilyn's public image, but there was another reason also. A childhood spent in various foster homes had taught Marilyn to react to the threat of unfamiliar surroundings by hiding. The bedroom had always been the place where she felt safest.

In anticipation of the tests, Marilyn met with Jack Cardiff, the Academy Award-winning cinematographer known for his work on *Black Narcissus*, *The Red Shoes*, and *The African Queen*. Marilyn had asked that he be hired. She told Cardiff that she wanted to use the pearly-white makeup she'd worn in *Bus Stop*, but Cardiff warned that the pale makeup might cause her teeth to appear gray. As she hadn't yet seen a final print, they went to Twentieth's private screening room in London to look at *Bus Stop* together. Marilyn saw that Cardiff was right; the makeup she had worn as Cherie was all wrong for *The Sleeping Prince*. But she also saw something else. Her favorite scene, in which Cherie talks at length about her past, had been cut. Marilyn had been convinced that her performance in that scene would change the way people saw her. She had excitedly anticipated the day when Arthur would see it and know that his faith in her had been well placed.

The discovery that *Bus Stop* would be released without this scene was the first break in Marilyn's mood of perfect happiness. With terrifying suddenness, Marilyn fell into despair. Her whole world turned upside down in a moment. All of her anger was suddenly focused on Joshua Logan. She was convinced that he had betrayed her. She was certain that he had never really believed in her as he had pretended to do. She would never accept that, in fact, Logan had fought to keep the scene but had been overruled by Buddy Adler and Spyros Skouras, who thought it unnecessary to the narrative. As far as Marilyn was concerned, Logan— the first director she herself had selected—had deceived her. In terms of her future relations with Olivier, this crisis could hardly have come at a worse moment. Marilyn brooded obsessively about whether Olivier, too, would turn out to be her adversary.

On July 18, when she arrived at Pinewood Studios some thirty minutes late for the first makeup tests, Olivier was horrified. Her skin was badly blemished. Her hair was a tangled, matted mess. She was completely disheveled. She barely listened when Olivier tried to speak to her. During the tests, she paid attention only to Cardiff, who used every lighting trick in his considerable repertoire. Marilyn's behavior and appearance bewildered Olivier. He had no knowledge of her upset over Logan's perceived betrayal. He was unaware of all that Lee Strasberg had done in advance to plant the seeds of distrust. He was insensitive to the effect that his own remoteness had on her. By and large, Marilyn's only way of communicating with a man was to flirt, or to permit him to baby her. Olivier did neither. By the end of the day, he had begun to wonder whether he had made a terrible mistake in agreeing to work with her. Marilyn, sensitive to the slightest hint of rejection, picked up on his doubts. And that—as Olivier failed to comprehend—made her freeze even more.

The following morning, Olivier watched the tests in a screening room at Pinewood. Whatever Marilyn may have looked like when she arrived for the makeup tests, in front of the camera she had metamorphosed into something entirely different. She lit up. She came alive. In a true feat of acting, she became the gorgeous, enchanting, kinetic girl known as "Marilyn Monroe." All of Olivier's doubts evaporated. Suddenly, he was excited about working with Marilyn again.

On the night of July 24, Terence Rattigan gave a supper-dance in Marilyn's honor at Little Court, his country house in Surrey. The guests included Lady Diana Cooper, Tyrone Power, Sybil Thorndike, Margot Fonteyn, John Gielgud, Peggy Ashcroft, and other luminaries. Though her host would have been unaware of this, it was the American ambassador, Winthrop Aldrich, who would have been of greatest interest to Marilyn. In Washington, D.C., the next day, Congress was to vote on whether to cite Arthur Miller for contempt.

The garden at Little Court was decorated with colorful Chinese paper lanterns. There were white-draped tables and a buffet supper of lobster curry. Later, there would be dancing inside. At the front door,

Rattigan and Olivier greeted the guests, who started to arrive at nine. Vivien Leigh was to have come after the evening's performance *of South Sea Bubble*, but she changed her mind at the last minute when her dress didn't fit. Radie Harris was supposed to be the only journalist in attendance, Olivier having strictly forbidden her to write about the party afterward. Yet when Harris arrived at Little Court, Olivier quietly took her aside.

"Darling," he whispered, "you can write any fucking thing you want. Louella Parsons is here!"

Parsons, wearing a black mantilla, surveyed the crowd from an elevated armchair. Milton Greene, under pressure, had secured an invitation for the powerful Hearst columnist.

It was nearly eleven before the Millers made their entrance. Marilyn wore a low-cut white chiffon gown which had been rejected as one of her costumes in the film. Draped over her shoulders was the now ratty white mink coat she'd worn to announce the "new Marilyn." The center of the large drawing room had been cleared for dancing. Someone put on a recording of "Embraceable You." Marilyn and Arthur floated onto the empty dance floor. As everyone looked on, the Millers danced cheek to cheek and held each other tightly. They were so affectionate that one guest later declared that someone ought to have said, "Look, there's a bedroom upstairs!" On the one hand, Marilyn acted as if no one else were present. On the other, it was as if she were sending a message to the American ambassador. Hours before the vote in Congress, Marilyn's actions demonstrated that she supported her husband fully. Never one who trusted easily, Marilyn had put her faith in Arthur. Who better to trust than a man willing to go to jail rather than betray others? The American public adored Marilyn; there was a chance that they wouldn't tolerate Miller's being punished if she showed how much she loved and needed him.

Arthur was by no means the only one at risk in the vote before Congress. Marilyn was well aware that Spyros Skouras's refusal to intervene could mean that he was prepared to abandon her, or had already done so. So tonight, once again, she risked everything she had worked for and won. For Arthur's sake, Marilyn put her own career in jeopardy. But the language that Marilyn used was not one that the people watching her understood. Her sexuality had always been Marilyn's primary means of communication; it had brought her power over men, and success in Hollywood. That night, it brought her only amused derision. Instead of bravery, people saw no more than a girl's somewhat indiscreet behavior with her new husband.

It was past 4 a.m. when the Millers returned to Parkside House. They remained in the bedroom much of the following day. They had food and the papers sent up. At one point Miller emerged in a white terrycloth bathrobe, only to disappear back inside. If he seemed distracted, there was a good reason. Washington, D.C. was five hours behind London, so the Millers had to wait until late in the day to learn the results of the Congressional vote.

Precisely as Joe Rauh had anticipated, Representative Jackson was the loudest and most articulate voice against Miller. Jackson argued that "moral scruples, no matter how laudable, do not constitute grounds for refusal to answer questions propounded by a duly authorized committee." The California congressman pointed out that HUAC "was investigating charges of passport fraud in connection with forthcoming legislation" and the information they sought from Miller was important.

"Why can't you bring in such legislation without requiring this man to squeal to the committee?" asked Representative Multer of New York.

"Arthur Miller was not subpoenaed for the purpose of squealing to anyone," HUAC's Chairman Walter cut in, "but because of information that he was a Communist associated with Communist activities. The committee is interested in knowing who were participants in the Communist conspiracy."

Representative Yates of Illinois noted that Miller "denied ever being a Communist during the hearing."

"Mr. Miller is not being cited for denying he was a Communist," Jackson retorted, "but for refusing to supply information."

When it was all over, Lloyd Garrison conveyed the results to the Millers. By a vote of 379 to 9, Arthur Miller had been cited for contempt of Congress. The House of Representatives would transmit the citation to the Assistant United States Attorney for investigation and possible prosecution. Joe Rauh, puzzled by Spyros Skouras's refusal to protect Marilyn, expressed confidence that they'd win in court. All of the worry, including Marilyn's, centered on Arthur's fate. Still, though he was her primary concern, she could not forget what the vote might mean for her own career.

Marilyn was hardly in an ideal frame of mind to begin five days of rehearsals on Monday, July 30. Olivier, still under the spell of the tests, arrived at Pinewood Studios with exceedingly high hopes. He had scheduled rehearsals in order to put Marilyn at ease with the cast, and had been working with Sybil Thorndike, Richard Wattis, and Jeremy Spenser in an upstairs rehearsal room for about three quarters of an hour when Marilyn arrived with Paula in tow. Marilyn's lateness was the first strike against her. Her unkempt appearance and withdrawn manner were the second. Paula's presence was the third. Olivier, having been warned by Joshua Logan never to explode, did his best to stay calm. He read Marilyn's appearance as an expression of disdain for the very idea of rehearsal.

When Olivier had agreed to direct The Sleeping Prince, he didn't know that Marilyn would insist on bringing a dramatic coach. Only in the last weeks of pre-production did he discover that Paula was part of the package. For a man of Olivier's ego, the presence of a meddlesome coach would in itself have been bad enough. Worse was that Paula, as the wife of Lee Strasberg, was a reminder of Olivier's painful personal conflict with the Actors Studio style when he had directed the British stage production of A Streetcar Named Desire in 1949. In the end, when the play was filmed, even Vivien Leigh had preferred Kazan's direction to her husband's.

The oddly shaped Mrs. Strasberg, whose hands and legs had remained slender as her torso inflated, threw herself between Marilyn and the director. When Olivier talked, Marilyn would stare uncomprehendingly as though he were speaking in a foreign tongue. Paula, forever buzzing in Marilyn's ear, translated. Olivier had no way of knowing whether he was being accurately interpreted. In the days prior to Paula's arrival, he had had an opportunity to try to connect with Marilyn, but he'd kept his distance. Now, it was too late. With Paula around, there was no getting through to his leading lady. Marilyn was eager to have her coach at her side, but in fact Paula's presence sabotaged any remaining hope that Marilyn would be able to work effectively with Olivier.

Something else was wrong that first day, though Olivier certainly would not have noticed. This was a Marilyn Monroe production. Based on her long-ago talks with Charlie Feldman, Marilyn had initiated the project. She had negotiated with Rattigan. She had won the film rights to The Sleeping Prince. She had brought in Olivier as director, co-star, and co-producer. Presumably the situation was to have been different from any picture in which Marilyn had previously appeared. But from the moment she entered the rehearsal room with Paula Strasberg, it was as if she were working on someone else's film.

There were several reasons for this. The fact that The Sleeping Prince was being made at an English studio with an English cast and crew put Marilyn at a considerable disadvantage. She felt and acted like a guest. To make matters worse, Olivier had done this story before on the stage. He was already at home with the material. He had a set approach to his part and to the play, and seemed to want Marilyn to perform the role as Vivien had done it. Finally, there was his stature as an artist. Marilyn's choice of such a formidable figure to direct and co-star made it much more difficult to think of the project as hers. She longed for Olivier's approval. She hoped to be accepted as his colleague. She dreamed he would take her seriously. At the same time, she was intimidated by Olivier, and that paralyzed her.

Olivier had spent weeks planning the production in anticipation of Marilyn's arrival. He introduced her to the other cast members. He presented the Associate Director and some members of the production staff. He ran through the story. He distributed scripts and read selected scenes aloud. From first to last, it was very much Larry Olivier's show.

On the second day of rehearsals Olivier castigated Marilyn for arriving three quarters of an hour late. The next day, she didn't show up until noon. Her eyes suggested that she'd been popping pills. Was her extreme lateness an act of defiance, or had the scolding made her so upset that she couldn't sleep? Was Marilyn angry at herself for having ceded psychological control to Olivier? The word from Parkside House was that Marilyn had spent the morning rather noisily in bed with her husband.

The Millers were no longer alone at Parkside. Hedda Rosten had arrived from New York with Paula, ostensibly to serve as Marilyn's secretary. But Marilyn and Arthur, still not entirely at ease with each other, seemed eager to have a third party present, and in a way, Hedda was there for Arthur as much as she was for Marilyn. After all, Marilyn had

Paula Strasberg and Milton Greene to serve her various needs. When tensions ran high with Marilyn, Arthur talked to Hedda, an experienced psychiatric social worker. As his former wife's close friend, Hedda provided a link to a world in which Arthur felt comfortable.

At the time Arthur and Marilyn were married, Truman Capote, who knew her well, had predicted that at length the episode might be titled "Death of a Playwright." *The Sleeping Prince* was to be Arthur's first experience of living with Marilyn—and trying to work himself—while she was making a picture. He had never really had to deal with Marilyn's work-related anxieties and sleeplessness. He'd never had to endure the drinking and drug-taking with which she struggled to cope. On *Bus Stop*, he'd only been present at weekends during the last few weeks of filming. And, importantly, he hadn't been under pressure to finish a play as he was now. As he told Kermit Bloomgarden, he wanted *A View from the Bridge* to be vindicated in London. Marilyn was scheduled to begin filming on August 7. Perhaps then, with his demanding new wife out of the house, Miller would have a chance to apply himself to his work.

That morning, Olivier arrived at Pinewood at ten minutes to seven. A great deal was on the line today. Joshua Logan had warned Olivier not to allow Paula on the set, and Milton Greene had guaranteed that Paula would not show her face outside Marilyn's dressing room. By and large, they'd managed to keep Paula in the dressing room throughout *Bus Stop*; why not now? For the first time, Olivier would have an opportunity to deal with Marilyn without the shield provided by Arthur or Paula. If ever the director was to get through to his leading lady, it had better be today. What took place that first day would set the tone for all that was to follow.

Like Olivier, Marilyn was to have been at the studio before seven in order to be dressed and made up. She and Paula did not appear until 8:30. From the outset, it was evident that Paula did not intend to remain in Marilyn's dressing room. Greene's assurances had been hollow; in fact, he had been in no position to promise Olivier anything. Marilyn had stopped listening to him long ago. Yes, Joshua Logan had successfully barred Paula from the set, but *Bus Stop* had been a Twentieth Century–Fox picture. *The Sleeping Prince* was a Marilyn Monroe production, with Jack Warner's participation limited to financing and distribution. In this instance at least, Marilyn used her authority: Paula was going to be on the set and there wasn't a damn thing Olivier could do about it. Of course he could always quit. But he already had too much time and money invested to consider doing that. Logan had warned Olivier to avoid having a temper tantrum with Marilyn; she was quite capable of walking out and not coming back.

It was no longer just a question of Paula's being present to interpret Olivier's instructions. On *Bus Stop*, Paula had been content to operate as a coach; on *The Sleeping Prince*, she appeared to see a larger role for herself. She set herself up as Marilyn's private director. Lee Strasberg had done his best to undermine Olivier in Marilyn's eyes. Before the cameras rolled, Paula's emphatic presence on the set declared Olivier unfit to direct a Method actress. Once before, when he directed *A Streetcar Named Desire*, Olivier had struggled with the palpable off-stage presence of Elia Kazan, Marlon Brando, and all that they represented. Now it was the specter of Lee Strasberg with whom Olivier wrestled daily.

Like a medium at a séance, Paula was constantly communicating mystical messages from the other side. When she told Marilyn, "Honey, just think of Coca-Cola and Frankie Sinatra," presumably it was Lee speaking through her. If Paula's suggestions didn't work, she could always say she had misinterpreted Lee. In this manner, Paula preserved her husband's reputation for infallibility.

That first day, Paula proved adept at keeping Olivier from his leading lady. Though physically awkward, Paula was a master of body language. The moment the camera stopped, she hurtled forward, determined to take possession of Marilyn before the director could. Once there, she stuck close. The conspiratorial whispering seemed never to cease, making it hard for anyone else to approach. Olivier found the situation humiliating. Before long, he felt the urge to kill Paula. Marilyn appeared determined utterly to ignore Olivier. She stared at him blankly, if at all. When the first shot had been completed after eight takes, Marilyn and Paula withdrew to a portable dressing room. They slammed the door for all to hear. Olivier followed.

Even in that limited space, Paula tried to block Olivier's access to Marilyn. This time, however, Olivier was intent on having a chat. But whatever he said behind closed doors evidently had no effect. At the end of the day, lest Olivier try to talk to Marilyn again, Paula ushered her out of the studio before her makeup had been removed.

For all that, Olivier still had reason to hope. He had witnessed Marilyn's breathtaking transformation in the makeup tests. He had seen for himself what she was capable of. Despite all the nonsense on the set so far, he knew she had the capacity to be magical on camera. He knew it was in her power to turn into the luminous "Marilyn" character he had adored in The Seven Year Itch. But how on earth was a director to persuade her to do what she did so well?

Later in the week, Olivier tried a new tack with his leading lady. In full costume as a Carpathian Grand Duke, he stared at her through a monocle as they prepared to shoot a scene.

"All right, Marilyn," said Olivier. "Be sexy."

The remark misfired badly. Marilyn, indignant, ran off the set. Paula accompanied her to the dressing room. Olivier's words may have been ill-chosen, but all he had been asking her to do was to perform the miracle he'd witnessed previously. He wanted her to become "Marilyn." Olivier's remark had been nothing less than his acknowledgment that as an actress, she knew exactly what she was doing.

Marilyn interpreted the incident very differently. She took the words to mean that Olivier had never thought of her as an actress and never would. Suddenly, she was convinced that even on her own production, she was doomed to the same sort of disrespectful treatment she'd once received at Twentieth.

Marilyn called Lee Strasberg in New York. She poured out her anger and upset. Strasberg has to have known that Marilyn would be unable to work effectively in this condition. It was essential that her first independent production be a success; making the film work had to be her priority. At that moment, anyone who sincerely cared about her would have done his best to calm her down. But the incident played into Strasberg's hands, and he turned it to his advantage. Soon, he was as indignant as Marilyn. He was very angry at Olivier. And he would not let the matter drop—not then or later. Strasberg had found a wedge with which to drive Marilyn and her director permanently apart. Even if he guessed what Olivier had really been trying to say, he could never have admitted that to Marilyn; he did not want her to know that some people regarded her best Hollywood performances as acting of a very high order.

Olivier seems not to have realized quite what had happened, but the incident doomed his working relationship with Marilyn. From then on, she abandoned all belief in the transforming power of a role she had worked hard to make her own. It was as though Olivier's remark had torn the veil from Marilyn's eyes. As far as she was concerned, the dream was dead. Whatever she might have hoped, it was now clear that her association with "the greatest actor alive" was not going to change her life. Humiliated, she felt like a fool for ever having imagined that Olivier could take her seriously. Her anger at herself turned outward; after this, Marilyn not only distrusted Olivier, she actively hated him.

More than ever, Marilyn looked forward to Arthur's visits to the set. Her eyes would brighten when she spotted her husband. No matter what she was doing, she would rush into his arms and excitedly wrap herself around him. He was her protector. He was there to get her through all this. She clung to him as if for dear life. Olivier might have been about to film a scene, but he would look on helplessly as the lovebirds disappeared to Marilyn's dressing room, usually for about ten minutes. After that, it was said, Marilyn would return to the set visibly refreshed.

Nonetheless, when it became evident that Greene was virtually powerless to influence Marilyn or to do anything about the Paula situation, Olivier, overcoming his initial irritation, turned to Miller. Marilyn trusted Arthur and hung on his every word. Perhaps he could help to get her to the studio on time. Olivier calculated that it was certainly in Miller's interest to do so. Marilyn's own company lost money every time she was late or held up the production in some other way. The money came out of Marilyn's pocket—not Warner Bros.', as Miller seemed to think until Greene enlightened him. And her latenesses meant less time and solitude for Miller to work. It was no secret that Arthur was under intense pressure to get those revisions to Binkie Beaumont, a close friend of the Oliviers.

After the first week of filming, Vivien was due to join her husband at Notley Abbey after finishing her commitment to *South Sea Bubble*. She was five months pregnant. Following her farewell performance, she went to a cast party in her honor, then drove out to the country late on Saturday night. On Sunday mornings, the village church bells in Chearsley, Haddenham, and Long Crendon could be heard throughout the house. Vivien invited a group of friends for tea that day, including the dancer Robert Helpmann, the costume designer Bumble Dawson, and Terence Rattigan. There was talk of a party which Rattigan planned to give at Little Court on August 18, before he left for America. Vivien, who'd missed his last party, was eager to attend. In a naughty mood, Vivien asked Colin Clark how things were going with Marilyn. She was pleased when Clark rolled his eyes. Aware of what Larry's feelings for Marilyn had been, she took malicious pleasure in all the trouble Marilyn gave him now. In high spirits, Vivien could not bear to see the party break up. She kept her guests late. After they all left, she felt unwell. While Vivien was waiting for the doctor, she miscarried. The baby, it turned out, had been a boy.

After the miscarriage, Binkie Beaumont visited Vivien at Notley Abbey. He found her state of mind to be precarious. Once again, she was perilously unable to sleep. Her husband, who believed that her madness had started after she miscarried the first time, had reason to fear that history was about to repeat itself. He released a statement to the press. "We are bitterly disappointed and terribly upset. The main concern now is Vivien. The important thing is that she should make a complete recovery." On the morning of Monday, August 13, Olivier was made up, costumed, and at work on the set long before Marilyn appeared.

Filming went no more smoothly than it had the previous week. Yet again, Marilyn appeared to panic whenever it was time to leave the cocoon of her dressing room. Utterly distraught, she would clutch at any excuse to linger. Instead of getting better as the years passed, her fear of going in front of the camera had intensified. Yet again, on the set Marilyn forgot her lines and huddled with Paula. She repeatedly disappeared to confer by telephone with Lee Strasberg in New York.

By the second week, it was evident that each side, Olivier and Monroe, misperceived the other. Olivier entirely misread Marilyn's anxiety. As far as he was concerned, anyone who dared to behave as Marilyn did with Paula could hardly be afraid. Without insight into the terrors that drove her, he assumed she was merely being rude and disruptive. Marilyn, for her part, mistook Olivier for a man who was serenely in control of his world, when in fact he had a mad wife and a tormented personal life. Marilyn had no idea of what Paula represented to Olivier. She knew nothing of his psychological battle with Kazan and the Actors Studio, and she remained blind to the extent to which she was being manipulated by Lee and Paula. It was in the Strasbergs' interest for Marilyn to believe that Olivier was patronizing her.

Night after night, Marilyn vented her fury at home. She was constantly screaming about Olivier. Her long telephone conversations with Lee only made her angrier. A woman in crisis, she kept Arthur awake much of the night. The only way Marilyn could finally get to sleep was to drug herself into oblivion. Miller, accustomed to working in calm isolation, suddenly found himself in the middle of a great storm. It was as though the Tom Ewell character in The Seven Year Itch had married "the girl" only to discover that sex was perilous, after all. In fact, Marilyn was tormented and intensely needy. She had a violent temper and expected Arthur to share her indignation, as Joe had done. She interpreted any disagreement as a betrayal. Aware that Arthur had never seen her quite like this before, Marilyn was constantly on guard for the moment when he would pull back in disappointment and disgust. Conscious that she was no longer playing an innocent, she wanted him to love her for who she really was. That meant Arthur would have to accept, even love, what Marilyn described as the monster in her.

It seemed that things could not possibly get worse, but by the end of the second week they had. Marilyn, searching for a copy of her script, wandered into the music room. Her husband wasn't there. She saw the script of The Sleeping Prince on Arthur's desk, with one of his notebooks lying open beside it. Like Pandora, Marilyn was unable to resist. The notebook entry, in Arthur's hand, concerned her.

For a long time, it had been Miller's custom to jot down random impressions, ideas for plays, lists of possible titles, snippets of dialogue, and even drafts of entire scenes. Sometimes, he wrote in the third person about a character named "Miller." At least in this context, he was interested in other people less for themselves than for the conflicts they generated in him, conflicts that might provide the germ of a play. When Arthur was with his first wife, he had stockpiled his thoughts on marriage to a difficult, demanding woman. He had meditated on adultery and a husband's search for ecstasy. Now that he was with Marilyn, he continued to take notes.

Marilyn was shattered. She reported to Lee Strasberg that in the notebook entry, Arthur had expressed his disappointment in her. According to Marilyn, Arthur wrote that he had believed she was an angel but now he realized he'd been wrong. She had turned out to be different from his fantasy, and she was convinced that he was sorry he'd married her.

It is important to understand why Marilyn responded to this discovery in catastrophic terms. As Miller himself later recognized, she lived
with the expectation of being abandoned. Early on, life had taught her to
anticipate rejection. There were her father, her mother, and all the others
who for one reason or another couldn't or wouldn't keep her. Her mother,
according to Marilyn, had done more than just walk away; she'd actually
tried to kill her. Perhaps it was inevitable that the child would ask why
she had been abandoned so often. Perhaps it was inevitable that she
would conclude it was something in her that drove people away. Is it any
wonder her sense of self-worth was so fragile? This would explain
Marilyn's lifelong terror of criticism. To have even her slightest flaws
pointed out suggested that the familiar process of discovery and abandonment had begun. And it would explain why Marilyn reacted so
strongly to Miller's notebook. She feared that he had begun to perceive
her unworthiness. She feared he was on to who she really was. She feared
he was about to leave her.

On the night of Saturday, August 18, the Millers drove to Little
Court for the second Rattigan party. This time, the host greeted them at
the door alone. Olivier remained at Notley Abbey with Vivien. The
Millers seemed like a different couple tonight. There were rumors of discord at Parkside House, though at this point no one yet knew how badly
things had spun out of control. Arthur was handsome in a white dinner
jacket, Marilyn oddly disheveled. Colin Clark later noted in his diary that
Marilyn actually seemed a bit frightened of her husband. That was a far
cry from the impression she had given last time.

Back then, Marilyn had been certain that in Arthur she had
finally found someone who loved her. Confident in his feelings, she had
dared to feel worthy of being loved. But the discovery of the notebook
changed all that forever. Suddenly, Marilyn was convinced that he would
abandon her as all the others had done. After this, she would never feel
safe in Arthur's love again.

On Friday, August 24, Arthur Miller announced that he had decided to interrupt his honeymoon and fly to the United States "to see my children." He planned to leave on Sunday night. He did not anticipate any trouble at home. Assistant United States Attorney William Hitz, who handled contempt cases in Washington, had been out all summer on sick leave and vacation. Miller's file had been placed on Hitz's desk along with several others. Hitz was not due back at work until the second week in September. It was unlikely that anything would happen until then. Meanwhile, Miller planned to visit Jane and Robert for about ten days, then return to England.

For Marilyn, the announcement could not have come at a worse time. One week after she discovered the devastating entry in Arthur's notebook, his decision to go home can only have confirmed her worst fears of abandonment. It wouldn't be the first time he had chosen his family over Marilyn. Once before, in New York in 1951, Arthur, having decided to leave his wife, had abruptly changed his mind and gone back to Mary and the children. Marilyn was left alone in a Manhattan hotel room to be comforted by Elia Kazan.

On Friday afternoon, Miller appeared at Pinewood Studios to collect Marilyn. Things had been tense at Parkside House all week. In the past, when Arthur arrived on the set, he and Marilyn couldn't wait to be alone together. That was far from the case today. Instead of going home with Marilyn, Arthur decided to remain behind. It was a most unusual thing for him to do. Marilyn left with Paula Strasberg and other members of her entourage. Miller accepted an invitation to join Laurence Olivier and Milton Greene for a drink in Olivier's dressing room.

Olivier was at wit's end as the third calamitous week of filming drew to a close. He was having trouble at work with Marilyn and at home with Vivien. Now he had two sleepless, mad women to contend with, though he loathed one and loved the other. He jestingly announced that he planned to leave for China. Greene, increasingly disillusioned by what it meant to be a partner in Marilyn Monroe Productions, laughed that he'd join him there. Arthur chimed in that he'd like to come, too. Olivier, surprised that Miller would say such a thing, reminded the man of his new wife. Miller declared she was devouring him.

In making that remark, Miller was clearly trying to distance himself from Marilyn. And he went considerably beyond merely sympathizing with Olivier about Marilyn's behavior on the film. Miller was actually complaining to her director about Marilyn's behavior at home.

That once again Miller was thinking of himself in the role of the betrayer is suggested by the way he rewrote A View from the Bridge in this period. There was a noticeable softening in the play's attitude to Eddie Carbone. Instead of merely condemning the betrayer as in the earlier version, the two-act View sought to understand, even to love him. In part, this was probably a response to Eric Bentley's criticism that the original was preachy and melodramatic. But it may also have reflected the playwright's changing attitude to his new wife. Marilyn demanded that in her conflict with Olivier, Arthur take her side completely and unquestioningly. That, more and more, he was unable to do. In the past, when Miller identified with the betrayer, it had been in terms of his actions to Mary. Now for the first time, it was Marilyn he found himself turning against. This was the personal conflict that preoccupied Miller as he revised View; is it any wonder he had new sympathy for Eddie?

As it happened, Arthur did not leave on Sunday, but postponed his trip until Thursday, August 30. Before returning to America, he planned to stop in Paris to see Yves Montand and his wife, Simone Signoret, who were filming an adaptation of The Crucible with a screenplay by Jean-Paul Sartre. The Montands had appeared as John and Elizabeth Proctor in the highly successful French stage production. Meanwhile, Parkside House rocked with the Millers' quarrels. Marilyn roamed the corridors of the enormous house, her drugged trance leading Olivier to compare her to Ophelia.

On Monday, Marilyn stayed away from work altogether. She

reported to the studio on Tuesday in a barbiturate blur. Late that night, Greene had to be summoned to bring more pills to Parkside House. She and Miller had been fighting, and eventually the husband just seemed to withdraw. Finally, over the telephone, Marilyn's psychiatrist in New York was able to soothe her sufficiently to let the sedatives work and send her to sleep.

Marilyn didn't show up at the studio again on Thursday. Instead, she saw Arthur off at the airport. The next day, Milton Greene telephoned Irving Stein in New York to report that Marilyn was pregnant. A gynecologist visiting Parkside House confirmed the pregnancy. Fearful she was going to lose her baby, Marilyn began to drink heavily, liberally supplementing champagne with tranquilizers. Hedda Rosten sat with her. Three sheets to the wind, Marilyn grew maudlin. She wept that she simply had to complete *The Sleeping Prince*.

Marilyn called Arthur in New York and they talked for hours. Olivier, worried that his leading lady might not be able to finish, had a business associate check his insurance policy in the event that the production had to be shut down. Miller wasn't due back in London until September 12, but he returned suddenly on Wednesday the 5th, only six days after he had left. By Saturday, word was out that Marilyn had miscarried.

She would be in no physical or mental condition to go back to work until the middle of the week. *The Sleeping Prince* seemed hardly to matter to her anymore. Marilyn had never recovered from the moment when Olivier urged her to "be sexy." From then on, her hopes for the film had died. But Marilyn's attitude to her marriage was a very different story. She was utterly determined to keep that dream alive. It was clear that the notebook entry, followed by Arthur's departure, had terrified her. She could not bear the thought that she might really lose him. When Arthur returned from America, Marilyn intended to hold onto him. She would do whatever it took to prove herself worthy of his love.

Despite her condition, Marilyn insisted that she drive to London with Arthur on Sunday. She might not be well enough to return to work, but this was something she had to do for her husband. There was a problem with *A View from the Bridge*, and Marilyn was in a unique position to help. The Lord Chamberlain, taking objection to the notorious scene in which Eddie kisses Rodolpho full on the lips, had refused Binkie

Beaumont a permit for public performances at the Comedy Theater. The censor of plays demanded that the scene be cut.

Instead, Beaumont had decided to stage the play under the auspices of the newly constituted New Watergate Theater Club. The censor had no authority over private theater clubs. In order to see *View*, one had to join Beaumont's club at least forty-eight hours before the performance one wanted to attend. There was a small membership fee (which Binkie happily pocketed) and one had to be certified by another member as not "undesirable." Eager to sign up as many members in advance as possible, Beaumont invited reporters to what was billed as the club's "first meeting," its principal attraction being an appearance by Marilyn Monroe.

On Sunday night, Marilyn looked wan as she arrived at the Comedy with Arthur Miller. They were met by a crowd of photographers. Inside the theater, Marilyn made much ado of paying her membership fee. Her husband certified that she was not "undesirable." The publicity that followed Marilyn everywhere benefited ticket sales immeasurably. As a result of all the press coverage, Binkie Beaumont had to assign nine extra assistants to handle the torrent of mail. In the end, they signed up about thirteen thousand members. Miller exulted about the heavy advance ticket sales to Kermit Bloomgarden, neglecting to point out that Marilyn might have had anything to do with it.

Kermit Bloomgarden hadn't had a chance to see Miller during his brief stay in New York, but the producer and the playwright had talked on the phone. Upon Miller's return, Bloomgarden telegraphed inviting Marilyn to appear on Broadway as Athena in Paul Osborn's *Maiden Voyage*. Soon, a copy of *Maiden Voyage* followed. Osborn was the commercially successful author of such plays as *The Vinegar Tree* and *Point of No Return*. Bloomgarden was careful to say he didn't want Marilyn simply for her name but because he was sure she would be terrific in the role.

Miller declined on Marilyn's behalf. He made a point of reaffirming his belief that Marilyn was going to be a great stage star, but as far as he was concerned, making her theatrical debut in Paul Osborn's play was simply out of the question. He noted that Marilyn was exhausted and couldn't possibly work that winter. As soon as she completed *The Sleeping Prince*, the Millers wanted to go home and settle down. Arthur had reached a point where he believed that only when the film was in the can could their life together really begin. Marilyn's first independent production, once the object of such high hopes, had turned into something merely to be endured and put behind them.

Miller threw himself into the final casting of A View from the Bridge. That allowed him to spend much of his time in London. Peter Brook, who had directed Olivier in Titus Andronicus, began rehearsals of View on September 17. Miller attended, he said, in order to be certain that the line for each character was clear. When the director had the play all blocked out, Miller promised to leave him alone for a few days.

Olivier was annoyed by Miller's failure to take Marilyn in hand. The director could hardly overlook the fact that she had been well enough to publicize Miller's play, but not to work on her own film. Marilyn had returned to work seemingly enraged at everyone but Paula and Hedda. In her dressing room that morning, Marilyn spiked her tea with gin and grew furious when Greene tried to weaken it.

The ability to supply drugs seemed to be the only power Greene still had over Marilyn. He gave her uppers to counter the barbiturates she took in large quantities at night. When sleeping pills didn't work quickly, Marilyn took more, often forgetting how many she had already swallowed. It was a dangerous game. She tended to be groggy the next day, and needed to be jolted awake.

In England, uppers were a different color from those Marilyn was accustomed to, and she angrily accused Greene of giving her the wrong pills. Above all, Marilyn didn't want spansules, which had a time release. She wanted the speed to kick in immediately. Greene arranged for a doctor in New York to ship Dexamyl in little packages, each containing about a dozen pills. Often the uppers made Marilyn so edgy that she required a tranquilizer during the day. Eventually the vicious circle of uppers and downers left her scarcely able to function.

By this point, Marilyn was convinced that Olivier was trying to destroy her performance. Lee Strasberg, who called collect most nights, encouraged her to believe that Olivier was jealous of her. As far as Marilyn was concerned, Olivier was competing rather than working with her. She sensed he was photographing their scenes to his advantage. Maybe he was. Olivier was known to be vain, declaring on one occasion after seeing William Wyler's Wuthering Heights, "I was so beautiful, I could go down on myself!"

Paula was now openly at odds with Olivier. It wasn't just his directing that she criticized; she belittled his acting as well. For all to hear, Paula confidently informed Olivier that his performance was "artificial." Olivier stifled his rage on the set. He was famous for what Peter O'Toole once called "that gray-eyed myopic stare that can turn you to stone." It seemed to have no such effect on Paula.

When Olivier awakened at Notley Abbey on the morning of Wednesday, October 3, he knew that he faced an exceedingly long day. Due at the studio by seven, in the evening he was expected to accompany Vivien to London to see the Bolshoi Ballet at Covent Garden. Lady Olivier was in a mood to do and see everything. Binkie Beaumont had taken her to Portofino, but she returned early because she missed her husband. Even though Olivier was working, she wanted to entertain and go out until all hours. She had little sympathy for her husband's fatigue. She didn't care about his problems on the film. Smoking and drinking too much, staying up late, playing loud music, Vivien showed signs of having entered the manic phase.

This morning, two pieces of bad news reached Olivier in his dressing room. The first was hardly a surprise. Marilyn planned to stay home today. The second bit of information, however, was entirely unexpected. Lee Strasberg, having arrived in London one day previously, was on his way to Pinewood. From now on, he intended to be present on the set along with Paula to oversee Marilyn's performance.

Olivier went berserk. He wanted the studio security force to prevent Strasberg from setting foot on the lot. Paula—or "the beast," as Olivier privately called her—had been bad enough. Under no circumstances was Olivier willing to consider the idea of Lee Strasberg's participation. Finally, it was Milton Greene who was sent to head off Strasberg at the main gate. At their previous encounter, in July, Strasberg had given a perfectly disgraceful performance. But he'd had the upper hand, and Greene had been forced to pay Paula an exorbitant salary. Strasberg had been tough and aggressive then. He hadn't been bashful about making threats.

He seemed to be a changed man today. When Greene notified Strasberg that Olivier refused to see him, he hardly put up a fight. He could have insisted. He could have bullied. He could have threatened. He could have complained to Marilyn who, as a full partner in the production, had the authority to demand that he be permitted on the set. Yet Strasberg did none of these things. Instead, he left quietly. Why?

Marilyn, popping pills and drinking heavily, was in dreadful shape. It was one thing to have heard about all this on the phone. It was quite another to have seen for himself, as he had already done. If Strasberg remained, he would be expected to take action rather than to criticize Olivier from afar. Instead of merely pontificating, he would have to produce results. If matters did not improve while Strasberg was there, Marilyn might see how ineffectual he really was.

When Greene went back in to report to Olivier, Strasberg realized that he had no way of getting out of there. In anticipation of a lengthy session with Olivier, he'd sent his car away. Now he had to wait outside the gate for an agonizingly long time until the car returned.

But even Olivier's insult to Strasberg could not deter Marilyn from her determination to prove her own value to Arthur, as Olivier saw the very next evening. For Arthur's sake, Marilyn and Olivier temporarily buried the hatchet. On October 11, the Millers, the Oliviers, and the Jack Cardiffs attended the black-tie premiere of A View from the Bridge together. Binkie Beaumont, thrilled by the potential for publicity, had rented a Daimler to deliver them to the theater. From Olivier's point of view, being photographed with Marilyn in public might counter rumors of dissension on the set—rumors that, in the end, could prove damaging at the box office. Whatever Marilyn may have thought, Olivier very much wanted the film to succeed.

The three couples gathered for drinks at Lowndes Cottage in Belgravia. On arriving there, Marilyn went upstairs to change. Arthur busied himself with a platter of raw oysters on the mantelpiece. Olivier and Cardiff were discussing a small Daubigny landscape displayed at the end of the huge drawing room when suddenly they heard Miller emit a resounding whoop.

"Attagirl," Miller cheered.

Marilyn, wearing an off-the-shoulder, red satin sheath, slowly descended the staircase. Olivier was astonished. Intent on giving Arthur exactly what he needed, she had turned herself into "Marilyn Monroe"—something Olivier had been struggling to get her to do for weeks. Marilyn was doing everything she could to win Arthur's approval again.

"Why shouldn't she show off her God-given attributes?" Arthur declared. "Why should she have to dress like her maiden aunt?"

Husband Number Three's reaction to her dress couldn't have

been more different from what Joe DiMaggio's undoubtedly would have been. But Miller had a play opening tonight and Marilyn was certain to attract a good deal of press attention. Miller did not think highly of the English audience. He told Kermit Bloomgarden that the English tended to make hits out of the worst junk. Even when a serious play opened to fine reviews, Miller complained, English theatergoers usually avoided it, preferring the likes of *South Sea Bubble*. So Marilyn's help was very much welcome.

As the Daimler pulled up in front of the Comedy Theater, fans broke through police lines to get to Marilyn. Critics and audience in evening dress were pushed aside as the crowd fought for a better look. In the stalls, people stared unabashedly at Marilyn, who sat between her husband and Olivier.

Later, when the curtain came down, the Millers, holding hands, took a bow. Though there were a few snide remarks that the applause was more for Marilyn's red dress than for the play, in fact the premiere was a success. The reviews were excellent and Miller had his first hit in a long time.

"Nobody familiar with *The Crucible* or with Mr. Miller's recent political troubles could doubt his hatred of informers," wrote Kenneth Tynan in the *Observer*, "but art, in this instance, tempers hatred with charity. Eddie dies unforgiven, but not unpitied. The curtain falls, as in tragedy it should, on a great unanswered question: for this man what other way was possible?"

When Paula insisted that Marilyn Monroe Productions pay for her to fly to New York for a week to ten days, the demand could have been construed as retaliation for Olivier's failure to welcome Lee. Hedda Rosten had already gone home in order to be present when her daughter Patricia went back to school. In Paula's absence, Dr. Margaret Hohenberg flew to London to be with her patient. The very substitution highlighted the peculiar role Paula played in Marilyn's life. Suddenly, Marilyn and Olivier began to get along much better, suggesting how different things might have been without the influence of the Strasbergs. Soon, Paula called hysterically from America to report that her English work permit had expired and that someone seemed to have influenced the authorities not to allow her to return.

Marilyn, convinced that Laurence Olivier and Milton Greene

were responsible, went into a tailspin. She vowed to walk out if Paula didn't get a work permit immediately. At this point, Marilyn had no compunction about abandoning the picture. Olivier vehemently denied that he was behind Paula's problems. So did Greene. Yet no sooner did Olivier intervene than a work permit was issued.

Olivier regarded Paula's return on October 31 as the final blow. That day he arrived at the studio after Marilyn and her dramatic coach. Informed that Marilyn was waiting, Olivier, utterly dispirited, replied, "Fuck her." As far as he was concerned, The Sleeping Prince was already ruined. All the things that Olivier had hoped Marilyn would provide— money, glamor, an opportunity to feel young and to reinvent himself— were obviously not going to materialize.

Miller, too, believed that he and Marilyn had failed to transform each other's lives as he'd once hoped. That sense of failure had come with astonishing rapidity. A mere five months had passed since he had divorced Mary. Already, Miller was telling himself that he and Marilyn were worse off than they'd been before. He was tormented by the feeling that somehow they had misled each other.

Probably it was a desire to turn back the clock to a more hopeful time that guided Miller's thoughts back to Nevada. In the music room at Parkside House, Miller started a short story based on an experience he'd had while waiting to file for divorce and to begin a new life with Marilyn. In Nevada he had spent time with two cowboys who hunted wild horses. "The Misfits," as the short story would be called, seems to have begun in a wish to eradicate the ghastly nightmare of Miller's life with Marilyn in England and to start over again.

Miller was at work in the music room when a policeman summoned him to appear at the British Foreign Office immediately. There he was questioned about his plans. The film would soon be finished. Did he intend to return to the United States? As Miller knew, Assistant United States Attorney William Hitz, back on the job, was then contemplating presenting his case for contempt to a grand jury. Joe Rauh was working to avert that by arguing that the questions HUAC had asked Miller had not been relevant to the purpose of the hearing.

Miller, who had just had a success on the London stage, would hardly have been the first American artist to resettle in England during the McCarthy era. Obviously, the U.S. government was eager to know his—and Marilyn Monroe's—plans. And the British authorities wanted to avoid being put in an awkward position should Miller be indicted and refuse to return. Miller informed the Foreign Office that he intended to go home.

On November 20, the Oliviers saw the Millers off at the airport, it having been decided that they must all put on a good face in public. Each of their lives had changed dramatically since the last time they were here together. Vivien Leigh had lost her baby and, as it happened, a chance to save her marriage. Laurence Olivier had missed an opportunity for the personal renaissance he'd hoped to achieve before turning fifty. Arthur Miller had realized that life with Marilyn Monroe was going to be unlike anything he had imagined. He had arrived in England believing in the fantasy of "the girl." He was going home with the knowledge that Marilyn was very different from the sweet, angelic, innocent creature he thought he had married. Marilyn, still reeling from the discovery of Arthur's notebook, had reason to believe that both her marriage and her first independent film were already failures.

Her suspicions about *The Sleeping Prince* were confirmed several weeks later in New York. Olivier brought a cut to America to show Jack Warner and there was a good deal of nervousness that the picture was intolerably slow and not particularly funny. (The reviews later said much the same thing.) It's a safe bet that Charlie Feldman, had he bought the rights, would have made sure that *The Sleeping Prince* was filmed as a sharp, sexy, fast-paced, modern comedy. He would have guaranteed that Laurence Olivier and Marilyn Monroe came across as, in Joshua Logan's words, "the most exciting combination since black and white."

Warner Bros., with an eye on ticket sales, insisted on changing the title to *The Prince and the Showgirl*. It was the studio's thinking that Marilyn, the box-office draw, had to be represented in the title. Milton Greene, perhaps realizing too late the sort of the film they should have made, decided to shoot a publicity poster that would show Larry and Marilyn in a steamy embrace. The image, or anything even remotely like it, might appear nowhere in the film, but it wouldn't hurt to hint that it did. Images of a stiff, stodgy Olivier, with heavy makeup, plastered-down hair, and a monocle, were unlikely to draw people in to movie theaters. When Greene proposed a stills session, Olivier initially declined. He hoped to pass through New York without seeing Marilyn. The idea of being in a room with her horrified him. But he did very much want the picture to make money. After a bit of prodding, he warily accepted.

Lush music filled the immense photography studio on Lexington Avenue in the East Forties. Greene was in his element here as he had never been on a film set. As a portrait photographer, he was famous for an ability to put people in the mood. There were caviar sandwiches. The liquor flowed freely. Marilyn, on best behavior, appeared in a floor-length brown dress encrusted with glittering sequins, with a plunging halter top and no back. It was the costume she had worn on December 18 to the premiere of Elia Kazan's *Baby Doll*, a benefit for the Actors Studio.

Not so long ago it had been Marilyn Monroe, white skirt flying up to her shoulders, whose image loomed over New York City. Now it was Carroll Baker, blonde and sensual, who hovered above Broadway. In an eye-catching billboard, Baby Doll Meighan, lying in a crib, sucked her thumb provocatively. For Marilyn, the image was a painful reminder of a missed opportunity. Baker had the hottest film role around, while Marilyn was about to open in the less-than-exciting *Prince and the Showgirl*.

That day in Greene's studio, Marilyn posed against a black backdrop. She gave the illusion of being filled with desire for Olivier. She parted her moist, crimson lips. She shut her eyes. She threw back her head to permit Larry, in a black silk dressing gown, to nuzzle her bare right shoulder. She compelled him to respond strongly. He closed his eyes, he squeezed Marilyn's hand, he gripped her waist tightly. The stills session was a huge success, the poster generating more electricity than all of their scenes together in the film combined. Perhaps it would fool the public; but it didn't fool Marilyn. To her, being sexy was never what *The Sleeping Prince* had been about.

+   +   +

On February 18, 1957, a federal grand jury indicted Arthur Miller on two counts of contempt of Congress. Each count was punishable by up to one year of prison and a $1,000 fine. Joe Rauh and Lloyd Garrison planned to argue that the questions Miller had refused to answer had nothing to do with the hearing's stated purpose. HUAC was supposed to be investigating passport abuse. Miller, the lawyers insisted, should never have been asked to name names in the first place. Rauh and Garrison were confident of winning the case. Still, as Garrison told the Attorney General, whatever the outcome the indictment would do Miller irreparable harm.

The Millers had returned to America intent on settling down. To Arthur that meant being able to write. In England, Marilyn's problems had drained his energies. He was often up half the night. He had revised *A View from the Bridge* in extremely stressful circumstances. Kermit Bloomgarden, eager to have a new play for the fall, expressed the wish that Miller would be able to calm down enough to plunge into his own work.

In England, Marilyn's belief in her own ability to become a serious actress had been badly shaken, if not destroyed. *The Sleeping Prince* seemed to have killed something in her. She was no longer confident of finding salvation through her work. She no longer felt certain that things were going to change because of her new contract. She'd pinned her hopes on the success of her first independent production, yet in the end the experience had left her feeling utterly defeated.

Marilyn, having lost one dream, was terrified of losing her marriage as well. In New York, she did everything possible to be certain that did not happen. Intent on disproving Arthur's sense that their life together was worse than it had been before, Marilyn threw herself into creating what she thought of as the ideal life for him. She put her own needs aside. She struggled to be, as one of Miller's lawyers fondly called her, "Mrs. Arthur." She would create a perfect home. She would make it possible for her husband to write. She would be at his side throughout his political troubles. And above all, she would give him a baby. Marilyn began treatments at Doctors Hospital in order to allow her to carry a baby to term.

Though she certainly didn't care to return to work right now, Marilyn owed Twentieth Century–Fox three films on her four-picture deal. In December 1956, the studio had paid the second $75,000 installment for the screen rights to *Horns of the Devil*. The money enabled Marilyn to take some time off, as Miller told Bloomgarden she very much needed to do. Still, the payment was a reminder that her second contract year commenced on December 31. Any time after that, Twentieth had the right to ask her to start a film.

The studio came up with the idea of putting Marilyn in a remake of *The Blue Angel* with Spencer Tracy as the obsessed Professor Unrat.

Marilyn would play the seductive, unscrupulous Lola Lola. Tracy agreed in principle, but there was a scheduling problem because of difficulties in completing *The Old Man and the Sea*. The need to postpone *The Blue Angel* on Tracy's account played right into Marilyn's hands.

Meanwhile, she decorated a new apartment at 444 East 57th Street, Arthur having sold the Roxbury farmhouse. She set up a cozy writing room off the living room, and furnished it with a desk, bookshelves, and a sofa. Jack Cardiff's black-and-white portrait of Marilyn as a windswept Renoir girl, Arthur's favorite picture of her, adorned the wall. Cardiff had photographed her through a Vaseline-smeared glass. Marilyn tiptoed about the white-carpeted, mirror-filled MGM film set of an apartment solemnly warning the servants not to make noise while Mr. Miller was at work. Arthur told Joe Rauh how pleased he was to be back in the business of writing.

Once he was indicted, however, inevitably the case stole the playwright's time and sapped his brainpower. That, in part, is what Lloyd Garrison meant when he said that, win or lose, the damage would be irreparable. A good deal of preparation for the trial was required, which of course meant huge legal bills. On March 1, Miller was arraigned before Judge Charles F. McLaughlin in Washington, D.C. He pleaded not guilty and a May trial date was set. He was released in Rauh's custody until he could post a $1,000 bond.

The waiting period was hardly a tranquil one. Marilyn, eager to turn her affairs over to Arthur and his associates, had gone to war against Milton Greene. In England, Greene had had reason to believe that his days with Marilyn Monroe Productions were numbered. Certainly he had outlived his usefulness. In New York, Marilyn announced that she was severing all ties with him. She accused him of mismanaging her company and said she had expected more of him. She declared that they had been at odds for a year and a half.

Greene, who had once engineered her break with Charlie Feldman, now found himself in Feldman's position. Like Feldman, Greene had worked hard to advance Marilyn's career, only to be banished before he could profit. Like Feldman, Greene had become the object of Marilyn's anger, resentment, and derision. Ironically, at this very moment, Feldman was badgering Marilyn to be repaid the money he had advanced for *Horns of the Devil*.

Asked about the breakup and about Marilyn's unflattering remarks, Greene exercised restraint. "It seems Marilyn doesn't want to go ahead with the program we planned," Greene declared. "I'm getting lawyers to represent me. I don't want to do anything now to hurt her career, but I did devote about a year and a half exclusively to her. I practically gave up photography. You can't just make a contract with someone and then forget it."

He wanted $100,000 to end the partnership. The sum was hardly excessive, Greene having financed Marilyn for a year before she signed her new studio contract. Marilyn returned his investment. In one fell swoop, Greene, Irving Stein, and their accountant were removed from the board of Marilyn Monroe Productions. Marilyn replaced them with George Kupchick, George Levine, and Robert H. Montgomery, Jr.— respectively Arthur's brother-in-law, Arthur's boyhood friend, and an attorney at the law firm Arthur used in New York.

Marilyn also broke with the psychiatrist Greene had recommended. Margaret Hohenberg was replaced by Dr. Marianne Kris. Dr. Ernst Kris, her recently deceased husband, had been the writing partner of Rudolph Loewenstein, Arthur's former psychoanalyst. Marianne Kris was the daughter of Sigmund Freud's great friend Oscar Ries. Freud called her his adopted daughter, and all her life she remained close to his real daughter, Anna. Conveniently, Dr. Kris's office was in the same Central Park West building where the Strasbergs lived. An elevator carried Marilyn from her psychoanalytical sessions to private acting lessons upstairs.

She continued to take treatments at Doctors Hospital. As Arthur's trial date approached, Marilyn learned that she was pregnant. Euphoric, she seemed to put out of her thoughts the physician's warning that she might have an ectopic pregnancy, in which the fertilized ovum develops outside the uterus. It seemed to Olie Rauh, the attorney's wife, that Marilyn regarded having a baby as the most important thing in her life.

On May 13, the day before the trial, Marilyn accompanied Arthur to Washington, D.C. She insisted on going with him this time. In order to avoid a circus, it was agreed that Marilyn would steer clear of the courthouse. Miller, fearful that Marilyn would be mobbed at a hotel, asked to stay at the Rauhs' Appleton Street home. Marilyn remained with Olie during the day while Arthur and Joe were in court. They hoped to keep Marilyn's presence there a secret for as long as possible.

The Rauhs hadn't met Marilyn before, but Joe Rauh had talked briefly to her on the phone when Arthur was out. From first to last she had taken an active interest in the case. When the lawyers prepared a public statement about the indictment, Marilyn as well as Arthur had reviewed the text. In Washington, she barraged the Rauhs with questions. At night, she studied transcripts of the proceedings, which were delivered to the house every evening around dinnertime.

During the day, Marilyn would not leave the house in case Arthur called or showed up suddenly. Marilyn was there to support Arthur, and she craved an intense emotional connection. His tendency to close himself off when in crisis made her feel like a rejected wife.

By Miller's own account, he had difficulty showing weakness to women. Perhaps he inherited that from Isadore Miller, who had always preferred to keep his troubles bottled up inside. As a boy, Arthur had regarded his father's stoic refusal to disclose bad news as a sign of strength. But Marilyn was frightened by Arthur's inability to share his troubles with her. Sensing her fear, Arthur found himself apologizing to her for the first time.

On the first day of the trial, Federal District Court overflowed with reporters; it had been rumored that Marilyn Monroe was to appear. During a break, Miller explained her absence to the disappointed press corps. "I think we should keep the issue where it is." Many fewer journalists attended in the days that followed.

The trial lasted six days. There was no jury, since Judge McLaughlin had determined that the case hinged on a point of law which was strictly for the courts to decide. Rauh argued that the identity of those present at the 1947 Communist writers' meetings was not pertinent to the topic of passport abuse. Assistant United States Attorney William Hitz contended that it had been necessary to ask Miller for those names in order to assess his credibility. Miller did not testify. He sat silently in a green leather swivel chair at the defense table. But his demeanor differed from what it had been at HUAC. Then Miller had been low-key and respectful. Now he let his anger show. During the testimony, he bent over a legal pad to draw caricatures of the government witnesses. When Richard Arens took the stand, Miller's dancing pencil depicted the committee counsel as a scowling vaudeville villain. Sketched in full view of reporters, this appeared to be Miller's comment on the proceedings.

It was only a matter of time before the press discovered that Marilyn was in town. Soon, the phone at Appleton Street was ringing incessantly. But Marilyn refused to take calls until she had a chance to confer with Arthur. On May 23, the last day of the trial, she talked to reporters on the phone in the morning and met four journalists in the Rauh living room at 2 p.m. Wearing a brown and white knit dress and white gloves, Marilyn, having steadied herself with a glass of sherry, announced that she had come to Washington in the belief that "a wife's place is with her husband." Asked what she had been doing for the past few days, Marilyn replied, "Mostly reading all of the time. Just odds and ends from Mr. Rauh's library. And I've been poring over the court records, learning a little about law." Marilyn's appearance was most effective. Lillian Hellman later jestingly told Joe Rauh that perhaps during her own troubles with the government, she would have done well to marry Clark Gable.

Nonetheless, Miller was convicted on two counts of contempt of Congress. Rauh implored the judge not to send him to jail. Soon afterward, a Supreme Court decision on a related case compelled Judge McLaughlin to reconsider his verdict. He reduced the conviction to one count, fined Miller $500 and gave him a suspended one-month jail sentence. Miller promptly appealed. The case was passed on to the Court of Appeals.

In an intensely hopeful mood, the Millers spent the summer on Long Island. They rented a weatherworn, brown-shingled house overlooking potato fields and horse trails in Amagansett. Norman and Hedda Rosten had a summer retreat in Springs, and the Bloomgardens were also nearby.

A few steps from the house was an artist's studio where Arthur could write in tranquility. Bloomgarden was making noises in the press that he planned to stage Miller's new play on Broadway in the fall. According to Bloomgarden, Miller had been working on the as yet untitled drama about "marital complications" since 1952. Indeed he had. It was the autobiographical play that Miller had begun after meeting Marilyn in Los Angeles with Kazan. At one point, he read aloud to

Bloomgarden and his wife, the actress Virginia Kaye, a fragment about Mary. Miller probably could have used Kazan's help at that moment; he was admired for his ability to infuse a play with narrative drive. Miller kept writing and writing, but the material had yet to take shape.

On the morning of Thursday, August 1, Marilyn was working on her hands and knees in the cottage garden. Suddenly she was overcome by excruciating pain. She screamed and Arthur ran out. They were more than one hundred miles from New York City, but Marilyn felt certain that if only she could see her regular doctor, the baby might be saved. Arthur, frantic, called Bloomgarden, who arranged for an ambulance to take them to New York.

It was noon before they reached Doctors Hospital at the edge of the East River. Marilyn, partly covered by a white sheet, was wheeled in on a stretcher. Dr. Hilliard Dubrow examined his patient and told the Millers that he wanted to operate immediately. Precisely as feared, Marilyn had had an ectopic pregnancy. The baby could not be saved. In the interest of protecting Marilyn's life, the pregnancy had to be terminated.

Marilyn, terribly depressed, remained in the hospital for ten days. The doctor's opinion that she might be able to have a child later did nothing to reassure her. She said little. It seemed to Virginia Kaye that Marilyn acted as though she were "ashamed." Kaye's heart broke for her. Arthur was constantly at her side; nonetheless, Marilyn seemed sure that her husband really would abandon her now. In England, Marilyn had lost her dream of being a serious actress; in New York, she seemed about to lose the dream of being a wife. Though it was all in Marilyn's mind, Arthur knew she believed she was going to lose him. He was desperate to find some way to show Marilyn how he felt about her.

+   +   +

The screenplay for The Misfits began as Arthur's effort to show Marilyn how much he loved her. But these things have a way of backfiring. The script—and the fears, suspicions, and hurt feelings that swirled around it—would at length lead to a divorce. Meanwhile, the struggle to film The Misfits would bind the Millers to each other long after, to all intents and purposes, the marriage was over. If The Sleeping Prince had been Act

One of the Miller–Monroe marriage, the debacle of The Misfits was Act Two.

It started sweetly and innocently enough. Sam Shaw came to see Marilyn at Doctors Hospital. Shaw, it will be recalled, had a keen eye for movie material. He regularly made suggestions to Feldman and others about things he had seen, read, or heard that would make a good film. That's what he did now as he and Arthur sat on a bench overlooking the East River near the hospital. Marilyn took the loss of her baby as a sign that something was wrong with her. Miller was saying that perhaps the right sort of role would make her feel better about herself.

The conversation turned to his short story "The Misfits." Miller related the plot. The intensely visual story, full of light and color, was about three cowboys who hunt wild horses in the Nevada back country. One of the men has a girlfriend named Roslyn. In the story, the reader knows about Roslyn through what others think and say about her. Obviously, her character would have to be filled out in the screenplay, but Shaw was convinced it would be a great part for Marilyn.

Marilyn was released from Doctors Hospital on Saturday, August 10. That morning she put on a full-skirted, sleeveless sundress that made her look a bit like a child on the way to a birthday party. She applied lip liner and an eye pencil. She had her hair curled by a hairdresser. There was something terribly poignant about the elaborate preparations. Marilyn knew the press would be waiting downstairs. Her costume, hair, and makeup were a tacit acknowledgement of their right to be there. She put on a good face as photographers clamored grotesquely at the windows of her ambulance.

During the slow, three-hour drive to Amagansett, she and Arthur hardly spoke. He could think of nothing to say to comfort her. She was devastated that she was probably never going to give him a child. Not long after she arrived home, Marilyn took an overdose of sleeping pills. Her husband found her collapsed in a chair, her breathing irregular. In the course of the marriage, that sound would become terrifyingly familiar. But now he needed a moment to grasp what it meant. Once he did, he phoned for help, saving Marilyn's life.

In hopes of giving Marilyn a gift, Miller put his autobiographical play aside—it hadn't been going particularly well anyway—and began work on The Misfits. The author of Death of a Salesman intuitively knew the importance of retaining one's dream. Isn't that what Willy Loman had been desperately struggling to achieve? And wasn't it a failure to do so that drove Willy to suicide? Perhaps Miller could write a script that would enable Marilyn to live up to her ideals.

He burrowed in his studio from breakfast until suppertime. He had not worked in such a sustained fashion since the marriage began. Knowing the degree to which he valued and protected his work, how could Marilyn fail to see that writing a screenplay for her was Arthur's way of publicly declaring his faith in her?

At the same time, spending hours away from her may have been the worst thing Arthur could have done. In the weeks after Marilyn left the hospital, there was a substantial change in his work habits. If he wanted to reassure her of his love, disappearing all day was likely to have the opposite effect. At a moment when, as he understood, Marilyn most intensely feared rejection, their days apart could only feel like a confirmation that, yes, Arthur was withdrawing.

Probably there was some truth to it. Though Miller told himself he was doing this for Marilyn, he seems to have retreated from the emotional chaos of his marriage to the familiar safety zone of work. He couldn't handle Marilyn's problems any better than she could. Bent over a typewriter in the quiet of his studio, a cigarette or pipe stem jammed between his teeth, at least he had the comfort of being in control.

To understand the fears on both sides of the marriage, it's useful to consider the metaphors Arthur and Marilyn used in speaking about themselves. On Miller's side, there was a sense of threat. He had complained to Laurence Olivier that Marilyn was devouring him. He compared her to a vase—lovely when intact but dangerous broken, the shards having the capacity to cut and kill.

Marilyn, for her part, focused on what was driving Arthur away. She spoke of the monster inside her. By that she seems to have meant the rage that was in sharp contrast to the shyness and sweetness she tended to project. In the beginning, Marilyn said, Arthur had perceived her as a victim, beautiful and innocent. She tried to be those things for him. When inevitably the monster disclosed itself, Miller was shocked and disappointed. He started to pull back.

Whether motivated by love, a desire to retreat, or most likely a mixture of both, Miller wrote *The Misfits* at a feverish pace. He seemed to be writing against death, as though his words were capable of saving

Marilyn. It was as though once he finished the screenplay, by an act of sympathetic magic the shattered vase would be whole again. But the idealized portrait of her he was writing—a picture of the woman he'd fallen in love with—was also clearly an attempt to hold onto his own image of Marilyn. After the horror of England, he seemed to be trying to reassure himself that she really was the beautiful innocent he thought he'd married. On a conscious level, *The Misfits* may have been intended to show Marilyn he loved her; but in a deeper sense, Miller also seemed to be trying to convince himself.

Soon he had pages to show her. As she read, he watched and listened. Marilyn laughed out loud reading about the cowboys. But her reaction to Roslyn was hardly what Arthur expected. Suddenly, she was cautious, reserved, unenthusiastic. Arthur sincerely believed that in creating the character of Roslyn he had done something wonderful for Marilyn, but she certainly didn't act as though he had. She wouldn't even commit to appearing in *The Misfits*. No wonder he later admitted to having been hurt.

What accounts for her response? Marilyn believed that for Arthur to love her, he also had to accept the monster in her. The extent to which he idealized Marilyn in his script suggested that, far from accepting the monster, he wanted to pretend that it didn't exist.

There was also the fact that Marilyn was vastly more experienced in film than Arthur. She had read a great many scripts over the years. Did she immediately perceive flaws in her husband's screenplay? That would certainly constitute a change in the relationship, a shift in the balance of power. Had Miller written a stage play for her, it would have been different. The stage was his domain. But film was something she actually knew a great deal about. In this area, he was no longer the teacher, she no longer the pupil. Suddenly Marilyn was in a position to judge, to criticize, even to reject what Arthur had written. Until this point, Marilyn had regarded Arthur as the great writer, the man of principle, the idol. It had always been a question of whether she was worthy of him.

In writing a screenplay, Arthur made it possible for Marilyn to suspect his motives. When they met in 1951, Miller had been in Hollywood trying to sell a script. For one reason or another, he never managed to get *The Hook* made. Back then, Marilyn had been an obscure starlet, a nothing. Since that time, she had become a star. Her name attached to a script could mean the difference between it being produced and it languishing in a desk drawer. It could mean an important director and costars. And of course, it could mean a great deal of money.

Had Arthur offered Marilyn a stage play, there could have been no doubt that he was doing it for her. He would have been providing her an entrée into his world, the world of the theater. He would have been conferring his prestige as a playwright upon her. As it was, he needed Marilyn's prestige to get The Misfits made. Whatever his intentions, there was at least the appearance that an ambitious husband was using a movie-star wife to cash in.

Marilyn had checked out of Doctors Hospital convinced that she was about to lose Arthur. Now, by writing The Misfits he permitted Marilyn, in her paranoia, to construct a self-loathing explanation for why he remained after her failure to give him a child—he wanted to jumpstart his film career. Marilyn had a history of suspecting people of using her. With the best will in the world, Joe DiMaggiò, by example, had encouraged her to be wary of others' motives. Arthur's screenplay, begun as an attempt to make Marilyn feel better about herself, soon appeared to have very much the opposite effect. It seemed only to confirm that, childless, she was no longer of interest as a wife. From then on, the only way Marilyn would be able to believe that Arthur still loved her was if he stopped trying to get The Misfits made.

PART THREE

✦

+ THIRTEEN +

Back in Manhattan that fall, Marilyn, knocked out by too many sleeping pills, tended to stay in bed late. Sometimes she did not stir until lunchtime. She required as many as five to doze off; seven were known to be lethal. Wearing a black eye-mask, she slept naked amid a tangle of white sheets. Her pubic hair was bleached blonde. The large bed had a powder-gray satin quilt and no headboard. A small lamp and a framed photograph of Gladys Baker, with sunken cheeks and a prominent widow's peak, sat on Marilyn's night table. On the dog-stained, deep white carpet were a portable record player, a stack of records, and a black telephone. Mirrors covered two walls. The blackout curtains remained tightly shut. The small, close, squarish room lacked a clock, so Marilyn never knew the time.

Long before she had awakened, Arthur would already be at work on his screenplay at the other end of the apartment. He rarely slept past seven. A visitor compared Arthur's tiny, book-filled study to "the stoke hold below the first-class lounge." Arthur tended to remain there from morning until night, emerging only to walk their basset hound, Hugo, or to order food. When the cook brought in Miller's tray, she usually found him at the desk gazing into space. It was his habit to chew a cigarette, rolling it thoughtfully from one tooth to another. The servants chattered among themselves, wondering what he did in there all day.

By the time Arthur and Marilyn had come home from the country, the nature of his project had changed. Marilyn had not responded to the script as he had hoped. Yet he kept writing. Perhaps she would agree to play Roslyn, perhaps not. He wasn't going to force her. *The Misfits* was

293

no longer entirely, or even primarily, a gift for Marilyn. Even if she didn't want it, Miller was going to finish it—for himself. Kermit Bloomgarden would have to be disappointed. There would be no new Arthur Miller play on Broadway this year.

Arthur tried unsuccessfully to hide Marilyn's drug and alcohol problem from his family. Still, even his young nephew Ross, Kermit's son, could see that something was going on. Marilyn often absented herself when she was drinking. Arthur, embarrassed, appeared willing to hurt others rather than disclose the trouble with his wife. On one occasion, at the last minute, he announced that he and Marilyn could not attend a family gathering. Later, rather than call his brother to smooth things over, Arthur composed an awkward letter, giving the impression that he had an important life now and that family matters were secondary. He couldn't admit the real reason for his failure to appear—he couldn't produce Marilyn.

In late September, Twentieth Century–Fox's executive manager, Lew Schreiber, flew to New York to talk to Marilyn about The Blue Angel. The studio knew Marilyn had lost her baby in August, and there were disturbing reports from New York that she wasn't well, whatever that might mean. Because of fuzzy wording in her new contract, it was open to question whether Twentieth needed to collect its four pictures in four years or seven, so they would have to proceed soon. Besides, there was concern about Marilyn's age. She was thirty-one. An entire year that should have been immensely profitable to Twentieth had already been lost in the dispute over her contract. So it seemed advisable to start filming The Blue Angel as soon as possible. Technically, as studio executives nervously reminded each other, they didn't need Marilyn's approval to replace Spencer Tracy, who had signed to appear in John Ford's The Last Hurrah and might not be available until the following summer. By contract, on this picture the director had to be one of the men on Marilyn's list. Her co-star, however, was strictly for Twentieth to select.

As they knew, even in the best of times, Marilyn was volatile. In the interest of averting a crisis, Schreiber came east to propose Curt Jurgens—the studio's first choice for the role of Professor Unrat—or Fredric March. Schreiber, who had tangled with Marilyn before, hoped to communicate in person rather than through a battery of agents. He also wanted Marilyn to accept Charles Vidor, though Vidor was not on her list of approved directors. Both Vidor and Jurgens were ready to begin *The Blue Angel* immediately.

There remained those at Twentieth, notably studio counsel Frank Ferguson, who were convinced they had made a drastic mistake in capitulating after Marilyn walked out in 1954. According to this school of thought, Twentieth had shown a fatal weakness in falling for her "bluff." To have done so, it was believed, was to make Marilyn even more of a loose cannon than before. In late September 1957, it certainly did not bode well that every time Lew Schreiber talked to MCA, the agency reported having been unable to reach Marilyn. When at last MCA did get through, Marilyn insisted she could not see Schreiber until the following week. On the day of the appointment, she called to cancel at the last minute.

In this period, Marilyn's day began with a Bloody Mary. Upon hearing that she was awake, the cook prepared eggs and toast in the small, old-fashioned kitchen. Another assistant served Marilyn's morning cocktail. There were times when Marilyn, still wearing the black eyemask, flailed about in the bed linens, seemingly unable to get up.

Intolerant of the sun, Marilyn insisted that the blackout curtains remain closed, preferring to gulp her red drink in gentle lamplight. She thought nothing of washing down her poached eggs with a champagne split. Soon, Frank Sinatra might be heard singing softly on the portable record player. The trip across the room to Marilyn's large but overcrowded closet—Arthur had a separate closet of his own in the hall—was known to be a huge production.

Somehow, on Tuesday, October 2, Marilyn put herself together in order to give the illusion that nothing was wrong. She bathed and washed her hair. She had herself beautifully dressed and made up. A hearse-like black Cadillac limousine carried her crosstown to Twentieth Century–Fox's offices on West 56th Street. As she swept into the conference room, she was all smiles. She was friendly, cooperative, agreeable. She gave no sign of the despondency to which she had succumbed after losing her baby. If Lew Schreiber had been apprehensive, she instantly put his mind at rest.

Schreiber got right down to business. He asked when Marilyn was prepared to start. She indicated that she was ready, no, eager to do *The Blue Angel*. But she still preferred to wait for Spencer Tracy. Though

Marilyn certainly did not mention it, even more than previously she welcomed the opportunity to put off having to return to a film set.

Schreiber announced that Charles Vidor was most enthusiastic about working with her. He pointed out that Vidor had a reputation as a fine "women's director". Marilyn said she knew Vidor's work. She liked his films with Rita Hayworth: *Cover Girl*, *Gilda*, and *The Loves of Carmen*. Marilyn declared that she was less worried about her director—she didn't say that in any case she would insist on having Paula Strasberg—than about who her co-star would be. In the interest of expediting matters, Schreiber proposed Curt Jurgens or Fredric March. Though Marilyn cheerfully agreed to come in for a screening of Jurgens's new picture, she made it clear that her heart was set on Tracy. Schreiber wanted to be absolutely sure Marilyn understood that if she insisted on waiting, they probably would not be able to start before next summer. Unmentioned was the worrisome ambiguity in Marilyn's contract about whether Twentieth needed to collect its second film before the end of the year.

Marilyn emphasized that Twentieth need not concern itself about the late starting date. Shooting the picture next year was fine with her. This wasn't quite what Schreiber had hoped for. The studio wanted to start right away. But he seemed relieved that at least Marilyn was set on the project, and that apparently she had no problem with doing it in 1958. Schreiber planned to begin work on signing Tracy as soon as he returned to Los Angeles.

Afterward, Schreiber sat and talked to Marilyn for a long time. Then he took her over to see Spyros Skouras. It cannot have been an easy encounter, Skouras having pointedly refused Joe Rauh's request that he intervene with Representative Donald Jackson on Arthur's behalf. Still, it was very much in Marilyn's interest to make peace with Skouras at a moment when her husband was about to submit a first-draft screenplay to Twentieth.

The beige club chairs in Skouras's office were as soft and inviting as quicksand. Marilyn, laughing deeply and licking her lips, perched on the cold marble desktop in front of the huge world map. After the meeting, Skouras alone escorted Marilyn to her hired limousine. As Marilyn was driven off, he blew her a kiss and urged her to give serious consideration to Curt Jurgens.

Arthur, as anticipated, completed *The Misfits* in October. There was every reason to assume that Twentieth would be delighted with *The Misfits* as a vehicle for Marilyn. The satisfaction of finishing something he liked in a matter of months seems to have impelled Miller to tackle other literary projects with new fervor. He began a novel based on *The Misfits*. He returned to his autobiographical play. He exulted to Joe Rauh that his life was filled with action. Rauh, for his part, was nervous about their not having heard yet from the Court of Appeals. But the lawyer remained confident that even if the court rejected his motion for a summary reversal, he would be able to overturn Miller's conviction by December at the latest.

Arthur secured a mortgage to buy an old dairy farm in Roxbury, Connecticut. It was on Tophet Road, a short walk from the smaller house he had once shared with Mary and the children. The property, just past the stony fields of the old Coyle farm, had been in the Tanner family for 175 years. The white farmhouse, built in 1783, had high ceilings and thick beams made from ships' timbers. In the attic were shoeboxes containing old family photographs and picture postcards. In the milking room, elsewhere on the property, was a stack of nineteenth-century portraits in gilded frames. Marilyn and Arthur, intent on making a home, planned to drive up on weekends until the dirt roads became icy.

Marilyn pinned her hopes for the future on the idea of building a modern house on top of a hill. She might not be eager to return to work, but she was full of plans for the property. The site had sweeping views in all directions. Marilyn wanted to hire Frank Lloyd Wright, whose design for the Guggenheim Museum was then under construction in New York. Meanwhile, they fixed up the old farmhouse as a temporary residence.

It did not go unnoticed at Twentieth that Marilyn had dropped out of sight again. She broke three appointments to see Curt Jurgens's new picture. She claimed to be ill. On two occasions, Schreiber had almost had a deal with Tracy, but both times the actor changed his mind about terms. Schreiber carefully documented the negotiations, and kept Marilyn's agents apprised of his efforts to get Tracy.

As the year drew to a close, there was much nervousness at the studio about their having permitted 1957 to pass without collecting the second of Marilyn's four films. In light of the ambiguity in her contract, the studio's legal department was particularly wary. Some consideration was given to refusing to pay the third $75,000 installment due on the film rights to *Horns of the Devil* until Marilyn actually started her next picture. At the time she signed her new contract, there had been talk behind closed doors at Twentieth of using the payments on *Horns of the Devil* as leverage in the event that she made any more trouble.

Schreiber, however, reviewed the notes of his October meeting with Marilyn and ordered the New York office to release the check. A meeting with MCA on January 2 shored up Schreiber's confidence that Marilyn intended to make *The Blue Angel* so long as Twentieth was able to get Tracy. The next day, Tracy's agent indicated that the actor was ready to make a deal. One problem remained. Before Tracy signed, he wanted to be certain of top billing. In other words, Tracy insisted that his name precede Marilyn's. If she agreed to that, he'd do the picture.

Schreiber asked Marilyn's agents to talk to her. Seven days later, MCA got back to him. It seemed that Marilyn was sick and her agents hadn't seen her yet; but they were sure she had no objection to her name being listed below Tracy's. Twentieth drew up Tracy's contract. Talks were simultaneously under way with George Cukor, who had often directed Tracy and was a close friend. Thus, as 1958 began, Twentieth appeared to have successfully concluded its dealings with Marilyn. Tracy had agreed, they looked likely to sign a director on her list, and *The Blue Angel* was set to go into production in June.

On January 9, Marilyn canceled a meeting at MCA in New York to approve Tracy's billing. For the moment, even Marilyn's agents seemed to be in the dark about her intentions. When she did come in on Monday the 13th, it wasn't to say yes to Tracy. Suddenly, as far as Marilyn was concerned *The Blue Angel* was off, and there was doubt as to whether she had ever really intended to make the picture in the first place. Marilyn declared that her attorneys in New York had reviewed her contract. It was their opinion that Twentieth's failure to put Marilyn to work in 1957 meant that she was owed $100,000 for the unmade picture.

Two days later, the second shoe dropped. Robert H. Montgomery sent a letter reminding Twentieth of its contractual obligation to have used Marilyn in a film in 1957. As it turned out, the attorney was claiming something more than just the $100,000 Marilyn's agents had demanded. He argued that Twentieth had sacrificed one of the pictures to which the studio was entitled under the 1955 agreement. In other words, it was now being asserted that Marilyn owed Twentieth two pictures instead of three. Considering how much revenue a Marilyn Monroe picture was likely to bring in, that was a very substantial claim. Studio vice-president Joseph Moskowitz shot back that Twentieth had postponed *The Blue Angel* at Marilyn's request. Should she pull out now, Twentieth would sustain major losses for which Marilyn would be held responsible.

As it happened, *The Blue Angel* was not the only Marilyn Monroe project being discussed at Twentieth. On December 30, 1957, Lloyd Garrison had reported to Joe Rauh that *The Misfits* was under active consideration. It soon became clear, however, that Spyros Skouras had no intention of acquiring *The Misfits* unless Arthur's contempt conviction was reversed. The appeal was taking considerably longer than Rauh had anticipated.

In mid-January, the Court of Appeals declared that until the Supreme Court ruled on a related case, Barenblatt v. United States, oral arguments would not be permitted in Miller's appeal. That meant a reversal, if one were to occur, could be a long way off. Obviously, Twentieth was not about to buy Arthur's screenplay. He announced publicly that he and Marilyn planned to do *The Misfits* as an independent production.

On January 27, Miller opened the second of two brown spiral notebooks in which he had written a draft of *The Misfits*. He turned to the last page of the script. A frugal man, he was not one to waste paper. On the very next lined page, he began to take notes. He started in pencil, later shifting to a pen. When he was finished, thirty-three pages would be covered.

Five months had passed since Arthur started *The Misfits* in an effort to show Marilyn how much he loved her. Back in August, he evidently still had hope, however slim, that Marilyn might yet be healed. He thought that perhaps he could help her to get better. Since that time, his notes suggest, that hope had vanished. He believed he had entered a cul de sac. Instead of saving Marilyn, he began to worry about saving himself.

After he met Marilyn in 1951, Miller's notebook had become the repository of his guilt. Finally, in *The Crucible*, he had worked out a way of absolving himself; he blamed everything on his wife. Now again, in 1958, Marilyn provoked a moral crisis, but of a very different sort. Seven years previously, Arthur had felt guilty for being drawn to Marilyn. Now he felt guilty for wanting to flee. That these feelings were just beginning to rise to the surface of consciousness is suggested by the veiled manner in which Miller wrote about them in a private notebook intended for no one's eyes but his own. It is as though the knowledge of his changing attitude to Marilyn were still too painful to be dealt with directly, as though he was fighting to repress his feelings even as he struggled to commit them to paper in order to examine them.

In the notebook are scenes and notes about characters based unmistakably on Mary Miller and Elia Kazan, material that would eventually find its way into the play *After the Fall*. The Mary section drew on the notes Miller had taken in 1952 for an autobiographical play about adultery. In January 1958, Miller apparently was not yet ready to write directly about Marilyn as he would in a later draft of *After the Fall*. But he had, however unconsciously, already reserved a place in the dramatic structure for her. And he had temporarily filled that place with a figure who elicited the same kind of guilt, fear, and tortured ambivalence.

Several years previously, when Miller was still unhappily married to his first wife, he had been accosted on the street by a Columbia University student, a visitor from Latin America. The young man turned out to be quite mad, his reason for wanting to meet Miller being his own belief in the power of witches. He assumed that the author of *The Crucible* would understand. The delusional young man made Miller uneasy; his problems seemed so severe as to be beyond the reach of a psychiatrist. While Miller was eager to get away, the student remained in his life for some time. He required a degree of attention and sympathy that Miller was not temperamentally inclined to offer. At the same time, Miller realized that he must not be cruel. The student was sick. It wouldn't be right to abandon him. How could Miller accuse Mary of coldness if he himself acted coldly? To do so would be to undermine the tortuous self-justification Miller had worked out in *The Crucible*. Thus, Miller found himself being unnaturally kind to the student. Eventually, the young man entered a mental hospital and Miller was freed.

In his guilt-ridden dealings with the young man, Miller had been trying to live up to his own image of himself. A man of conscience, he had been struggling to do the right thing. Yet, as he wrote in the notebook, he believed that guilt was an inadequate basis for morality. He did not want to be good just because one ought to; he wanted to act properly because it was his nature to do so. Now, after his HUAC testimony, things had become more complicated still. Miller had to live up to the world's image of him as an ethical hero. That he was wondering whether he could is suggested by the notation that even as the mad student had been making a god of Miller, Miller had been involved with Marilyn.

As Miller made these notes, a new production of The Crucible was being prepared in New York. It was to open off-Broadway at the Martinique Theater in March. The playwright attended rehearsals, so it is hardly surprising that the characters and situations would be much in his thoughts. Though he seemed to have resolved a number of personal issues in that play, his life had changed substantially since writing it. Most importantly, as he certainly had never expected to do at the time, he had left Mary for Marilyn. In light of that, Miller, in his notebook, revisited territory already explored in The Crucible.

Again, there is a cold, unforgiving wife. Again, there is a tormented husband—here called "Miller"—paralyzed with guilt. Again, there is a betrayer from whom Miller hopes to differentiate himself. But now, there is someone else: a fragile, emotionally needy, mentally unstable figure from whom Miller can find no excuse to extricate himself. In this embryonic version of After the Fall, that figure is the Latin American student. Later it will be a character based on Marilyn Monroe.

Miller once said he couldn't write about anything he fully understood. If he had already come to the end of an experience, he couldn't write it. After the Fall would not be complete until the author had worked out a justification for leaving Marilyn. In the process of writing, he would find that justification, and the search for it would produce the drama of the play. The play would be finished when Miller had reassured himself, and the audience, of his own goodness.

As Miller was starting to write about all this in his notebook, Laurence Olivier arrived in New York, having finally decided to leave Vivien Leigh. Olivier confessed to Noël Coward that he couldn't bear to live with her anymore. According to Kenneth Tynan, it had been watching Arthur and Marilyn that had helped Olivier to clarify his own circumstances. Olivier's choice, as he saw it, was between nursing Vivien and getting on with his own life and career. Put another way, Olivier explained his decision to ask for a divorce by saying that he just had to "get some sleep."

The experience of working with Marilyn Monroe had not

provided the personal renaissance Olivier had hoped for. As chance would have it, however, an opportunity to reinvent himself was precisely what he did get from his trip with Arthur Miller to see *Look Back in Anger*. As a result of Olivier's backstage encounter with John Osborne, the playwright sent him *The Entertainer*. Archie Rice, a pathetic, seedy, music-hall performer, was, as Kenneth Tynan would declare, "one of the great acting parts of our age." To achieve just the right note of lechery, Olivier pictured how Archie might look as he imagined fondling Marilyn Monroe's breasts—not the real Marilyn, but the character she played in *The Sleeping Prince*.

The role was a triumph for Olivier in England. Now, he had brought the show to the United States. After previews in Boston, it was to open on Broadway at the Royale Theater on February 12. Appearing in the role of Archie's daughter was the young actress Joan Plowright, whom Olivier hoped to marry after divorcing Vivien. It was said that Plowright had not broken up the marriage; she had simply been present "at the crucial turning point in Larry's life."

In New York, Olivier also took care of some unfinished business. Since directing *A Streetcar Named Desire* in London in 1949, he had been passionately resentful of the Actors Studio and all it stood for. That resentment was intensified many times over as he endured the Strasbergs on *The Sleeping Prince*. Now, Olivier visited the old white brick church on West 44th Street. He wanted to see for himself what all the fuss was about.

Strasberg liked to fill the Studio with celebrities—"visiting potentates," as Frank Corsaro called them—who dropped in once or twice to watch. The impression they carried away depended entirely on chance. Some days the exercises worked. Some days they did not. Strasberg, working as he did, could not be expected constantly to produce results. The particular day Olivier appeared turned out to be "most unfortunate in terms of results," Corsaro recalled.

Olivier did not fall under Strasberg's spell. He found his long, rambling, off-the-cuff lecture pretentious. And he found his severe criticism of one young actor misguided and cruel. After the session, Olivier confronted Strasberg and pointed out that totally undermining the young man's confidence could only make things worse. Strasberg waved Olivier away as though he were an imbecile.

Marilyn hid in the ladies' room when Olivier visited the Studio. His very presence was a painful reminder of a dream that had died. Appearing in a film with Olivier was supposed to have established Marilyn's credentials as an actress. It was supposed to have proven her worth. It was supposed to have prevented her from ever having to play another dumb blonde on screen.

That would explain Marilyn's violent reaction when Billy Wilder sent her a script he had written with I. A. L. Diamond. It had been inspired by the 1932 German film *Fanfares of Love* about two musicians who travel about in disguise. To Marilyn's way of thinking, the role of Sugar Kane in *Some Like It Hot* asked her to return to a past she had worked very hard to escape. Marilyn grew enraged as she read the story of two musicians who have the misfortune to witness the St. Valentine's Day Massacre. Suddenly they need to escape the mob. Disguised as women, "Josephine" and "Daphne" join an all-girl band run by Sugar Kane. Sugar is a singer and ukelele player.

Marilyn, throwing the screenplay on the floor, declared that she had played dumb characters before, but never this dumb. Would anyone really believe Sugar failed to guess that the musicians were really men? In her anger, Marilyn failed to notice that *Some Like It Hot* was probably the most literate and intelligent script she had ever been offered. Miller urged her to do the picture. Her agents urged her to do it.

Even Spyros Skouras appeared to like the idea, though Twentieth would make not a penny on the film, which was to be produced by the Mirisch brothers and distributed by United Artists. Where Twentieth would profit handsomely was in the immeasurable good that *Some Like It Hot* would do for Marilyn's reputation. *The Prince and the Showgirl* had been a critical and box-office dud. If the Billy Wilder picture was the smash hit almost everyone but Marilyn predicted it would be, that could only enhance her value as a studio property.

Marilyn called the script ridiculous. She accused her husband of caring only about money. She insisted she would not accept the part. She accused her representatives of trying to trick her. To read the documents in Marilyn Monroe's studio legal file pertaining to the negotiations between MCA and Twentieth is to sense that those talks proceeded without—almost in spite of—Marilyn herself. The opposing sides seemed to concur that it was in everyone's interest to have Marilyn working again.

The agents and the studio reached an agreement on April 15. There were major concessions on both ends. MCA backed off on its claim that Marilyn owed Twentieth two additional pictures instead of three. Twentieth relieved Marilyn of the obligation to appear in *The Blue Angel*.

Spyros Skouras went so far as to agree to pay $100,000 for a film Marilyn had not made. That seemed a very small price for the vast sums Twentieth stood to earn on three more Marilyn Monroe films. Skouras would never have considered forfeiting that third picture. The $100,000 may also have been Skouras's way of making amends for his failure to buy *The Misfits*.

To guarantee that he saw Marilyn again, Skouras stipulated he would pay the money, in addition to her regular fee, after she had finished her next picture at Twentieth. The studio had until January 14, 1959, to put her in a film. Meanwhile, the Old Greek gave Marilyn permission to appear in *Some Like It Hot*. In view of past problems, Frank Ferguson urged that Marilyn be compelled to sign the papers before someone else talked to her and she changed her mind again.

In the dark bedroom on East 57th Street, Marilyn, sitting naked in bed, drank champagne and stuffed herself compulsively. The servants marveled at her ability to cram vast quantities of food down her throat. She devoured lamb chops, steaks, hamburgers, veal cutlets, and home-fried potatoes. She was particularly fond of chocolate pudding. She vowed to make herself so fat that no one would want her to appear in *Some Like It Hot*.

Nonetheless, on April 21, 1958, Marilyn signed a contract amendment accepting the new terms. Eight days later, MCA officially notified the studio that Marilyn had agreed to do *Some Like It Hot*. Shooting was to begin sometime between July 15 and August 1. Marilyn would be required to work for about sixteen weeks.

At times, she actually seemed resigned to doing the film. In bed, she taught herself to play the ukelele. As Arthur worked on *After the Fall* in his study, Marilyn's baby voice wafted through the white-on-white apartment. She sang "I Wanna Be Loved By You," one of her songs from the movie. At other times, panic seized her. Weeping, Marilyn pleaded with Arthur not to send her to Hollywood. He remained calm and sensible. He tried to reassure her. But in doing so, he inadvertently said the one thing certain to plunge her into a deeper terror. He reminded Marilyn that it was up to her to make *Some Like It Hot* a success.

✦   ✦   ✦

The Strasbergs had always loved to entertain. Even in their down-at-heel Hollywood days, Paula had been known to delight guests with smoked salmon flown in from a favorite Manhattan delicatessen. Friends affectionately called Paula "the Big Wet Tit." At her Sunday open houses in New York, platters overflowed with cold cuts. Sometimes, the menu consisted of three kinds of Chinese takeout. The atmosphere was free and easy. Paula, who wore a copious black caftan, took pride in feeding as many as four hundred people at a time.

It was a rare occasion when Arthur would agree to accompany Marilyn to the Strasbergs'. By this time, he made no secret of his dislike for Lee. One evening, however, the Millers did stop by for drinks on their way to the theater. Marilyn was in a hypercritical mood. In front of the other guests, she excoriated her husband.

There had once been a time when Marilyn would never have dared to contradict Arthur. Now she seemed to disagree with everything he said. There had been a time when she gazed at Arthur adoringly. Now she seemed intent on humiliating him. If he was angry and embarrassed—and it would have been hard to imagine he wasn't—he kept his rage within. At such moments, he refused to fight. He declined to take the bait. He withdrew into himself. That would infuriate Marilyn. She hated it when, as she would say, Arthur wasn't there. She wanted him to pay attention. She attacked even more viciously in an effort to elicit some response, any response.

Finally, on this particular occasion, Marilyn loudly ordered Arthur to get her mink coat. The Strasbergs' guests were theater people. In this crowd, Arthur Miller was not just any husband being belittled by a wife. He was one of the finest post-war American playwrights. He was an artist who, whatever one might have thought of him personally, commanded respect both for his life and work. When Arthur obediently went out for Marilyn's coat, one horrified guest felt he simply had to say something.

"Marilyn, how can you talk to that man that way, like he's a shit? It's degrading, it's terrible."

Suddenly, Marilyn didn't seem angry anymore. Her tone was cool, rational. "You think I shouldn't have talked to him like that?" she asked. "Then why didn't he slap me? He should have slapped me."

The honeymoon, it was being said about town, was over. More and more, Marilyn's idealization of Arthur seemed to have turned to contempt. The shift appeared to hinge on his efforts to write and sell a screenplay. After Twentieth failed to buy *The Misfits*, Miller submitted it to the French director René Clément. That, too, was a dead end. The excuse given was that Clément had trouble understanding the script. Miller said he had been exhausted by the prospect of having to translate the story's specifically American nuances to the filmmaker.

Whatever the reason, the fact remained that Arthur had suffered another setback. That seemed only to confirm Marilyn's opinion of his screenplay. If she was sometimes mercilessly cruel, that cruelty was probably nothing more than an expression of her own fear. The curtain had been wrenched aside, the Wizard of Oz revealed for who he really was. The knowledge seemed to terrify her. If Arthur was less than the god Marilyn had imagined him to be, how was he possibly going to protect her?

He discovered that he could not anticipate her moods. He was in a state of perpetual apprehension as Marilyn veered between extremes. She lashed out one moment, and wept that he was ignoring her the next. She was desperate to have his baby. She was eager to make a real home with him in Connecticut. She urged him to buy more land, though he feared being plunged into debt. She talked excitedly about adding a nursery wing to the farmhouse. At the same time, she attacked her husband precisely where he was most vulnerable. Sniffing failure and defeat, she assaulted Miller's stature as a writer. Her initial lack of enthusiasm for *The Misfits* had festered into overt and strident criticism. It was only a matter of time before his confidence was eroded.

Marilyn did not hesitate to disparage *The Misfits* to others. Worse, more often than not her complaints were devastatingly on target. She was correct that the script desperately needed to be rewritten. It was talky. It was static. It was thin on character and action. The writing was fuzzy. The story often failed to make sense. Marilyn did not, however, appear sincerely interested in fixing the script. Her real purpose seemed to be to vent her rage at her husband.

She complained to Norman Rosten that the character Arthur wanted her to portray was passive. She was right, of course. But Marilyn had put Rosten in a most awkward position. He was one of Miller's oldest and closest friends. At the very least, he could not be expected to take sides, Arthur having failed to show him the script. Soon after Norman and Hedda went to Long Island for the summer, a copy of *The Misfits* arrived in the mail. It came from Marilyn. A week later the phone rang. Marilyn was calling from Roxbury. She announced that Miller was listening on the other phone. She asked Rosten what he thought of the script.

Rosten, put on the spot, said he believed it would make a good picture. The remark elicited a grunt from Miller. Marilyn instructed Rosten to turn to a key speech, which she characterized as "lousy."

"The speech is too goddamn long," Marilyn declared. "And anyway, it isn't right."

Marilyn paused, obviously expecting Rosten to concur. He discreetly said nothing.

"I want this speech rewritten," she barked. When her husband remained silent, Marilyn called, "Arthur, are you there?"

"I'm here," said a gravelly voice.

"Well, what are you going to do about it?"

"I'm going to think about it."

"Norman agrees with me."

"I don't agree, Marilyn," Rosten interjected, the conversation getting sticky. "I agreed to read the screenplay, which I did. If Arthur asks my opinion on certain scenes or speeches, I'll tell him. Look, it's a draft. I'm sure there'll be more work on it. I mean, it's not final, is it?"

"It's a draft," said Miller apathetically. After two disappointments, he admitted he didn't know what to do with the script.

"Maybe that section can be trimmed," said Rosten in a conciliatory manner. "If Marilyn has specific objections . . ."

"I object to the whole stupid speech," Marilyn insisted, "and he's going to rewrite it!"

Meanwhile, Miller was being pressured to complete *After the Fall*. Kermit Bloomgarden had confidently announced plans to bring Arthur Miller's new play to Broadway, and had already booked theaters for previews. He had an eye on Jason Robards, Jr. for the "Miller" role. At length, he gave the date of the premiere as December 18, 1958, ignoring the fact that, though Miller had already filled a great many pages—at one point he counted as many as 2000—he had not yet found a way to make it all work as a play. When Marilyn went to Los Angeles on July 7, Miller, under the gun, planned to keep writing in Connecticut. She was scheduled to report to Billy Wilder on July 14 for two weeks of tests and pre-production.

As the time to go approached, Marilyn grew increasingly apprehensive. She talked about suicide. She sat on a windowsill in Willard Maas's penthouse overlooking the Brooklyn Bridge. Maas and his wife, Marie Menken— later said to be the basis for the battling married couple in Edward Albee's *Who's Afraid of Virginia Woolf?*—held a salon for avant-garde artists.

"I'm thinking it's a quick way down from here," Marilyn told Norman Rosten, who brought her to the gathering. "Who'd know the difference if I went?"

"I would," said Rosten, "and all the people in this room who care."

On the July 4 weekend, Arthur invited Frank Taylor to Roxbury to talk about *The Misfits*. Miller knew the prominent editor from the days when Mary had worked as Taylor's secretary at a New York publishing house. "She was typing away, so he could stay at home and write plays," recalled Taylor's wife, Nan. Mary's boss had published Miller's novel, *Focus*, in 1945. When Miller completed *Death of a Salesman*, he had asked Taylor to pitch the film rights in Hollywood. Since that time, Taylor had spent four years at MGM. He was now back in publishing. That Miller would use Taylor to get a copy of *The Misfits* to John Huston suggests the degree to which Marilyn had distanced herself from the project.

Miller said that even before he finished writing, he had hoped the script might be something Huston would direct. To date, Marilyn had done nothing to make that happen. She was conscious of her power, and knew how to use it. All she needed to do was to call Huston. She could have written to him. She could even have instructed her agent or lawyer to send Huston *The Misfits* on her behalf. That she had not done so suggests she wanted no part of this. Miller's decision to bring Taylor to Roxbury during Marilyn's last weekend there seems almost like an act of defiance. It was as though he were telling her that if she would not provide him an entrée into the film world, he was perfectly capable of getting it himself.

The farmhouse was then being extensively remodeled, Frank Lloyd Wright's plans having proven impractical. The old Tanner place would not be torn down after all, but it would be dramatically enlarged and renovated. There always seemed to be some structural change under way. As the Miller–Monroe marriage disintegrated, the Roxbury house slowly neared completion.

When the Taylors arrived, Miller greeted them alone. There was no sign of Marilyn. Pointedly, she did not come downstairs. A year before, when Miller had shown her his first pages, he failed to get the reaction he had hoped for. When he sent The Misfits to Twentieth and later to René Clément, he met with further disappointment. This time, he took no chances. He told the story to his guests. He acted out all the parts, modulating his voice and accent appropriately. He paused now and then to clarify the action.

William Styron, a Roxbury neighbor, once called Miller an "actor of intuitive panache." His excruciating reserve would vanish as he lost himself in telling a story. He was consummately theatrical. His eyes sparkled. His timing was perfect. His laughter was infectious. He had a flair for comedy. He knew how to draw listeners in. His pleasure in connecting with an audience—when he found the right audience—was palpable.

Arthur was by no means the only one to put on a show that day. As the author performed his work, the sound of a vacuum cleaner could be heard. Marilyn, a one-woman Greek chorus, ceaselessly pushed the vacuum cleaner back and forth on the creaky old floor upstairs. Ostensibly, she was ridding the house of plaster dust. But the noise was also Marilyn's sardonic comment on her husband and his goddamn screenplay.

Later, Taylor said he would call Miller from home with John Huston's address in Ireland. When Marilyn learned that Arthur was going to offer Huston The Misfits, the obvious thing to say was that she would send it herself. But Marilyn did not intercede, though she must have known that her husband would soon find himself in the awkward position of having to explain her silence. To make matters worse, she indicated that Huston was Miller's last chance. If Miller failed to attach Huston, she intended to pull out of the film. So a great deal depended on Miller's letter asking Huston to read the script. At one point, Arthur had seemed to think he could get the picture made without Marilyn. By now, however, it was increasingly obvious that her withdrawal would be fatal to the project. If Marilyn refused to play Roslyn, *The Misfits* would end up like *The Hook*. Almost certainly, it would never be produced.

Miller drove Marilyn and an assistant to the airport on Monday evening. Just before seven the next morning, Marilyn emerged in Los Angeles, dressed in shades of vanilla. Her hair was platinum. The Hollywood press corps had not seen her in two years, and there were a good many jokes about the new, "definitely chubby" Marilyn. All that eating and drinking in bed had taken its toll.

Barraged with questions about her weight, Marilyn admitted that she might have put on a few pounds.

"It's still in the right places, isn't it?" she teased.

The pressmen weren't certain.

"My weight goes up and down like everyone else's," said Marilyn, a bit nervously, "but I'll be in good shape in two weeks because I intend to do lots of walking and exercising."

Arthur, she explained, had remained in Connecticut to finish a new play.

Would there be a role for her?

"Who knows?" Marilyn laughed.

One week after Arthur saw Marilyn off at the airport, he wrote to John Huston. When Miller finished a new work, his pride was known to border on arrogance. True to form, upon completing *The Misfits* nine months previously, Miller had been cocky. Since that time, however, Marilyn had done her best to cut him down to size. The experiences of recent months formed the subtext of Miller's letter. His posture was uncharacteristically defensive. He wrote as though he could still hear Marilyn barking on the phone, "Well, what are you going to do about it?"—as though he half-expected John Huston to ask the same thing. He emphasized that his screenplay was an early draft. Before Huston had even agreed to read it, Miller said he hoped to tell him his ideas for revisions. He welcomed any suggestions the director might offer. Clearly, he was hoping to forestall rejection.

By way of explanation for why he was approaching Huston through Taylor, Miller alluded to the bad feeling over Huston's having failed to be hired to direct *The Sleeping Prince* in 1955. The implication was that Marilyn would have liked to contact Huston herself about *The Misfits*, but that she was too nervous and frightened. Even as Miller seemed to distance himself from her girlish silliness, he made it clear that Marilyn was attached to the project.

Huston was then in Paris finishing *The Roots of Heaven*. He had recently hired Jean-Paul Sartre to write a script on the life of Sigmund Freud. Fascinated by Marilyn Monroe (had he sensed her presence in *The Crucible* when adapting it for the screen?), Sartre very much wanted her to play the female lead in *Freud*. Huston wrote to Miller that he was delighted to be offered *The Misfits*. He promised to read it and get back to him right away. Meanwhile, Huston asked him to reassure Marilyn and to give her his love. Huston, of course, was well acquainted with Marilyn, having directed her in *The Asphalt Jungle* in 1950 when she was Johnny Hyde's protégée. Though *The Asphalt Jungle* was not her first film, Howard Hawks credited Huston with having discovered Marilyn.

As promised, Huston wasted no time in getting back to Miller. Yes, he very much wanted to do the picture. He would come to America in a few months to meet Miller. Characteristically ebullient, Huston declared the script perfect. He said he would not presume to make any suggestions. At this point, Huston gave no clue of his intention to require a complete overhaul. He would have assumed that as a working professional Miller was sincerely prepared to rewrite extensively. Huston expected film scripts to need revision.

A gifted writer himself, Huston was famous for his ability to work with screenwriters. If Miller was having trouble writing for the cinema, Huston would cheerfully tutor him. Flaws in a first draft did not bother Huston. So long as he was drawn to the material, problems could be ironed out later. Huston loved the idea of making a picture about the hunt for the last of the mustangs up in the Nevada mountains. Curiously, the subject matter seemed closer to the sort of thing Huston tended to do than Miller. And Huston loved the idea of collaborating with the author of *Death of a Salesman*. Miller, unaccustomed to Hollywood hyperbole, was mistaken if he believed Huston really thought the script was already perfect. He would discover the director's real plans soon enough.

On August 7, the local workmen who were renovating the Roxbury farmhouse surprised Miller with a case of beer and a bottle of whisky to celebrate the news from Washington. Miller's contempt

conviction had finally been overturned. He proceeded to get drunk in
the company of the mason, the back hoe operator, the steamfitter, and
the carpenters. Spyros Skouras wasted no time dictating a letter warmly
congratulating Miller. Insisting he was delighted with the outcome,
Skouras commended Miller on his courage and perseverance. Three
years after he had implied that Marilyn's career would be destroyed if her
husband declined to name names, he conceded that his advice had been
wrong. Skouras prided himself on having what he called a "jungle
instinct" for survival. More than any public event, perhaps, Skouras's
gesture to Miller quietly marked the end of HUAC's power and influence.

Marilyn, at the Bel Air Hotel, called Arthur as soon as she heard
about the decision. They talked for over half an hour. Afterward, Marilyn
celebrated alone with a bottle of champagne. Reporters caught up with
her in her dressing room at the Samuel Goldwyn studio.

"Neither I nor my husband ever had any doubt about the outcome
of the case," said Marilyn as she shifted poses for photographers. She
wore a flimsy, beige chemise dress and strummed a white ukelele. When
Marilyn disclosed that she had talked to Arthur on the phone, one news-
man asked whether Miller planned to join her in Hollywood.

"He said he would probably be out before the picture ends,"
Marilyn replied. "I never know when to expect him. He's always surprising me. Maybe he'll even be coming this week."

The Strasbergs, to be sure, had already arrived. Their rented
beach house in Santa Monica was soon filled with certain indispensable
books and records transported from Central Park West. Film actors and
actresses who had passed through the Actors Studio at one time or
another arrived to pay their respects. There was often a group of acolytes
at Lee's feet.

Eleven years previously, Strasberg had been fired as a director of
screen tests at Twentieth Century–Fox. He had never actually directed a
film. He had left Hollywood a beaten man. Now he returned as counselor
to one of the industry's great stars. In a town where he had once failed
miserably, Strasberg's connection with Marilyn Monroe made him a force
to be reckoned with—or so he seemed to think. Paula accompanied
Marilyn to Billy Wilder's set every day. Lee, who had pasty, dark-stubbled
skin, sat on the beach staring serenely at the ocean.

When Billy Wilder had first heard that Marilyn Monroe was

studying at the Actors Studio in New York, he was horrified. Wilder would pace back and forth as he talked, slapping his thigh with a riding crop. "Here you have this poor girl and all of a sudden she becomes a famous star," Wilder declared. "So now these people tell her she has to be a great actress." He said it was as if the author of "How Much Is That Doggie In The Window" suddenly aspired to compose a classical symphony. He predicted that if she took such talk seriously it would be the end of Monroe. Having once warned her to stick to the great character she'd created, Wilder feared that Marilyn would lose her audience, and worse, lose everything that was uniquely her own. He worried that the general public would hate her. He insisted the last thing in the world Marilyn needed was acting lessons. Why would anyone want to spoil a good thing?

Once Wilder was reunited with Marilyn for *Some Like It Hot*, he freely admitted he had been wrong. To his astonishment, Marilyn, under Strasberg's tutelage, had indeed become a stronger actress. She was deeper. She had a better grasp of what she was doing. But in Marilyn's new, intense self-consciousness, Wilder perceived a potential problem. "Before she was like a tightrope walker who doesn't know there's a pit below she can fall into," Wilder said. "Now she knows."

Paula, clutching a huge black silk umbrella, accompanied Marilyn to the MGM back lot on the first day of filming. It was Monday, August 4. Wilder was to shoot the train sequence in which Marilyn makes her entrance at the station.

"Relax, relax," Paula whispered in Marilyn's ear.

Marilyn closed her eyes. She appeared to slip into a trance. She threw her neck forward and let her arms dangle. She violently flicked her fingers up and down. She flapped her arms and rotated her head, reminding Jack Lemmon of a chicken on a block. Marilyn, in her fury, seemed almost to be trying to detach her hands from her wrists. One might have thought she was having a fit. In fact, she was performing Paula's relaxation exercise.

During the rehearsal, Paula watched from the sidelines. She said not a word. But according to Tony Curtis, Paula somehow communicated the message, "I am King Shit here." Not for long.

As was Marilyn's custom, after the rehearsal she glanced over at Paula, as though the director didn't matter or exist. For Laurence Olivier,

Paula's presence had been psychologically loaded. Olivier went *mano a mano* with Paula, but he had been wrestling with ghosts. Billy Wilder didn't have that problem. He seemed to regard Paula as nothing more than an annoyance. After all, he had endured Natasha Lytess on *The Seven Year Itch*.

Wilder was famous for his corrosive wit. He was said to have a brain "full of Gillette blue blades." He was known to have a cruel, nasty, sour cast of mind. He actually seemed to prefer to be hated. He waited for precisely the right moment to establish who was going to be King Shit on this set.

Wilder got what he needed in a single take.

"Cut!" cried the director.

Marilyn turned to Paula, and Wilder rose from his director's chair. "How was that for you, Paula?" he inquired. His voice could be heard throughout the set.

The effect was devastating. Laurence Olivier, in the identical situation, had often worked himself into a lather, to no avail. With Billy Wilder, six words and a deadpan delivery were all it took. He had instantly punctured any authority Paula might have hoped to exert.

At the same time, Wilder, an artist at the peak of his powers, gave every sign of planning to treat Marilyn with dignity and respect. He made his intentions clear the following day as they all watched the rushes together. Wilder was delighted by what he saw on screen. Marilyn was not. She believed her entrance in the picture should have been sharper, funnier. Wilder listened carefully, but it wasn't a matter of courtesy. He sincerely admired Marilyn's comic sense. In this particular instance, he treated Marilyn as someone who knew what she was talking about. Wilder and his co-writer, Iz Diamond, rewrote in the light of Marilyn's criticism.

One might have expected things to go well from then on. Wilder had adroitly established his authority, as Olivier had never managed to do. More importantly, he had displayed an eagerness to have Marilyn's creative input, as Olivier had never deigned to do. Marilyn had once longed for a time when her opinions would be taken seriously by a director of Wilder's caliber. Unfortunately, however, the moment may have come too late. She seemed not to notice that Wilder was genuinely interested in what she had to say. Perhaps she just didn't care anymore. In any case, she continued to regard Wilder as an adversary.

It soon became evident that she was up to her old tricks, only worse. She came to work late. Indeed, she seemed to have lost all sense of time. She hadn't learned her lines. Her tendency to botch the simplest dialogue irritated the other actors. As Jack Lemmon noted, sometimes Marilyn required forty takes; sometimes she needed only one.

"Billy, how many fuckin' takes are we gonna do?" Tony Curtis inquired on one occasion.

"When Marilyn gets it right, that's the take I'm going to use," Wilder replied.

More often than not, Marilyn appeared to be tipsy. And it did not take long to see why. No sooner did the director yell "Cut!" than Marilyn shouted "Coffee!" The choreography hardly varied. An assistant would materialize with a red thermos. Marilyn, pretending it really was coffee, sipped vermouth all day.

If Marilyn often snarled at the director, there were times when she seemed even angrier at her husband. Her behavior toward Miller was wildly contradictory. One moment she was lamenting on the phone to Norman Rosten that Arthur was no longer eager to have a baby with her. The next, she was setting Miller up to be savaged by one of his literary idols.

John Huston had praised *The Misfits*, and Marilyn seemed intent on knocking Arthur off his high horse. What better way to accomplish that than to press a copy of the screenplay on Clifford Odets? Odets, the author of *Waiting for Lefty* and *Golden Boy*, wasn't simply a friend like Norman Rosten. He was a playwright Miller revered. In Odets, Marilyn had managed to find someone whose opinion would conceivably outweigh Huston's.

As it happened, Odets had no interest in Arthur's script, his real reason for hooking up with Marilyn being—what else?—to attach her to a screenplay of his own. It was called *The Story on Page One* and Odets also hoped to direct. He agreed to read *The Misfits* while Marilyn was on location in Coronado. They made a date to have dinner after she returned to Los Angeles.

On September 11, Marilyn, hands trembling, wrote a frantic letter to the Rostens. She compared herself and the production to a sinking

ship. She implored Norman and Hedda not to give up on her. At the top
of the Hotel de Coronado stationery was a picture of the oceanfront
resort. Marilyn drew a stick figure in the water. The figure, clearly meant
to represent herself, was shouting "help."

The following evening, Marilyn called Connecticut, pouring out
her upset to Arthur. Sometime that night, she swallowed an overdose of
sleeping pills. Precisely as Natasha had once done, Paula found her in
time. Had Marilyn expected to be discovered? She may not have known
the answer herself. She spent the weekend in the hospital. Miller, putting
aside *After the Fall*, rushed to California. Was that precisely what she had
hoped to achieve? As Marilyn later told Norman Rosten, she needed
something to hold onto.

That week, visitors at Coronado were treated to a curious sight.
Billy Wilder had been permitted to rope off a small patch of the beach for
the actors and the film crew. Marilyn, wearing a 1920s-style bathing suit,
repeatedly blew her lines. Paula Strasberg, who wore a tent-sized, hooded
black robe, threw a short, white terrycloth robe over Marilyn's shoulders
with one hand, with the other gripping a black umbrella to shield
Marilyn from the sun. But Paula was no longer alone in comforting
Marilyn between takes. Arthur Miller also danced attendance. Marilyn,
the center of attention, resembled a cosseted child.

Things improved drastically once Miller was present. He did
everything to lift Marilyn's spirits. In the beginning, she appeared to
respond. Once again, Marilyn gazed at him adoringly. Once again, she
addressed him as Papa. Once again, she looked to him for protection.
The tensions of recent months, particularly those generated by *The
Misfits*, evaporated. Not long after Arthur joined her in California,
Marilyn became pregnant.

Back in Los Angeles, Arthur moved in with Marilyn at the Bel Air
Hotel. Visiting the Strasbergs in Santa Monica, she actually seemed
happy. On the night she was to dine with Clifford Odets, Marilyn, insisting she was tired, sent Arthur alone. At that moment, she was in no
mood to drag her husband over the coals.

Her contentment, however, was short-lived. Very soon, the old
fears and suspicions beset her. Part of the problem seemed to be finding
herself with Arthur in the company of so many people who, as the
expression goes, knew her when. This, after all, was the first time Arthur

had tarried with Marilyn on a Hollywood film set; during *Bus Stop*, his visits by and large had been confined to a few stolen weekends at the Chateau Marmont. At least three men connected with *Some Like It Hot* had been to bed with Marilyn in years past. She had spent a night with Tony Curtis in 1949 or 1950. She had had a fling with Edward G. Robinson, Jr., in the early fifties. She had had sex with the entertainment journalist James Bacon in 1949 while she was living in the guest cottage on Joe Schenck's estate. Wherever Arthur turned, he might see one of Marilyn's former lovers.

Arthur, having observed Marilyn at Charlie Feldman's eight years previously, was well aware of her past on the Hollywood party circuit. But by his own account, something prevented him from acknowledging that past as hers. That was precisely what Marilyn had objected to in his screenplay-in-progress. If Arthur couldn't accept who she really was, she feared she was being rejected.

As it often did, her fear erupted in cruelty and anger. She lashed out at Arthur. She fought with him on the set. She taunted him with her sexual past. She French-kissed Tony Curtis in an effort to make her husband jealous. In despair that Arthur was ashamed of her, she pretended not to care. She seemed intent on provoking him. When Marilyn introduced him to the gregarious James Bacon, she cooed suggestively, "Jim and I used to be real close." It was as though she and Bacon were in on a joke that the stiff, moody husband didn't quite get.

Miller's failure to react strongly, as Joe DiMaggio would have done, made it possible for Marilyn to suspect his motives. He had permitted Kermit Bloomgarden to announce a new stage play. The date of the premiere was fast approaching, yet *After the Fall* remained unfinished. His screenplay, on the other hand, was ready to go. John Huston would soon be in America to make plans. Was that why Arthur dutifully tagged along, carrying Marilyn's purse and makeup case? Did he just want to be sure she was available for *The Misfits*?

Late in the production, Miller approached Wilder on the set. Telling him in confidence that his wife was pregnant, he implored Wilder to go easy with her, and asked him to consider releasing Marilyn at 4:30 each day. Wilder wasn't amused.

"Look, Arthur, it is now four o'clock," he snapped. "I still don't have a take. She didn't come on the set till half past eleven. She wasn't ready to work until one. I tell you this, Arthur, you get her here at nine, ready to work and I'll let her go—no, not at four-thirty—I'll let her go at noon."

Marilyn, for her part, seemed at once to long for and to dread motherhood. She wanted to protect her baby even as she put it in jeopardy. She worried about Billy Wilder's pushing her too hard. She did not want to lose this child. Yet she disregarded a gynecologist's warning that her steady intake of booze and barbiturates could kill the child. She was told in no uncertain terms that due to the build-up of barbiturates in her system, a single drink could trigger a miscarriage. Yet the red thermos remained a fixture on the set. And though Marilyn insisted that she wanted a baby more than anything, she continued to take drugs. On one occasion, she gobbled four whole Amytal sleeping tablets—the equivalent of eight regular-sized tablets—on an empty stomach, and washed the pills down with sherry. In a letter to Norman Rosten, Marilyn worried she had "killed" her child.

Marilyn finished Some Like It Hot on November 7. Twelve hours later, it looked as though she were about to miscarry. Weeping "I don't want to lose my baby again," she was rushed to Cedars of Lebanon Hospital. As it happened, there was no miscarriage. Doctors released her with a warning to stop the pills and the drinking. The baby, she was informed, was in grave danger. After a week of bed rest at the Bel Air Hotel, Marilyn was taken by ambulance to the airport for the flight home. On East 57th Street, there was a gift waiting for her. Next to the framed photograph of Gladys that adorned her night table, she discovered a miniature cradle with a toy baby. It was a present from her maid. The sight caused Marilyn to burst into tears of gratitude.

Suddenly, she appeared to wake up and attempt to control herself. She stopped drinking. She took no more drugs. Convinced that the baby would be a girl, Marilyn insisted repeatedly that she did not want to harm her daughter. Yet, as the doctors in California had warned, it might already be too late. At any time, the barbiturates in Marilyn's system might end the baby's life. Fearful that any exertion might cause her to miscarry, Marilyn remained in bed, nervously playing with the miniature cradle which she had placed on the pillow beside her.

Soon after the Millers returned, Kermit Bloomgarden delayed the December 18 Broadway premiere until February or March 1959, when he hoped Miller would be finished. Under intense pressure to work on his play, Arthur focused on a short story. On December 3, he completed a first draft. "I Don't Need You Anymore" depicted a small boy's bitter resentment of his mother's pregnancy.

The pregnancy theme was also very much on the minds of Twentieth Century–Fox executives, rumors of Marilyn's condition having reached the studio. Now that Marilyn had completed *Some Like It Hot*, Twentieth had until April 14, 1959 to summon her for a film. But if the rumors were true, the studio hoped to be granted an extension. There was a lot of nervous debate about how best to approach Marilyn without triggering one of her rages.

Finally, on December 2, Frank Ferguson wrote to inquire whether she was pregnant. If so, he notified Marilyn that Twentieth wanted to extend the period during which it was obligated to use her. Unmentioned was the fact that Skouras and his colleagues did not yet have a project ready for their biggest star. The studio, having fumbled badly, would by no means be upset to delay the second of Marilyn's four films. At the same time, Twentieth did not want to repeat past mistakes. No one wanted to pay Marilyn, as Skouras had done, for another film she failed to make. And certainly no one wanted to forfeit a Marilyn Monroe picture. Twentieth was eager to hear from her as soon as possible.

Marilyn sent the letter on to her attorneys—who also represented Miller—but they were clearly in no hurry to reply on her behalf. Miller did not yet know when Huston would be available to film *The Misfits*. The director was about to go to Los Angeles to prepare *The Unforgiven*, which was to be shot in Mexico in January. But first, he planned to meet Miller in New York. *The Misfits* would not necessarily be Huston's next project, Sartre having recently delivered a ninety-five-page treatment for *Freud*. Huston anticipated being busy with *The Unforgiven* until about May. If Marilyn gave birth in June, he would probably go on to direct *Freud* while she did a picture for Twentieth. But the fact remained that doctors had warned Marilyn she might miscarry. After Ferguson's letter, her attorneys were silent for two weeks.

Meanwhile, Huston arrived on Sunday, December 14. He and Miller met for the first time. Contrary to anything he had said previously, Huston indicated that he expected a rewrite. As far as Huston was concerned, the screenplay was by no means finished. Now there were two unfinished projects on Arthur's desk. Now there were two men—Huston and Bloomgarden—waiting for pages.

As Arthur worked in his study, he heard Marilyn scream from the bedroom. The pain, mental and physical, was excruciating. Frenzied, she wept that she was going to lose the baby. Arthur and an assistant accompanied her in an ambulance to the Polyclinic Hospital. That night, Miller returned to the apartment alone.

In the past, when Marilyn lost a baby, she had blamed fate. She had blamed her body. She had blamed some defect within. But this time was different. This time, she held herself responsible. She embraced her own guilt. She had been warned to give up barbiturates and alcohol, she knew that her addictions could harm the baby. And she had ignored those warnings until it was too late.

For a long time, Marilyn had feared that one day she would become like her mother. Many years previously, Gladys had tried to smother Norma Jeane in her crib—or at least, Marilyn believed she had. Now, Marilyn had succeeded where Gladys had failed. She was convinced she had killed her own daughter. When Marilyn came home, she spotted the miniature cradle next to Gladys's picture on her night table and threw it on the floor. She began to weep uncontrollably.

On December 17, the day the miscarriage was announced to the press, the Fox legal department finally heard from Marilyn's attorneys. In reply to Frank Ferguson's December 2 letter, Robert H. Montgomery, Jr. notified the studio that Marilyn Monroe had completed *Some Like It Hot* and was now "ready, willing, and able" to begin work on her next picture for Twentieth.

+ FOURTEEN +

The ball was in Twentieth's court. Studio executives had until April 14 to put Marilyn in a picture. By the terms of her amended contract, that was the latest possible start date. On January 20, 1959, Frank Ferguson and Lew Schreiber reviewed Marilyn's list of approved directors. The studio attorney reminded Schreiber that they could not notify Marilyn to report to work until they had a commitment from one of the sixteen men on her list.

Billy Wilder was on the list, but after *Some Like It Hot* he never wanted to work with Marilyn again. Joshua Logan was on the list, but Marilyn had been furious with him since her big scene in *Bus Stop* was cut. John Huston was on the list, but his dance card was filled. Lee Strasberg was on the list, but he had never directed a picture.

One name, however, presented distinct possibilities. Elia Kazan remained under contract to Twentieth. In 1950, Lew Schreiber had been sent to New York by Darryl Zanuck to urge the board to approve the largest salary the corporation had ever given a director. Four years later, though Zanuck refused Kazan's request to call off the contract, the production chief did not succeed in getting a fourth picture. Zanuck, confident that his personal relationship with Kazan would enable him to prevail, pleaded with Skouras not to intervene. Since that time, however, Zanuck had quit Twentieth. And the matter of Kazan's contract had been left unresolved.

Twentieth, eager to come up with a picture for Marilyn, seized on a pet project of Kazan's. It was a script about the Tennessee Valley Authority, based on the novels *Mud on the Stars* by William Bradford

Huie and *Dunbar's Cove* by Borden Deal. In *Time and Tide*, Twentieth saw a vehicle for Marilyn. That Kazan and Miller, once close, had been at odds for seven years seemed to concern the studio not at all.

Before a deal could be put together, Kazan had to accept officially. Only then could Twentieth order Marilyn to work. On February 19, Frank Ferguson advised Lew Schreiber that in order to be certain there was time to give Marilyn thirty days' notice, they must notify Kazan no later than the 25th.

Kazan was then in New York directing Tennessee Williams's *Sweet Bird of Youth*, produced by Cheryl Crawford, which was set to open on Broadway on March 10. Kazan, accompanied by Abe Lastfogel, met with Skouras and officially agreed to direct *Time and Tide*. Twentieth gave him a terrific deal. When he completed the picture, he would be relieved of the obligation to direct the fifth and sixth films in his 1950 contract.

On March 4, Kazan wired production chief Buddy Adler promising to report no later than April 1 for conferences with Calder Willingham, who was being put to work on the script. Immediately Lew Schreiber directed the studio attorney to draft a letter informing Marilyn that she was officially assigned to *Time and Tide*, to be directed by Elia Kazan. Marilyn was to report on April 14. Suddenly, at a moment when Arthur was having trouble revising *The Misfits*, it looked as though Marilyn was going to appear in Kazan's picture first. This state of affairs recalled the strange, awkward situation in 1955 when Marilyn, her love affair with Miller notwithstanding, hoped to go off with Kazan to film *Baby Doll*. This time, however, the fact that Marilyn was Arthur's wife made things even more complicated and highly charged.

Matters were already tense in the Miller household. Marilyn was in despair after the preview of *Some Like It Hot* on February 5. Arthur, like most of the critics, thought she had been wonderfully comical in the film. "I don't want to be funny," Marilyn declared. "Everybody's going to laugh at me. And not because of my acting. I looked like a fat pig. Those goddamn cocksuckers made me look like a funny fat pig."

Billy Wilder had scrupulously used only those takes in which Marilyn—not Tony Curtis or Jack Lemmon—was particularly effective. The result was to privilege those moments when she had been at her most brilliant, to enable her to shine. Yet, in her paranoia, Marilyn sincerely believed Wilder had been determined to make her look bad. She blamed Arthur for having made her appear in the film in the first place. Shrieking that it was his fault, she burst into his study after Wilder joked about her in an interview in the *New York Herald Tribune*.

The interviewer had inquired about Wilder's health now that he was finished working with Marilyn. "I am eating better," said Wilder. "My back doesn't ache anymore. I am able to sleep for the first time in months. I can look at my wife without wanting to hit her because she's a woman." Wilder emphasized that his physical and mental health precluded doing another picture with Marilyn.

Egged on by Marilyn, Arthur sent an angry telegram to Wilder, declaring he could not permit the attack on Marilyn to go unchallenged. He cited his wife's ill health during the making of *Some Like It Hot*, and mentioned her pregnancy and miscarriage. He called the director's comments contemptible, accusing him of being unjust and cruel. He claimed to take solace in the fact that, despite Wilder, Marilyn's beauty and humanity shone through in the finished film.

Wilder's reply enraged Marilyn all the more. He said he had actually protected her from the press. He noted that he had lied repeatedly to cover up her unprofessional behavior. The *Herald Tribune* piece, he argued, would have been twice as harsh if he had failed to cooperate. He pointed out that Marilyn's lateness and unpreparedness had cost the studio eighteen shooting days and hundreds of thousands of dollars. He insisted that had Arthur been not Marilyn's husband but her director, he would have "thrown her out on her can, thermos bottle and all, to avoid a nervous breakdown."

On March 30, three weeks after *Sweet Bird of Youth* opened on Broadway, Kazan reported to Twentieth. Despite the fact that the play was a hit, Kazan had been badly wounded by criticism that, with an eye to commercial values, he had altered Tennessee Williams's work and distorted his vision. Kazan's influence on the playwright was widely deplored; the Williams–Kazan collaboration was said to have "reached the point of diminishing returns." Though no one knew it at the time, *Sweet Bird of Youth* would be the last Williams play that Kazan would direct.

Marilyn was due in the studio two weeks after Kazan. She had voiced no objection to the assignment. By the time Kazan had been at the studio for ten days, however, it became evident to Buddy Adler that things were not proceeding as he and Skouras had anticipated. Kazan, relentlessly self-critical, remained dissatisfied with the screenplay. He wanted Paul Osborn to be brought in. Osborn, who had written the script for *East of Eden*, would not be available until July 21. Kazan insisted on waiting.

Thus, four days before Marilyn planned to fly to the west coast, Lew Schreiber notified MCA that the studio was not ready for her. Marilyn was advised to wait in New York until needed. Her salary for *Time and Tide* would, however, start on April 14 as originally scheduled.

Again, it seemed, Kazan held Miller's fate in his hands. Indeed, by accepting the assignment to direct Marilyn in the first place, Kazan appeared to be reminding Miller of the power he still had over him. Once that had been accomplished, Kazan pointedly rejected Marilyn as he had done at the time of *Baby Doll*. He told Buddy Adler that he did not want to do the picture with her. He preferred to cast Lee Remick. Had Kazan chosen to go forward with Marilyn, it is impossible to say what would have happened with *The Misfits*.

Twentieth made no effort to find another project for Marilyn. From the first, the studio had viewed *Time and Tide* as a Marilyn Monroe vehicle. Astonishingly, no one at Twentieth seems to have paid attention to paragraph eight in her contract, which required principal photography to begin no later than ten weeks from the date she was ordered to work. Though Marilyn had been instructed to remain in New York, the clock had started ticking on April 14.

On June 25, Skouras and company were taken aback when a telegram announced that Marilyn was no longer obligated to appear in *Time and Tide*. It was signed Marilyn Monroe Productions. A lawyer's letter followed. Once again, Marilyn demanded to be paid $100,000 for a picture she had not actually made. She also demanded to be paid for *The Blue Angel*, as Skouras had promised she would be. And she demanded to be released from one of the three remaining films she owed.

That last demand was the most significant, $200,000 being as nothing compared to the sums Twentieth stood to earn from a Marilyn Monroe film. The legal department determined that in view of Kazan's refusal to proceed, Twentieth would have been within its rights to seek an extension of the ten-week period stipulated in Marilyn's contract. But no one had bothered to do so. For now, Twentieth needed to catch its

On December 31, 1955, Marilyn signed a new studio contract that gave her the right to make her own films and to select her own directors. It represented a complete victory in her long-running battle with Zanuck. She returned to Hollywood in triumph to shoot *Bus Stop* at Fox.

After Miller refused to name names to the House Un-American Activities Committee in June 1956, Marilyn risked her own career by publicly supporting the man she loved.

At Arthur's home in Roxbury, Connecticut, in June 1956, shortly before he and Marilyn were married. The news of their engagement unleashed a media frenzy in the small, rural village.

Marilyn and Arthur were married twice—first in a civil ceremony and then in a religious ceremony.

Laurence Olivier and Vivien Leigh welcome the Millers to England in July 1956, where Marilyn was to film *The Prince and the Showgirl* under Olivier's direction. This was to be her first independent production for her own company.

From the first, Marilyn's working relationship with Olivier was a disaster. The high hopes with which she had begun the project ended in despair and mutual recriminations.

The Millers and the Oliviers attended the London premiere of *A View from the Bridge* together.

Back in New York, Marilyn was determined to prove herself the perfect wife. She was pregnant in July 1957 when this picture was taken.

Leaving the hospital in August 1957, Marilyn had just lost her baby. Miller began to write his script for *The Misfits* shortly after this.

With Billy Wilder in
8 on location for *Some Like It
ot*. Marilyn had not wanted to
ake this film, but she gave her
finest performance in it.

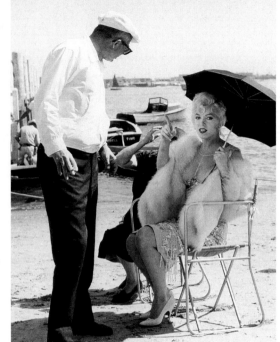

Arthur, Marilyn, and
Paula Strasberg, who
had replaced Natasha as
Marilyn's coach. Marilyn
became pregnant again
during the shooting of
Some Like It Hot, but
she lost this baby too.

By the time Marilyn started *Let's Make Love*, her marriage was in trouble. Her costar Yves Montand had appeared in both the stage and screen versions of Miller's *The Crucible* in France.

While Marilyn was working with Montand in California in early 1960, Miller went to Ireland to work on the screenplay for *The Misfits* with John Huston, who had been hurt in a riding accident.

With director George Cukor and Montand on the set of *Let's Make Love*. When both Miller and Simone Signoret, Montand's wife, left California, Marilyn began a love affair with Montand.

With director John Huston and Arthur Miller. Filming of *The Misfits* finally began in Nevada in July 1960. By the time they finished shooting in November, Marilyn's marriage to Miller had ended.

The press mobbed Marilyn in March 1961, as she left Columbia–Presbyterian Hospital. After her divorce from Miller, Marilyn, depressed and suicidal, had to be hospitalized.

Joe DiMaggio had returned to Marilyn's life as her most loyal friend in these desperate months. When the hospital released her, Joe took her to Florida to regain her health.

Back in New York. Grateful as she was for Joe's loyalty, some part of Marilyn didn't want to be rescued anymore.

Marilyn, with Elizabeth
Taylor and Dean Martin,
watches Frank Sinatra in
Las Vegas in June 1961.
She had begun to date
Sinatra, and before
long her drinking and
drug-taking were again
out of control

With Peter Lawford.
Upon her return to Los
Angeles in 1961, Marilyn
became a regular visitor
to Lawford's oceanfront
home in Santa Monica.

Marilyn sings "Happy Birthday" to President John F. Kennedy at Madison Square Garden on May 19, 1962. After the party, Kennedy, concerned about all the press attention, ended their affair.

A few days after her return from New York, Marilyn posed nude for photographers on the set of her final film, *Something's Got to Give*. She was fired from the film in June 1962.

On August 5, 1962, Marilyn, age thirty-six, was found dead of a drug overdose in her Los Angeles home.

A distraught Joe
DiMaggio orchestrated
Marilyn's funeral on
August 8, 1962.

Arthur Miller and Elia
Kazan. In October 1962,
it was announced that
Kazan would direct
Miller's new play. When
After the Fall opened in
1964, its harsh portrait
of Marilyn created a
huge scandal.

breath and decide how to respond. One thing was certain, however. Before Paul Osborn had officially started work with Kazan, Marilyn was off *Time and Tide*.

Miller, in the meantime, had been having scant success with *The Misfits*. John Huston had stopped in New York in May on his way back to Ireland after *The Unforgiven*, but Miller had had nothing to show him. Miller's stage play also seemed to be stalled, February and March having passed without the Broadway premiere Kermit Bloomgarden had been endlessly announcing. In June, Miller finished reworking the beginning of *The Misfits* and sent it off to Huston. The pages were hardly the complete overhaul Huston had expected. Seven days later, Huston wired Miller. Consummately diplomatic, he praised the revisions and announced his own imminent arrival in New York. Whatever Huston may have assumed at the start, obviously Miller was going to need a good deal of prodding and guidance.

When Huston met with Miller that month, he made it clear that *The Misfits* needed to be substantially revised. If Miller could finish rewriting by the end of the summer, Huston hoped to shoot in April 1960. Otherwise, he might direct *Freud*, though there were problems with Sartre's script as well.

One night at 3 a.m., Norman Rosten's phone rang. Marilyn's maid begged him to come immediately. Arthur, as he sometimes did, had gone up to Connecticut alone to write in peace and Marilyn was alone in New York that night. She had taken another overdose. By the time the Rostens arrived from Brooklyn, a doctor had finished pumping Marilyn's stomach.

Norman followed Hedda into the small, softly-lit room. He could hear Marilyn crying. In a whisper, he asked how she was.

"Alive," said Marilyn in a low, sad voice. "Bad luck."

Her overdoses were not always intentional. Another time when Arthur had gone up to the country alone, Marilyn, frustrated by her inability to sleep, devoured a large number of pills all at once. In the morning, the maid discovered Marilyn unconscious on the white bedroom carpet. A physician pumped her stomach and Arthur was summoned from Roxbury.

As Laurence Olivier had been with Vivien Leigh, Miller was faced with a choice. He could try to take care of Marilyn, or he could get on with his life and work. Olivier chose the latter, and it was beginning to look as though Miller would do the same. A decade had passed since *Death of a Salesman*. Miller was generally considered never to have matched the brilliance of that work. After *Salesman*, his only new full-length play seen in New York had been *The Crucible* in 1953. The expanded version of *A View from the Bridge* had only been seen in England. Recently, all of Bloomgarden's announcements and cancellations, however well intentioned, had clearly done the playwright's reputation no good. Miller was painfully conscious that he appeared to be idle. His priority was to get his screenplay produced. He had to finish *The Misfits* to Huston's satisfaction. He had to complete a work he could speak of in the same breath as *Salesman*.

That summer he holed up in Connecticut. He wrote seven days a week. He resisted the temptation to contact Huston. He wanted to send the director not mere promises but results. Though Marilyn accompanied Arthur to the country, by and large he retreated into himself and his work. Miller had started *The Misfits* in order to permit Marilyn to hold onto her dream. Now he seemed to be trying to do the same thing for himself. He seemed to be fighting for his own personal dignity, not hers.

Miller, in his studio, sat at an austere slab desk near a fireplace and little louvered windows. Workmen were in and out of the main house, where walls were forever being moved and wings added. Glass walls were installed in the rear to take advantage of a spectacular view. While he wrote, Marilyn was intent on making the old place entirely her own. She added dark wood ceiling beams. She added dormer windows. She added a room over the kitchen. She filled the sunroom with photographs of Arthur and posters for his plays. She never stopped buying and rearranging furniture. But as Norman Rosten perceived, a sense of having finished evaded her to the end.

Marilyn shopped in Roxbury and nearby Woodbury, sometimes twice a day. She walked in the green and yellow fields and along stone-wall-lined dirt roads. On one occasion, Marilyn paid a call on their neighbor, old Percy Beardsley. As he often did with visitors, Percy invited Marilyn to inspect his father's famous coal cellar.

Local farmers still talked about the time, many years previously, when a motion picture company used Nate Beardsley's red Devon cows and steers as a backdrop. One night the leading lady, Norma Talmadge—

Joe Schenck's wife—had accompanied Nate to the coal cellar, where she left her long, white kid gloves on a cider barrel. In later years, though Nate and his son drank one barrel of cider a month, they religiously avoided disturbing the movie star's gloves. In these parts, the Beardsley cellar was thought to be better than any museum. Even after old Nate died, his boy Percy faithfully maintained the shrine. The white gloves, thick with dust, gave the appearance of having been mummified.

After her visit, Percy tried to preserve the marks left by Marilyn Monroe's spike heels in the dirt floor. When a drover stepped on the spot, inadvertently obliterating the marks, Percy, furious, refused to speak to him again.

Marilyn often spent hours searching for Hugo, the basset hound, who tended to wander. He moved very slowly, leading Arthur to nickname him "Flash." He was known to appear on doorsteps miles away, or even to fall asleep in the middle of the road, forcing cars to a halt. He barked in agitation whenever a man, whether Arthur or Norman, entered the room; something about their voices distressed him. But the dog adored Marilyn. And she doted on him, going so far as to give him brandy when he seemed depressed. That caused him to run about hysterically, one droopy ear to the floor. Then he turned around sharply, running with his other ear to the floor. Suddenly, poor Hugo collapsed in a corner and fell asleep. "Maybe that'll help," Marilyn declared.

Much of the summer passed with no sign of how Twentieth intended to react to Marilyn's demands. In fact, for some time studio executives seemed unable to develop a plan of attack. At length, it came to the attention of the New York office that, during the period when Marilyn was supposed to have been ready, willing, and able to report for *Time and Tide*, she had entered Lenox Hill Hospital for gynecological surgery. That in itself provided Twentieth with grounds to fight her in court.

But to the bewilderment of the New York office, their counterparts on the west coast were suddenly most eager to pay Marilyn. They wanted to avoid a lawsuit at all costs. On August 26, Twentieth officially capitulated to all of Marilyn's demands. The studio notified her that she would be paid for both *The Blue Angel* and *Time and Tide*. More importantly, she was relieved of the obligation to do one of the three pictures she still owed.

Buddy Adler had the reputation of being a weak, indecisive production chief, who was not quite up to the job. He was anxious to settle with Marilyn because an opportunity had unexpectedly presented itself to put her in a film. *Some Like It Hot* had been a huge critical and box-office success. Marilyn was very hot right now. Adler wanted to get her in front of the studio cameras before she signed to do another outside film. Marilyn, after all, had not appeared in a picture for Twentieth since *Bus Stop*, three years previously.

As it happened, a project had been sitting under Adler's nose all summer. For the past few months, the producer Jerry Wald had been putting together a film to star Gregory Peck. Based on a screenplay by Norman Krasna, *The Billionaire* was a comedy of mistaken identity. So far, no leading lady had been cast. In the beginning, Marilyn's name had not even come up, because it was assumed she was to do *Time and Tide* with Kazan. In July, Wald had approached the director George Cukor. By August, Cukor definitely seemed interested. But he had reservations about the script and he wanted to know who the female lead was going to be.

Wald was also the producer of Clifford Odets's *The Story on Page One*. Like Odets, he had very much wanted to cast Marilyn. But Odets was not on Marilyn's list of approved directors. As chance would have it, George Cukor was. Marilyn had met Cukor several years previously when she was studying with his friend Constance Collier. According to Marilyn's contract, if Twentieth signed Cukor she would have no choice but to report to work on *The Billionaire*.

In the last days of summer, as Twentieth negotiated with Cukor, Miller was rushing to complete his second draft. On September 2, he wired Huston in Ireland that he was almost finished. Miller thanked God for that, explaining his own long silence by insisting he wanted to deliver the screenplay itself instead of merely talking about it. Yet as the fall approached, Miller clearly felt the need to give Huston some indication of progress. In contacting the director, he seemed to be giving himself a final push. Miller put further pressure on himself by talking about *The Misfits* to the *New York Times*. He announced that he had been at work on the script in Roxbury. He disclosed that they hoped to shoot in April 1960 and that the picture would star Marilyn and perhaps Jason Robards. It is possible that Miller sensed he was about to encounter difficulty with the last three pages, which would prove the hardest part of the script to write. Contacting Huston and agreeing to talk to the press may have been a way of leaving himself no choice but to finish.

On September 16, Twentieth made a deal with Cukor, and the next day a letter went out notifying Marilyn that she was to report for pre-production on November 2. Filming was scheduled to start the following week. Thus, before Marilyn could even think about appearing in Arthur's picture, she would be required to fulfill her obligation to Twentieth.

Gregory Peck needed to be finished by February 1. So, though it would be a tight fit, if all went well Marilyn would be available in time for *The Misfits*. Still, the last-minute commotion over *The Billionaire*—would Marilyn accept? would she be finished in time? would she agree to come out right away to meet with Jerry Wald?—was hardly what Miller needed as he struggled with two very different versions of the ending.

He did not accompany Marilyn when, at Skouras's behest, she flew to Los Angeles to attend a lunch in honor of Nikita Khrushchev at Twentieth Century–Fox. Though it was rumored that Miller had stayed away for political reasons, the truth was he remained in Connecticut to work.

The Khrushchev lunch, hosted by Frank Sinatra, was billed tongue-in-cheek as "the greatest spectacle ever staged in a motion picture studio." Many stars, studio executives, and journalists attended. In the crowd were Elizabeth Taylor, Debbie Reynolds, Judy Garland, and Kim Novak. To publicize her upcoming picture, Marilyn appeared on George Cukor's arm. She actually arrived early, prompting Billy Wilder to remark that Twentieth ought to hire Khrushchev to direct *The Billionaire*. Skouras, though he hosted the event, seemed eager to challenge the Communist leader to a public "sparring session."

"I was just a poor boy," Skouras began in a thick accent, "and now I'm head of a studio."

"I was just a poor boy," Khrushchev replied through a translator, "and now I'm head of Russia."

And so it went. Afterward, the consensus was that Khrushchev had "clobbered" the Old Greek.

The real reason for Marilyn's trip was a four-hour meeting the next day with Wald, Krasna, and Cukor. It was Sunday, September 20.

Marilyn was due to fly back to New York afterward. Yves Montand, who had played John Proctor in the French stage and screen versions of *The Crucible*, was to appear in concert on Broadway, opening the following evening. Since Arthur was busy putting the finishing touches on *The Misfits*, Marilyn was to attend the premiere in his place. He had arranged for her escort to be Montgomery Clift, who was about to leave for Tennessee to film *Wild River*, as *Time and Tide* had been renamed.

The fact that Marilyn had not yet read *The Billionaire* seemed to bother no one at the meeting, especially since Cukor had already demanded a rewrite. Norman Krasna used the opportunity to tell Marilyn the story in detail. To everyone's relief, when he finished, Marilyn seemed pleased.

"It's wonderful," she cooed. "I'm so enthusiastic. I can't wait to get started."

She promised not to peek at the script until the revisions were completed. She did, however, have certain requests of her own. Though Marilyn's contract gave her no say about the cameraman for this film, she made it clear that she preferred Harry Stradling, who had shot *A Streetcar Named Desire* for Kazan. And she wanted Jack Cole for her song-and-dance numbers.

Wald, said to be the model for Sammy Glick in Budd Schulberg's novel *What Makes Sammy Run?*, promised to try to "pin down" the people she wanted. Marilyn reiterated that she was thrilled with the package. She adored the idea of working with George Cukor and Gregory Peck. She emphasized that she had been discussing Norman Krasna with her husband. She wanted the screenwriter to know that Arthur had great faith in Krasna's ability to produce a script that would be good for her. The tensions in the marriage notwithstanding, Marilyn appeared to love quoting Arthur. She used every opportunity to throw his name around.

On Thursday, September 24, Miller finally sent off a second draft of *The Misfits*. He still planned to do some work on the ending. Nearly two years had passed since he had completed the 149-page first draft. The new version was nineteen pages longer. He was very excited about the rewrite, but of course it was Huston's reaction that counted. On Sunday, Miller could not resist wiring Huston to confirm that he had received the screenplay. The response he had been hoping for came two days later. "SCRIPT MAGNIFICENT," Huston wired from Ireland. Miller read the message with delight.

It is enormously revealing that before Miller replied to Huston, he dashed off a letter to Brooks Atkinson, the critic who had dubbed the postwar years on Broadway the Williams–Miller era. That, of course, was no longer the case. At the time of *The Crucible*, Eric Bentley had argued that Miller needed a Kazan. Whether or not one agreed, there could be no denying that Williams had been remarkably prolific in recent years while Miller, more and more, seemed to be devoid of inspiration. Eager to counter that impression, Miller wasted no time in contacting Atkinson, who had continued to warmly support the playwright and his work. On October 1, Miller declared that he hoped soon to repay Atkinson's faith with a new stage play. In the meantime, he informed Atkinson that, appearances to the contrary, he had hardly been inactive. In fact, he had been exploring a broader universe than he had known previously. Miller announced that, as a first leap into that new world, he had just finished *The Misfits*. Bursting with pride, he called it the most fully realized work he had written.

Did Miller really mean to suggest that *The Misfits* was superior to *Death of a Salesman*? Apparently so. At this point, he seemed very much to need to believe that to be true. Miller's exaggerated sense of what he had just accomplished sounds like a reaction to months of self-doubt, and to years of having repeatedly disappointed people's expectations.

Four days later, when Miller wrote to John Huston, he crowed that not since *Death of a Salesman* had he been so eager to see his work acted. He assumed the director would see why he had taken such a long time. In revising the screenplay, Miller had discovered an exciting new realm that he had needed time to explore. He felt certain that together they would be able to create something entirely new. He predicted that *The Misfits* was going to be one of those unique creative undertakings in which every aspect would instantly come to life. He assured Huston that Marilyn was getting in shape for the day when they began.

Even as Miller wrote this, however, Marilyn was launching a campaign for the lead in the film of *Breakfast at Tiffany's*. If it turned out to be successful, she would probably be unavailable for *The Misfits*. Truman Capote had put a good deal of Marilyn into the original novel. When Marilyn had first arrived in New York, she had been bright and hopeful, with everything seemingly ahead of her. In portraying Holly Golightly, perhaps she sought to recapture something of that earlier, more innocent period. At the same time, she seemed eager to subvert Arthur's plans. If he was willing to put up with anything to get his picture made, then Marilyn, apparently, was ready to do anything to stop it. She prepared two scenes from *Breakfast at Tiffany's* for Lee Strasberg's private class. She also performed the scenes for Capote. He insisted she was perfect for the part. But all the bad publicity about the trouble she had given Billy Wilder on *Some Like It Hot* made her *persona non grata* at Paramount. At length, over Capote's objections, the role went to Audrey Hepburn.

Now that the script was finished, the Millers spent most of their time in the city, driving to Connecticut on weekends in a Jaguar. In letters to Brooks Atkinson and John Huston, Arthur made a point of cheerfully mentioning Marilyn as if nothing had changed. Norman Rosten, at work on a screenplay based on *A View from the Bridge*, often stayed with the Millers in Roxbury. He could see that the image of marital harmony had become a façade.

When the couple fought in town, Marilyn sometimes spent the night at the Strasbergs. Paula would give her a soothing cup of tea and rub her shoulders. Lee, in striped pajamas and a decrepit bathrobe, would perch on the edge of Marilyn's bed. He was not known for being warm or affectionate, yet he abundantly provided the physical and emotional comfort she missed at home. Marilyn rested her head on his shoulder. He wrapped his arms around her. He stroked her hair. He tenderly sang a lullaby. She closed her eyes and smiled.

Strasberg was feeling rather needy himself lately, having been rejected for a top post at the new repertory theater at Lincoln Center. The Actors Studio had been conferring with the Lincoln Square Project (as Lincoln Center was then known) since 1956. Elia Kazan, Lee Strasberg, and Cheryl Crawford had offered their ideas for the theater that would be part of a cultural complex housing the Metropolitan Opera, the New York Philharmonic, and the New York City Ballet. Strasberg assumed the Actors Studio would be the resident company, and believed a leadership position his rightful place. Instead, Robert Whitehead, appointed to set up the theater, invited Kazan to be his partner.

Kazan, for his part, wasn't so sure he wanted the job. Tennessee Williams urged him to say no, reminding him that he was an artist, not an administrator. Whitehead, who had co-produced A *View from the Bridge* in New York, arranged a meeting between Miller and Kazan. They talked. They enjoyed each other's company. They both refrained from mentioning why they had been at odds since 1952. Miller agreed he would like to write for the new theater. For Kazan, a chance to work with Arthur Miller again was a major incentive to take the job at Lincoln Center.

Though Kazan would never forgive Miller for having walked past him that day with Kermit Bloomgarden, there could be no denying that Miller remained the playwright to whom he felt closest. In the past, Kazan had had occasion to think that he and Miller were actually the same person. He often felt he could share things with Miller that he could not with Williams. Kazan believed that in the aftermath of HUAC, Williams had been his most faithful friend, but it was Miller to whom Kazan, still admittedly tense, was ineluctably drawn.

Miller viewed Kazan as the best possible director for his autobiographical work-in-progress. Perhaps Eric Bentley had been right; perhaps Miller really did need a Kazan. At a deeply troubled moment in the Williams–Kazan collaboration, Miller stepped into the breach. At a deeply troubled moment in Miller's own marriage to Marilyn Monroe, he renewed his passionate friendship with the man he once called brother. Miller agreed to give his plays to the new company. Kazan, as in the old days, would direct.

On October 14, Kazan left to shoot *Wild River*, the film he was originally to have done with Marilyn. Seven days later, there was an official announcement that he had accepted a post as "an associate in the development and direction of the Lincoln Center Repertory Theater." Neither the reunion of Miller and Kazan, nor Miller's plans, was announced publicly. Even in New York theatrical circles, few people were aware that the momentous reconciliation had occurred, or had any inkling that one of the great creative teams of the modern American stage was due to be revived.

+   +   +

On October 14, Jack Cole arrived at the Dance Players Rehearsal Hall in New York City. He had a slight, bony physique, with a finely-lined, cadaverous face, a large, hooked nose, and a cast in one eye. He wore baggy blue jeans and a gray sweatshirt, the sleeves hiked up above his elbows. The dance director had first worked with Marilyn on *Gentlemen Prefer Blondes*. At her request, he had also been brought in on *River of No Return* and *There's No Business Like Show Business*. More recently, he had done uncredited work on *Some Like It Hot*.

Three and a half weeks previously, Marilyn had informed Jerry Wald that she wanted Jack Cole on *The Billionaire*. Twentieth, eager to please, went to considerable lengths to hire him. As a choreographer, he was very much in demand. He had television and Broadway commitments and would only be able to work on the picture a few weeks at a time. But in light of the fact that Marilyn believed she needed him, he was willing to squeeze her in.

Today, Cole waited at the rented rehearsal space in anticipation of working on "My Heart Belongs To Daddy." Thus far it was the only musical number definitely chosen for the film. Others were soon to follow. Gregory Peck's requirement that he be finished by February 1 meant George Cukor would be working on a tight schedule. Jerry Wald thought it best for Marilyn's numbers to be fully rehearsed before she arrived in Los Angeles. At this point, the plan was to shoot the musical numbers before anything else.

Cole knew that Marilyn was not a skilled dancer. He also knew she was a perfectionist. So they would need plenty of time to develop her first big number. He intended to go over the music with the rehearsal pianist and the drummer before Marilyn arrived. Knowing Marilyn as he did, he was certainly not surprised that she didn't appear on time. He was astonished, however, when she failed to show up altogether. The entire day was squandered. Cole, known for a hot temper and a foul mouth, was not amused.

The rest of the week was no better. Sometimes Marilyn didn't appear at all. Other days she came in but didn't work. By October 19, Cole was no longer sure he could have even one number ready to be filmed on November 3. And he was beginning to wonder if he really wanted to work on this picture after all. He was sufficiently alarmed to urge Twentieth to send someone to New York immediately to sort out the problems with Marilyn. Something was definitely wrong.

In Los Angeles, Jerry Wald grew nervous. At their last meeting,

Marilyn had given every indication that she was going to be the soul of cooperation. She had loved the story. She had gushed over the Cukor–Peck–Krasna package. What had changed in three and a half weeks? Wald had no idea that in that time John Huston had given the green light to The Misfits. From first to last, Twentieth would fail to grasp the degree to which The Misfits complicated both Marilyn's and Arthur's actions with regard to The Billionaire.

On October 24, George Cukor arrived in New York to talk to Marilyn and to select locations for three days of unit work. He held court at the Plaza. Cukor had a reputation for being "an actor's director." "He thought like an actor," recalled Tony Randall. "He knew what you were thinking when you were working. He knew what your problem was. He just got inside you. He was especially effective with women. He was all sympathy." With Marilyn, however, Cukor was prepared for the worst, being well-versed in Larry Olivier's and Vivien Leigh's horror stories. Hero-worshipping the Oliviers as he did, Cukor might actually have been disappointed had Marilyn behaved any other way. When she bitterly complained about the script, it became apparent that shooting might be held up until the story was revised to her satisfaction.

Arthur Miller signed up to do two weeks of rewrites. John Huston had announced an April start date and nothing must be done to force him to postpone. So it was in Miller's interest, every bit as much as Twentieth's, to get The Billionaire in the can. For once, Arthur Miller and Spyros Skouras found themselves on the same side. Miller met with Cukor and Jerry Wald, and a letter of agreement was prepared.

For a $15,000 fee, Arthur agreed to develop Marilyn's role. He did not, however, want any credit on screen or off. He wanted there to be no publicity about his involvement. Obviously, the news that he had been working on Cukor's picture would make it impossible to bill The Misfits as Arthur Miller's screenwriting debut, as well as the first work he had written expressly for Marilyn. By contract, Miller was to complete his work on The Billionaire by November 14.

He had reason to be excited about The Misfits. Huston was close to a deal with Clark Gable. In the beginning, Huston had been particularly keen on Robert Mitchum as Marilyn's co-star. When Mitchum was shooting The Night Fighters in Ireland, Huston suddenly appeared with Miller's screenplay. Mitchum read The Misfits and was baffled. The first draft made no sense to him. But Huston would not take no for an answer.

"If John Huston calls," Mitchum jestingly declared, "tell him I died." That didn't deter Huston either. Hardly had Miller completed a second draft when a copy was put in Mitchum's hands as he was boarding a plane to Australia. The second draft made no more sense to Mitchum than the first.

At the suggestion of Lew Wasserman, Huston shifted his sights to Clark Gable. Huston sent the script and a personal note to Gable in Rome, then flew in for a follow-up chat. On October 31, Huston wired Miller that he believed Gable was theirs. The actor would not commit, however, until he returned to Los Angeles and talked it over with his agent.

Arthur's revisions on The Billionaire were well under way when Marilyn reported to the Fox lot on November 9. Though she was consistently late to rehearsals, and though on the third day she inexplicably failed to return after lunch, Cukor and Wald weren't worried. Everyone seemed to be patting everyone else on the back about the brilliant decision to hire Miller. On Friday, November 13, he delivered his pages a day early. Wald rushed the script over to Gregory Peck.

The production was plunged into crisis when Gregory Peck, dismayed by the extent to which Marilyn's part had been built up, asked to cancel his contract. Peck was willing to return a $100,000 advance if Twentieth would release him. Buddy Adler reluctantly approved. The casting department called frantically all over town for a replacement. The candidates included Charlton Heston, James Stewart, Kirk Douglas, Cary Grant, Peter Lawford, Tony Curtis, and Rock Hudson. But nothing could be arranged. For a moment, with Twentieth scrambling to replace Peck, it looked as though the April start date on The Misfits was about to have to be put off. Once again, however, Arthur Miller saved the day. He recommended Yves Montand. Montand's one-man show had been a triumph in Los Angeles as it had been in New York. He was now performing in San Francisco.

In order to hire Montand, Twentieth would have to overlook the fact that the comedy of The Billionaire was based on the notion of a man who can't sing or dance pretending to be a song-and-dance man. That's why Gregory Peck had been cast. Montand, by contrast, was well known precisely as a song-and-dance man. Twentieth would also have to over-look the fact that Montand had very little English. And Spyros Skouras would have to overlook that Montand and his wife, Simone Signoret, were leftists.

In the interest of starting principal photography, all these draw-backs were instantly forgotten. Signoret, currently enjoying immense success as the sad older woman in the film *Room at the Top*, spoke fluent English. She took the call from Twentieth's casting department. She indi-cated that they planned to return to France for Christmas. Montand was to tour Japan after that. Signoret would, however, read the screenplay on her husband's behalf. A script was rushed to San Francisco and Montand nervously said yes. An opportunity to appear in a Hollywood film with Marilyn Monroe was a major incentive, of course. But no less important, apparently, was Miller's participation.

Montand deeply admired Miller both for his politics and his art. In 1953 Montand and Signoret had read a translation of *The Crucible* and decided it must be performed in Paris. The couple appeared in the highly successful French adaptation, *Les Sorcières de Salem*, as well as in a film version. The role of John Proctor, caught between his wife (played by Signoret) and his lover, was widely regarded as Montand's breakthrough as an actor.

Soon, Montand and Miller were to be seen exploring the residen-tial streets near the Beverly Hills Hotel. They passed gated, meticulously landscaped Spanish and Tudor-style mansions. On one occasion, a policeman stopped them to inquire what they were doing there. They usually walked while Marilyn was rehearsing with Cukor. Montand, who had a loping stride, welcomed the chance to strike up a friendship with his hero. These walks also served as impromptu English lessons, Montand having discovered that for some reason he understood every word Miller said. Montand was one of those rare individuals with whom Miller seemed to open up. The men talked about politics, their families, Hollywood.

Miller said it was impossible to think of this place as a city. "It doesn't smell like anything," he insisted. "In Europe, you can smell every-thing—cooking, garlic . . . " As he had been when he came here to sell *The Hook*, Miller was ambivalent. He both disdained and desired success Hollywood-style. He took pains to distance himself from the wealth and glitter even as he dreamt that *The Misfits* would be released as a road show—screened only at prestigious theaters with reserved seats and a high ticket price.

Hardly had Miller provided Twentieth with Montand when *The Misfits* lost its leading man. Clark Gable, upon returning to Los Angeles, changed his mind. Out of range of Huston's charm, Gable, like Robert Mitchum, decided the script didn't make sense. He read it several times, then told his agent he didn't want to do it. Huston urged Miller to talk to Gable. They were already acquainted, having met at Charlie Feldman's in 1951. Huston knew from Miller's letter of October 5 that he was confident his screenplay was a major work of art and *The Misfits* was going to be a great movie. Perhaps Miller's enthusiasm would convince Gable he'd be missing the boat if he turned this project down. As it happened, Miller's pitch was convoluted. He earnestly described *The Misfits* as an Eastern Western about the meaninglessness of life. But the gobbledegook seemed to work. Gable reread the screenplay and decided to take the part of Gay Langland after all. The offer of a $750,000 salary (excluding overtime) may also have influenced his decision.

Eli Wallach and Thelma Ritter having agreed to play Guido and Isabelle, one major part remained to be cast. For Perce, Miller thought of Montgomery Clift. Miller asked to see some of the footage of *Wild River* which Kazan had sent back to Twentieth. Later, he called Kazan in Tennessee to find out when he expected to finish. Kazan said Clift would be free by early January. Miller indicated he was going to send *The Misfits* to Clift, and asked Kazan to read it when Monty was done. On December 4, Miller offered Clift the role, adding that Marilyn was excited by the prospect of working with him. The start date, Miller announced, was now March 24. Clift accepted and the cast was complete.

John Huston swept through Los Angeles. He approved the casting. He wanted to cut the script. United Artists would not consider distributing a picture longer than two hours and ten minutes. Miller, however, seemed to believe that length was an advantage for roadshowing. Huston, it became clear, didn't see the film that way at all. He certainly didn't think it should be roadshowed. That, he pointed out, was for spectacles.

Huston, evidently, had a more realistic view of what Miller had actually written. He saw *The Misfits* as essentially a small picture. He argued it should be as modest and unpretentious as they could make it. Miller wanted to shoot the script as it was, then cut it down later. Huston was appalled. That kind of thinking, he said firmly, led to an atmosphere of waywardness and uncertainty that could prove fatal to a picture. He always found it to be a grave error to shoot scenes and speeches he wasn't certain were going to be in the film.

Nothing had been decided when Huston left in time to spend Christmas at St. Cleran's, his Georgian manor house in Galway. He invited Arthur and Marilyn to join him there as soon as she was finished at Twentieth. That Huston extended the invitation suggests he had no idea Cukor had yet to start filming *Let's Make Love*, as *The Billionaire* had been renamed.

Between November 9 and December 4, Marilyn's late arrivals, recorded at the studio gate, cost Cukor more than twenty-seven hours, or approximately three and a half days, of rehearsal time. The week of December 7, she kept Cukor waiting more than twelve hours. In the early part of the following week, nearly ten hours were lost.

Wilder, once he had settled the delicate matter of who was boss, had been known to rely on Paula Strasberg to reason with Marilyn. Cukor did not have that luxury, Marilyn having temporarily decided that she distrusted Paula. Paula sensed that Marilyn had begun to confuse her with her own mother. Gladys remained at Rockhaven Sanitarium in Glendale, where there were constant problems. Gladys insisted that the hospital staff wanted to poison her. She fought with her fellow patients. She tried to escape. She tried to kill herself. Paula, who had often played a mother's role with Marilyn, was the beneficiary of a good deal of Marilyn's anger at Gladys. That anger came to a head in November. Marilyn, in Los Angeles for the first time since her miscarriage, filed a petition in Superior Court appointing Inez Melson, her business manager, Gladys's conservator. Fearful that in killing her baby she had become just like Gladys, she pushed the mad mother away.

Marilyn finally consented to do the first wardrobe and makeup tests on Tuesday, December 15. Two days later, Buddy Adler, George Cukor, Jerry Wald, various studio executives, and Marilyn herself settled themselves in a screening room to look at the tests. The day began a new phase in her career.

When the tests for *The Sleeping Prince* were shown at Pinewood

Studios in 1956, three years previously, the relief and delight in the room had been palpable. Whatever Marilyn may have looked like in person—and initially Olivier had been horrified by her appearance—she was enchanting on screen. She had an extraordinary ability to project. She had what cinematographers call "flesh impact." The naked eye might not perceive it, but the camera certainly did. But on Thursday, December 17, 1959, when Marilyn appeared on screen, Buddy Adler was shocked and dismayed. The color tests were disastrous. Marilyn, it seemed, could no longer be relied on to be utterly magical on camera. Her makeup was peculiar. Her hairdo was unflattering. Her blue gown didn't work. She didn't look like herself. How was Marilyn supposed to look? Certainly not ordinary.

Adler advised Wald and Cukor to run a scene from Bus Stop. He instructed them to view The Seven Year Itch as an even better example of what he had in mind. Above all, he urged them to study any reel of Some Like It Hot to see Marilyn Monroe "as she should be."

What did Marilyn think? Before anyone had a chance to ask, she had vanished. On Friday, Marilyn called in sick. On Monday, she called in sick. On Tuesday, she called in sick. On Wednesday, she called in sick. On Thursday, Christmas Eve, a half-day, she called in sick. Marilyn's opinion of the tests was clear.

Meanwhile, Twentieth had once again brought in Arthur to work on the script. On December 23, he officially began a second set of revisions, for which he was to be paid an additional $5,000. The pages were due on January 4. That day, Marilyn reported for a wardrobe fitting, leaving after only twenty minutes, and a physician called Twentieth to say she was ill. In her bungalow at the Beverly Hills Hotel, Marilyn had been feasting on a suicidal smorgasbord of drugs: Demerol, sodium pentothol, Amytal, phenobarbital. Her speech was slurred. She could barely carry on a conversation.

Marilyn attempted to rehearse on January 6, 1960, but remained on the studio lot for a mere half hour. Obviously, at this rate the picture was never going to get made. Two days later, Lew Schreiber had a call from George Chasin at MCA. Marilyn's agent indicated that she would return to work in ten days. Chasin said he'd had a long talk with her. Marilyn promised to report on time and to work diligently. With a January 18 start date, if all went well principal photography was now scheduled to conclude on March 25.

That meant Marilyn would have to go directly from *Let's Make Love* to *The Misfits*. It was hard to imagine how she could do that in her present condition, but technically it was possible. Miller certainly appeared eager to get her through. The same day her agent talked to Schreiber, Arthur began a third set of rewrites on *Let's Make Love* for an additional $7,500 fee.

Meanwhile, he was supposed to be trimming *The Misfits*. Frank Taylor, who had signed on to produce, did a good deal of fast talking to avoid answering United Artists' queries about length. When Taylor talked to the author about cuts, Miller was a bit stubborn. He did, however, promise to take another look at the script. In particular, he would see what he could do about removing process shots, because Huston had complained there were too many. The action in a process shot is filmed against a background of previously filmed footage.

On January 11, Huston informed Taylor that he, too, was trying to cut. He was confident that together they'd be able to bring the script down to size. Huston was immobilized, having managed to break his knee in a riding accident. Proposing to mix work with a holiday, he invited Miller and Taylor to St. Cleran's for a few weeks. If Marilyn hadn't yet finished *Let's Make Love*, she could join them a bit later. In fact, she had yet to begin.

On Saturday, January 16, Twentieth hosted a press party to welcome Yves Montand. Shy and awkward, he read a short speech in broken English. He had squinty eyes and pronounced ears. When he grinned, huge teeth flashed beneath a rubbery upper lip. The Millers and the Montands posed together, laughing and smiling. Marilyn looked adorable. She gave every indication of being ready to return to work. With a twinkle in her eye, she told reporters that besides her husband and Marlon Brando, Yves Montand was the most attractive man she knew. She did not, however, mention what she had been saying in private, that Montand reminded her of Joe DiMaggio. Studio executives went home confident the picture's problems were behind them. With principal photography set to begin, Arthur made reservations to fly to Ireland on February 3 or 4.

On Sunday, in a green-carpeted bungalow at the Beverly Hills Hotel, Montand said his "English prayers," as he jestingly called learning lines by rote. Signoret worked with him for hours, endlessly reviewing

Monday's scenes. He was admittedly terrified of going in front of the camera and, especially, of having to do it all in English. He would have felt considerably worse if he'd had any idea of what was going on next door.

In the hours since the party, Marilyn's composure had shattered. At 5 p.m. the studio received word that she would not be coming in tomorrow after all. A frantic call was made to Montand. Cukor planned to shoot material that did not require Marilyn. Montand scrambled to memorize new lines. Soon, his brain was a porridge of words and phrases he barely comprehended. When, full of anxiety, Montand left for work the next morning, the curtains in the Miller bungalow were ominously shut. They remained shut throughout the week as Marilyn repeatedly called in sick. Day after day, Montand found himself shifting gears at the last minute. By Thursday, he was no longer able to cope, and the entire production ground to a halt. The next day, John Huston received word that Miller's arrival in Ireland was to be delayed.

Clearly something had to be done. From New York, Marianne Kris had recommended a distinguished colleague in Los Angeles, Ralph Greenson. Marilyn's psychoanalyst did not take lightly the matter of referring a patient to a new doctor; her dying husband had used his last breath to recommend new doctors for his patients. Dr. Greenson was in the circle of Marianne Kris's lifelong friend Anna Freud. He was Clinical Professor of Psychiatry at the University of California Medical School at Los Angeles, Dean of the Training School at the Los Angeles Institute for Psychoanalysis, and on the Medical Advisory Board of the Reiss–Davis Clinic. He counted many Hollywood personalities among his patients, including Peter Lorre, Frank Sinatra, and Vivien Leigh. The doctor had pouchy brown eyes and a shaggy moustache. His New York-accented speech was forceful and deliberate. He prided himself on meeting people easily. He boasted that he was exceptionally good in the first hours with a new patient. He contrasted himself with most analysts who, in his view, suffer from stage fright; afraid to be seen, they prefer to hide behind the couch. Dr. Greenson insisted on encountering patients face to face. He was outspoken and confrontational. He wanted patients to react to him not as a god but as a fallible human being. He was the first to enumerate his own flaws. He readily admitted his tendency to exaggerate and to be too sure of himself. When, as Marilyn did, a new patient mentioned a previous doctor, he relished the opportunity to ask, "And what do you think about me?"

Greenson came to Marilyn's bungalow at the Beverly Hills Hotel. He drastically limited her intake of drugs. He insisted that Marilyn discontinue her longtime practice of getting prescriptions from a number of different physicians. He listened patiently to her grievances about the picture she was making and about her husband.

Marilyn reported to George Cukor on Monday, January 25, and filmed part of "My Heart Belongs To Daddy." Yves Montand had no call that day. She returned on Tuesday. Again, she worked on her own. Her first scene with Montand was to be shot on Wednesday. She arrived on time at 7 a.m. But two hours later, Marilyn, in full makeup, abruptly announced that she had to go home. Before anyone knew quite what had happened, Marilyn had disappeared. Yet again, Montand was left in the lurch. He frantically closeted himself with his English coach, trying to learn by rote a new set of lines. The company took three hours to move to Stage 14 in order to shoot an office scene.

After Marilyn departed, Buddy Adler screened Monday's dailies. He was anxious to see what she looked like. After his complaints about the wardrobe and makeup tests, he assumed her appearance would be improved. Watching the rushes, he went wild. Nothing in the tests had quite prepared him for this. Marilyn didn't look well at all. He grumbled that she was fat, and that in the dance number she actually looked pregnant. Though Adler had stated plainly that he didn't want Marilyn to use the chalky white makeup from Bus Stop, that's precisely what she had done.

Jerry Wald called Adler to smooth things over. Wald was famous for his ability to talk people to death. To explain what he delicately called the "bumpy look" around Marilyn's middle, the fat producer claimed her sweater had been sewn to her leotard. Wald insisted that if Marilyn's sweater were loose, the problem would be solved. Confidently he assured Adler that once the dance sequence had been edited, the speed and intensity of the number would cause viewers to be less conscious of Marilyn's appearance. But in private, Wald was extremely worried. He sent a copy of Adler's critique to Cukor in the hope that something could be done.

Meanwhile, no sooner had Marilyn disappeared from the studio lot than MCA officially notified Twentieth that she was scheduled to begin *The Misfits* between April 1 and April 14. The agents' timing could hardly have been worse. At a moment when Marilyn had yet to appear in a single shot with Yves Montand, Buddy Adler had had about all he could take.

At long last, on Friday, January 29, Marilyn prepared to go in front of the cameras with her co-star. It was 10 a.m. and they were on Stage 11. Marilyn approached Montand.

"You're going to see what it means to shoot with the worst actress in the world," she declared.

"So you're scared," Montand replied, a pleading expression on his furrowed face. "Think of me a little bit. I'm lost."

His display of vulnerability did the trick. Marilyn worked with him that day, and every day of the week that followed. Yes, she was constantly late. Yes, she wasted time postponing the moment when she emerged from her dressing room. Yes, she sipped gin from a teacup. Yes, she appeared unable to remember more than one line at a time. But it seemed that Cukor was finally getting the picture made.

Arthur was able to slip off briefly to New York to concentrate on cutting *The Misfits*. By the time he flew back to Los Angeles on February 4, Twentieth was estimating that Cukor would finish shooting on April 6. With post-production, that meant the start date for *The Misfits* would have to be rolled back.

Marilyn had been working steadily for eight days when Arthur flew to Ireland, planning to stay with Huston for two weeks. At seven that morning Marilyn called in sick. Her decision to stop the production again was clearly tied to Arthur's departure. She did come in the next day, February 11, but was quickly sent home when it became apparent that she was in no condition to work.

That morning, the studio attorney responded to MCA's notice that Marilyn had to be ready to start another picture on April 1, by declaring that the studio would need an extension to complete *Let's Make Love*. He included a day-by-day breakdown of all the time that had been lost due to Marilyn. Exactly how long it would now take to finish the film was impossible to say.

In the days that followed, Marilyn alternated between working partial days and calling in sick. On Thursday, February 18, she escalated matters. She stayed out without notifying the studio. Twentieth called her bungalow repeatedly, but there was no answer. The hotel switchboard reported that Marilyn had made at least one outgoing call, so at least they knew she was alive.

Montand, boiling with rage, sent Signoret to see what was going on. She knocked on the door and called, but Marilyn refused to answer. Later, Montand put a note under her door. Presumably, Signoret had assisted in writing it. "Don't leave me to work for hours on end on a scene you've already decided not to do the next day," Montand implored. "I'm not the enemy, I'm your pal. And capricious little girls have never amused me."

That night, Miller called the Montands from Galway. Marilyn had asked him to call. Fearful and ashamed, she wanted Montand and Signoret to come back to her door. When they arrived, Marilyn, weeping, begged their forgiveness. She admitted she had been bad. She promised not to do it again. Arthur, though he had been given an idea of his wife's torment, remained at St. Cleran's for one week more, working on *The Misfits* with Huston.

Everyone was walking on eggshells when Marilyn came in on Monday at 10:30 a.m. The Academy Award nominations had been announced. Billy Wilder had been nominated as Best Director for *Some Like It Hot*. Wilder and I. A. L. Diamond had been nominated for Best Screenplay. Jack Lemmon had been nominated for Best Actor. The film had other nominations in the categories of cinematography, art direction and set decoration, and costume design.

In what a good many people considered a glaring omission, Marilyn Monroe had not received a Best Actress nomination. As it happened, Simone Signoret had, for *Room at the Top*. Marilyn showed no irritation. When she saw Signoret, she made a point of cheerfully congratulating her. Marilyn seemed to take the affront well. Day after day, she dutifully reported to work. She viewed the rushes with interest. Yet something was bothering her. She seemed to do everything in slow motion. On Monday, Cukor had been more than seven days behind schedule. By Friday, he was running ten days late.

On Saturday afternoon, Lew Schreiber, at work in his office, had a call from the front gate. George Chasin wanted to see him. Schreiber told the guard to send Marilyn's agent right in. Marilyn, it seemed, was terribly upset about being scheduled to work on Monday with an actress named Mara Lynn. She had complained to Chasin that Lynn had put blonde streaks in her hair. Unless Lynn's hair was changed, or the actress was dismissed, Marilyn would not report to the studio lot next week. Schreiber was surprised she would take such an adamant position on a minor player's hair color. Yet the fact remained that Marilyn had been angry enough to get her agent to show up on a Saturday. So something had better be done to humor her. Schreiber called Billy Gordon. He demanded to know why a blonde had been engaged for the scene. The casting director insisted that in fact Lynn was a brunette. They had put a red wig on her to be certain that her hair coloring was completely different from Marilyn's.

As Schreiber listened, an even more disturbing fact emerged. Schreiber, like Chasin, had assumed Marilyn was talking about a bit actress who was to start on Monday. Now he realized that Lynn, in the role of Lily, was already established in the picture. She had started on January 29. Schreiber realized that he had seen Lynn in the rushes and that her hair was definitely red.

Chasin departed, faced with the unenviable task of getting back to Marilyn. For hours she did not answer the phone. Arthur being due back that night, the agent resolved to talk the matter over with him. Meanwhile, Schreiber called all around town. He tracked down Cukor. He tracked down Wald. They confirmed that Lynn had been ordered to wear a red wig. There was no way any sane person could mistake her for a blonde. Clearly, Marilyn had been seeing things. That realization put the fear of God into everybody. No one guessed, however, that Marilyn had found a way to express her worst fear. Though Marilyn was a blonde, she was terrified of being confused with "the woman with the red hair." She did not want to turn into her mother.

The incident drastically changed the studio's view of Marilyn. In the old days, Zanuck had dismissed her as an idiot who didn't know the first thing about filmmaking. But now, she wasn't merely being difficult, or stubborn, or capricious. Her mind appeared to have been addled by drugs. Like her mother, she had delusions of persecution. From this point on, Twentieth treated Marilyn as though she were mad.

For weeks, Buddy Adler had been criticizing her appearance. He had complained about her weight. He had complained about her makeup. He had complained about her hair. Suddenly, Twentieth sent word to Marilyn that Mr. Adler, Mr. Wald, Mr. Cukor, and Mr. Schreiber all believed she looked fine. Nobody intended to utter another peep about her looks. The studio was concerned with one thing only—getting the picture made.

Eventually, Chasin reached Arthur by phone. No sooner had he walked in the door of the bungalow than he was swept up in Marilyn's problems again. Chasin, relating the situation to Arthur, pointed out that there was no similarity between Marilyn and the other actress. Marilyn's own agent now was insisting that she was trying to make an issue out of a trivial matter. He warned that Cukor was ready to throw in the towel. He suggested in strong terms that Marilyn would be wise to get on with it and finish Let's Make Love.

Twentieth wanted Cukor to go more quickly. And he would have been happy to do so, except that he was worried about the effect of pushing Marilyn. Cukor was an old hand at working with drunks and crazies. He had directed John Barrymore, Spencer Tracy, Vivien Leigh, and Judy Garland. He very much wanted to keep Twentieth happy. After the traumatic experience of having been dismissed from Gone with the Wind, he had gone out of his way to please studio executives. At the same time, he certainly didn't want to trigger a paranoid episode in his leading lady.

Cukor feared that might happen when a production executive visited the set on March 2. Marilyn had not yet arrived that morning, when Sid Rogell had a chat with Cukor. Rogell complained that Cukor was over-covering. He protested that the director was making far too many takes, and criticized him for repeatedly giving in to Marilyn. Instead of worrying about Rogell's objections, Cukor seemed vastly more concerned that Marilyn would discover the men in conversation. She was likely to assume that Cukor and Rogell were plotting against her.

As it happened, the discussion had been pointless anyway. The Screen Actors Guild went on strike at the end of the week. On March 4, the cameras on Let's Make Love recorded their last scene. Three days later, production was officially suspended for the rest of the strike. After all the delays, this latest complication left everyone concerned completely up a creek. Only recently, Wald had been hoping that he would have Let's Make Love in the can by April 13. If the strike dragged on—and there were indications that it might—there was no telling when they would finish.

Yves Montand was desperate to finish in order to get to Japan in time to keep his concert commitments. Arthur needed to get Marilyn out of this film and on to The Misfits. Cukor was in a state. He had shot only seventy-four pages of a 150-page script. During the strike, he put in frequent appearances at the studio. He tried to get ahead on the editing. He did what he could to move things along. But his efforts were in vain; he could accomplish little without actors. Finally, he consoled himself for the shutdown by ordering a new Rolls Royce, proof that at least he was being well paid for his headaches.

It looked as if it would be a considerable time before the strike was settled, so Arthur and Marilyn decided to fly back to New York for the duration. Though she had been seeing Dr. Greenson regularly, back in New York she would be able to see Dr. Kris, and perhaps regain some sort of balance during the break from work. Arthur needed to finish the third draft of The Misfits, which still had to be submitted to United Artists for final approval. The Montands would remain in Los Angeles. Before Marilyn could leave, however, she had to appear the following evening, Tuesday, March 8, at the Golden Globe Awards. Though she didn't feel it was a proper compensation for her failure to be nominated for an Oscar, the Foreign Press had nominated her for Some Like It Hot as Best Actress in a comedy. Marilyn had promised to attend the ceremonies.

Sam Shaw was then in Los Angeles to photograph John Wayne. He had just checked in at the Chateau Marmont that Tuesday evening when he got a call from Marilyn, asking him to come to the Beverly Hills Hotel right away. He had no idea what she wanted. Not long afterward, Shaw walked into the living room of Marilyn's bungalow. There were three people sitting in the room—in total silence. Montand and Signoret sat in one corner as though waiting patiently for someone to arrive. On the other side of the room sat Arthur.

Since his return from Ireland on February 27, Arthur had worked ceaselessly as he tried to complete a new draft of The Misfits which incorporated his discussions with Huston. Even now, he was still not quite finished, and he knew that there could be additional weeks of delay on Let's Make Love because of the strike. He had a look of total distraction, as if he were off in some other world with his screenplay. He was bedraggled and unshaven. On the table in front of him was a plate with a huge steak, recently delivered by room service. Arthur stared at the plate, methodically cutting off a piece of meat. He lifted the fork to his mouth, chewed, then cut another piece. Meanwhile, no one spoke until suddenly Marilyn could be heard calling cheerily, "Sam Spade, come in here!"

Shaw entered the bedroom. There he discovered an equally silent and nearly catatonic Whitey Snyder. Marilyn's makeup man sat on a bench in front of a table with a mirror and many little makeup jars. But there was still no sign of Marilyn.

Then she called out again: "In here!"

Shaw entered the bathroom. Marilyn, in the bath tub, was "encased in ice cubes." There was no water in the tub, only ice.

Shaw and Marilyn had been friends for years, and he was rarely surprised by anything she did. He sat down on the edge of the tub as if there were nothing odd about his having just walked through a silent cast of characters to be greeted by a naked movie star in a bath of ice. Marilyn, by then having passed into full character in anticipation of the evening ahead, offered a deadpan and sincere explanation: "The ice cubes will keep my body up and firm!" Sam responded in kind, pointing out that Katharine Dunham used much the same technique. Before going on stage, the dancer always put her feet in a bucket of ice.

The two friends talked for a while until finally Marilyn stood up out of the ice. Sam, scrutinizing her naked body, declared approvingly that the ice had done its work. Soon they moved into the bedroom, Sam continuing to chat with Marilyn as she was dressed and made up. Whitey painted her face. Signoret was called in to fiddle with Marilyn's snug bodice to be certain her breasts did not unexpectedly pop out.

By this time, a publicist was waiting in the living room. As Marilyn entered, Arthur, who in all this time seemed not to have said a word, rose silently from his dinner. He picked up the long train of Marilyn's gown, dutifully following her out to a chauffeur-driven car. It was an unforgettable image—the great playwright carrying Marilyn's train—one that reminded Shaw of nothing so much as Emil Jannings and Marlene Dietrich in The Blue Angel.

Marilyn, evidently, had worn them all down. Yet that night at the Golden Globes, no one would ever have guessed that she was anything but the delightful, enchanting character that Billy Wilder had captured on film one last time. When Marilyn won the award, it was richly deserved—as well as a poignant reminder of what might have been, and of how truly sad this whole thing had become. By the next morning, the fairy-tale princess had become the nervous, despondent Marilyn again.

+ FIFTEEN +

On March 24, 1960, Billy Wilder and his wife Audrey drove up Charlie Feldman's driveway in Coldwater Canyon. So did the Gary Coopers and the Irving Lazars. Tony Curtis put in an appearance. Warren Beatty arrived with Joan Collins. Beatty, touted as the next James Dean, was about to be directed by Elia Kazan in *Splendor in the Grass*. Kazan, though on the guest list, was not in town yet on account of the Screen Actors Guild strike. Had he attended, there might have been some awkwardness with Simone Signoret. Disdainful of Kazan's politics, Signoret had refused to consider being directed by him in an adaptation of Colette's *Chéri*.

Charlie Feldman would soon be fifty-six. Though he still kept a black book, he was no longer preoccupied with having a new girl every night. He was then involved with Capucine, a twenty-seven-year-old French model who had come to Hollywood with the hope of becoming a star. When the question of acting lessons arose, Feldman knew just the woman for the job. Natasha Lytess was hired to do for Capucine what she had once done for Marilyn.

These days, Yves Montand and Simone Signoret were often to be seen at Feldman's. Twentieth paid their expenses during the strike. In the aftermath of her Academy Award nomination, this was very much Signoret's moment. She quickly became a beloved figure in Hollywood. She was smart, witty, sexy, self-assured. She wasn't obsessed with aging. She had no particular interest in stardom. She had a terrific marriage—or at least she seemed to.

Montand, who wore an identical wedding ring, claimed not to be upset about playing second fiddle to his wife. Tonight, his sole disappointment was that Frank Sinatra had sent regrets. Montand was eager for Sinatra to do a guest spot in *Let's Make Love*. He hoped to make the pitch himself, Sinatra having already said no to Jerry Wald. Montand had asked that Sinatra be invited to this evening's party in honor of the French designer Hubert Givenchy.

On April 4, Simone Signoret was named Best Actress at the Academy Awards ceremony at the Pantages Theater, ahead of Elizabeth Taylor, Katharine Hepburn, Audrey Hepburn, and Doris Day. It was an extraordinary achievement for a French actress in a small English film. Signoret believed that her Oscar had less to do with her performance than with Hollywood's need to prove to itself that McCarthyism was a thing of the past. Five days later, she returned to France. She left calmly, with every reason to anticipate being separated from her husband for no more than a month. *Let's Make Love* was about to resume production, the strike having been settled on April 8. Montand's Japanese concert tour was scheduled to begin in May.

Signoret also had every reason to expect that Marilyn would not be alone in Los Angeles. Arthur had accomplished most of what he had gone to New York to do. He had completed a fresh draft of *The Misfits*, and Frank Taylor reported to Huston that the script was substantially improved, down to a running time of two hours and twenty minutes. That was still long, but Miller hoped to cut a bit more in the final third. He continued to have problems with the end. Nonetheless, the script was almost ready to be sent over to United Artists. If all went well, Huston planned to start filming on June 13.

Marilyn returned to Los Angeles on April 11. Arthur accompanied her on the flight from New York. The couple again checked into a bungalow at the Beverly Hills Hotel. Montand was still in residence as well, but this time he was alone.

The day after her return, Marilyn reported for rehearsals. Then, on April 13, she stepped before the cameras again. Immediately, the pace of filming slowed. Montand tried to postpone his Japanese tour, but the promoters declined; they also refused Spyros Skouras's offer to buy out Montand's contract. Jerry Wald, hoping to expedite matters, urged Cukor not to shoot so many closeups. The director explained that it was hard to get a decent closeup of Marilyn anymore. Evidently, he was unaware that Adler and other studio executives had ceased to be particularly concerned with her appearance. Cukor, choosing his words, said Marilyn did not "look her best" in profile. She had gained a good deal of weight during the strike. He had to stage scenes in a way that permitted him to shoot her favorably. That took time.

It did not help that Marilyn almost never put in a full day. She tended to give Cukor four hours at most. Lew Schreiber summoned George Chasin, imploring the agent to explain the facts of life to her. If Marilyn didn't hurry up, she would never get to make *The Misfits*. To the perplexity of studio executives, the argument seemed to impress her not at all. And Cukor was more aware than anyone that if he were to show the slightest impatience no matter how late Marilyn arrived or how many takes she required, she was likely to shatter into a million pieces and be completely useless to him.

The sixty-year-old Cukor, however, was not an easy-going person, even in the best of circumstances—and this was hardly the best. Highly-strung and nervous, he fought a lifetime battle with his weight, alternating between diets—controlling his appetite with diet pills which only sharpened his already fierce temper—and episodes of bingeing on food. At the moment, he was in a diet phase. Thus, he could not comfort himself by eating during the seemingly endless hours he had to wait for Marilyn on the set. Instead, he developed a most peculiar alternative: he would stifle his rage by tearing bits of paper off the script, stuffing them into his mouth. It was as though he could silence himself that way, keep himself from exploding at Marilyn when she arrived. Cukor, pacing back and forth, would chew pieces of the script until finally, Tony Randall said, "his mouth was white with paper." Upon seeing Marilyn, Cukor would swallow the paper in a great gulp before greeting her with a burst of effusive delight.

It was evident to everyone that Marilyn was deeply depressed. Tony Randall, also in the picture, studied her one night in the rushes. "Her eyes would be kind of dull," he said. "On the word 'Action!' her face would light up and the eyes got bright and she did the scene. With the word 'Cut!' she drooped in the most desperate depression." Watching Marilyn, her head down on her chest, Randall was reminded of a deflated tire. "You saw the real Marilyn there," he recalled, "how unhappy she was with herself."

Randall observed something similar when they all left after the rushes. "She got in her car," he remembered, "and she slumped all the way down in the back seat so that she was almost out of sight. It was just such self-loathing, such disappointment in oneself. It was pitiful."

Arthur remained in Los Angeles with Marilyn for only a few days. After he had attended to some *Misfits*-related business, he returned to New York to try to finish his screenplay. That April of 1960, as he had done nine years before, Miller left Marilyn alone in Los Angeles with his friend. This time, Marilyn remained behind not with Kazan but with Yves Montand. In 1951, Marilyn had reacted to Arthur's departure with a certain sadness. This time, she reacted with anger. For months, Marilyn had given Arthur every possible signal that she was distraught, yet *The Misfits* remained his priority. Nothing she did cracked his self-absorption. The man who had once written, "Attention, attention must be finally paid to such a person," should have known that Marilyn would keep trying to get his attention in whatever way she could.

Marilyn stayed home from work with a fever. At the end of the day, Montand ran into Paula. Had she been sent there to intercept him? Paula urged Montand to visit Marilyn. She said Marilyn was distressed about having called in sick. She insisted a visit would make her feel better.

Marilyn greeted him in bed. He sat on the edge of the mattress, made small talk, and stroked her hand. Then, he said, he really had to go home to prepare for tomorrow. He planted a goodnight kiss on her cheek. She moved slightly. Their lips met. He felt a pang of guilt. And matters proceeded from there. Marilyn had seduced John Proctor. The following night she came to his bungalow. When she took off her mink coat, she was naked.

That Marilyn may also have been feeling guilty is suggested by the fact that during the first week of her affair, she made prolonged lunchtime visits to Dr. Greenson. His Beverly Hills office was a few minutes from the studio. After these sessions, either she did not return to work at all or she locked herself in her dressing room for an hour before assistants were permitted to do her hair and makeup. She had a lot to think about. Greenson told Marilyn that he would not help her to spite her husband.

But was it mere spite that motivated her? Or was Marilyn testing

Arthur? By this time, she had tried almost everything to provoke him. One thinks of that night at the Strasberg apartment when Marilyn was abusive all evening, then asked why Arthur hadn't slapped her. If sleeping with his friend didn't do the trick, what would? Marilyn's affair with the actor who had played John Proctor was not just an on-the-set fling; it was a calculated gesture on her part. She later told Kazan that she resented what she saw as Arthur's tendency to cast himself as morally superior to her and others. The author of *The Crucible* may have been a master of self-justification, but Marilyn did not plan to let him get away with it this time. She was not about to let Arthur tell himself that *The Misfits* was a gift for her. If he went ahead with his film after Marilyn's betrayal, Miller would have to face the fact that, in his wife's eyes at least, he was a user like all the rest. In challenging Arthur to proceed with *The Misfits*, Marilyn brutally assaulted his core sense of himself. She attacked his posture of moral superiority. She cried out that he was no better than she. For Marilyn, this wasn't about Yves Montand at all; it was about Arthur Miller.

Arthur, in New York, clearly had no idea of what was going on. Perhaps he refused to know. He knew only that Marilyn appeared to be in excellent spirits. He did not seem suspicious about why his wife, who had barely managed to drag herself through the film, was suddenly so pleased. As though he had blinders on, he attributed the change not to Montand but to Cukor. On April 30, he wrote to thank Cukor for all he had done for Marilyn. He was effusive. He said he had never known Marilyn to be so happy in her work or so full of hope. He commended the director for his patience and for his skill. He guessed that by now Cukor understood why Marilyn was so precious to him. He explained that he still had work to do in the east but didn't know how much longer he could bear to live as a bachelor. Miller's letter must have made interesting reading for Cukor, who had been among the first to know about the affair.

Perhaps it was her husband's very lack of suspiciousness that caused Marilyn to flaunt the relationship. Dr. Greenson's departure for ten days of lectures in Detroit and Atlantic City seemed to liberate her. In Montand's bungalow one morning, she permitted herself to be seen by a room-service waiter, and soon people were talking all over town.

A little over a week after he had written to Cukor, Arthur appeared in Los Angeles. By then he may have been the last person to find out. Even when he did discover that his wife had been sleeping with her co-star, he proceeded with his plans. He suppressed his anger. Yet at least one old friend discerned the feeling in Miller's voice, the hurt in his face.

Elia Kazan, at work on *Splendor in the Grass*, had heard all about Marilyn's affair. He was struck by the flagrancy of her actions. From the first, Kazan had believed that Marilyn was not the sort of girl one married. He wondered whether Miller, in his view an innocent, would be able to handle the punishment. He contacted Miller and suggested they meet. Nothing could be more ironic than the fact that it was Kazan who felt called on to comfort Miller. Nine years before, Kazan, like Montand, had carried on an affair with Marilyn when his friend Miller returned to New York.

Kazan and Miller, at their first meeting after seven years, had refrained from talk of HUAC. This time, they avoided mention of Marilyn. Yet that painful topic formed the subtext of the encounter. Kazan regarded Miller's restraint as manful. Much had changed in the five months since Miller's call to Kazan on location, when Miller had looked like a winner again; five months later, he was a cuckold and many people in Hollywood knew it. Kazan reached out, and Miller appeared to welcome his sympathy and interest.

When Arthur returned to the east, Marilyn was seen everywhere with Montand. They attended a screening of Billy Wilder's *The Apartment*. She took him to a party at Romanoff's. When Tennessee Williams brought his mother to Cukor's set to say hello to Marilyn and invite her to lunch, Marilyn left no doubt in his mind that she was having an affair. She appeared increasingly shrill and desperate. At times, the burly Montand actually seemed afraid of her. He, like everyone else on *Let's Make Love*, had abundant evidence that Marilyn was unstable. He did not want to offend her, but he didn't want matters to get out of hand either. This was his first Hollywood film, and he didn't want to ruin his chance.

Cheryl Crawford, who hoped to cast Montand in a Broadway musical, took him and Marilyn to a party at David Selznick's house. The evening was a disaster. Simone Signoret had endeared herself to Hollywood. Montand was winning no popularity contests for having betrayed her. Late in the evening, Marilyn overheard Greg Bautzer,

Howard Hughes's lawyer, in conversation. Bautzer, massive and powerful, was a rough number, always prepared for a tussle. He remembered Marilyn from the days when she was on call at Uncle Joe's. In his deep, booming voice, Bautzer announced that Joe Schenck was near death. Aged eighty-one, he had had a heart attack and later slipped into a coma. Marilyn went wild, screaming that it couldn't be true. She knew she would have been called. She insisted she had to see Uncle Joe immediately. Bautzer responded angrily, contemptuously. He reminded her of who she was. He told her to save her tears. He berated her for having failed to visit when Schenck might actually have enjoyed seeing her.

Montand could not understand why Bautzer addressed her so disrespectfully. Marilyn knew only too well. It was her first taste of what life was going to be like now that she had discarded the protective shield of being Mrs. Arthur Miller. In the beginning, she had been drawn to Miller precisely because he was capable of absolving her of all she was ashamed of in her past. Now, as Johnny Hyde would have said, she was right back on her ass with all the other girls. And she had done it herself.

Meanwhile, Marilyn had not heard Montand declare he wanted to leave. Montand liked to say that having been born poor, he always had his eye on the emergency exit. He took Marilyn's car. When she found out he was gone, she drunkenly ran down the hill in pursuit. She disappeared into the darkness, insisting at the top of her lungs that she would catch up.

The affair had started as a way of testing Arthur, but now it became something else. Marilyn, having seen for herself what life was going to be like without Miller, looked to Montand as her new protector. She decided he must divorce Signoret and marry her. Montand intended to do no such thing. His worst fears were realized; the situation was flying out of control. A minute ago Marilyn had been livid that Miller was using her; now she was intent on proving how useful she could be to Montand.

Marilyn seized on Montand's desire to have Frank Sinatra make an appearance in their film. Twentieth was ready to go with Bing Crosby, but Marilyn insisted she could get Sinatra. For more than ten days, making that happen became her obsession. She swore everyone to secrecy. Jerry Wald joked that there was more "hush-hush" about the operation than about the U-2 flying over the Soviet Union. But the jokes soon fell flat. Marilyn's efforts became embarrassing.

She hounded Sinatra, calling him repeatedly in Honolulu. Obviously, he did not want to be in the film. She pleaded with him to say yes. She promised to do something for him in exchange. She would not take no for an answer. She begged Wald for more time. Finally, on a Friday afternoon, Wald told Marilyn that a decision had to be made. He gave her until next week. If she could not get a firm commitment, he planned to call Bing Crosby. Marilyn, who had a reputation as "a phone person," spent the better part of the weekend dialing Sinatra. On Monday, she charged onto the studio lot with the news that Frank had changed his mind. Asked exactly when Sinatra planned to come in, Marilyn couldn't say.

She demanded a telephone. In moments she had Sinatra on the line. For all to hear, she said that Jerry Wald wanted him to send a cable to George Cukor. She said Jerry was nervous he'd back out. She listened a moment, then hung up. Triumphantly she announced that Frank had agreed. He would contact Cukor immediately.

An hour and a half later, Wald and Cukor met privately. Wald doubted Sinatra would be in touch, guessing he had said yes in order to get Marilyn off the phone. At length, Wald was proven correct. There was no confirmation from Sinatra. Everybody was worried about how Marilyn would react, but in the end she watched silently as Montand did the scene with Bing Crosby. She actually seemed pleased, as though this were what she had wanted all along. But she was probably putting on an act so that Montand would not see her defeat.

Jerry Wald spoke ruefully of their all trying to inch their way to the finish of the picture. The pace was so agonizingly slow, Cukor said he felt as though he were being photographed in slow motion. He kept telling himself the production could not go on forever. Jack Cole, though hired at Marilyn's behest, finally exploded at his old friend.

They had been filming a scene in which she was required merely to watch Montand. Marilyn demanded that Cole give her something to do.

"Do you want me to give you something to do?" he shot back.

"Yes."

"Then stick a finger up your ass. I think that's quite within the realm of your technical facilities."

He walked off, leaving Marilyn in tears. Cole later apologized, but the incident suggests the degree to which everyone's patience had worn thin.

By now, Twentieth had almost no hope that *Let's Make Love* would be a success. This was no *Bus Stop* or *Some Like It Hot*. Montand was hard to understand. Marilyn looked awful. The film would have to be publicity-driven. As in the early days of her career, a bad picture would have to be sold with a vivid personal story. But this time it wouldn't be Marilyn who adroitly played the press. At the moment, she was in no condition to do that. This time it was Twentieth who tipped off Hedda Hopper and other columnists about Marilyn's affair. Darryl Zanuck had once feared the nude calendar story would destroy Marilyn. Now the studio seemed to think only a scandal might help.

The co-stars had shot their final scene together on Thursday, June 16. Montand filmed without Marilyn on Friday. His only remaining work was a considerable amount of dubbing, which, to Cukor's amusement, he called "dumbing." Montand spent a last, tense weekend with Marilyn. As always, he had his eye on the emergency exit. Marilyn seemed to panic as the end grew near. Montand's priority had ceased to be humoring her in order to complete the picture. He just wanted to return to his wife. He feared Marilyn would make a scene in the press. There was no telling what she might do.

On Monday, as Marilyn was being driven to the studio, John Huston arrived in New York. He was to conduct four days of meetings with Miller, then fly to Reno to inspect the locations. He intended to start filming *The Misfits* on July 18. At this point, Huston had no idea of the situation with Marilyn. In Europe, he hadn't heard about the affair with Montand. He was oblivious to the Millers' marital difficulties. He knew nothing of her drug problem. Miller gave no indication that anything was wrong. Huston had no reason to guess that if Marilyn's current, rather confused plans regarding Montand came to fruition, she might not show up in Nevada at all.

On Monday evening, Marilyn completed her last shot. Principal photography on *Let's Make Love* ended twenty-eight days behind schedule, not counting the strike. Buddy Adler had been dismayed by her appearance, but there were to be no retakes. That was a mark of how bad Twentieth considered the picture to be, and how eager everyone was to finish. For Marilyn, all that remained were two or three days of dubbing.

If she gave Twentieth that, at least there would be something to release.

On Tuesday, she appeared at the studio with laryngitis. Obviously, dubbing was out of the question. On Wednesday, she failed to show up at all and refused to answer the phone. When Marilyn remained incommunicado on Thursday, Twentieth resorted to sending a wire to the Beverly Hills Hotel. The studio implored her to come in before she left town.

Finally, on Thursday afternoon, Wald called Frank Taylor and explained that they had been trying to reach Marilyn. Taylor said he was under the impression that Marilyn planned to return to New York on Saturday night. Wald pointed out that *Let's Make Love* was not finished. The implication was clear: Marilyn would not be free to start Huston's picture until she had fulfilled her commitment.

That same day, Miller went into action. He may have been powerless to stop Marilyn from sleeping with Montand, but he was not prepared to stand by while she brought down his film. Like Montand, Miller seemed to regard her as dangerously unpredictable. He took steps to get her back to New York immediately. She had betrayed him, and she had humiliated him. Still, it would be safer to have Marilyn close by, where she could be watched until Huston was ready for her.

Miller instructed George Chasin to notify Twentieth that Marilyn should be sent home to recuperate. He wanted the studio to permit her to dub in New York. Miller's intervention struck an awkward note. Did Marilyn's husband really speak for her anymore? Or did he simply represent his own interests with regard to *The Misfits*? Miller may not have known the answer to those questions himself.

Unexpectedly, Marilyn appeared at the studio on Friday afternoon. She watched the film with Montand. By the time she left the screening room, she was saying that perhaps she would not go home after all. Perhaps she could recuperate in Los Angeles. She hoped to come in next Thursday, June 30, to dub. Not by chance, that was the day Montand was scheduled to return to Paris. Signoret had sent him a hurt letter and some newspaper cuttings about the affair. Montand needed to explain, and he had to do it in person. But if Marilyn insisted on coming in next week, he would not be able to go. Suddenly, the lover was as eager for Marilyn to be on that Saturday night flight to New York as the husband was.

On Sunday morning, Marilyn arrived in New York. Huston had left town two days previously. She focused on Thursday. That's when

Montand would be changing planes in New York. Somehow, between now and then, Marilyn had to convince him not to go back to Signoret.

Marilyn reserved a hotel suite near the airport. She ordered champagne and flowers. She hired a limousine. When Montand's plane touched down, she was waiting. His layover was extended, someone having phoned in a bomb threat. Montand had not expected to find Marilyn, and he certainly had not anticipated that his plane would have to be searched for explosives. He refused to accompany her to a hotel, but he did welcome the shelter of her black Cadillac.

They drank champagne and ate caviar. He did his best to be diplomatic. He did not want to provoke her. The last thing Montand needed was for Marilyn to sound off to reporters before he had smoothed things over at home. He kissed Marilyn and said he had enjoyed himself, but he made it absolutely clear that he did not plan to divorce. He was returning to Simone. He assumed Marilyn would go back to Arthur. He looked forward to a day when the couples could be friends again. He even invited the Millers to visit the Montands in France.

Later, Marilyn cried that she had been a fool. She pictured Montand and Signoret having a good laugh at her expense. But that did not stop her from wanting to speak to Montand. She worked the phone, desperately trying to reach him.

There had been a time when Marilyn had lovingly set up a cozy writing room for her husband, when she tiptoed about, warning the servants not to make noise while Mr. Miller was at work. Now, she banged her fists on his office door, demanding he come out. He was known to hide from her in there. Pretending to work, he would nap on the sofa. When he didn't stir, she marched to the bedroom, knocking over furniture along the way. She hurled a liquor bottle at a floor-to-ceiling mirror. Glass shattered all over the queen-sized bed. Repeatedly, Marilyn threw herself against a closet door until a maid restrained her.

By the time Huston returned on July 4 to shoot some tests, he had heard all about the Montand business. But as the husband was ready to proceed, it was fine with Huston. Marilyn's peaky appearance was attributed to the fact that she had recently been ill and was resting between films. Meanwhile, since Twentieth had refused to permit Marilyn to dub in New York, Miller arranged for her to stop in Los Angeles en route to Nevada. Initially, Twentieth protested that July 14 was too late. In the end, however, Lew Schreiber reluctantly said yes. Cukor, who had completed all of his other chores on July 1, agreed to stand by until then. On July 11, Miller called MCA to report that Marilyn was not feeling well again.

Montand was to stop in New York in three days' time on his way back to Hollywood. Having made peace with Signoret, he had agreed to appear in the film *Sanctuary* with Lee Remick—who had eventually played the part in *Wild River* that Marilyn had thought was hers. Marilyn hoped to see him between planes.

Cukor refused Miller's request that he come in on Saturday the 16th to do the dubbing. As far as he was concerned, he had indulged Marilyn at every turn. Despite all the trouble she had given him, he had signed up to work with her again. (Twentieth was eager to collect Marilyn's last film before it was too late. On July 1, the studio assigned her to *Goodbye, Charlie*, to be shot after *The Misfits*.) But on one matter, Cukor would not bend. Vivien Leigh had arrived in Los Angeles with the play *Duel of Angels*. It was her first visit since the announcement that Olivier wanted a divorce to marry Joan Plowright, and she worried that her Hollywood friends would take Larry's side and abandon her. Cukor, intent on proving her fears groundless, had planned numerous parties and poolside lunches in Vivien's honor. So this was a very busy time for him. Marilyn would just have to wait until Monday. Cukor offered to pick her up and escort her to the studio. He promised to have her finished in time to start *The Misfits* on the 20th.

Montand arrived in Los Angeles on Friday, July 15. The city was at a pitch of excitement, the Democratic convention having been going on all week at the Sports Arena Center. John Fitzgerald Kennedy had been nominated for president two days previously. His acceptance speech was being broadcast on television the night Montand checked in at the Beverly Hills Hotel.

Marilyn boarded a plane for Los Angeles on Sunday, July 17. She had missed Montand in New York but planned to call him on the coast. She looked utterly exhausted. There were pouches under her eyes, bloodstains on the rear of her beige skirt. Arthur went to Nevada alone, expecting that Marilyn would join him there as soon as Cukor had the fifty dubbed lines he needed. But would she actually show up for *The Misfits*?

In recent weeks, Arthur had done everything to guarantee that she appeared. He had kept her in New York until the last minute. He had dealt with her agents. He had haggled with the studio. He had endured her rages. But the next few days were in Marilyn's hands. Arthur had no way of controlling what happened once she was back in Los Angeles with Montand.

+   +   +

The cabin where Arthur had spent six weeks in 1956 was still standing near Pyramid Lake. But the windows no longer gave out on the gray water, a marina and a hot dog concession having been erected since he was here last. Four years previously, he had been waiting to divorce Mary. He had been soaking in the atmosphere that would form the basis of *The Misfits*. He had been looking forward to a calm year, perhaps the year after next, or the year after that.

Pyramid Lake, once serene, was awhirr with motorboats. The chilly, unlit phone booth, to which Arthur had often been summoned when the breathy-voiced Mrs. Leslie called, had vanished. Temperatures soared over one hundred degrees. John Huston went shirtless beneath his well-cut bush jacket.

Some things did seem to be the same, however. Yet again, Arthur waited in Nevada while Marilyn worked in Los Angeles. Yet again, she was terrified that she would not be able to do what was expected of her. Yet again, she was despondent. But this time it was not Arthur whom Marilyn persisted in trying to reach by phone; it was Yves Montand.

Principal photography was scheduled to begin in Reno on Monday, July 18. First, Huston, tall and thin, with a pugilist's shattered face, insisted that nearly two-thirds of the screenplay be revised. Miller may have called *The Misfits* his most complete work, but at the last minute he found himself prodded by Huston to rewrite extensively. If, as Arthur seemed to think, his work was already complete, why was Huston demanding it be redone now?

At this point, the script certainly had its champions. Not a foot of film had been shot, and already phrases like "the ultimate motion picture" and "the great American movie" were being used—though not by Huston. Frank Taylor informed *Time* magazine that *The Misfits* was the best screenplay he had read. United Artists vice-president Max Youngstein predicted that it would turn out to be one of the great films. But it was Arthur himself who seems to have set the bar the highest. In speaking of his screenplay, he casually referred to *King Lear*, *Hamlet*, and *Oedipus Rex*. Miller's eagerness to believe that his script was a masterwork, and Huston's cool awareness that it was in fact deeply flawed, would lead to repeated clashes in the weeks to come. Huston pressed for more revisions, and Miller delivered rewrites of lines and scenes without ever undertaking the fundamental reappraisal of the material which might, even then, have given him the great film he wanted.

Marilyn, scheduled to arrive two days after Huston started filming, was another source of pressure on Miller. Would she appear on time? Would she appear at all? And in what condition? Even if Marilyn did show up in Nevada, there was no guarantee she would get through the picture. Still, Miller suggested that Paula Strasberg was the most significant difficulty Huston faced. After a meeting, everybody agreed to freeze Paula out.

Paula was hardly the problem anymore. A good deal had changed since *The Sleeping Prince*. Marilyn's intake of barbiturates had escalated dangerously. It was no longer the Method that was at stake; it was Marilyn's life. One has to wonder whether in focusing on Paula, Miller was denying a horror he had no way of coping with emotionally. The bumptious Mrs. Strasberg made an easy scapegoat. Were Miller to face the real problem—the fact that Marilyn was in no condition, physically or emotionally, to be appearing in his picture—he might have to shut down *The Misfits*. And that, apparently, he was not prepared to do. But, as sometimes seemed to be the case, was he merely doing everything necessary to get his picture made? Or were his motives more complicated?

Perhaps the answer lay in the screenplay. "He fears he's losing her," Miller told an interviewer, in an effort to explain why it's important to Gay that Roslyn be present during the hunt for the wild horses. "He asserts his identity. He wants to call up his powers. When he's doing his work he feels most himself. He wants her to see the power within himself." Miller might have been talking about his own situation with Marilyn.

On July 20, at a quarter to three in the afternoon, he waited at Reno airport as a DC-7 flight from Los Angeles landed. He wasn't alone. A United Artists publicist waited. Local newsmen waited. The governor's wife and daughter waited. And some two hundred fans waited.

Marilyn and her helpers lingered on the plane a good half hour after the other passengers left.

When Marilyn finally did appear, she looked as though she were coming home at the end of an arduous location shoot. She wore a platinum wig she planned to use in *The Misfits*. She had a white silk blouse and a snug white skirt with a bulging zipper in back. She clutched a white leather purse. Arthur hovered protectively as she signed some autographs. She accepted a bouquet from the governor's family. She posed for pictures. She was determined not to let the press see her real feelings about her husband. She was determined to hide her sense that the marriage was over. She might not have shown up here at all but for the fact that in Los Angeles, Montand had refused to take her calls.

Huston was horrified by his first sight of Marilyn. She reminded him of an invalid. Her hands quivered. Her eyes were glazed. Arthur had assured Huston that Marilyn was getting in shape for the great day when filming began. Huston, for his part, had serious doubts whether her physical and mental condition would permit him to finish the picture.

The first days of filming in Reno went smoothly. As he leaned forward in his director's chair, ditch-digger hands dangling between long, bony legs, Huston seemed to calm Marilyn. Instead of being threatened or annoyed by Paula, Huston was amused. His concerns about both the script and the leading lady led Huston to distance himself emotionally from the project. It was as though the director had decided to protect himself from the inevitability of disappointment. There were moments when Huston would ignite; suddenly, he would appear to see again what all this might have been. But, particularly in the beginning, his thoughts seemed to be elsewhere. In a group of exceptionally tense people, he seemed to enjoy some of the off-screen performances far more than those on-camera. For Huston's money, Paula was the best show in town.

Paula, who wore a kind of black dunce's cap, shooed away flies with an orange palmetto fan. Her face was covered with white powder. She wore several watches in order to know the time in different cities around the world, though why she required that information no one had any idea. She annotated Marilyn's script with cryptic comments like "You are a bird" and "You are a tree." Huston was reminded of the Cumaean sybil, a prophetess who guided Aeneas through the underworld. But unlike Paula, the sybil didn't devote her spare time to reading a book entitled HOW AND WHY only a very few WIN AT CRAPS.

On July 27, Huston and company moved to the Stix Ranch in Quail Canyon, a forty-five-minute drive from Reno. The surrounding hills were covered with sage and wild rye. The cowboys who inspired Miller's short story had lived in the ranch house. Miller, as he inspected the premises, realized that a number of features seemed to have been altered. Or perhaps he had misremembered. Whatever the reason for the discrepancies, he penciled changes into the screenplay.

The changes did not appear to be the problem for Marilyn so much as the psychologically loaded nature of the material. On Saturday, July 30, she was to film a sequence in which Roslyn dances with Gay. Guido walks in on them and senses that he's lost Roslyn to his friend. The sequence echoed the pivotal moment nine years previously when Elia Kazan entered Charlie Feldman's house to discover Marilyn dancing with Miller, and the sight of them made it clear that the trio's dynamics had changed drastically. That moment had been a plot point in their lives, and so it was in Miller's screenplay. Once again, Miller returned to the primordial theme of the triangle. Identifying as he did with Gay, Miller imbued Guido with characteristics that bring Kazan to mind. Guido, in order to get what he wants, is willing to change his tune. He's complex and devious. He's ready to become an animal lover, rather than a hunter, if that will get him the girl. In the role of Guido, Miller had cast Eli Wallach, who had played the role of Kazan's surrogate in Baby Doll. But, strong as the echoes of that long-ago evening are in Miller's fictional scene, there is one particularly striking change: the Kazan character now has never slept with Marilyn.

On Saturday morning, Marilyn called in sick. The company had Sunday off. On Monday, she stayed out again. When she returned on Tuesday, her agitation was evident. She did not approach the material as Arthur did. He had sentimentalized Roslyn. He wanted the scene to convey joy and abandon. Instead, Marilyn went deeply within herself to dredge up the terror of a woman hunted by various men. Marilyn had experienced those feelings as a starlet on the Hollywood party circuit. She recalled being chased by Charlie Feldman, Pat De Cicco, and Raymond Hakim after Johnny Hyde's death. She recalled being held down in an upstairs bedroom as a group of men tried to rape her. And going even further back, she recalled the sexual assaults to which she had been subjected in the foster homes she had lived in as a child. As written by Miller, Roslyn is almost too sensitive to exist in the world. Marilyn made the character darker and more complex. Instead of the innocent whom Miller depicted, Marilyn saw Roslyn as a survivor. She gave her the ugly backstory Miller had left out.

Huston also had problems with the way Roslyn's character had been written. The director, after all, had observed Marilyn on the party circuit. He had known her as a "house girl" at Sam Spiegel's. He knew the brutal treatment she had endured. When Marilyn tried to bring some of that experience to bear on her character, it felt right to Huston. He, too, was eager to go after a much darker story than Miller seemed willing to write. But no matter how many times he sent Miller back to revise, the sentimentality remained.

For Huston, this was strictly an artistic problem. For Marilyn, it was something much more. Some people thought she felt betrayed because Miller had taken so many of her lines and private thoughts and put them into his script. That wasn't it at all. Marilyn felt betrayed because Arthur seemed unable to acknowledge her past. From the first, the whole point of marriage was to be accepted by such a man. She needed Arthur to love her in spite of all the shameful things she had done. Marilyn saw the script as proof that he had never really accepted her. How could he, when he seemed to refuse to acknowledge who she was in the first place? Had Arthur only married her because he thought, or pretended, that she was someone else, someone like Roslyn? Instead of a husband's loving portrait, the script seemed to Marilyn like another rejection. Given all that she had hoped for in the marriage, this may have been the most painful rejection of them all.

In anger and frustration, Marilyn lashed out at Arthur. She quarreled with him publicly. She shouted obscenities for all to hear. At the end of a day's filming, she and Paula disappeared into a white Cadillac, pointedly slamming the door in Arthur's face. They drove off, leaving the husband stranded in the desert. Miller's face remained mask-like, the expression unchanging. Huston, who witnessed the humiliation, offered him a ride back to Reno.

At one point, Miller wandered into the bar at the Mapes Hotel. One half of the hotel had been given over to the cast and crew. Huston, laughing uproariously, was seated at a table with a slim, handsome young

Austrian woman, Ingeborg Morath of Magnum Photos. The international photographers' cooperative had exclusive rights to cover the production for newspapers and magazines around the world. Every two weeks, a new pair of photographers arrived in Reno, the first being Morath and Henri Cartier-Bresson. Morath had covered Huston's *The Unforgiven* for *Paris-Match* and *Life*. As Miller entered the bar, she and Huston had been reminiscing about the time she saved the film's star, the war hero Audie Murphy, from drowning in a lake in Durango. Murphy, who could not swim, had fallen out of a small boat. Morath, on shore, stripped to her underwear and dove in. She swam about half a mile. Then she pulled him to safety, Murphy holding onto her bra strap. Huston adored her. Miller, noting her bobbed hair and her blue eyes, was struck by Morath. But for the moment, other matters absorbed him.

"You've got to get Marilyn off the drugs," Huston warned Miller on another occasion. "You're her husband and the only one who can do it. If you don't, you'll feel guilty as long as you live. If she doesn't stop now, she'll be in an institution in two or three years—or dead!"

The situation deteriorated rapidly. Marilyn had built up an astonishing tolerance for medication. She took as many as twenty Nembutals a day, pricking the capsule with a pin in order to make it work more quickly. When she found a willing doctor, she had Amytal injections. Some mornings, she could barely be roused. An assistant put her in the shower. Another painstakingly constructed her makeup as she lay on the bed. She drifted between sleep and wakefulness. "Is Marilyn working today?" the cast and crew took to asking.

The long hours of waiting for Marilyn placed enormous stress on Clark Gable, who was not in the best of health. When, if at all, Marilyn finally appeared, she worked in a drugged daze. Huston grumbled that whoever allowed her to take barbiturates ought to be shot. She was mortified to be behaving this way in front of Gable. He had powerful personal associations for Marilyn, who, encouraged by her mother, had once fantasized that Gable was actually her father. Marilyn had finally met Gable on the magical night Charlie Feldman and Billy Wilder gave her a party at Romanoff's after *The Seven Year Itch*. When she danced with him and confessed her childhood fantasy of being his daughter, he had been kind and understanding. It was almost as if Marilyn really had found her father at long last and shown him all she had achieved. So for reasons that few people on *The Misfits* understood, it pained Marilyn greatly for Gable to see her like this. And she certainly didn't want to do him any harm. But the truth was, she couldn't help herself.

Her disputes with her husband were beginning to embarrass all concerned. Marilyn's trailer rocked with their arguments, requiring the costumer Shirlee Strahm to step outside repeatedly. On one occasion, Nan Taylor entered the Millers' hotel suite to discover Marilyn screaming furiously at Arthur. Marilyn went on and on about Yves Montand. She told Arthur she really loved Montand. She insisted Montand really loved her. She was certain he was going to leave Simone Signoret for her.

As Marilyn shrieked, Miller just stood there. "You know that isn't true, Marilyn," he said gently. But there was no reaching her.

Marilyn was not about to let Arthur forget what she had done. If she screamed long enough about Montand, perhaps Arthur would be forced to stop pretending she was Roslyn. Perhaps even at this late date, she could provoke him into accepting and loving her for who she really was.

For once, Miller seemed relieved when Lee Strasberg arrived. Perhaps he could help. He and Paula were staying at another hotel. Miller went to him immediately. When Strasberg came to the door, Miller was taken aback. Strasberg was not wearing his usual dark, loose-fitting, priestly clothes. He was dressed as a cowboy, in a braided shirt, rigid trousers, and ornate, pointed leather boots. He flexed his knees to show off the fit. He had even bought a cowboy hat. He might have been auditioning as one of the bronco-busters in *The Misfits*.

Strasberg was eager to discuss his new clothes. He did not, however, wish to talk about Marilyn. That was not why he was in Nevada. He had come to sound off about his wife. He was indignant that Paula was not being taken seriously, enraged that Huston refused to confer with her. He vowed to take her back to New York. If that meant that *The Misfits* would have to be shut down—almost certainly Marilyn would never agree to work without her coach—so be it. As might have been expected in view of Paula's $3,000 weekly salary, Strasberg did not carry out his threat.

Another visitor seemed to pose a more substantial danger. There was talk that Yves Montand might come to Reno on August 21 for the premiere of *Let's Make Love*. Montand, intent on patching things up with his wife, had been ducking Marilyn's calls. However, the Fox executives were determined to keep the Monroe–Montand affair in the public consciousness, believing it was the best way to promote a film that almost everyone agreed was a stinker.

Soon, Huston, in addition to his other problems, was being barraged with communications regarding the premiere. Jerry Wald had reserved the Crest Theater in Reno. He had hired an airplane and arranged to fly in journalists from around the world. Simone Signoret was reported to have arrived in Los Angeles. Did she plan to accompany her husband to Sunday's premiere?

Marilyn never found out. On Saturday, the Sierras burst into flame. Plumes of black smoke obscured the sun. Firefighters in emergency aircraft dumped chemicals, to no avail. The following day, fire devoured the power lines to Reno. The city went dark. Air-conditioners stopped. Elevators halted between floors. That evening, a chartered bus carried reporters through the spectral city, Wald having arranged for them to be flown back to Los Angeles. Noisy auxiliary generators powered the large casinos; otherwise, one saw only car headlights. A single white light blazed eerily on the top floor at the Mapes Hotel. Arthur, still rewriting, had requested that a line be run from the film crew's mobile generator to his ninth-floor room. Marilyn slipped out. Down the hall, she joined some company members as they sipped champagne and watched the distant fires.

It was the calm before the storm. By the end of the week, Huston had despaired of working with Marilyn. The company physician declined to give her more drugs, but she persisted in getting them elsewhere. On Thursday evening, Huston sent word advising Marilyn to stay home the following day. The suggestion that she use the opportunity to rest triggered enormous upset.

"I said I would be there!" she sobbed. "I promised John!"

On Friday, Marilyn was up first thing. She insisted on being driven to the location. She shot a scene with Gable, but it was just no good. Russ Metty, one of the best cameramen in the business, noticed that Marilyn's eyes weren't focusing. During lunch with John Huston, Frank Taylor, and Arthur Miller in a little pink house in the desert that had been rented for the production, he voiced his concerns.

"I can't photograph her," Metty declared. "That's it. The pills . . .

Her eyes are gone. She can't be photographed. If this is going to go on day after day, we're finished here."

Finally, it was decided that the picture had to be shut down so Marilyn could be hospitalized. But who would tell her? Not one of the men was willing to face Marilyn. In the end, they sent the producer's wife.

Paula Strasberg, beneath a black umbrella, sat in front of Marilyn's trailer as Nan Taylor entered. Inside, Nan found Whitey Snyder, the makeup man. Marilyn was lying down.

"I have a message for you from Frank," said Nan. "We're going to shut the movie down."

Marilyn flew into a rage. "That goddam sonofabitch of a husband of yours!" she screamed. "That Frank Taylor! I never want to talk to him again! And you . . . you idiot! Why don't you leave him? What's the matter with you?"

"Marilyn, stop it!" Nan said firmly. "I don't want one more word out of you about my husband. Not one more word. That's it."

On the morning of Saturday, August 27, Huston arranged for Marilyn to enter a small Hollywood hospital under the name Mrs. Miller. She was flown out in a private plane. Her secretary May Reis and Paula Strasberg accompanied her, Miller staying in Reno for now. Huston had not made the decision lightly. He was aware that if Marilyn failed to complete *The Misfits* she would be virtually uninsurable on future pictures. That could mean the end of her career.

At Westside Hospital, Marilyn was in the care of Ralph Greenson and his associate Hyman Engelberg, a Beverly Hills internist. On the telephone, Greenson assured Huston that he would have Marilyn working in one week. It was the same thing he had said seven years previously, when the production of *Elephant Walk* halted on account of Vivien Leigh. On Monday morning, Huston's cast and crew learned that the film was being closed down temporarily. Huston indicated that he hoped to resume in a week or so. Privately, however, he believed the chances of finishing were slim.

News of the star's hospitalization could not be kept out of the press. "Miss Monroe is suffering from acute exhaustion and needs rest and more rest," Dr. Engelberg announced. And Frank Taylor told reporters, "Miss Monroe has been working continuously under a heavy six-day-a-week schedule and under trying physical conditions. The heat has been 95 to 105 degrees throughout and almost all the shooting has been out-of-doors and physically demanding." The producer also pointed out that Marilyn had gone directly from *Let's Make Love* to *The Misfits* without a break.

Meanwhile, Dr. Greenson cut off Marilyn's barbiturate supply. She was given mild doses of chloral hydrate, Librium and Placidyl. Dr. Engelberg injected her with vitamins. She was given a good deal of vitamin B-12 and liver.

When Marilyn entered the hospital, Montand had been winding up *Sanctuary*. He was to fly to Paris on September 2 to join Signoret. Would he visit Marilyn at the hospital? He adamantly declared he would not. "If I do, it will be talk, talk, talk," Montand told Hedda Hopper when she visited his bungalow at the Beverly Hills Hotel on August 30. Montand's English had improved considerably since his walks with Arthur Miller.

Montand knew perfectly well that anything he said would be printed at once. That he talked to Hedda Hopper at all was surprising, since the columnist was no friend to the Montands, whose politics she abhorred. That he talked to her when Marilyn was in the hospital being detoxified was crass and unconscionable.

"Perhaps she had a schoolgirl crush," Montand said of Marilyn. "If she did, I'm sorry. But nothing will break up my marriage."

The phone rang. The switchboard operator announced that Marilyn Monroe was on the line.

"I won't talk to her," Montand informed the operator.

"You deliberately made love to this girl," said Hopper. "You knew she wasn't sophisticated. Was that right?"

"Had Marilyn been sophisticated, none of this ever would have happened," Montand replied. "I did everything I could for her when I realized that mine was a very small part. The only thing that could stand out in my performance were my love scenes. So, naturally, I did everything I could to make them good."

After Hedda Hopper's column of September 1, Marilyn could harbor no illusions about Montand. He had been a user like all the rest. Now that the lover had publicly humiliated her, the husband stepped back up to the plate. Arthur had arrived on Monday. His hope that theirs might be a happy ending after all was reflected in the conclusion he wrote for his film. It was no secret that Arthur identified with Gay. It was no secret that he thought of Roslyn as Marilyn. Perhaps if, in spite of everything, Gay and Roslyn got together at the end of the story, Arthur and Marilyn would too. Aside from being a cliché, the love-conquers-all ending did not follow from the rest of the film. Yet, over Huston's objections, Miller insisted on it.

Huston flew to Los Angeles to check on Marilyn's condition. First, he talked to Dr. Greenson. The encounter provided Greenson with an opportunity to size up the enemy. As chance would have it, the analyst had been working since 1958 to make it impossible for a film about Sigmund Freud to be shot in Hollywood. He knew all about the screen-play Huston had hired Sartre to write. And he knew that a respected director's involvement was particularly distressing to Anna Freud, as that would lend credibility to the project. But Huston was not here to discuss *Freud*. He wanted to know about Marilyn. Greenson declared her ready for work, a week without barbiturates having made all the difference. Though she resembled an addict in some respects, she did not exhibit withdrawal symptoms. Marilyn's appearance seemed to confirm the doc-tor's remarks. She was vibrant. She was wide awake. She indicated that she knew what the barbiturates had done. She was embarrassed by her behavior. She was grateful Huston had intervened. She was eager to come back, if he would have her.

Marilyn returned to Reno on September 5. At midnight, when she and Arthur stepped off the plane, she heard a marching band, with cheers and applause. She saw signs proclaiming "WELCOME MARILYN." The warm reception was not really for her benefit, however. United Artists had staged the event to give reporters something to write about other than the rumors of a drug overdose. She went before the cameras the following day.

Marilyn's hopes of pleasing Huston were quickly dashed. Three days after she returned, she faced her most technically demanding scene. It took place in the litter-strewn rear of the bar where Roslyn and Perce have been dancing. It consisted of five minutes of dialogue between Marilyn and Montgomery Clift. Huston viewed it as a directorial chal-lenge; he had never shot a scene that long.

Miller had begun *The Misfits* in an effort to provide Marilyn with her first truly serious and important role. The film, intended to make her feel good about herself, was to have been Marilyn's chance to show the world what she was capable of as a dramatic actress. Her inability to memorize was notorious; yet somehow she had always believed that only a long dialogue scene would test her worth. So this was to have been her big opportunity.

They shot intensively beneath a black tarpaulin and ten-thousand-watt lights, the torrid air thick with flies. But Huston remained dissatisfied. The pace needed to be faster. The actors persisted in blowing their lines. At the end of two days, Marilyn sensed that she had failed.

Huston, having lost a good deal of money in the casinos, went to San Francisco, where he collected an advance of $25,000 to direct Freud for Universal. That enabled him to pay off his gambling debts. Upon his return, they reshot a bedroom scene in which Clark Gable awakens Marilyn. He is fully clothed, she is naked beneath a sheet. Gay kisses Roslyn and she sits up. Magnum photographer Eve Arnold could see that Marilyn was eager to please Huston.

In the seventh take, she did something not in the script. She had failed to impress Huston in her five-minute dialogue scene, so now she gave him the one thing that always seemed to work for her. It was as though she could hear Olivier urging, "All right, Marilyn. Be sexy." As she sat up, she dropped the sheet, exposing her right breast. The moment was a sad one, suggesting as it did Marilyn's sense that, despite her dreams of being an actress, this was all she really had to offer. If she thought Huston would be pleased, she miscalculated badly. After the take, Marilyn cast a hopeful glance in his direction.

"I've seen 'em before," said Huston, unimpressed. He later grumbled that he had always known girls have breasts. Huston demanded two more takes, with the breast covered.

Four days later, Huston insisted on reshooting the big dialogue scene with Monroe and Clift. It was Friday, September 23. In the retakes, Marilyn surprised herself. By an act of will, she finally gave Huston the performance he wanted. She and Clift were brilliant together. Huston exulted that it was Marilyn's best work in the film. In spite of everything, he offered her the female lead in Freud. She was to play Cecily, a patient. Clift would play Freud. Marilyn was delighted.

Still, she could not stay away from drugs. She moved in with Paula at the Holiday Inn. When Huston visited Marilyn there, he was appalled to find her in the worst shape yet. Her hair was matted, her nightgown and body filthy. She veered between euphoria and trance. It was as though she had never been detoxified. On another occasion, Miller arrived to discover a doctor probing for a vein in the back of Marilyn's hand, preparing to inject her with Amytal. When Marilyn spotted him, she angrily ordered her husband to leave.

The hunt for the wild mustangs remained to be shot. Gay takes Roslyn along because he senses he's losing her, but the adventure does not have the hoped-for effect. Instead of Gay's power, Roslyn sees what he's become. He's so much less than she thought. Gay, once a heroic cowboy, has been reduced to selling wild horses for dog food. Something similar happened when Marilyn observed Arthur at work on *The Misfits*. He talked of *Death of a Salesman*. He mentioned *Hamlet*, *King Lear*, and *Oedipus Rex*. In fact, the playwright had devoted the better part of three years to a mediocre screenplay.

Never was that more evident than during the calamitous final days of filming. By then, Miller should have been able to connect the story's two dominant lines, that of Roslyn and that of the wild horses. He should have shown that Roslyn seeks to stop Gay from hunting the mustangs because of the pain she's experienced in being hunted herself. Instead, Miller has Roslyn protest at the hunt because she cannot bear to see anything killed. Miller gives her a heart of gold. In sentimentalizing Roslyn, he fails to provide a convincing explanation for her behavior. That explanation had been under his nose all along. It lay in the conflict between Gay and Guido, a conflict that Miller mysteriously never develops. We never see the men struggle over Roslyn. At a moment when, in life, Miller was moving back in Kazan's direction, perhaps that was a conflict he preferred not to probe. In the end, Roslyn's emotions during the hunt are not as moving as they ought to be, because they seem disconnected from the story.

Location shooting concluded on Tuesday, October 18. The company moved to Los Angeles. Process shots were to be done the following week. The Millers took up residence at the Beverly Hills Hotel. Marilyn, in atrocious condition, was treated by Dr. Greenson. As the end drew near, she had reason to believe that her questions were finally about to be answered. Had Arthur been using her? Had he endured betrayal and humiliation in order to get his film made? Would he abandon her once

The Misfits was finished? As though Marilyn could not bear to learn the truth, she threw him out first. His things were carted away in a station wagon. He moved to another hotel.

On Friday, November 4, Huston shot a retake of the happy ending that showed Gay and Roslyn starting a life together. Forty days behind schedule, *The Misfits* was finished. Before Marilyn left, she approached the director. She had waited until the very last minute to say this. She was in awe of Huston, so it cannot have been easy to announce that she had decided to turn down a role in *Freud*. Anna Freud, she declared, did not want the picture made. Clearly, Dr. Greenson had gotten to Marilyn. Perhaps because Marilyn herself wanted to do the film so very badly, she disappeared quickly, giving Huston no chance to reply.

That weekend, she and Arthur flew back to New York separately. Marilyn returned to their apartment. Arthur moved to the Adams Hotel on East 86th Street. Despite everything, she called him there to ask gently, "Aren't you coming home?"

He did. But it was only to collect his possessions. Their marriage was over.

+ SIXTEEN +

Marilyn studied the black-and-white contact sheets of *The Misfits* through a watchmaker's loupe. She wore a white bathrobe and her feet were bare, the nails painted silver. As though the filming itself had not been painful enough, now she had to relive it in excruciating detail. She was particularly distressed by some of the photographs taken when Henri Cartier-Bresson and Inge Morath were on duty. Again and again, Marilyn scratched a red X over the tiny images that showed the Millers together. At the time, she had been intent on hiding the truth that the marriage was finished; now she thought the pictures dishonest. The world would probably think so too, since the Millers' decision to divorce had been widely reported.

"MILLER WALKS OUT ON MARILYN," the *New York Daily News* had blasted on November 12, 1960. Journalists didn't know where to find Arthur, but they all knew Marilyn's address. They staked out the front of her building near the East River, lining up on both sides of the awning, requiring her to run a gauntlet of flashing cameras and shouted questions when she left to see Dr. Kris. They were usually still there when she came home. Marilyn felt like a prisoner. Almost certainly, it was rage that caused her, bent over the contact sheets with grease pencil in hand, repeatedly to cross out images of Arthur alone or with others. She ignored Eve Arnold's patient reminders that she had the right to approve only pictures in which she was present.

She had to choose quickly. United Artists had decided to move up the premiere of *The Misfits* after Clark Gable died on November 16. From then on, among the questions regularly shouted at Marilyn was whether she felt guilty. Gable's frustration over Marilyn's constant lateness was rumored to have led to his heart attack. Marilyn, for her part, wondered whether it might be true. Gladys had hinted that Norma Jeane was Gable's child. Though Marilyn certainly did not believe that now, she was tortured by the possibility that on some unconscious level she had harmed Gable in order to punish her absent father. Each time she spotted Gable in the contact sheets, Marilyn, desperate to do something for him, advised Eve Arnold at length on how the photograph ought to be retouched.

"I will not discuss my personal life," Marilyn whispered to reporters as she rushed to a waiting black Cadillac limousine. She wore a black coat, the collar pulled up to her chin. The white-gloved doorman helped her in. The hired car carried her to 135 Central Park West.

Her analyst's office-apartment had the air of a museum. Dr. Kris's husband, in addition to being a psychoanalyst himself, had been a renowned art historian and curator, a collector of ancient cameos, intaglios, and cut stones. He had advised Sigmund Freud on the purchase of Egyptian, Greek, Roman, and Asian antiquities. Marianne Kris was motherly and deeply caring. It was said that when her husband died, her first concern, typically, was for other people. Dr. Kris, in her dealings with Marilyn, was utterly without self-interest.

Because Marianne Kris and Lee Strasberg lived in the same building, and because Strasberg focused so intensely on matters of psychology, it was easy for Marilyn's sessions with her analyst to blur into her sessions with the acting teacher. She often saw him directly after therapy. The process of pouring out her pain, her fears, and her anger in Dr. Kris's office would continue upstairs in Strasberg's study. At best this was confusing. At worst it was destructive.

Strasberg's efforts were tainted with self-interest. When Marilyn returned from The Misfits, she was sick, depressed, and extremely upset about the end of her marriage. She was haunted by the possibility that she had killed Gable. She needed to rest, having made two difficult films without a break. Yet Strasberg wasted no time in pushing a project of his own. As far as he was concerned, Marilyn mustn't let the studio force her into doing another light comedy. Strasberg wanted to direct her in a television production of Somerset Maugham's Rain. He lacked credits, so her participation was vital. She accompanied him to meetings with executives at NBC.

Marilyn had been notified to report to George Cukor on April 14, 1961. Suddenly, on December 13, to the apparent bewilderment of everyone but Lee Strasberg, Marilyn informed Twentieth that she would not appear in *Goodbye, Charlie*. She offered no reason. The studio replied that her contract obliged her to make this picture. As long as Twentieth had Cukor, one of her approved directors, Marilyn could not legally refuse.

She lay cloistered in her dark bedroom, refusing most calls. Lee and Paula, however, were always able to get through. When Hedda Rosten finally talked to her, Marilyn's voice had an indistinct, faraway quality. As the holidays approached, her depression deepened. On Christmas night, the kitchen door opened and a mountain of poinsettias was brought in. Marilyn, who had resumed her desperate calls to Yves Montand, may have thought that he, or Arthur, had had a change of heart. If she did, she was disappointed. A helper had already opened the card. It said, "Best, Joe."

"Well, there's only one Joe," Marilyn declared.

Unlike Montand, DiMaggio was waiting for her call. She asked why he had sent the poinsettias.

"First of all, because I thought you would call me to thank me," Joe replied. "Besides, who in the hell else do you have in the world?"

What could she possibly say to that? Joe asked what Marilyn was doing tonight. When she admitted she was free on Christmas, he asked if he could stop by. Marilyn later told Dr. Greenson that, though she had been tired and depressed, she was happy to see Joe.

From then on, Joe appeared regularly. Sometimes he was accompanied by George Solotaire. In order to avoid the press, he would arrive late. He used the service elevator, entered by the kitchen door and left at dawn. Yet her staff knew that he had come back into her life. The milk in the refrigerator was for Joe; his ulcer prevented him from drinking coffee. His visits persisted until he was required to go out of town on business.

On her publicists' advice, Marilyn chose January 20, 1961, to file for divorce, hoping that the inauguration of John F. Kennedy as president would overshadow the news. She flew to El Paso, Texas, where a car was waiting to take her to Mexico. Arthur had signed a waiver, so he did not have to appear in person.

As it happened, that day Miller was in Washington, D.C.,

attending the inauguration with Joe and Olie Rauh. Joe Rauh, a prominent backer of Hubert Humphrey, had played a pivotal role at the Democratic convention, helping to persuade Humphrey to withdraw when it became clear he could not win. Rauh's only regret, expressed privately to Miller, was that Kennedy had double-crossed the liberals by choosing a conservative vice-presidential candidate, Lyndon Johnson. Olie, when she saw Arthur in Washington, told him how sorry she and Joe were about the divorce.

"I am, too," Arthur replied, "and I know Marilyn is. But if I hadn't done this, I would be dead."

A question lingered. What did a man who had been married to Marilyn Monroe do next? Watching Miller with the Kennedys gave Joe Rauh an idea. After the inaugural festivities, he and Olie agreed that Arthur was going to make a play for Jacqueline Kennedy. The Rauhs were jesting, of course. But the idea bears thinking about. The First Lady was one of the few women alive capable of topping Marilyn Monroe.

Marilyn returned from Mexico in a state of utter despair. This was more than just the end of a marriage. For Marilyn, it was the end of all hope that she would ever be able to see herself as worthy of being loved. For a short time, Arthur had given her that hope. For a short time, Marilyn had believed that she might actually find happiness. Now, Arthur was gone from her life forever, and his departure felt like a verdict.

On January 31, 1961, she attended a preview of *The Misfits* at the Capitol Theater on Broadway. Escorted by Montgomery Clift, Marilyn looked completely ravaged, aged beyond her years. Miller was there with his two children. He and Marilyn conspicuously avoided one another. This was the first time Marilyn saw the film that had once been intended to prove Arthur's love for her. For three years, this project had been the force that simultaneously held their marriage together and tore it apart. Watching *The Misfits* was a painful experience for Marilyn. The moment the film was over, she fled the theater. The next day, *The Misfits* opened to mixed reviews. Arthur had not brought off the Great American Film after all.

Marilyn blamed herself for the failure of the marriage. She blamed herself for having come so close to realizing her dream, then losing it. Finally, in her anguish, she came up with an excuse to call Arthur. She

asked if she could drive to Roxbury to collect some of her possessions.
The Connecticut property, the home where Marilyn had dreamed of a
family and a future, had gone to him, while she kept the apartment in
Manhattan. He told her to come up any time, adding that if he was not
there when she arrived, she knew where the key was. If that was a warning, Marilyn did not register it as such. She told herself Arthur would be
there. Maybe he would ask her to have coffee with him. When she
arrived, the house was empty. Obviously, he did not want to see her. He
had fled the cul de sac he had written about in his notebook, and now he
was all too clearly wary of being drawn back in.

Nor, as Joe Rauh had presumed, was he inclined to try to top
Marilyn. Like Olivier after Vivien Leigh, Miller entered a relationship with
a sane, sensible, self-sufficient woman, who was the antithesis of the mad,
devouring second wife. It was said that Joan Plowright had not broken up
Olivier's marriage; she had simply been present "at the crucial turning
point" in his life. The same could be said of Inge Morath with Miller. The
Magnum photographer had been in Nevada as Miller's marriage was coming apart. He had run into her again in New York after it was over. The contrast between Inge and Marilyn could hardly have been stronger. One had
saved a man's life; the other needed to be saved. At Inge's suggestion,
Arthur moved downtown to the Chelsea Hotel, where she preferred to stay.

He had his typewriter. He had his notebooks. He had his autobiographical work-in-progress. But he was blocked. After The Misfits, he
could not seem to shake his own embarrassment. Only recently he had
crowed about his new work to Brooks Atkinson, so he was uneasy when
Atkinson paid a call in Roxbury. Miller felt he had disappointed the
critic. But Atkinson was there to show support for an artist he valued. He
was there to convey the hope that Miller, having had his fill of
Hollywood, would soon emerge with a new Broadway play.

After Marilyn's visit to Roxbury, it seemed to Norman Rosten that
he'd never seen her so depressed. Her marriage having ended, she
appeared to stop fighting her mother's judgment; she accepted that she
was unworthy to go on living. And so it was that a maid walked into the
living room to discover Marilyn preparing to jump out the window to her
death. Following this latest suicide attempt, as far as Dr. Kris was concerned there could be no question of Marilyn's being left alone in her
apartment in this condition.

On February 7, 1961, some three weeks after her divorce, Marilyn acceded to Dr. Kris's pleas that she sign herself into the Payne–Whitney Psychiatric Clinic. Dazed and confused by the drugs she had been taking in such alarming quantities, Marilyn probably was not entirely clear on what she was agreeing to do. She registered under the name Faye Miller. When Arthur, at the Chelsea Hotel, learned about Marilyn's hospitalization, he was extremely upset. Her greatest fear, after all, had always been that she would go insane like her mother and find herself committed to a mental hospital. John Huston, apprised of Miller's state of mind by Frank Taylor, called from Ireland to comfort him.

Arthur, debating whether to go to Marilyn, called Nan Taylor.

"Nan, should I go to see her?" he asked. "I care for her so terribly. Should I go to see her? What do you think?" In the end, he followed Nan's advice to stay away.

Marilyn later insisted that she had not known Payne–Whitney was a psychiatric hospital. When she realized where she was, she hurled a chair against a glass door and retrieved a shard of glass, threatening to cut herself if she was not released. Four attendants carried her face down to the elevator. Marilyn, transferred to the violent ward, was sedated and restrained. She contacted Lee and Paula. She contacted Joe. She needed someone to get her out.

On February 10, DiMaggio came through the door. He had rushed to the hospital as soon as he heard. The doctors insisted that Marilyn was in no condition to leave, but Joe warned that if Payne–Whitney did not let her go right now, he was prepared to take the building apart brick by brick.

"Thank God for Joe," Marilyn said.

In consultation with Marianne Kris, he arranged for Marilyn to be transferred to Columbia–Presbyterian Medical Center in upper Manhattan. It was a hospital, but at least it was not a mental hospital, and that was important to her. Joe promised to remain until she felt safe. Meanwhile, Dr. Kris planned to fly to Los Angeles in mid-March to confer with Ralph Greenson.

Marilyn was at Columbia–Presbyterian for three weeks. When the Rostens visited, a nurse was sponging Marilyn's pale forehead. Marilyn listlessly raised her arm to greet them. She smiled, yet the sparkle had vanished from her eyes. It seemed to Norman that Marilyn's illness had spread from her body and her mind to her very soul.

Some nights she did not sleep at all. She lay awake reading Freud's published correspondence. His photograph, opposite the title page, made her cry. She thought he looked depressed, disappointed with life. She guessed he was near death. Even when Dr. Kris pointed out that at the time the photograph was taken Freud had been in acute physical pain, Marilyn insisted it was disappointment she saw in his gentle face.

In a letter from Columbia–Presbyterian, Marilyn informed Dr. Greenson that she knew she would never be happy. She reminded the analyst of something she had once told him about Elia Kazan. Kazan had called her the gayest girl he had ever known. According to Marilyn, he had loved her for a year. Now, in her despair, she contemplated playing the happy girl again. That's what men wanted. She would not really be happy, of course, but at least she could pretend.

Even in the hospital, the pressures did not go away. Twentieth was not about to drop its demand that Marilyn report for *Goodbye, Charlie*. Spyros Skouras, Marilyn's old ally, was now increasingly under attack by business rivals anxious to replace him. He was sensitive to charges of being extravagant and sentimental, and of repeatedly capitulating to Marilyn Monroe and other stars. Eager to look tough in front of stock-holders and to show his enemies on the Fox board that he was the boss, Skouras was prepared to take Marilyn to court. Despite her condition, the studio continued to regard her as a valuable property. So, astonish-ingly, did Lee Strasberg, who was still trying to put together a deal for *Rain*. He behaved as though on a sacred mission, as though he were doing it all for her. He believed it might be years before psychoanalysis helped, and he was convinced that a serious dramatic role would enable Marilyn to channel her rage into art. He would not permit Twentieth to force her into *Goodbye, Charlie*.

Only Joe seemed to believe that Marilyn's career was killing her. Things were very different from the days during their marriage when Marilyn still believed that becoming a star could make her life right. Then, Joe's opposition to her work had often appeared to be based on little more than selfishness. But now, perhaps, Joe was right. As the end of her hospital stay approached, Joe invited Marilyn to join him in Florida where, after a decade of discord, he was working with the Yankees in spring training at St. Petersburg. Joe, always concerned about his dignity, was pleased finally to have been asked to give the benefit of his knowledge and experience to young players. Some time in the sun, with Joe there to protect her, would get Marilyn away from everything, at least for a little while.

Joe wanted to take Marilyn for walks on the beach. He wanted to take her fishing. He wanted to take her to the training camp. Most of all, he wanted to divert her from her troubles. Though Joe admitted he was still in love with Marilyn, he had no desire that they would marry again. Asked by her maid, Lena Pepitone, if marriage were a possibility, DiMaggio clutched his stomach as though in excruciating pain. He said he loved Marilyn. He would always be there for her. But he could not live with the woman without quarreling.

Marilyn welcomed the chance of an escape and some more time to enjoy the security of Joe's friendship. She accepted his invitation and prepared to leave New York. She had been released from the hospital, but she was by no means well. The hospital had provided a measure of calm, but no doctor could give her back her lost hope.

Before Marilyn went to Florida, she saw Arthur. He had not come to her aid in Payne–Whitney. She never knew that he had been extremely upset about her hospitalization, though it would have meant everything to her if she had. But when Arthur's mother died suddenly on March 8, only three days after Marilyn was released from the hospital, Marilyn knew what she wanted to do.

Isadore Miller had been preparing to undergo surgery when his wife passed away. He left the hospital to bury her. When the old man arrived at his wife's funeral, he was astonished to find Marilyn there waiting to comfort him. Marilyn was well aware of her father-in-law's fondness for her, and she was determined to do whatever she could for him now that he needed her. Throughout the service, she gripped Isadore's hand and tried to calm him. Arthur's nephew Ross thought it took guts for Marilyn to show up there alone.

After the service, she asked Isadore, "Dad, shall I come to the cemetery?"

"Marilyn, you've been sick," Isadore replied. "Don't come."

In the days that followed, Marilyn called Isadore regularly at the hospital. She talked to his doctor. She sent flowers. She continued to call from Florida. There were all too few people in her life who had loved her as sincerely as he did, and she was going to show her gratitude.

Meanwhile, Marilyn's situation at Twentieth was growing more complicated. George Cukor had withdrawn from Goodbye, Charlie, and was now tied up at MGM with Lady L. He had assumed that he would be finished in time to report to Twentieth on March 1 to work with Marilyn—which, considering the fragile state of her health, would have meant rushing her from her hospital bed directly to a sound stage—but he had not even begun to shoot by March, his film having been plagued by script problems. MGM refused to release him. Legally, Twentieth had only until April 14, 1961, to put Marilyn to work, or they risked losing her services altogether. While the legal department threatened Cukor with a lawsuit, studio executives frantically checked the availability of the other directors on Marilyn's list.

As long as Twentieth had one of her sixteen approved directors, Marilyn would have to make Goodbye, Charlie. At the very least, the studio was required to make a reasonable effort to approach them all. They contacted Billy Wilder, John Huston, Joshua Logan, Elia Kazan, William Wyler, George Stevens, John Ford, Alfred Hitchcock, and Carol Reed. Again and again, they struck out.

Marilyn returned from Florida to find a letter from Frank Ferguson, the studio attorney, announcing that Cukor had quit. Ferguson had long been of the opinion that Twentieth had made a dreadful mistake in capitulating after Marilyn walked out with Milton Greene. Ignoring her plans to do Rain that summer, which had been reported in the press, Ferguson informed Marilyn that Twentieth had put off the start of her film. In the event of a director's resignation, the studio had the right to postpone for four weeks. Marilyn was not expected to report until further notice.

Marilyn, accompanied by Paula, arrived in Los Angeles intent on forcing a settlement that would permit her to do Rain with Strasberg. On April 20, Ferguson told Marilyn that every effort had been made to get one of her directors. As no one on her list had been available, Twentieth wanted to consult with her about a substitute. The following day, a team of MCA agents appeared in the office of Robert Goldstein, Twentieth's new production chief. Buddy Adler had died during pre-production for Cleopatra, the $30 million white elephant that was supposed to have reversed the studio's post-Zanuck decline. Goldstein, the former head of the London office, was known as Skouras's man. There were those at Fox who muttered that he was not really the production chief, Skouras was.

Marilyn's agents knew for a fact that one of the directors on her list had not heard from the studio. The studio had failed to approach Lee Strasberg, and therefore it had not lived up to the letter of her contract. After discovering that Strasberg did not have a Hollywood agent, Twentieth had made no further effort to reach him. Strasberg was thought of as an acting teacher; no one took him seriously as a director. There was every reason to assume that his place on Marilyn's list had been a whim. Obviously, the studio executives were going to have to rethink that.

Meanwhile, MCA struck again. As of April 25, four weeks had passed since Ferguson's letter informing Marilyn that her picture was being postponed. George Chasin called Spyros Skouras on April 26 to announce that Twentieth had missed the date by which it was obligated to start Goodbye, Charlie. If Skouras still wanted to use Marilyn, he would have to make a deal with her production company. He would have to give her a say in what project she did, and with whom she did it. And, of course, he would have to give her a lot more money. After the phone call, Skouras checked Marilyn's contract. He saw that in fact the clock had started ticking on April 14, the date she was supposed to have reported to Cukor; the studio clearly had until May 12 to put Marilyn to work. Skouras told Bob Goldstein that should Marilyn refuse to report on the 12th, he would seek an injunction to prevent her from working elsewhere. If she remained adamant about Goodbye, Charlie, Twentieth would consider substituting Celebration, a film Jerry Wald had been developing. Otherwise, the studio intended to proceed with efforts to replace Cukor. By now, those efforts had focused on Lee Strasberg.

Strasberg was rumored to be planning to go to Europe in June, but when Twentieth finally reached him in New York, he indicated he'd be willing to make himself available for a project that interested him. On May 4, eight days before the scheduled start date, Frank Ferguson wired Marilyn's lawyer, Aaron Frosch, to announce that Strasberg was reconsidering his travel plans. He might be able to direct Goodbye, Charlie. Twentieth was eager to confer with Marilyn.

Strasberg, for his part, was eager to know how much the studio intended to pay him. Fourteen years earlier, he had suffered the disgrace of being fired by Fox. He did not plan to be insulted again. He insisted on being paid what he was worth. He suddenly cast aside his conviction that Marilyn must not do another light comedy. He seemed to forget his belief that it was in her best interest to appear in a serious dramatic role. For the moment at least, Strasberg abandoned his staunch opposition to *Goodbye, Charlie*.

The studio offered $22,500, the same fee Daniel Petrie had received for *A Raisin in the Sun*. Petrie had one prior film directing credit; Strasberg had none. Yet Strasberg indignantly shot back that the studio's offer must be commensurate with his standing. Bob Goldstein, down to the wire, approved a new offer of $50,000. That wasn't enough either. On May 8, Strasberg, now communicating through an agent, turned the offer down. If he calculated that Twentieth would keep going, he was mistaken.

At the last minute, Skouras decided not to take Marilyn to court after all and unexpectedly released her from *Goodbye, Charlie*. In return, her lawyer agreed that she still owed Twentieth a film, the start date to be postponed until November 15. Meanwhile, Skouras gave Marilyn permission to do *Rain*, the only stipulation being that she finish by October 30. Supposedly, the deal let everyone save face, both Skouras and Strasberg. But it didn't work out that way. Strasberg fared worse at NBC than at Twentieth. The film studio had been willing to hire an inexperienced director; the television network was not. In the end, Marilyn refused to do *Rain* without him.

During this period, Marilyn had been seeing a good deal of Dr. Greenson. In March, Marianne Kris had come to Los Angeles expressly to talk to him about Marilyn. Marilyn's resentment over the Payne–Whitney episode made it advisable for another doctor to take over her treatment, but as her permanent residence was in the east Greenson was excluded for now. Meanwhile, he worried about her being alone in the world. He worried about her being drawn back to drugs. He worried about her attraction to destructive people. He was particularly distressed about her having canceled several hours' worth of appointments with him in order to go to Palm Springs with Frank Sinatra. Greenson lifted his eyes to the ceiling, his mustache curling into a frown, whenever Marilyn mentioned his former patient. He worried about her being used, and hurt, by men. That, perhaps, seemed inevitable the more deeply involved she became with Sinatra and his clique.

Frank was by turns generous and cruel. Ava Gardner once said that he could be "the sweetest, most charming man in the world when he was in the mood." Indeed, he was all that and more with Marilyn. In New York, Sinatra had been exceedingly kind to her at the hospital. He called. He visited. He gave her gifts, including a fluffy white poodle, whom she named Maf (short for "Mafia," a reference to Sinatra's ties to the mob). Determined not to let Joe DiMaggio find out about Frank, Marilyn claimed the puppy had been a gift from a publicist.

In California, she visited Sinatra's modern, light-filled Palm Springs house on the edge of the Tamarisk Country Club golf course. Frank enjoyed having lots of friends around. The regulars included Peter Lawford, Sammy Davis, Jr., and Dean Martin. By this time, Marilyn, drinking from a flask, was in bad shape again. That seemed to bring out a very different aspect of Frank's personality. He turned vicious, insulting her in front of the others.

Marilyn accompanied Frank to Las Vegas. At the Sands Hotel, she shared a front-row table with Dean Martin, Eddie Fisher, and Elizabeth Taylor. Marilyn leaned on the railing, a champagne glass in hand. She gyrated pleasurably to the music. She drummed the stage with her palm. She cheered each number. She was said to have stolen Sinatra's show. Sinatra was furious. At a party afterward, Frank told Marilyn off and she abruptly departed.

Yet she kept coming back for more. Frank introduced her to the alcohol-drenched scene at Peter Lawford's oceanfront home in Santa Monica. There were pool parties. There were all-night card games reminiscent of those she used to attend at Uncle Joe's. Sinatra, besotted with the Kennedys, dubbed their host Brother-in-Lawford, as he was married to the President's sister Pat. Jack Kennedy had yet to visit California after the election, but when he did, it was a safe bet he planned to spend a good deal of time at the Lawfords'. Sinatra, not to be outdone, was intent on his Palm Springs home being unofficially designated the Western White House. At the inauguration, he had produced a star-studded show-business tribute. Now, he built a heliport and other facilities at his compound in anticipation of playing host to Chicky Boy, as he liked to call the President.

For Sinatra and many others in Hollywood, Lawford's Kennedy connection was the basis of his new allure. It gave a boost to his undistinguished acting career and made his parties the place to be. Marilyn knew him from the days when he was a regular at Charlie Feldman's. Now, in her visits to the Lawford home, she seemed to drift back to a life she'd once worked very hard to escape. The failure of her marriage had led her to believe that this was where she belonged and, for all the grand hopes she'd had, all she really deserved.

Marilyn returned to New York on June 14 for gall bladder surgery, her condition said to be the result of barbiturate abuse. Accompanied by Joe DiMaggio and George Solotaire, she entered Polyclinic Hospital on a stretcher. The doctors found her frightened and disoriented. Marilyn appreciated Joe's devotion, but she also seemed to want to give herself space. So when she came home from the hospital, she was cared for by her half-sister, Berniece Miracle. Gladys's daughter by Jap Baker came up from Florida at Marilyn's request.

When Marilyn was able to go out again, her masseur, Ralph Roberts, carried a favorite chair of Arthur's down to a station wagon. He also loaded two beds from the guest room, and drove the sisters to Connecticut. Marilyn wanted Berniece to see the white colonial farmhouse on Tophet Road. Roxbury was another world from the life Marilyn had re-entered with Sinatra. She was immensely proud of the improvements she had made to the property. She pointed out the dormer windows, the room she'd added over the kitchen. Sadly, Marilyn had never lived in the finished house, as the carpenters had hammered in the last nail as *The Misfits* was being completed. She loved the old place. Yet she had signed it over to Arthur, insisting that that seemed appropriate.

In the sunroom, Arthur served the two women tea. He puffed on his pipe. After four years of Marilyn Monroe, he craved stability. Friends knew of his happy relationship with Inge. *The Misfits* had been a critical and commercial disappointment, and he had recently sold a number of his manuscripts in order to pay taxes. He was under pressure to come up with a new play for Kazan to direct at Lincoln Center. Yet he indicated that he was not actually writing at the moment, just thinking a lot.

In the distance, Maf and Hugo played together, darting past Arthur's studio on the way to the pond. The sight encapsulated the recent changes in Marilyn's life. Maf, small and light, was portable. The miniature poodle could easily be taken on an airplane. Evidently, that's the sort of existence Sinatra saw Marilyn as having from now on. Hugo, long and heavy, was very much a house dog. Marilyn had loved and fretted over the basset hound. She had searched for him when he wandered off. She had fed him brandy when he seemed depressed. But Hugo was Arthur's now. Roxbury was his home.

Marilyn collected some cheap glasses, and took a television set from the second floor. As she picked up an old coat she'd left behind, an unfamiliar perfume filled her nostrils. When Marilyn first came to Roxbury in 1956, she had taken possession of another woman's house. Mary Miller had not actually been there, of course, but her traces were everywhere. Now, Marilyn realized that a new woman had come onto the scene. Upset, she threw the coat in the trash.

On August 8, she returned to Hollywood. Though she kept her rented Manhattan apartment, her base of operations shifted. As Norman Rosten perceived, she went back because she had nowhere else to go. She stayed temporarily in Sinatra's Los Angeles house, while he was in Europe, and during that time she learned about a vacancy in the small, white apartment house on Doheny, where she used to live. On one side lived Sinatra's secretary; on the other was an apartment Frank kept for his personal use. Marilyn signed a lease and prepared to move into the tiny apartment. The gesture, like scratching out the images of herself and Arthur in the *Misfits* contact sheets, appeared to be an attempt to revise the past. As Marilyn re-entered the iron-gated courtyard lined with black-enameled doors, it was almost as though she had never left. In her desperation, perhaps it seemed less painful to pretend that her lost dreams of the years in New York had never existed at all.

Marilyn's stated reason for moving to California was that she owed Twentieth a film. But she hated the studio. The great victory her contract had once represented meant nothing to her now. If she had triumphed over Twentieth in December 1955, she had long ago lost the upper hand. By and large, Marilyn was treated less respectfully there than ever. The general perception at the studio was that her money-making days were grinding to a halt as she moved into her late thirties, prematurely aged by drugs, drink, and pain.

Taking more drugs and drinking more heavily than she ever had in the past, Marilyn seemed to be chasing death. Yet, after a lifetime of struggle against Gladys's judgment, part of her still refused to give up. The war between Marilyn's will to live and her desire to die had always been intense. Though the latter seemed more powerful at the moment, Marilyn's decision to seek help from Dr. Greenson suggested a wish that she might yet survive. In the months that followed, the psychiatrist would become Marilyn's lifeline, the single most important force connecting her to the possibility of going on.

+   +   +

Ralph Greenson kept a rowboat in his swimming pool, and there he liked to sit for hours. He fondly referred to the spot as Lake Greenson. The gentle, hypnotic rocking motion put him at peace. Roses and camellias scented the air. He read. He meditated. Sometimes he smoked a cigar.

Greenson was fifty on September 20. He saw the day as a turning point. A heart attack six years previously had left Greenson acutely aware of his own mortality. He told Anna Freud that he did not really feel older; he felt more serious. He viewed time as precious and longed to concentrate on his own creative work. He was in the throes of writing *The Technique and Practice of Psychoanalysis*, and had just completed a 105-page chapter on resistance. He was about to begin a chapter on transference: the transfer of feelings about a person in the past to someone in the present. Anticipating that this chapter would be even longer than the previous one, he was eager to confer with his publisher on the east coast.

Greenson, determined to finish his book by the end of the academic year, worried about devoting too many hours to patients. He resigned as dean of the training school and chairman of the education committee at the Los Angeles Institute for Psychoanalysis. He also limited his professional activities. He was weary of meetings. He was weary of speaking and of delivering papers to groups of psychoanalysts. Though he had long been active in the American Psychoanalytical Association, he planned not to attend this year's midwinter meeting. His time, he declared, would be better spent writing.

Yet he did not hesitate to take responsibility for Marilyn's treatment. Greenson, for all his stridency, was a decent, compassionate man. He liked Marilyn and sincerely wanted to help. He recognized that she was painfully alone in the world, and admitted he had a weakness for damsels in distress. He hoped he might be able to defeat what he saw as the destructive forces life had stirred up in her. He believed he might actually learn something in the process. Still, at a moment when Greenson was very much clearing his plate, he remained ambivalent. From the first, Marilyn was exceptionally demanding of his time and emotions. He had to improvise, since Marilyn, as he told Anna Freud, was too sick to begin psychoanalysis.

His task was not made easier by the Lawfords' return from Europe. Her visits to their house often seemed to undo everything the doctor hoped to achieve. Soon after they arrived back in Los Angeles, they invited Marilyn to a dinner party in honor of Attorney General Robert F. Kennedy on October 4, 1961. Kennedy planned to be in town to confer with local law-enforcement officials about mob activity in Los Angeles, as part of the Justice Department's crackdown on organized crime.

The dinner would be Marilyn's first chance to meet one of the Kennedy brothers, and she intended to make herself the center of attention. She gave her dressmaker precise instructions for the dress she wanted to wear that night. Marilyn saw herself in a slim, floor-length column of black that would set off the whiteness of her skin. But it was the top of the dress that was to be its most strategic component. For the strapless bodice, she selected an openwork fabric of black eyelet that would permit her bare nipples to stick out. Marilyn, giggling wickedly, described her plan: At the dinner table, she would make sure the President's younger brother noticed as she casually played with the hair on her exposed left nipple.

This was the sort of self-destructive behavior Dr. Greenson was then fighting to persuade Marilyn to stop. She certainly didn't have to do this sort of thing anymore to attract attention. Marilyn had once worked hard never again to have to do anything she was ashamed of. Yet, self-loathing as she now was, she seemed intent on degrading and punishing herself. She acted in this manner precisely because she believed it was wrong. It was as though Marilyn were trying to prove—to others and to herself—why her dreams had failed. Once, in a more hopeful time, it had meant everything to her to make sex appear innocent and fun. That had been the basis of her immense appeal. But that refreshing innocence no longer reflected how she felt, or even hoped to feel, about herself.

According to plan, on the evening of October 4 Marilyn arrived at the Lawfords' in her new peekaboo dress. One of Marilyn's proudest hours had been her behavior during Arthur's political troubles, and now again she found herself in a political context. Clearly distressed, Marilyn proceeded to get more and more drunk. The brave, dignified person she had been five years previously had vanished. By the end of the evening, it became obvious that she was in no condition to get home by herself. Kennedy and his press aide, Edwin Guthman, offered to drive her back.

At Doheny, Kennedy and Guthman carried Marilyn into her apartment. A queen-sized bed with a hideous electric-blue cover dominated the tiny, dark, depressing living room. Marilyn was on the point of passing out, so the men put her into bed, leaving her there to sleep it off. Guthman would later remember that both he and Bobby found her sweet that night—and very, very sad.

On October 16, Twentieth assigned Marilyn to be directed by George Cukor in *Something's Got to Give*, a remake of the 1939 Irene Dunne comedy *My Favorite Wife*. The notice triggered what her doctor characterized as a severe depressive and paranoid reaction. After *Let's Make Love*, Marilyn was convinced that Cukor had it in for her. She spoke of abandoning motion pictures altogether. She threatened to take her own life. Greenson believed she was potentially suicidal. She needed to be detoxified again. In light of the Payne–Whitney episode, however, he was wary of institutionalizing her. So he put her under round-the-clock nurses' care in her apartment. The living room became Marilyn's hospital, with heavy, blue, triple-lined curtains blocking out the sunlight.

If Marilyn was in turmoil, so was the studio that had ordered her back to work. Twentieth was no longer the great company Darryl Zanuck took pride in having built. It didn't make great pictures anymore, and it certainly didn't make money. In 1961 alone, Fox would lose more than $22 million. Much of that could be attributed to the deeply troubled production of *Cleopatra* in Rome. Skouras was the subject of a good deal of speculation. He was said to be gravely ill. He was said to be seeking a scapegoat for the studio's operating losses. He was said to have been implored by Jerry Wald, George Stevens, and other Fox veterans to bring back his old adversary Zanuck as production chief. He was said to have been given an ultimatum by his enemies on the board to step down. But there were also those at Twentieth who believed that if *Cleopatra* were ready in time for the May stockholders' meeting, Skouras might yet save his job.

On October 26, Fox executives met with the attorney Mickey Rudin about a proposed contract for his client Frank Sinatra. The studio contingent included the new production chief, Peter Levathes. Levathes, once thought of as Skouras's protégé, was rumored to be a candidate for his mentor's job. As the meeting drew to a close, Rudin made a surprise move. He brought up "the Monroe problem." Rudin, as it happened, was married to Ralph Greenson's sister. Greenson, concerned about Marilyn, had asked Rudin to get involved. The doctor believed it was in Marilyn's interest to do the picture and get out from under the burden of her Fox contract.

Rudin cut to the heart of the matter. He suggested that Marilyn's problem with Twentieth was psychological. It was not simply how much she was being paid or what approvals she had in her contract—though naturally he was very much concerned with these issues—but how Marilyn felt about her treatment by the studio. He emphasized the importance of their taking her opinion seriously. He urged them to come up with an arrangement that would permit Marilyn to feel that she had a degree of control over her work. For the first time in Marilyn's tumultuous saga at Twentieth Century–Fox, someone had articulated what the fight had always been about. Charlie Feldman, for all his expert negotiations, had never understood that money meant little to Marilyn. He never saw that what really fueled her was a desire for respect. Rudin, with the benefit of his brother-in-law's insights into her personality, had finally made that point clear. Twentieth might have everything in its favor legally and still not get a picture. Marilyn had to feel that she was being treated with dignity.

Rudin also dropped the bombshell that he knew Twentieth did not yet have a contract with Cukor when Marilyn was summoned. When Cukor was mentioned for Something's Got to Give, Twentieth knew that he might be busy at Warner's on The Chapman Report until as late as December 26, more than a month after the date by which Twentieth had to call Marilyn back to work. Her contract did not, however, require the studio to begin principal photography by then. So, rather than risk the last picture she owed, Twentieth decided to keep her on salary as long as Cukor took to finish The Chapman Report. The studio and the director came to terms verbally, but Cukor had yet to sign. The technicality—and that's all it was—provided grounds to contend that Marilyn was no longer under contract. Rudin made clear he had no interest in pursuing this avenue but would do so if Twentieth failed to consider his suggestions.

What exactly was he suggesting? Studio executives seemed unsure. It was almost as though they were constitutionally unable to hear what Rudin had just explained to them. As Frank Ferguson saw it, Rudin wanted two things: money and script approval. Levathes offered a bonus if Marilyn finished *Something's Got to Give*. Meanwhile, Ferguson expressed confidence that the studio's position was sound. He expected Marilyn to report on November 15. Whether she would remained in question. Rudin had another meeting at Twentieth on November 9. This time the screenplay was the issue. Frank Tashlin had written it without Marilyn in mind. At Cukor's suggestion, Twentieth had recently hired Arnold Schulman to tailor the material for her. The studio promised to send Marilyn a copy as soon as it was finalized, but reminded Rudin that she did not have script approval.

That afternoon, Marilyn put in an appearance at the Beverly Hills Hotel. The new production chief had asked to have lunch with her and her lawyer in an effort to establish a friendly relationship. Levathes returned to the studio in the belief that he probably had been successful. Still, Marilyn had not said yes to *Something's Got to Give*. And she still had not said yes on November 13, two days before she was due to come in. On the 14th, Rudin again asked for a copy of the screenplay, saying that Marilyn would not report before being shown a script. It did not arrive. The next day, Marilyn failed to appear and Twentieth suspended her. Suddenly, Rudin began to talk about other projects Marilyn might do to fulfill her obligation. Tennessee Williams had advised her to do *Celebration* for Jerry Wald. Rudin also mentioned Vera Caspary's *Illicity*.

By this time, Marilyn's daily life had settled into a routine. Late in the day, she would be driven to Santa Monica in a green Dodge. Her housekeeper (provided by Ralph Greenson), Eunice Murray, would drop her off in front of a five-bedroom, white stucco house. Perched on a hill, it had a large, velvety lawn, with sparkling ocean views in one direction and city views in another. In a front window, Marilyn could usually see Dr. Greenson, in shirt and tie, at a wooden desk. He sat in a leather chair, under a wood-beamed ceiling, with a vase of roses from the garden nearby. Marilyn, on her first visit, had been some thirty minutes late. The doctor declared that lateness communicates dislike. After that, Marilyn made a point of being early, pacing palm-lined Franklin Street until it was time to go in. She tended to be his last appointment.

Ten months previously, Dr. Greenson had made a promising discovery. For some time he had been immensely frustrated in his treatment of a young schizophrenic. Filled with guilt about what he perceived as his own therapeutic failures, he asked Anna Freud to come from England as a consultant, but she declined. The case seemed to be stalled when Greenson happened to ask his daughter, Joannie, an art student, to drive the patient home one day. The patient's response was electric. As she chatted with Joannie in the car, she seemed like any other healthy young person. After that, Greenson regularly assigned Joannie to take her home. Though the change vanished as soon as she and Joannie were apart, the fact remained that the patient had made her first significant progress when Greenson involved her with a member of his family.

Thus, Greenson's unorthodox and potentially controversial decision to integrate Marilyn into his home life was a deliberate one. As he told Anna Freud, he had to improvise. Yet he often found himself wondering where this was going. Joannie, as a little girl, had been taught to keep out of sight of the patients, so her role with the schizophrenic had been very much a departure. Her involvement with Marilyn was even more unusual. When Marilyn arrived, the twenty-one-year-old Joannie would meet her at the door. On the days when Greenson lectured at the university and thought that he might be late for Marilyn's session, he asked Joannie to take her out for a walk.

Marilyn, with the doctor's permission, kept a bottle of Dom Perignon at the house so that she could have a glass of champagne at the end of her hour. Afterward, she often stayed for dinner. She adored the Mexican kitchen where the family tended to gather, and the beamed, wood-paneled living room filled with books and art. Its focal point was a grand piano. An immense fireplace was decorated with colorful Mexican tiles. From a balcony, one could see the garden and the swimming pool. There was a bo tree, a descendant of the sacred Indian fig tree beneath whose branches the Buddha gained enlightenment. Beneath it stood a Polynesian Tiki god, five feet tall, with an open mouth and a bedazzled expression, which Greenson had given to his wife for Christmas.

Ralph and Hildi, after twenty-five years of marriage, remained devoted to each other and to their children. He described himself as a Brooklyn Jew who had married a good Swiss girl. He called Hildi the one who made everything possible. She saw him as her other half; when she was scattered, he was organized; when she was timid, he opened doors. Their twenty-four-year-old son, Danny, a medical student, was also living at home that year. An accident had left him on crutches, his leg in a cast.

Dr. Greenson hoped to expose Marilyn to the warmth and affection of a happy family. He hoped to compensate for the emotional deprivation she had suffered since childhood. He hoped to assuage her painful loneliness. But in welcoming her into the household, he was also trying to make himself real and human in her eyes. He believed patients must be allowed to see that the analyst has emotions and weaknesses of his own. He believed the doctor must provide a model of someone who can be trustworthy and reliable despite his frailties. He strove to teach his patients to accept that human beings are imperfect, that one must learn to live with uncertainty.

Greenson diagnosed Marilyn as a borderline paranoid addict. Borderline personalities dread abandonment. They fear that being left means they are evil or bad. Faced with even a routine separation, they react with anger, cruel sarcasm, and despair. They cast certain people—a lover, a teacher, a doctor—in the role of savior, abruptly and viciously turning against them for not being sufficiently "there." Borderline personalities, perceiving themselves to have been abandoned by those whom they have idealized, are apt to threaten or to attempt suicide. The diagnosis fit Marilyn to a tee. No wonder Greenson was wary of being idealized. Yet he risked bringing Marilyn into his home, aware of what might happen to her if he did not.

More and more, Marilyn was being pulled between two households in Santa Monica. On the one hand, she loved to attend the chamber music concerts held regularly in Dr. Greenson's living room. On the other, she continued to be very much drawn to the Lawfords'. There, on Sunday, November 19, the event everybody had been waiting for finally occurred. A motorcade pulled up. Jack Kennedy, who had spoken at the Hollywood Palladium the night before, emerged from an open convertible that had been intended for Secret Service agents; on the way out to the beach, he'd insisted on changing cars. He had only a few hours to relax before returning to the Beverly Hilton to prepare for the first of a series of talks with West German Chancellor Adenauer, and he planned to enjoy himself.

Kennedy, whose father had been active in the film business in the twenties and thirties, was decidedly at home in Hollywood. Inside his sister's house, he swapped the dark business suit he'd worn to church for a sports shirt and blue denims. Before long, he was out on the sunny beach mingling with the Lawfords' guests. Lawford, in the words of Gore Vidal, was "Jack's Plenipotentiary to the Girls of Hollywood." From the first, the President seems to have viewed Marilyn as a particularly desirable scalp to add to his belt.

Marilyn discovered in the President the perfect vehicle to play out her own emotional contradictions. After the failure of her third marriage, she had lost the chance for absolution that being Mrs. Arthur Miller was supposed to have provided. With Sinatra and Lawford, she plunged back into precisely the world she had once been desperate to flee. The President was very much of that world, though most people didn't see him that way. Marilyn's personal history gave her a unique perspective. Both Charlie Feldman and Joe Schenck had been close to Joseph P. Kennedy. Both had assisted, in one way or another, his mistress Gloria Swanson. Both had entertained young Jack in Hollywood. From the outset, Marilyn recognized the President as one of a particular group of men. She knew who he was and what he was after.

At the same time, Marilyn, like many Americans, was caught up in the romance of the Kennedy administration. He was young. He was modern. He was charismatic. He was passionate about ideas. He spoke to youth as perhaps no president had in recent years. In this light, Marilyn saw Jack Kennedy as a moral figure on a par with Arthur Miller. Certainly, Kennedy's Saturday night speech at the Hollywood Palladium, an attack on right-wing "crusades of suspicion," would have been familiar political terrain. As Marilyn later indicated to Dr. Greenson, she was prepared to do anything to help the President. The psychiatrist's dilemma was that politically his own heart was very much with Kennedy.

Lawford arranged another meeting two weeks later. On December 5, howling winds rocked New York. Gusts of up to sixty-eight miles per hour pried loose a stone ornament on a building directly across from the Hotel Carlyle on East 76th Street at Madison Avenue. An emergency crew secured the huge, heavy cresting with a rope in time for the presidential motorcade to pass beneath shortly before 3 p.m. There were fifty police motorcycles and twenty-five cars. Jack Kennedy, wearing neither hat nor topcoat, rode in a bubble-top limousine, accompanied by a contingent of city officials who had met him at the airport. The President, on his way to Palm Beach, Florida, was to spend Tuesday night at the Carlyle. In view of the danger, he entered by a side entrance.

That evening the President was guest of honor at an awards dinner given by the National Football Foundation and Hall of Fame at the Waldorf-Astoria. Afterward, he went to a party at the Park Avenue apartment of Mrs. John Fell, the widow of a prominent investment banker. That's where he was to see Marilyn again, Lawford having arranged for her to fly in for the occasion. But when the President arrived, Marilyn wasn't there yet. As usual she swept in late, much to Lawford's annoyance. It was his responsibility that such encounters ran smoothly.

Lawford wasn't the only one frustrated in efforts to pin Marilyn down to a schedule. That month, Twentieth finally let her read *Something's Got to Give*. A nervous accompanying letter pointed out that the screenplay had been revised specifically as a vehicle for her and was still in the process of being polished. It stressed the studio's recognition that she would probably have suggestions of her own. Two copies of the script were delivered to her lawyer. Four days before Christmas, Rudin called Ferguson. Marilyn demanded changes, but that was not all. She wanted Twentieth to hire the cameraman from *Some Like It Hot*. She wanted a say in the casting. She wanted a say in the publicity. She reluctantly agreed to work with Cukor, but not with his color consultant. Afterward, Ferguson found himself wondering whether it was coincidental that "each calendar year seems to end in a crisis which has been created by this girl."

The negotiations resumed after Christmas. Nothing was settled right away, yet the studio had a sense that progress was being made. Marilyn insisted that a good picture was her sole concern. It is significant that what she meant by "good" had changed drastically. She had once rejected the crowd-pleasing, money-making formula of *Gentlemen Prefer Blondes* and *How to Marry a Millionaire*. At the moment, however, her needs were different. She believed she had "slipped" in the past two years. She needed a hit.

When Twentieth proposed Nunnally Johnson to rewrite *Something's Got to Give*, Marilyn was enthusiastic. He had done the screenplay for *How to Marry a Millionaire*. He knew how to write "Marilyn Monroe." Marilyn feared he was still angry about her having turned down *How to be Very, Very Popular*, but Johnson declared: "Tell Miss Monroe that if everybody who turned down a script I wrote was no longer a friend of mine, I wouldn't have any friends." They reconciled over three bottles of champagne at the Polo Lounge. On January 24, 1962, Ferguson gave the go-ahead for a contract to be drawn up. Johnson went to England to work. Marilyn agreed to do the film if the script turned out as she hoped.

The nurturing atmosphere of the Greenson household appeared to have had a stabilizing effect. When the doctor advised Marilyn to exchange her depressing apartment for a home of her own, she chose a house in Brentwood expressly because it reminded her of the Greenson residence. It was on Fifth Helena Drive, a secluded cul de sac. Marilyn hoped to replicate the colorful tiles and other Mexican decor she associated with her happy evenings at the Greensons. She was particularly eager to reproduce the family kitchen.

Clearly, Marilyn missed the life, or more precisely the dream of a life, she had left behind in Roxbury. Her eyes would cloud over as she spoke of the white farmhouse that she and Arthur had redone. At the last minute, she seemed uncertain whether she wanted to go through with the purchase of the Brentwood property. She left the room, returning ten minutes later to sign. Later, she disclosed that she had been struck by the sadness of buying a house all by herself.

On February 1, Marilyn attended a dinner party for Robert and Ethel Kennedy at the Lawfords'. Remembering the fiasco of her previous meeting with Bobby, she did everything to make a good impression. Marilyn, seated beside the Attorney General, interrogated him about civil rights and other issues. Dr. Greenson's son had helped her prepare a list of political questions. Never one for memorization, she peeked in her handbag intermittently. Bobby, delighted, spent much of the evening in conversation with her. The next day, she wasted no time in writing about the dinner party to Isadore Miller in Florida. She had every reason to expect Isadore would tell his son. Her timing suggests she was sending a message to Arthur. If the Attorney General thought well of her, shouldn't he?

Marilyn flew to New York. She conferred with Lee Strasberg about *Something's Got to Give*. While Johnson finished the script, she planned to go to Mexico in search of furniture and art for her new home. She seemed to be feeling pretty good about herself. Then she heard something that plunged her into despair. Arthur was to be married on February 17. Apparently, only a few people had been invited. The ceremony was to take place in a model home in New Milford, Connecticut, part of a development built by his cousin Morty. Arthur and Inge had been travelling in Europe together. She was now two months pregnant.

Marilyn fired off a telegram to Miami Beach, asking Isadore to meet her at the Eastern Airlines terminal that very evening. When she arrived, it was evident that he did not know his son's plans. They dined at the Fountainbleau and took in a show at the Sea Isle. They strolled crowded Collins Avenue, her arm locked tightly in his. On Saturday, Marilyn took Isadore and a few of his friends to dinner. Afterward, she arranged to be alone with him in her suite at the Fountainbleau. They'd been sitting comfortably for a while when she disclosed that Arthur was getting married today. Marilyn, realizing the old man was upset, added that a letter must be on the way. She was there to comfort Isadore. She was there to seek comfort. But in spending the evening with Arthur's father, she was also inserting herself, however indirectly, into his wedding.

Four days later, Joe, then at the Yankee training camp, escorted Marilyn to Miami International Airport for her flight to Mexico. By the time she came home on March 2, she was in dreadful shape again. Only a few weeks before, buying and decorating her own house was supposed to have marked the start of a new life. In the aftermath of Arthur's marriage, her attitude changed. Marilyn swallowed too many pills the night before she was to leave Mexico. At the airport, she had liquor on her breath. As she made her way to the plane, she could barely walk straight.

She was still unsteady on her feet three days later at the Golden Globe Awards in Los Angeles. She arrived drunk, a Mexican lover in tow. She wore a backless, green beaded gown. When it was time to collect a gold statuette as the World's Favorite Female Star, she could scarcely get to the podium. Her acceptance speech was boozy and indistinct. The sight of her like this at a major industry event led some people to say Marilyn was finished. Yet the next afternoon, she kept an appointment with Peter Levathes at Fox. After the Golden Globes, the production chief had reason to be concerned. He asked if she was "with us."

"I guess I'm reporting back," Marilyn replied.

It was hardly an enthusiastic statement, but as far as Frank Ferguson was concerned, it meant that on March 6 Marilyn Monroe had reported ready, willing, and able to work. It meant that she had agreed to do *Something's Got to Give*. At least, everyone at Twentieth hoped it did. Just to be sure, studio wardrobe people were sent to Marilyn's apartment. They took her measurements so a form could be made to create her costumes. Marilyn seemed cooperative. But was she in any condition to work? The studio attorney, for his part, viewed the situation as precarious.

Under the circumstances, Dr. Greenson had to rethink his own plans. Before Marilyn's calamitous trip to New York, he had been looking forward to a trip of his own. In the spring, Hildi intended to visit her mother, who had recently suffered a mild stroke, in Switzerland. The Greensons hoped to do a bit of traveling in Europe together. On the way back, he planned to stop off in New York to see his publisher.

Two days after the Golden Globes, however, he was not sure he should leave. Hildi had to go in any event. He still very much wanted to meet her there, but whether that could be arranged was another matter. Greenson, having diagnosed Marilyn as a borderline personality, was well aware of her fears of abandonment. Though his reasons for going abroad had nothing to do with her, how would she react to his departure? Her dependence seemed to have intensified. Marilyn had transferred certain of her feelings about her former husband to her doctor. Now it was Greenson whom she idealized and cast in the role of savior. Coming on top of Arthur's marriage, Greenson's departure could prove devastating.

He kept changing his mind. Now he planned to go, now he did not. The trip seemed to be on again after Marilyn reacted favorably to Johnson's script. She stipulated that it needed additional comedy. Otherwise, she was quite pleased. Greenson had reason to think everything was finally going to be all right. On March 21, he seemed utterly confident that he would be able to get away. Hildi was to leave in the middle of April. He intended to follow in May. He particularly looked forward to seeing Anna Freud in London.

Three days later, Marilyn turned up at her doctor's home. It was early Saturday morning, long before she customarily awakened. A water heater was being installed in her house, and the plumber had informed her that there would be no hot water for thirty minutes. Marilyn wanted to wash her hair at the Greensons'. Greenson was happy to accommodate her, but bemused as to why she was up so early, and in such a rush. She told him that Peter Lawford was coming to pick her up to take her to Palm Springs.

President Kennedy was spending the weekend there, though not at the Sinatra compound, since in his brother's view it would be inappropriate for the President to accept Sinatra's hospitality at a moment when the Justice Department was engaged in a crackdown on organized crime. Sinatra, informed by a nervous Lawford that Chicky Boy would not be his guest after all, flew into a temper and wrecked his new concrete helicopter pad with a sledgehammer. Lawford, in the meantime, drove Marilyn to Bing Crosby's house, where it had been arranged for Kennedy to stay instead. She spent the night in the President's quarters.

If Marilyn wanted to prevent Dr. Greenson from "abandoning" her, she could hardly have come up with a more effective scenario. The desert weekend was precisely the sort of situation that set off alarm bells, concerned as Greenson was about her being hurt and exploited. And that may have been very much Marilyn's intention, in choosing Greenson's house to wash her hair on Saturday morning before she left. She may have been playing the happy girl, but whether consciously or not she was letting her doctor know she was in trouble. Indeed, he was soon lamenting to Anna Freud that he was no longer certain he could break free.

He had reason to be worried. Marilyn, from the start, regarded her relationship with Jack Kennedy as a good deal more serious than it actually was. "Well, it wasn't a big thing as far as he was concerned," said Senator George Smathers of his close friend's involvement with Marilyn. According to Smathers, Marilyn was "like a lot of the pretty girls who had fallen very much in love with the Kennedys just by being around him a little bit." But Marilyn wasn't like most other women. She had known the most extravagant of her fantasies to come true. On the basis of only a few days' acquaintance in 1951, she had captured Arthur Miller's imagination, and eventually the great writer had left his wife for her. Now, she seemed to assume she'd have a similar effect on the President. Therein lay the seed of disaster.

Arthur and Inge, who had been on honeymoon in Europe, came home on April 10. That night, Marilyn could not sleep. Her house was empty, the furniture and art not yet having arrived from Mexico. The living room had a chair and a low coffee table. Maf, never properly housebroken, had already stained the new white carpet. In the kitchen, cabinets, fixtures, and wiring were in the process of being ripped out. According to a nightly ritual, two phones, one white, the other pink, both with long cords, had been smothered with pillows in a guest bedroom. Shopping bags, a record player, and records littered the floor in Marilyn's own bedroom. Marilyn once told Dr. Greenson that she did not know what nights were for. On this particular night, she tried Nembutal. She tried Librium. She tried Demerol. She tried chloral hydrate.

A studio limousine came for her in the morning. The house, which had barred windows in front, looked deserted. No one answered the door. Afterward, Greenson discovered Marilyn, under her white satin comforter, in a drug coma.

Two days later, she flew to New York to confer with Strasberg. She and Cukor were already at odds, the director having brought in yet another writer. Marilyn had agreed to do *Something's Got to Give* strictly on the basis of Johnson's draft. Her only stipulation had been that it needed some funnier lines and more comical situations. Strasberg concurred. Cukor and his writer Walter Bernstein pressed ahead anyway, and some forty blue pages of changes materialized. Marilyn found them unacceptable. Nunnally Johnson, she believed, had written first-rate "Marilyn Monroe." The rewrite, in her view, failed to accomplish that.

Marilyn declared she could not do the part as it had been revised. She was to play a wife believed to have been dead for seven years. She objected to the character's going after her husband when he remarries. Marilyn preferred to encounter him by chance. "Marilyn Monroe" would never pursue a man, she insisted; men pursue "Marilyn." There was some puzzlement about Marilyn's speaking of herself in the third person. Of course, she wasn't really. She was talking about a comical character she had created, much as Charles Chaplin might have talked about the Tramp. It was the character Billy Wilder had once urged her not to abandon. At the time, she had rejected Wilder's suggestion. Now, she seemed to have had second thoughts.

Though Marilyn did not have script approval, Rudin informed Levathes that she would film only those portions to which she had no objection. So before the picture even began, Marilyn and Cukor were at war. At times, Cukor insisted that he liked Marilyn. But the fact was he loathed her. He described her as erratic, inconsiderate, ruthless, tough, and willful. In speaking of her, Cukor used language that, said Nunnally Johnson, "would have brought a blush to Sophie Tucker's cheeks."

Suddenly, there were hints that Marilyn might not do the film after all. Rudin revived the claim that she was no longer under contract, since Cukor had not signed in time. The lawyer insisted that if Marilyn appeared in Something's Got to Give, it was merely in an effort to compromise. Far more alarming to Twentieth was her lawyer's refusal to bill the studio for Marilyn's services. Ostensibly, she preferred to be paid in a lump sum, along with the bonus Levathes had discussed. But there were fears that the real reason was to avoid compromising the claim, should Rudin decide to press it, that her contract had expired.

Cukor started shooting on Monday, April 23. The night before, he received word that Marilyn would be unable to work. Apparently, she had caught a cold from Lee Strasberg. Rudin told Levathes that she had a fever. She failed to come in for the rest of the week. Cukor, forced to shoot without her, was exasperated.

So was Dr. Greenson. He adored Marilyn. He sincerely wanted to lessen her pain. At the same time, as he never tired of pointing out, he was only human. She'd exhausted him. He craved peace and relaxation, and needed a vacation for his health. His wife's departure had been delayed until May 1, and he wanted to meet her in Rome on the 10th. He had been invited to Jerusalem to deliver a paper on transference, a subject with which he'd had a good deal of experience lately. He longed to visit some of the Greek islands. He longed to spend some quiet time with his Swiss in-laws. Yet, as he growled to Anna Freud, there would be uncertainty about his trip until he left.

On the eve of the second week of filming, Greenson reviewed the situation for Anna Freud. Marilyn was either teetering on the edge of establishing her independence, or of regressing and wrecking his vacation. He insisted Marilyn would probably succeed in living without him.

But, he said, probably only half in jest, he wasn't sure he himself would survive the turmoil. Thus the analyst expressed his fear that Marilyn—a borderline personality, after all—might react to his departure with a suicide attempt. Greenson desperately wanted to believe that she was no more likely to die as a result of his trip than he was. But he was aware that might not be true. He was overwhelmed by the responsibility and more than a little resentful.

Marilyn wanted to please her doctor. She could never bear to leave matters between them unresolved. On Monday, April 30, she arrived at the studio twenty-five minutes early for a 6:30 a.m. makeup call. She worked until 4 p.m. It was a different story the next day, however—the day Hildi left for Switzerland. Marilyn, upset by the prospect of Greenson's following his wife to Europe, could hardly work. Thirty minutes after she arrived at Twentieth, she collapsed and had to be taken home. She called in sick for the rest of the week.

On the night of Sunday, May 6, Marilyn notified the studio that she couldn't come in on Monday morning. By that time, Cukor had run out of material to shoot without her. He closed down the production, resuming on Wednesday with a bit of location work. Greenson, due to leave the next day, could put off a decision no more. After months of intense daily contact with Marilyn, he believed he had earned a rest. After months of storm and stress, he was even looking forward to a little boredom. Perhaps he told himself that if he did go, Marilyn's reason for staying in bed would vanish. On Thursday, May 10, Greenson flew to Europe, leaving Marilyn in the care of an associate. It was a decision he would never entirely forgive himself for having made.

SEVENTEEN

By the end of the third week, Marilyn had worked only one day. Late on the afternoon of Friday, May 11, Peter Levathes called Mickey Rudin. It had come to the production chief's attention that Marilyn planned to be in New York the following Thursday and Friday, before performing at a Democratic Party event at Madison Square Garden on Saturday the 19th. The gala, designed to raise money to pay off the deficit from the presidential campaign, was billed as a forty-fifth birthday salute to President Kennedy. Levathes indicated he couldn't possibly let her attend. Her absences had already put *Something's Got to Give* considerably behind schedule. Twentieth expected Marilyn to report every day during the week of May 14 to 18.

If there ever had been the slightest chance she would acquiesce, it was dashed by events in Washington. That very evening, Arthur Miller attended a black-tie dinner at the White House for André Malraux, the French Minister of Culture. Jacqueline Kennedy, in a strapless pink Dior gown, greeted some of America's most distinguished artists, including the novelists Saul Bellow and Robert Penn Warren, the poet Archibald MacLeish, and the critic Edmund Wilson. Andrew Wyeth and Mark Rothko represented painting, Leonard Bernstein music, and George Balanchine the dance. From the theater came Tennessee Williams, Elia Kazan, and Lee Strasberg.

It was Arthur Miller who, to his astonishment and delight, found himself seated with Mrs. Kennedy and Malraux. The First Lady was known to have agonized over the seating charts, which she had spread out on her sitting-room floor. Placing Miller near her was a bold stroke. It left no doubt that McCarthyism was dead. Eisenhower's Washington had taken a dim view of Miller; Kennedy's made him an honored guest. Miller, for his part, reveled in an administration that valued artists and intellectuals as much as "showbiz stars."

Marilyn called the Rostens in Brooklyn to announce her impending arrival, characterizing her trip as a secret mission. She disclosed she was going to sing at the President's birthday. She exulted that the press would be surprised by her escort. Isadore Miller had agreed to take Marilyn to Madison Square Garden. The choice of Arthur's father as her cavalier guaranteed that, in Roxbury at least, attention would be paid.

All weekend, the white-carpeted, unfurnished rooms at Fifth Helena echoed with Marilyn's whispery voice. She lay in the tub singing "Happy Birthday." She sat on the living-room floor, endlessly tape recording and listening to herself. A manic energy propelled her. On Monday, she arrived at Fox twenty minutes before her 6:30 a.m. makeup call. She was eager. She was diligent. She was cooperative. She made it clear, however, that she simply had to go to New York. On Thursday, May 17, she planned to work only until noon.

Marilyn could not have picked a worse time to challenge the studio. On May 15, Spyros Skouras faced three hundred jeering stockholders at the annual meeting in New York. Contrary to plan, *Cleopatra* was not yet finished; all Skouras could do was to make promises and excuses. The standing-room-only crowd responded with skepticism and derision. There were angry remarks about the excesses of Hollywood stars (i.e. Elizabeth Taylor and Marilyn Monroe) and the highly-paid studio executives who indulged them. The next day, Twentieth sternly warned that if Marilyn went to New York she'd be in violation of her contract. Mickey Rudin replied that the studio seemed to have forgotten something; as far as she was concerned, she didn't have a contract. Marilyn, preoccupied, was still singing "Happy Birthday" on the airplane with Peter Lawford and Paula Strasberg.

She continued to practice in her New York apartment. Her interpretation grew sexier. It grew outrageous. Paula worried that it verged on self-parody. But Marilyn insisted it had to be "sexy." Her song was the finale. Ella Fitzgerald, Peggy Lee, Jack Benny, Maria Callas, Bobby Darin, Harry Belafonte, and other stars preceded her. Marilyn was convinced this was the way to top them.

Paula believed that only Lee might be capable of stopping Marilyn. But he gave the impression he had more important things to think about. His tacit comment on the proceedings was to decline to attend. Strasberg, insulted that Lincoln Center had spurned him and indignant that Elia Kazan had accepted a post there, was then planning to launch his own competing repertory company, the Actors Studio Theater. He wanted to direct Ben Gazzara and Marilyn Monroe in *Macbeth*. The absurdity of the casting was not lost on Strasberg. When he spoke of Marilyn as Lady Macbeth, he would actually laugh. "It's a wonderful little portrait of his own ego," said Frank Corsaro. "It wasn't so much that she was going to do this. It was the fact that he was going to accomplish this miracle. The poor girl looked at him with amazement, surprise, and fear."

On Saturday night, Marilyn was high when she emerged from the shadows behind master-of-ceremonies Peter Lawford on stage at Madison Square Garden. She walked like a geisha. She threw off her white fur. She had on a flesh-toned gown encrusted with rhinestones. She flicked the mike with her finger. She shielded heavy-lidded eyes to survey the audience of fifteen thousand whooping, whistling Democrats. The arena was adorned with red, white, and blue balloons and streamers. In the presidential box, Jack Kennedy mauled a cigar, his feet up on the railing. Mrs. Kennedy had pointedly declined to attend.

Marilyn began to sing. She closed her eyes. She licked her lips. She ran her hands up her thighs and stomach, aborting the gesture at her breasts. The Broadway columnist Dorothy Kilgallen, commenting on the telecast, described Marilyn's act as "making love to the president in the direct view of forty million Americans." The nation was titillated. Yet the performance was also a cry for help. Marilyn believed she had been left—by Miller, by Greenson—because she was bad. Tonight she showed how bad she could be. She let them see what abandonment had done to her. She warned of what was to come.

Arthur's father picked up Marilyn backstage. When Jack Kennedy entered the dressing room, Marilyn, flustered, introduced Isadore. A moment's awkwardness followed. "I should have said 'Happy birthday, Mr. President,'" Marilyn added, "but I was so excited about Dad I introduced him first."

The old man escorted her to a small party at the house of Arthur

Krim, chairman of United Artists. Jimmy Durante played the piano and sang. Marilyn found a chair for Isadore. He looked on as Bobby Kennedy and Arthur Schlesinger, Jr. engaged in "mock competition" to dance with her. The historian had one advantage over the Attorney General; he could talk to Marilyn about their mutual friends Joe and Olie Rauh. The reference would have been bittersweet, recalling a moment when she had risked everything to prove she was worthy and good. Tonight, Marilyn again put her career at risk, but to a very different end. Back then she had reached out to life. Now she seemed to embrace self-destruction.

But not entirely . . . not yet. After the party, she took Isadore home. She kissed him good night, leaving him at the elevator in his daughter's apartment building. Marilyn was on her way out when something caused her to turn back. She implored Isadore to come to the Coast with her the following day. He promised to come later.

Marilyn flew back to Los Angeles. After the sensation she had created in New York, she wanted to go further. After her "skin and beads" costume, there really was only one way to go. Cukor planned to shoot a skinny-dipping scene on Wednesday, May 23. Magazine photographers were alerted, presumably for shots of Marilyn in a flesh-toned bikini. Instead, when Marilyn emerged from the turquoise swimming pool, she was naked. She had removed her flimsy swimsuit underwater.

Marilyn posed in the nude. She performed a striptease with co-star Dean Martin's copious blue robe. At length, the images would appear on more than seventy magazine covers in thirty-two countries. Many people interpreted it as a masterful publicity stunt, a return to the old "carefree" Marilyn Monroe. Marilyn, having lost fifteen pounds, was said to be back to her "calendar-girl shape." She lapped up the attention. She was gratified by the prospect of knocking Elizabeth Taylor and *Cleopatra* off magazine covers around the world.

So, on one hand, the pictures read as a triumph. On the other, they seemed like a defeat. Posing in the nude was everything Marilyn had fought to put behind her. Why had she chosen to do it now? Would no one get the message?

In recent days, Marilyn had soared emotionally. That weekend she seemed to crash, her sense of power turning to shame. She failed to come in on the morning of Monday, May 28. Cukor had nothing to shoot without her. Again the company lost a day's work. After that, Marilyn worked intermittently. And when she did work, Cukor thought it wasn't any good. Worse, she knew it was no good. Marilyn had always been her own harshest critic. That was what made it all so painful now.

Also painful were her attempts to maintain a connection with Jack Kennedy. After Madison Square Garden, he had decided to pull back. On the basis of Marilyn's over-the-top performance, everybody was talking about the President and the movie star. Kennedy assigned staff members to kill potential news stories. Ordinarily, gossip about his promiscuity did not particularly distress him. The possibility of publication—whether in *Time*, *Newsweek*, or some other periodical—was another matter entirely. Once a story appeared in print, it was likely to be picked up. And that, as he well knew, could be politically disastrous. So the President put out the word that rumors linking him with Marilyn were false.

Even as the President was distancing himself, Marilyn was looking for ways to penetrate his inner circle. She summoned Kennedy's hair stylist, Mickey Song, who had done her hair at Madison Square Garden. Excitedly he assumed she wanted to hire him. But when Song arrived at Fifth Helena, he discovered that Marilyn was interested in a very different sort of arrangement. After a few minutes of small talk, she got to the point.

"I'm really trying to find out some information about what's going on," she said. "I don't know whether there's other people coming in or not. And I thought maybe you and I could team up."

Marilyn wanted to know whether there were other women in Jack's life. Song prided himself on his discretion, but the pressure he felt from Marilyn was extremely intense. "I don't know anything," Song insisted. "I don't know anything."

Marilyn called the President at the White House. She wanted to see him. She wanted to come to Washington. She would not take no for an answer. She phoned again and again. "He wanted to stop it," said Senator George Smathers, "because it got to be to a point where it was somewhat embarrassing." According to Smathers, Kennedy sent their friend Bill Thompson, a railroad executive, to try to control Marilyn. He may also have asked Peter Lawford to intercede. The President, for his part, refused all further calls. That seemed to work. "She stopped bothering him," said Smathers, "because he quit talking to her."

On Friday, June 1, Marilyn turned thirty-six. After work, a birthday cake, with crackling Independence Day sparklers, was wheeled out, the cast and crew singing "Happy Birthday." Two days later, Marilyn summoned her psychoanalyst's son and daughter. She was lying naked beneath a sheet, her night table cluttered with pill bottles. She wept that her life wasn't worth living. She said she was ugly. She said she was unloved. She complained of being used. She agonized about never having had a baby. The visitors, alarmed, called their father's associate, who confiscated Marilyn's pills, dumping the bottles in his black leather bag. Another physician was brought in to sedate her.

Ralph Greenson had already been to Greece, Israel, and Italy. He was about to spend some time with his Swiss in-laws when Eunice Murray called. Unable to talk on the phone, Marilyn had given her housekeeper a list of "urgent" personal questions for the doctor. But the individual questions were less significant than the subtext: Aren't you coming home?

On Monday morning, Twentieth received word that Marilyn would not be coming in. Cukor found some material to shoot with Dean Martin and Cyd Charisse, who played his new wife. Afterward, Cukor dismissed the company, letting it be known that if Marilyn failed to report the next day, he had nothing left to film. A call was issued for Tuesday. If she didn't show up then, the studio had two options: hire a replacement or shut down the picture. Kim Novak, Shirley MacLaine, Doris Day, and Lee Remick were among the actresses being discussed. Late on Monday afternoon, Phil Feldman, the executive vice-president for studio operations, conferred with Mickey Rudin, who described her as exhausted. His efforts to persuade her to work had been fruitless.

Rudin was unable to do anything with her in the morning either. In a fit of paranoia, she accused her own lawyer of being "with them." At Marilyn's request, Rudin summoned Dr. Greenson. He promised to return by Wednesday evening, leaving Hildi with her family for ten days.

While Marilyn waited for the doctor, her publicist Pat Newcomb cared for her in her room, spending the night at the foot of her bed. Eunice Murray provided meals. Meanwhile, Rudin agonized about whether to send a strong letter advising Marilyn of the possible consequences of her actions. He believed that professionally he probably should do it. At the same time, deeply concerned about her as he was, he hesitated to do anything to upset her further.

Cukor evidently felt no such compassion. He didn't want to be blamed for the trouble on the film. He was convinced that even if he managed to finish *Something's Got to Give*, it wouldn't be much good. After the trauma of *Gone with the Wind*, he certainly didn't want to be fired. His fears were not entirely baseless; Nunnally Johnson later urged Cukor's dismissal as an alternative to replacing Marilyn. Still, in light of the fact that Marilyn was obviously very ill, it's hard to excuse Cukor's decision to leak a story about her to Hedda Hopper on Wednesday, June 6. Indeed, he must have sensed how bad it would look. Before Cukor vented his spleen, he was careful to stipulate, "Please, Hedda, this is not from me."

Cukor disclosed that Twentieth was looking for another actress. He said Marilyn should have been replaced weeks ago; she was over the hill. As though intent on feeding her paranoia, he revealed that she had accused her own attorney of being against her. He alluded to her mental problems. He chronicled her behavior on the set and criticized her acting. She couldn't remember lines; she behaved as though under water; her work was just no good. He suggested it was the end of her career.

That night, Dr. Greenson flew in. He drove directly to Marilyn's home. She was "comatose." But at least she was alive. On Thursday morning, Greenson, speaking through Rudin's law partner Martin Gang, informed Twentieth that Marilyn would be back on Monday. By the afternoon, the psychiatrist had seen reports that Kim Novak had been offered Marilyn's role. Greenson reiterated, "I am convinced that she can finish this picture in the normal course."

It was estimated that Twentieth lost $9,000 each day Marilyn failed to work. Phil Feldman wanted a guarantee that she would be at the studio regularly from Monday on. If necessary, was Greenson willing to lead her there himself? It seemed he was. On Friday, Greenson had lunch with Phil Feldman in Fox's executive conference room. Mickey Rudin and Frank Ferguson also attended. Peter Levathes was absent; the production chief had gone to Rome for a few days to see what could be done about the *Cleopatra* mess. Clearly, the studio's concerns about *Cleopatra* had a significant bearing on Marilyn.

Greenson pointed out that he had "pulled" Marilyn through *The Misfits*. After a week in the hospital, she'd been able to finish the Huston film. He insisted he could do the same now. Greenson, though he did not wish to be compared to Svengali, claimed to be able to persuade Marilyn to do "anything reasonable." And he was prepared to do far more than get her to the studio. With characteristic chutzpah, he offered to assume responsibility for artistic decisions as well. In disputes over, say, which scenes Marilyn would do, her psychoanalyst was ready to step in. On this matter, Rudin appeared to try to slow his brother-in-law down.

Phil Feldman posed an intriguing question. Greenson seemed to be the only person capable of influencing Marilyn. What would happen to her if he were called away? What would happen to the production? Greenson, for his part, had no satisfactory answer.

That afternoon, Phil Feldman notified Marilyn's lawyer that Twentieth was not interested in further talks. Greenson had failed to convince the studio that Marilyn was capable of completing the picture. In short, she'd been fired. Spyros Skouras wasn't around to bail her out. The rumors of his failing health had proven correct, and Skouras had entered St. Luke's Hospital for prostate surgery on May 19. George Cukor called Marilyn's dismissal a shot heard round the world. He rejoiced that Twentieth had finally thrown her out "on her keester."

Peter Levathes's press release stated matters somewhat more delicately: "Marilyn Monroe has been removed from the cast of *Something's Got to Give*. This action was made necessary because of Miss Monroe's repeated willful breaches of her contract. No justification was given by Miss Monroe for her failure to report for photography on many occasions. The studio has suffered losses through these absences and the Twentieth Century–Fox Film Company will take legal action against Miss Monroe." Twentieth sued Marilyn for $750,000.

Marilyn had been absent from most of the footage Cukor managed to shoot, but Dean Martin appeared extensively. So it came as quite a blow when he threatened to quit. "I have the greatest respect for Miss Lee Remick and her talent and all the other actresses who were considered for the role," he declared, "but I signed to do the picture with Marilyn Monroe and I will do it with no one else." He insisted he had the right chemistry with Marilyn. He pointed out that she meant more at the box office than Lee Remick, who had replaced her. He reminded studio executives that in the picture he left Cyd Charisse for Marilyn; who would believe he'd leave for Lee Remick?

An emergency Saturday morning meeting at Twentieth with Peter Levathes, Phil Feldman, George Cukor, and others failed to persuade Dean Martin to continue. As far as Martin was concerned, if the studio refused to rehire Marilyn, he was through. He sent an assistant to collect his wardrobe. Twentieth sued Martin, and he in turn sued the studio. Mickey Rudin, apprised of the situation, quipped that maybe the studio ought to hire President Kennedy as the leading man.

On the evening of Monday, June 11, Twentieth, having already poured more than $2 million into *Something's Got to Give*, suspended production. Cukor diverted himself with talk of doing a film based on all that had happened backstage: Marilyn, manipulative and outrageously demanding, would be a character. So would the pretentious Paula. So would various inept studio executives who repeatedly give in to the troublesome star. Cukor insisted it would be the definitive Hollywood tale, a tragicomedy with a most dramatic denouement. The one thing Marilyn Monroe has always feared finally occurs; she really does goes mad.

After the events of recent days, Marilyn's camp was eager to counter the rumors that she had had a major breakdown. In order to save her career, she had to show her face in public right away. She needed exposure in national magazines. She had to prove she was viable. Posing for photographs to be published in *Vogue*, *Life*, and *Cosmopolitan* also just might convince Twentieth to rehire her. She didn't want to do the picture, but she didn't want to be sued either. Once again Marilyn used the power of publicity to influence her studio. In the past, she'd wanted Darryl Zanuck to give her better parts. Now all she asked was for Twentieth to take her back.

As it happened, the first salvo was a *Life* cover story featuring one of the nudes taken on the set. It was billed, tantalizingly, as an image from the skinny-dip scene readers would never see. Yet at least one reader failed to be convinced by Marilyn's latest impersonation of the happy girl. A decade ago, when Arthur Miller had gone back to his first wife, Marilyn liked to imagine that he would wander into a movie theater in New York and see one of her films by chance. Now, he was buying a paper at a Manhattan newsstand when he spotted the June 22, 1962, issue of *Life*.

Turbulent emotions welled up as he saw the nude within. The image saddened him. He couldn't help thinking Marilyn should not be doing this anymore. He couldn't help sensing the supposedly carefree look on her face was forced. For the playwright, all drama sprang from what he once called the "wound of indignity." This photograph suggested Marilyn's struggle was over. It suggested to Miller that she had "given up trying to cease being the immemorial prey."

At night, Japanese stone lanterns illuminated the garden of the Bel Air Hotel. In a secluded pink bungalow—Number 96, the hotel's best—empty film cartons, discarded liquor bottles, and Marilyn's shoes littered the bedroom floor. Strobe lights flashed, an Everly Brothers record playing in the background.

It was past midnight. Marilyn, in bed, had been posing for hours, her Dom Perignon spiked with one-hundred-proof vodka. She removed a frilly black chiffon bed jacket. Beneath the white sheet, she was naked. As she retrieved a champagne glass from the floor, the sheet dropped off. She seemed to find that very funny. Bert Stern, on assignment for *Vogue*, photographed her rolling about drunkenly. For Stern, it was a dream come true. From the age of thirteen, he had fantasized about encountering a woman like this who would do anything he desired. Tonight, Marilyn seemed to be that woman.

Finally, she lay still. Under the sheet again, she was utterly passive and vulnerable. Stern's thoughts raced. He and she were locked in, while a *Vogue* editor, a hairdresser, and others waited in an adjoining room. He contemplated taking off his own clothes and climbing into bed with her. He perched on the mattress. Marilyn's eyes were shut. The sound of breathing reassured him she was alive.

He kissed her.

"No," said Marilyn from the depths of her trance.

Stern slid his hand under the sheet. He touched her. She did not resist. Indeed, he thought she actually moved closer. Stern told himself Marilyn wanted to make love. He told himself she was ready. But at the last minute he removed his hand, deciding to go no further.

Her eyes opened partly. "Where have you been so long?" she asked dreamily, before falling asleep.

+   +   +

On June 27, half a dozen journalists waited at Fox headquarters on West 56th Street in New York. Rumor had it that the man they called "Hollywood's last king" was being dethroned. Spyros Skouras, still recovering from prostate surgery, had returned to work on Monday. Colleagues noted that the fight seemed to have gone out of him. This morning, he faced the eleven-man board. Peter Levathes and Charlie Einfeld, vice-president in charge of advertising and publicity, were also present. Skouras answered for the studio's financial crisis, for operating losses of nearly $35 million in the past twenty-four months, and for the excesses of stars like Elizabeth Taylor and Marilyn Monroe. He answered for *Cleopatra*, the most expensive picture ever made. He answered for the cancellation of *Something's Got to Give* at a cost of some $2 million. He answered for his own penchant for lavish foreign travel and other perks. In sum, he answered for his reputation as "the last of the big-time spendthrifts."

By midday, the press contingent had doubled. Sandwiches and sodas were delivered from the Stage Delicatessen. By late afternoon, it seemed as though every reporter in town was there. The tumultuous meeting lasted past 7 p.m. During a break, Charlie Einfeld emerged and nervously announced that Skouras had stepped down after twenty years as president. One reporter demanded to know the exact vote. Which board members had been for Skouras, which against?

"There was no vote," publicist Jack Brodsky interjected. "How could there be a vote? The man just resigned."

Skouras, to save face, claimed to have retired for health reasons. In fact, he had been forced out, several board members having vowed to quit if he stayed. His resignation became effective on September 30, or earlier if a new president could be found immediately. Skouras, who remained on the board, was put on the search committee. Peter Levathes was a leading candidate. So were former United Artists vice-president Max Youngstein, CBS television president James Aubrey, and director Otto Preminger. Skouras was thought to favor Youngstein. The Wall Street faction liked Aubrey and Levathes.

The next day, Darryl Zanuck threw the process into chaos. "The board of directors is primarily composed of very successful and important industrialists," said Zanuck from Paris, where he was completing *The Longest Day* for Twentieth. "Unfortunately the majority of them, while eminently successful in their own fields, have no working knowledge of or experience in the motion picture industry. Their financial interest is negligible. I have a larger financial interest in Fox than the combined membership of the board of directors. I have been inaudible for too long. Now, as the largest individual stockholder, I intend to make my position clear on all major matters."

Hours after Zanuck spoke out, a contingent of Fox executives descended on Marilyn's home. The June 22 issue of *Life*—particularly the nude photograph that had so disturbed Arthur Miller—had generated immense public curiosity. By this time, it was in both Marilyn's interest and the studio's to finish *Something's Got to Give*. But first, Twentieth needed to see if she was in any shape, physically and mentally, to work. Three weeks previously, Phil Feldman had certainly had his doubts. Today, Marilyn, coiffed and made up as though for a film role, was intent on putting all such fears to rest.

Twentieth also needed to see if Marilyn would agree to its "conditions." At a moment when film studios were being ridiculed in the press for ceding power to stars, no one wanted to be accused of giving in to Marilyn Monroe. Twentieth's list was a long one. Among the most significant items: Marilyn was asked to give up all say on the choice of director, cameraman, and co-stars. She was forbidden to consult on the script. She was forbidden to request additional takes or to attend the dailies. She was forbidden to bring her dramatic coach or other helpers onto the set without the studio head's permission.

Twentieth hoped to erase every major concession Marilyn had fought for in her December 31, 1955 contract. The studio claimed back everything she had won—and more. In one fell swoop, all the work of Charlie Feldman, Milton Greene, and, above all, Marilyn herself was undone. Instead of allowing Marilyn to feel that she had a degree of control, Twentieth asked her to accept no control at all. And as if that were not enough, before she came back she would be required to make a strong public apology. Eight months after being urged to treat Marilyn with dignity, Twentieth sought to strip her of the shreds of dignity she still had.

Marilyn's talks with the studio occurred in an atmosphere of deep uncertainty. The men vying to lead Fox seemed bent on destroying one another. Executives in charge one week might be out of a job the next.

The present administration did its best to show it was in control. "Fox pictures will be made under a new set of rules," Peter Levathes announced. "The old method has failed. We are determined to break the hold that has produced failure." Nonetheless, each day brought fresh rumors about Zanuck. The former production chief dismissed his rival Levathes as "devoid of any production experience." He arrived in New York to place his bid for the presidency. He let it be known he was gearing up for a proxy fight.

In the middle of all this, Marilyn had a call from Milton Greene. Their partnership had ended badly, but Marilyn was thrilled to hear from him. She and Greene talked for some ninety minutes. They shared a sense of disappointment. Marilyn, a wonderful light comedienne, longed to do serious roles. Greene, a gifted photographer, dreamed of being a film producer. Neither seemed to value what he or she could actually do so well. Perhaps, as Biff Loman says of his father Willy at the end of *Death of a Salesman*, they had "the wrong dreams." Marilyn reviewed her circumstances. She said it was as though the past ten years had never happened. She said she was right back to where she didn't want to be.

On July 12, Marilyn returned to Twentieth. Fifteen out of its sixteen sound stages were dark. Twentieth, eerily deserted, resembled a ghost town. A single picture, *A Woman in July*, was in production.

The classic studio era had come to an end. Time had passed Twentieth by. While in recent years other major companies had concentrated on the distribution of independently produced films, Twentieth had struggled to go on producing most of its own pictures. Competitors called Skouras a dinosaur from the pre-television period. In a sign of the times, the day before Marilyn came in, Levathes had announced plans to modernize by renting space to independent film and television producers.

But the current administration did very much want to resume *Something's Got to Give*. George Cukor was off the film, having agreed in the interim to direct Audrey Hepburn in *My Fair Lady* for Warner Bros. It was a break for Cukor, whose career had been waning. He certainly had no complaint about missing a chance to be reunited with Marilyn.

The studio brought in Jean Negulesco to direct a mildly revised version of Nunnally Johnson's script. On the face of it, she seemed to have won. But that was hardly the case in view of the numerous conditions she was required to accept. Once Twentieth had her signature, it could change its mind about Negulesco. It could substitute a different screenplay. It could do almost anything and Marilyn would be powerless to object. As she told Milton Greene, Marilyn Monroe Productions might never have existed.

Twentieth persisted in demanding an apology. Marilyn knew that if she didn't do the picture, she would be sued. So she agreed to go in sackcloth and ashes. One might have thought the studio, eager not to lose a $2 million investment, would leave matters at that. But this wasn't strictly about money. It was about looking tough. It was about machismo and menace. It was about bringing a recalcitrant star to her knees.

Jack Brodsky, in the New York office, was asked "very confidentially" to draft Marilyn's apology. Even if the words weren't her own, at least they'd be the right words. The publicist crafted a mild document that permitted Marilyn to save face. The studio, displeased, removed Brodsky from the assignment. Clearly, the intent was to humiliate her. A leak was given to *Time* magazine: "No public apology, no Marilyn."

Meanwhile, something unexpected happened. Skouras threw his chips in with Zanuck. And those chips were valuable indeed, Skouras holding some 98,000 shares of Fox stock. Suddenly, the presidency seemed very much within reach for Zanuck, who had approximately 110,000 shares of his own. It was a curious alliance, there being no love lost between the men once known as New York and the Coast. More than anything, the Old Greek wanted to frustrate the board members who had toppled him.

And so he did. After Zanuck became president on the 25th, two prominent enemies of Skouras resigned. Skouras was appointed board chairman. "I believe the president of a motion picture company today should be its production head as well as its administrative head," Zanuck said. His election put everything at Fox on hold—including Marilyn Monroe's talks with the previous administration. Zanuck evicted Skouras. Out went the slab-like marble desk, the beige club chairs, and the gallery of family photographs. Skouras's office became the new boardroom. A broken man, he moved to humbler quarters near the elevators.

Many people believed it was Zanuck who had once made

Twentieth great. Some studio veterans predicted (erroneously) that he would usher in "a new Golden Age." For Marilyn, he had no such happy associations. He had never liked her. He'd always treated her disrespectfully. He'd once threatened to destroy her. Zanuck, complaining about the power of stars and their agents, had left in 1956 as Marilyn was about to start *Bus Stop*, new contract in hand. Now that she seemed to have lost everything, Zanuck was back. The timing may have been coincidental, but it was ominous all the same.

The day Zanuck became president, Marilyn had two sessions with Dr. Greenson, one in his office, the other at her home. Dr. Engelberg sedated her by injection. Greenson, hoping to wean Marilyn off drugs, had appointed the Beverly Hills internist to supervise her medication. In the light of her history of suicide attempts, the doctors had an arrangement. If in addition to an injection Engelberg prescribed Nembutal, he would inform Greenson. Since the analyst had returned from Europe, he'd seen Marilyn almost daily. She was constantly on the phone to him. It was not unusual for her to call in the middle of the night, often at 2, 3, and 4 a.m.

Marilyn also phoned Bobby Kennedy a good deal in this period. Unlike the President, he almost always took her calls. For Marilyn, it was a way of maintaining a Kennedy connection despite the President's decision to cut her off. Besides, the Attorney General had a reputation for being "a good shoulder to cry on." Marilyn wasn't the only Hollywood actress to reach out to him. Judy Garland often phoned, Edwin Guthman recalled, "just to have someone to talk to." When Bobby was unavailable, Marilyn chatted with his secretary, Angie Novello. On several occasions she talked to his wife, Ethel. At the time of her firing, Marilyn had declined an invitation to a party for the Lawfords at Hickory Hill, Bobby and Ethel's estate near McLean, Virginia. Since then, Bobby had seen Marilyn at a dinner party at the Lawfords' on June 26. At her request, he had stopped by to inspect her new home the following day. He knew firsthand that she was on edge.

Marilyn was often enraged at others, and at herself. She knew what she wanted. But she also knew she had done much to sabotage her own dreams. In a telling gesture, when the nudes she had drunkenly posed for at the Bel Air Hotel were sent for her approval, she slashed the color transparencies with a hairpin.

Despite evidence to the contrary, Greenson insisted that Marilyn was much better. This may have been his way of dealing with the guilt of knowing that his absence had led to her dismissal. It may also have been a way of reassuring himself that she would eventually improve, freeing him from being on call seven days a week, twenty-four hours a day, indefinitely. He saw himself as the prisoner of a method of treatment that, however necessary for Marilyn, had proven nearly impossible for him. Marilyn, sensing his need to see improvement, may sometimes have pretended to be getting better. She was an actress, after all. She knew how to play a happy girl, even with her doctor. The important thing was not to be left.

There was a very real threat that might happen again soon. Greenson planned to go away as early as next month. When he interrupted his vacation, he had canceled a stop in New York to see his publisher. Now, he intended to go east sometime in August, September or October. Work on *The Technique and Practice of Psychoanalysis* proceeded slowly, as so much of his time and emotion was devoted to Marilyn. Greenson wanted to coordinate his travel plans with Anna Freud. His mentor was about to come to the United States, and he hoped to be invited to join her at the Menninger Clinic in Topeka.

As August began, the central drama of Marilyn's life was being played out with her analyst. Her other saviors had abdicated in one way or another. Though he wanted to direct her in *Macbeth* at the new Actors Studio Theater, Lee Strasberg, Marilyn believed, had ceased to pay enough attention to her. Miller, of course, had a new wife and was soon to be a father. Joe DiMaggio was away on business. So Greenson was all Marilyn had left. On Saturday, August 4, he had a call from her at approximately 4:30 in the afternoon. Dr. and Mrs. Greenson were going out that night. Still, Marilyn sounded depressed, so he agreed to visit her at home.

There was something he did not know. One day previously, on August 3, when Engelberg came to sedate her, she lied that Greenson had approved her being given some Nembutal. Assuming he was acting on instructions from Greenson, Engelberg neglected to tell his colleague about the prescription he gave Marilyn for twenty-five capsules. Marilyn had it filled immediately. On Saturday, when Greenson arrived, she had enough drugs in the house to take her own life.

The rooms at Fifth Helena remained bare; the pieces Marilyn ordered in Mexico had never been delivered. A *Cosmopolitan* photographer who'd recently worked with her had preferred not to shoot in her home because, with so little furniture, the place had a depressing air. Marilyn had spent much of Saturday in bed. Lately, she had been reading the book *Captain Newman, M.D.*, a thinly fictionalized account of Ralph Greenson's World War II experiences. The rickety wooden night table overflowed with plastic pill bottles, though the Nembutals were nowhere in sight. Shopping bags and dirty clothes littered the floor.

Greenson conferred with Marilyn in her room, while Eunice Murray and Pat Newcomb waited in the living room. Marilyn struck him as despondent and disoriented. Once, perhaps twice, the doctor, absorbed in thought, wandered out into the hall. Greenson was quite tense himself, for reasons having nothing to do with Marilyn. He was trying to give up smoking.

It was certainly a bad sign that Marilyn had failed to take Isadore Miller's call on Saturday morning. She was invited to dinner at Peter Lawford's that evening, but she was in no shape to go. The previous day she'd asked her publicist, who had bronchitis, to stay in the spare room. But the fact that her guest slept soundly until noon seemed to enrage Marilyn, who had lain awake all night. As was frequently the case, Marilyn's anger was irrational. Still, in the interest of peace, Greenson asked Newcomb to leave. He arranged for the housekeeper to stay instead.

After Greenson had been there for about two and a half hours, Marilyn did seem calmer. Inevitably, the moment approached when he would have to go home and change for his dinner party. He left at seven, telling Marilyn to call when she got up in the morning. Greenson, mindful of her fears of abandonment, reassured her that he'd be available again in a few hours.

Marilyn couldn't wait that long. She appeared to focus all of her anxiety about his impending trip east on the prospect of his being out of reach this evening. She seized the first opportunity to connect with him again. Hardly had Greenson arrived home when the phone rang. It was approximately 7:40 and he was shaving. Marilyn excitedly announced that Joe DiMaggio's son had just called. Joe, Jr., serving in the Marine Corps, was stationed in San Diego. She assumed Greenson would want to know he'd broken off his engagement.

"Isn't that great?" asked Marilyn, who believed that Joe, Jr., at twenty-one, was too young to settle down. Her high spirits contrasted with the bleak mood Greenson had observed less than an hour ago. She would have known a tearful call would irritate him after he'd just spent a good deal of time with her. The news about Joe, Jr. offered a pretext to talk happily, as though that were what this desperate call were really about. Marilyn did, however, provide one important clue to what was on her mind, though Greenson failed to notice at the time.

"Did you take away my bottle of Nembutal?" Marilyn asked. The question signaled two things. She was informing him that she had a supply of the dangerous barbiturate, and she was warning that she intended to use it. Greenson, unaware of the prescription, assumed she must be mistaken. As far as he knew, Marilyn couldn't possibly have any Nembutals in the house.

By the time Marilyn's phone rang about twenty minutes later, she may already have begun to swallow the yellow capsules. When she was finished, the Nembutal bottle would be empty. And only ten green chloral hydrate capsules would remain in a container that held fifty.

Why did Marilyn take an overdose? A. Alvarez has compared the triggering event in certain suicides to "a trivial border incident which triggers off a major war." The event may seem insignificant to us, but not to the person in pain. One can never know exactly why someone takes her own life. In Marilyn's case, the triggering event, the specific incident that pushed her over the edge, seems to have been nothing more than her doctor's having gone to a dinner party with his wife. Earlier, Marilyn had been frantic at the prospect. By now, it would have become a life-and-death matter, his absence on a par with all the abandonments she had suffered, beginning with her father. Perhaps she thought she would punish Greenson for having left her tonight. Perhaps she thought she could force him to return. Perhaps she thought that, as others had done, he'd rescue her before it was too late.

Marilyn picked up the phone. It was Peter Lawford calling about dinner.

"Hey, Charlie," he asked, "what's happened to you?"

The party was already under way. Lawford's pals chattered in the background. Marilyn, in a dozy voice, said she couldn't come. He'd heard her like this before. Her thick, halting speech meant she was drunk or drugged, perhaps both. No matter; she'd be perfectly welcome like that. He shouted into the receiver, hoping to revive her.

Then she said something that brought him up short. Lawford had a hard time hearing over the din at the beach house, but he was sure Marilyn said, "Say goodbye to Pat. Say goodbye to Jack. And say goodbye to yourself because you're a nice guy." Silence followed. Had she fallen asleep? Had the receiver slipped out of her hand to the white rug? Had she hung up? Had the phone gone dead? Lawford called back repeatedly. Confronted with a busy signal, he couldn't stop thinking about the fact that Marilyn had just said goodbye.

He wanted to go to her, but his manager, Milt Ebbins, insisted it would be better to contact her lawyer or her doctor. Ebbins was unable to reach Greenson, but he did track down Mickey Rudin at a cocktail party. It was about 9:30 when the lawyer called to check on Marilyn. Eunice Murray, spending the night in the dressing room, answered the second phone. She reported that Marilyn was resting in her room. She insisted everything was fine. As far as she knew, it was. In fact, Marilyn was probably already dead or dying.

Murray awakened at 3 a.m., surrounded by full-length mirrors. Like Natasha Lytess twelve years previously, she sensed something wrong. She flicked on a light and put on a robe. What she saw in the hall distressed her. A phone cord ran under Marilyn's locked door. Ordinarily, the phone would have been "put to bed" under a stack of pillows in the guest room.

Moments later a phone rang at the Greenson home. The doctor wouldn't have been surprised to hear Marilyn's slurred voice. Instead, he heard the frightened housekeeper. She followed instructions to knock on the door and shout Marilyn's name. There was no response. She rushed outside. The night air was cool and damp. Marilyn's lamp was on, but heavy curtains blocked the view. Murray, reaching through an iron grille, pushed them aside. Marilyn, naked, lay sprawled face-down on the bed, one hand resting on the telephone receiver.

Greenson arrived at 3:40. He smashed a pane of glass with a fireplace poker and reached in, undoing the latch. Dr. Engelberg, who came ten minutes later, pronounced Marilyn dead.

Marilyn had finally given in to her mother's judgment. On the night of August 4, she finished what she believed Gladys had set out to do when she tried to kill her baby daughter.

Marilyn's life had been one of rare achievement. On her own, against almost impossible personal and professional odds, she had created something brilliant and magical—"Marilyn Monroe." Her creation had brought immense pleasure to millions of people, and would continue to do so long after she was gone. The world loved Marilyn. Yet in the end she felt utterly unloved and alone. For thirty-six years, Marilyn, with her immense life force, had fought against an equally strong pull towards death. Tonight, death triumphed, and her struggle was over.

The doctors conferred. Greenson, to his horror, learned about the twenty-five Nembutals. As often happens after a suicide, the "what ifs" and the "if onlys" hovered in the air. If Greenson had known about the barbiturates, almost certainly he would have been alert to Marilyn's cry for help. Her death might have been prevented. At 4:25 a.m., Greenson, devastated, called the West Los Angeles police station.

Now that Marilyn was gone, Greenson would confide to Anna Freud that he realized all his knowledge, desire, and strength had been insufficient. Marilyn's death was a blow to his pride, he admitted. And it was a blow to his science. But most of all, it was a blow to him personally, for he had cared about her very much. Anna Freud wrote back that she knew exactly what he was going through. She had once returned from a trip abroad to discover that a patient of hers had committed suicide two days previously. She explained to Dr. Greenson that one goes over and over in one's thoughts how one might have done better, the process inevitably leaving the survivor with a terrible sense of defeat. "But, you know," Anna Freud continued, "I think in these cases we are really defeated by something which is stronger than we are and for which analysis, with all its powers, is too weak a weapon."

Greenson knew it would take him a long time to get over Marilyn's death. It hurt even to think about it, yet he sensed it was only by remembering that someday he would be able to forget. He longed to spend a few days talking himself out with his own analyst, Max Schur, in New York. (Schur had been Sigmund Freud's personal physician.) But there was no time for that now. Greenson was interviewed at length by the police, by the district attorney's office, and by a panel of twelve psychological experts dubbed the "suicide squad." The latter had been appointed by Dr. Thomas J. Curphey, the chief medical examiner and coroner for Los Angeles County, to determine whether Marilyn had been capable of taking her own life.

When someone commits suicide, friends, family members, and other associates often question whether the person could possibly have done such a thing. So it was quite normal when Marilyn's housekeeper, makeup man, hair stylist, and others in her entourage suspected that she had died by accident (having lost track of how many pills she'd taken) or even by foul play. The haunting image of her hand on the telephone receiver led several people to believe that Marilyn's final act had been to try to call them. A natural death is hard enough to deal with; the idea that someone close died intentionally may be almost impossible to bear. Denial frees the survivors from endlessly examining whether there were any indications that a suicide was going to occur. And of course, it frees them from a certain amount of guilt.

In fact, everything pointed to the conclusion that Marilyn had killed herself. There had been prior attempts to take her own life. There was a family history of suicide. She had been feeling especially defeated in recent weeks. Though there had been talk of future projects, one had to wonder whether she was capable any longer of doing a film, let alone a play. Marilyn had been despondent the day she died. Toxicological tests showed that a combination of Nembutal and chloral hydrate had proven fatal. The only thing that could never be known was whether, as on previous occasions, she expected to be saved. The one person who might have disclosed that was Marilyn, and she was dead. Still, in light of all the rumors, the coroner ordered a "psychological autopsy." On the basis of the report, Dr. Curphey later ruled the death a "probable suicide."

Meanwhile, there was confusion about who would claim the body. Marilyn's sixty-two-year-old mother was her closest relative, but she was incompetent. At Rockhaven Sanitarium, Gladys appeared to have no reaction to her daughter's death. Initially, Marilyn's half-sister couldn't be reached in Florida. Joe DiMaggio came from San Francisco as soon as he heard about Marilyn. He hadn't seen her in two months, though they had often talked on the phone. He was prepared to make the funeral arrangements, but the coroner couldn't release the body without a family member's permission. Finally, Berniece, contacted by telegram, gave Joe the go-ahead. She flew to Los Angeles early on Monday morning.

On Wednesday, August 8, a small group of invited mourners entered the tiny Westwood Funeral Chapel. An organist played "Over The Rainbow," among other selections. Marilyn, in a green Pucci dress and a platinum wig, lay in a velvet-lined, open bronze casket. George Solotaire and Joe DiMaggio, Jr., in his Marine dress uniform, were present. So were the Strasbergs and the Greensons. (Lee Strasberg and Marianne Kris had been left the bulk of the estate, with the stipulation that the psychiatrist use her inheritance to further her work.) Also in attendance were Marilyn's housekeeper, makeup man, hair stylist, masseur, and driver. There were two of Marilyn's attorneys, her half-sister, her publicist, her former secretary, and a few others—but no movie stars, no studio executives, and no press. Frank Sinatra and the Lawfords had been excluded. Arthur Miller chose not to attend. A tearful Lee Strasberg, voice quivering, delivered the eulogy. But the most poignant moment occurred as the coffin was about to be closed. Joe DiMaggio leaned over to kiss Marilyn.

"I love you, I love you, I love you," Joe wept.

Something extraordinary happened after that. Joe's life with Marilyn had been messy and embarrassing. He frequently lost his temper and did things he was later ashamed of. The dignity he prized had often eluded him. He never seemed to understand why the relationship failed to live up to his ideal. But in his impeccable behavior following Marilyn's death, Joe finally recaptured some of the "deft serenity" he once knew on the baseball field. He was steadfast in never talking about her in public, yet he made it clear precisely how he felt. His silence, once a sign of awkwardness, became a form of grace.

+   +   +

The story that began when Arthur Miller and Elia Kazan arrived in Los Angeles to pitch The Hook came to an end on January 23, 1964. That evening, Miller's long-awaited autobiographical play After the Fall had its premiere in New York. Directed by Kazan, the production marked the first time the two men had collaborated in thirteen years. The origin of the play itself also dated back to that earlier time. Miller had been writing about Marilyn in one way or another since 1951, when he fled Los Angeles having known her for only a few days. The moral crisis Marilyn provoked exploded in his thin brown notebooks. As early as 1952, Miller had discovered his own alter ego in Quentin, a tortured, unfaithful husband, torn between the claims of ecstasy and morality.

For more than a decade, Miller's autobiographical work-in-progress proceeded in fits and starts. He worked at a cluttered desk in Brooklyn as children's voices wafted in from other rooms. He worked in his study on East 57th Street, while Marilyn, at the other end of the apartment, strummed a ukelele and sang "I Wanna Be Loved By You." He worked in a spartan one-room studio in Roxbury. But in all those years, Miller failed to bring his play to completion. Marilyn's death changed all that. Miller seemed suddenly to know why he was writing and where the play must go.

On October 25, 1962, two months after Marilyn committed suicide, the Lincoln Center Repertory Theater announced that Miller's new drama would be its inaugural production. From the first, there was a distinct air of scandal about the project. The news that Miller had agreed to work with Kazan, perhaps the most notorious of the informers, came as a shock to many people. The nightmare of McCarthyism was not yet so far in the past that people were willing to forget what Kazan had done. Too many careers had been wrecked, too many lives destroyed. In his decision to revive the collaboration, Miller seemed to confer a certain amount of his own moral authority on Kazan. It was said in Miller's own family that were Mary still his wife, she would never have permitted him to reunite with Kazan. A number of Miller's friends were baffled by his motives. Norman Rosten blamed ambition. In Rosten's view, Miller, unsuccessful in recent years, was "looking for a replay of his past triumphs" with Kazan. Indeed, there could be no denying that Miller's once brilliant career had faltered badly since he lost Kazan. In a sense, the production of *After the Fall* took both men back to 1951 as they set out to match the glory they had achieved together with *Death of a Salesman*.

It also took them back to the moment when the sexual triangle that had played such a vital role in Miller's imagination began. When Miller and Kazan first encountered Marilyn, she had recently attempted suicide. In awe of Kazan, Marilyn dreamed that the great director might give her a role. At that point, it would have been inconceivable that the author of *Death of a Salesman* would even consider writing for her. More than a decade later, Marilyn had succeeded in killing herself, and the former husband and the former lover seized the opportunity to reignite their partnership with a play devoted, in large part, to the star's sensational life and death. The package seemed to have all the ingredients of the triumph that had long eluded Miller. In speaking of his intimate life with Marilyn, the playwright would tell a story the public very much wanted to hear. And, of course, Miller had Kazan back. This time, no critic would lament the director's absence as Eric Bentley had done in his review of The Crucible. It was all rather like Kazan's fantasy of two men, recently enemies, happily going off together at the end of Baby Doll.

Questions of propriety aside, Miller did have the material for a fascinating and disturbing play. He might have probed a man's feelings of guilt, shame, anger, and defeat when a woman he once loved takes her own life. Miller had written about suicide with immense sensitivity in Death of a Salesman. Unfortunately, he did something entirely different in After the Fall. Instead of the sympathetic treatment he had given Willy Loman, he depicted Marilyn as a shrill, devouring harpy. He used her propensity for self-destruction to justify his own decision to leave her when she was obviously very ill. In the end, Marilyn's suicide had made it possible for Miller to finish his play. Importantly, it allowed him to sustain his self-image as a man of conscience. It provided the absolution he had been seeking. "A suicide kills two people," Quentin tells Maggie, the character based unmistakably on Marilyn, "that's what it's for! So I am removing myself, and perhaps it will lose its point." As in The Crucible, a man's act of betrayal is shown to be the woman's own fault; she drove him away. But in After the Fall, Miller goes further. He asks us to believe, and seems actually to have convinced himself, that he walked out for her own good.

There was every reason to expect that After the Fall was only the start of great things for both Miller and Kazan. Following the premiere, however, it quickly became apparent that matters would not work out that way at all. Miller's unctuous exercise in self-justification met not with praise but with disgust. The play generated a huge controversy in the press and Miller, to his bewilderment, found himself reviled by critics for his unremittingly harsh portrait of Marilyn. Ironically, in exposing Marilyn as he did, Miller, who had refused to name names, became something of an "informer" himself. He surrendered the moral authority that had sustained him through a decade of artistic disappointment. Even his friends were appalled by the play. Joe Rauh declared that he didn't see how a man could write about his wives that way. Norman and Hedda Rosten were furious that he had depicted Marilyn as nothing more than a "slut." Didn't he remember how brave Marilyn had been during the HUAC crisis? Couldn't he at least give her credit for having been ready to sacrifice everything for him? Why had he left out the powerful ideals that had been among Marilyn's defining characteristics?

Hedda Rosten viewed *After the Fall* as "a betrayal of Marilyn." She was speaking of Marilyn as an individual. But the play was also an attack on all that Marilyn symbolized as a star. In *After the Fall*, Miller reverted to the puritanical view of sex he had propagated in *The Crucible*. "It isn't my love you want any more," Quentin tells Maggie. "It's my destruction!" In 1951, Miller had guessed that Marilyn Monroe posed a threat to his existence; in 1964, he knew. Once again—but this time publicly, ritualistically, and forever—Miller fled Marilyn's embrace. Significantly, this time Miller staged his bleak cautionary tale in modern dress. This time, his preacherly warning about the perils of sex was set not in the Puritan age but in our own.

In a curious way, it is precisely American society's Puritan roots that account for Marilyn's enduring appeal. Despite the upheaval of the 1960s, despite the sexual revolution, feminism, and other developments, America remains at heart a puritanical culture, threatened by the power of sex and quick to point an accusing finger at anyone who may have transgressed. In the middle of all that, the vivid image of Marilyn Monroe sends out a contrary message; its power is in proportion to the depth of our own fears. As a symbol, she promises us that sex can be innocent, without danger. That, indeed, may not be the truth, but it continues to be what we wish. And that is why Marilyn remains, even now, the symbol of our secret desires.

Notes on Sources

I have tried wherever possible to base my reconstruction of events on primary sources. Where there are disparities between this biography and previously published accounts, I have followed the information given in the primary sources. In my effort to tell Marilyn Monroe's story, a number of archives were particularly helpful.

The vast Twentieth Century–Fox collection at UCLA is essential to any attempt to trace Marilyn Monroe's life. She spent the greater part of her career at Twentieth, and her legal files are crammed not just with contracts and notices, but huge numbers of detailed letters and memos documenting every aspect of her turbulent existence there. There are production files for all of her Fox films, as well as daily production reports. The drama of Marilyn's perpetual conflicts with Darryl Zanuck and other studio executives explodes in these utterly fascinating pages. As one of Marilyn's lawyers recognized late in her career, her problem with Twentieth was psychological. Her principal concern was never money or what approvals she had in her contract; it was whether the studio was treating her seriously and respectfully. For the biographer, one of the great virtues of the Fox collection is the opportunity it affords to eavesdrop on the studio executives' private discussions, and to comprehend something of their attitude toward Marilyn. In allowing us to know quite what Marilyn was up against, the papers make it possible to see why she felt and acted as she did.

The Charles K. Feldman collection at the American Film Institute offers a unique and remarkably vivid glimpse of a vanished world. Many of the major players in this story crossed Feldman's radar screen, and their comings and goings are all copiously recorded in his social and business files. To scrutinize Feldman's day book for 1951 is to learn exactly when Arthur Miller and Elia Kazan arrived at 2000 Coldwater Canyon Drive, how long they were there, and who was invited to lunch and dinner during their stay. Even the girls Feldman invited to the party for Miller are listed, including one described simply as Kazan's girl, because, in that milieu, no other description was necessary. By the time Marilyn Monroe was deemed worthy of a name, Feldman's papers document Famous Artists, Inc.'s extensive contacts with her. At the agency, any staff member who had even the most minor interaction with a client or would-be client was expected to keep a record of all that occurred. In Marilyn's case, because there was so much frenzied back-and-forth, those voluminous records offer an extraordinary chronicle of several of the most vital years in her professional life. The collection also illuminates Marilyn's personal life, disclosing as it does Joe DiMaggio's hitherto unknown, off-stage role in her great battle with Twentieth Century–Fox.

The Feldman papers note the date of Miller's departure from Hollywood after his cataclysmic first encounter with Marilyn Monroe. The Arthur Miller collection at the University of Texas at Austin shows what he did when he returned to his wife and family in Brooklyn. For the Monroe biographer, the great prize in the Miller papers are the slender, brown notebooks, in which the playwright-as-alchemist attempts to transmute private experience into art. Here are the notes for a contemporary adultery play, written out of Miller's ethical crisis over Marilyn. Here is the moment when that play metamorphoses into *The Crucible*. And here are the jottings that, after Marilyn's suicide, will finally take shape as *After the Fall*. The notebooks—raw, intimate, revelatory—make it possible to begin to understand the man, his work, and his tormented relationship with Marilyn Monroe.

Two other collections are invaluable to anyone trying to chronicle the Monroe–Miller marriage. The Joseph Rauh collection at the Library of Congress in Washington, D.C., in addition to offering tantalizing glimpses of Marilyn and Arthur's day-to-day existence, suggests the considerable extent to which the McCarthy era shadowed Marilyn's life from the time she first met Miller in 1951 until her painful encounters with the Kennedys a decade later. Reading the papers, one senses for the first time how very brave Marilyn was during the HUAC crisis, and how much she risked in publicly supporting the man she loved.

Marilyn's valiant efforts on Miller's behalf were a high point of their relationship. *The Misfits* was another matter entirely. But in order to assess its impact on Marilyn, one must see it as something much more than the isolated film shoot depicted in most biographies. The preparation of the screenplay and the efforts to get the film made dominated the second part of the Monroe–Miller marriage. The correspondence in the John Huston collection at the Academy of Motion Picture Arts and Sciences documents the slow, often painful evolution of a film whose completion would mark the end of the marriage.

The Anna Freud collection at the Library of Congress in Washington, D.C. is an invaluable resource for anyone hoping to make sense of the ineffably sad last period of Marilyn's life. Here one discovers letters written by Ralph Greenson to his cherished friend and mentor, Anna Freud, before, during, and after the time when Marilyn Monroe was his patient. The letters are important not only for Greenson's comments on Marilyn's case, but for the personal details that provide the essential context for understanding his interaction with her, as well as the background for certain of the controversial decisions he made in the course of her treatment. Read in conjunction with Greenson's own papers and tapes on deposit at UCLA, the materials in the Freud collection hold important clues to the events that led to Marilyn's suicide.

CHAPTER ONE

Chapter One is based on letters and memos by Kermit Bloomgarden, Charles Feldman, Frank Ferguson, Jack Gordean, Howard Hawks, Ivan Kahn, Elia Kazan, Joseph P. Kennedy, Ben Lyon, Grace McKee, Hugh Oliver, Joseph Rauh, Joseph Schenck, Lew Schreiber, George Wasson, John Wharton, Tennessee Williams, Audrey Wood, and Darryl Zanuck.

Collections include those of Kermit Bloomgarden (State Historical Society of Wisconsin), Charles Feldman (American Film Institute), William Gordon (Academy of Motion Picture Arts and Sciences), John Huston (Academy of Motion Picture Arts and Sciences), Arthur Miller (University of Texas), Joseph Rauh (Library of Congress), Tennessee Williams (University of Texas), Audrey Wood (University of Texas), and Maurice Zolotow (University of Texas). Oral histories include those of Nunnally Johnson, Raymond Klune, and Albert Maltz.

Miller's notebooks, as well as a script of *The Hook*, are in the Arthur Miller collection at the University of Texas. Miller and Kazan's trip to Hollywood in 1951 is traced in Charles Feldman's day book at the American Film Institute.

Marilyn Monroe's and Elia Kazan's Twentieth Century–Fox legal files are on deposit at UCLA. Also important are the production files and daily production reports for *As Young As You Feel* and *Viva Zapata!*.

A manuscript of Natasha Lytess's unpublished memoir is at the University of Texas.

Previous Monroe biographies consulted include: Peter Harry Brown and Patte Barham, *Marilyn: The Last Take*; Fred Lawrence Guiles, *Legend*; Marilyn Monroe, *My Story*; Randall Riese and Neal Hitchens, *The Unabridged Marilyn: Her Life from A to Z*; Carl Rollyson, *Marilyn Monroe*; Sandra Shevey, *The Marilyn Scandal*; Donald Spoto, *Marilyn Monroe*; Anthony Summers, *Goddess*; and Maurice Zolotow, *Marilyn Monroe*. Also helpful were the following memoirs: David Conover, *Finding Marilyn*; James Dougherty, *The Secret Happiness of Marilyn Monroe*; Berniece Baker Miracle and Mona Rae Miracle, *My Sister Marilyn*.

Elia Kazan tells his own story in *A Life*, and Arthur Miller his in *Timebends*. Other significant background on the men and their milieu is provided in the interview collections Christopher Bigsby, ed., *Arthur Miller and Company*; and Matthew Roudane, ed., *Conversations with Arthur Miller*. Also useful was Robert Martin, ed., *The Theater Essays of Arthur Miller*.

Additional information comes from: Brooks Atkinson, *Broadway*; Garson Kanin, *Hollywood*; Andrew Sinclair, *Spiegel*.

CHAPTER TWO

Chapter Two is based on letters and memos by George S. Ackerman, Kermit Bloomgarden, Harry Brand, Charles Feldman, Jack Gordean, Vernon Harbin, Lillian Hellman, Elia Kazan, R. A. Klune, Jason Joy, David March, A. L. Rockett, Lew Schreiber, Spyros Skouras, Minna Wallis, Jack Warner, George Wasson, Ralph Waycott, Jr., Tennessee Williams, and Audrey Wood.

Collections include those of Charles Feldman,. William Gordon, Arthur Miller, Tennessee Williams, and Audrey Wood.

A transcript of Elia Kazan's HUAC testimony is contained in "Communist Infiltration of Hollywood Motion Picture Industry—Part 7."

Also important are Marilyn Monroe's and Elia Kazan's Twentieth Century–Fox legal files, and the production files for *Love Nest*, *Let's Make It Legal*, and *Don't Bother to Knock*.

A number of books provide revealing glimpses of Joe DiMaggio and his world: Maury Allen, *Where Have You Gone, Joe DiMaggio?*; Jimmy Cannon, *Nobody Asked Me, But . . .*; Bob Considine, *Toots*; Joseph Durso, *DiMaggio: The Last American Knight*; David Halberstam, *Summer of '49*; Roger Kahn, *Joe and Marilyn*; Robin Moore, *Marilyn and Joe DiMaggio*.

Additional information comes from: Margaret Brenman-Gibson, *Clifford Odets: American Playwright*; Mel Gussow, *Don't Say Yes Until I Finish Talking: A Biography of Darryl F.*

Zanuck; Peter Manso, *Brando*; Berniece Baker Miracle and Mona Rae Miracle, *My Sister Marilyn*; Leonard Mosley, *Zanuck*; Victor Navasky, *Naming Names*; Anthony Quinn, *One Man Tango*; Sidney Skolsky, *Don't Get Me Wrong, I Love Hollywood*; Robert Vaughn, *Only Victims: A Study of Show Business Blacklisting*.

CHAPTER THREE

Chapter Three is based on letters and memos by Grace Dobish, Charles Feldman, Frank Ferguson, Hugh French, Jack Gordean, Jed Harris, Vivian Leslie, David March, Ned Marin, and A. L. Rockett.

Collections include those of Charles Feldman and Arthur Miller. Also important are Marilyn Monroe's Twentieth Century–Fox legal files, and the production files for *Niagara*, *Gentlemen Prefer Blondes*, and *Monkey Business*.

Additional information comes from: James Bacon, *Hollywood is a Four Letter Town*; Jane Russell, *Jane Russell: An Autobiography*. Eric Bentley's reviews are collected in *What Is Theater?*

CHAPTER FOUR

Chapter Four is based on letters and memos by Charles Feldman, Frank Ferguson, Hugh French, Jack Gordean, Ned Marin, Marilyn Monroe, Robert Quinn, A. L. Rockett, Lew Schreiber, Harry Sokolov, Ray Stark, Loyd Wright, Loyd Wright, Jr., and Darryl Zanuck.

Collections include those of Charles Feldman, Ralph Greenson (UCLA), and Jean Negulesco (Academy of Motion Picture Arts and Sciences). Also important are Marilyn Monroe's Twentieth Century–Fox legal files, and the production files for *How to Marry a Millionaire* and *River of No Return*.

Additional information comes from: Marlon Brando, *Songs My Mother Taught Me*; Jean Negulesco, *Things I Did and Things I Think I Did*; Otto Preminger, *Preminger: An Autobiography*.

CHAPTER FIVE

Chapter Five is based on letters and memos by Charles Feldman, Frank Ferguson, Hugh French, Jack Gordean, Milton Greene, Hedda Hopper, Lew Schreiber, Sam Shaw, Spyros Skouras, Harry Sokolov, Ray Stark, Loyd Wright, Loyd Wright, Jr., and Darryl Zanuck.

Collections include those of Charles Feldman and Hedda Hopper (Academy of Motion Picture Arts and Sciences). Also important are Marilyn Monroe's Twentieth Century–Fox legal files, as well as the production file for *There's No Business Like Show Business*.

Additional information comes from: George Barris, *Marilyn*; Kenneth Geist, *Pictures Will Talk*; Ezra Goodman, *The Fifty Year Decline and Fall of Hollywood*; Joshua Greene, *Milton's Marilyn*; James Haspiel, *Marilyn: The Ultimate Look at the Legend*; Sidney Skolsky, *Don't Get Me Wrong, I Love Hollywood*; Maurice Zolotow, *Billy Wilder in Hollywood*.

CHAPTER SIX

Chapter Six is based on letters and memos by Frank Delaney, Charles Feldman, Frank Ferguson, William Gordon, Milton Greene, Elia Kazan, Lew Schreiber, Sam Shaw, Harry Sokolov, Tennessee Williams, Audrey Wood, Loyd Wright, and Darryl Zanuck.

Collections include those of Charles Feldman, William Gordon, and Sidney Skolsky (Academy of Motion Picture Arts and Sciences). Also important are Marilyn Monroe's and Elia Kazan's Twentieth Century–Fox legal files.

Additional information comes from: Virginia Spencer Carr, *The Lonely Hunter: A Biography of Carson McCullers*; Cheryl Crawford, *My Fifty Years in the Theater*; Gilbert Maxwell, *Tennessee Williams and Friends*; Sam Shaw and Norman Rosten, *Marilyn Among Friends*.

CHAPTER SEVEN

Chapter Seven is based on letters and memos by Kermit Bloomgarden, Harold Collins, Charles Feldman, Frank Ferguson, Jack Gordean, Elia Kazan, Rudolph Loewenstein, Arthur Miller, Lew Schreiber, Sam Shaw, Spyros Skouras, Ray Stark, George Wasson, John Wharton, Tennessee Williams, Audrey Wood, and Darryl Zanuck.

Collections include those of Kermit Bloomgarden, Charles Feldman, Arthur Miller, Joseph Rauh, Martin Ritt (Academy of Motion Picture Arts and Sciences), Sidney Skolsky, Tennessee Williams, and Audrey Wood. Also important are Marilyn Monroe's and Lee Strasberg's Twentieth Century–Fox legal files. A copy of the original script for *A View from the Bridge* is on deposit in the Martin Ritt collection at the Academy of Motion Picture Arts and Sciences.

A number of books provide revealing glimpses of Lee Strasberg and his world: Cindy Adams, *Lee Strasberg: The Imperfect Genius of the Actors Studio*; Margaret Brenman-Gibson, *Clifford Odets: American Playwright*; Cheryl Crawford, *My Fifty Years in the Theater*; Harold Clurman, *The Fervent Years*; Frank Corsaro, *Maverick*; David Garfield, *A Player's Place*; Robert Hethmon, ed., *Strasberg at the Actors Studio*; Foster Hirsch, *A Method to their Madness*; Robert Lewis, *Slings and Arrows*; Maureen Stapleton, *A Hell of a Life*; John Strasberg, *Accidentally on Purpose*; Susan Strasberg, *Bittersweet*; Susan Strasberg, *Marilyn and Me*.

Additional information comes from: Marlon Brando, *Songs My Mother Taught Me*; Carroll Baker, *Baby Doll: An Autobiography*; Truman Capote, *Music for Chameleons*; Irene Mayer Selznick, *A Private View*.

CHAPTER EIGHT

Chapter Eight is based on letters and memos by Hugh Beaumont, Kermit Bloomgarden, Charles Feldman, Frank Ferguson, Vivien Leigh, Harry McIntyre, Arthur Miller, Laurence Olivier, Lew Schreiber, Irene Selznick, Spyros Skouras, Tennessee Williams, and Darryl Zanuck.

Collections include those of Charles Feldman, Ruth Gordon (Library of Congress), Joseph Rauh, and Tennessee Williams. Also important are Marilyn Monroe's Twentieth Century–Fox legal files.

Additional information comes from: Cindy Adams, *Lee Strasberg: The Imperfect Genius of the Actors Studio*; Eve Arnold, *Marilyn Monroe*; Philip Dunne, *Take Two*; James Haspiel, *Marilyn: The Ultimate Look at the Legend*; Laurence Olivier, *Confessions of an Actor*; Laurence Olivier, *On Acting*; Tarquin Olivier, *My Father Laurence Olivier*; Maureen Stapleton, *A Hell of a Life*.

CHAPTER NINE

Chapter Nine is based on letters and memos by Hugh Beaumont, Kermit Bloomgarden, Charles Feldman, Lloyd Garrison, William Gordon, Milton Greene, Ben Kadish, Elia Kazan, Arthur Miller, Joseph Rauh, Larry Rice, Sid Rogell, Lew Schreiber, Irving Stein, and Paula Strasberg.

Collections include those of Carson McCullers (University of Texas), Joseph Rauh, and Tennessee Williams. Also important are Marilyn Monroe's Twentieth Century–Fox legal files, as well as the production files and daily production reports for *Bus Stop*.

Additional information comes from Joshua Greene, *Milton's Marilyn*; Joshua Logan, *Movie Stars, Real People, and Me*; Arthur Miller, *Timebends*.

CHAPTER TEN

Chapter Ten is based on letters and memos by Charles Feldman, Lloyd Garrison, Lillian Hellman, Arthur Miller, Joseph Rauh, and Francis E. Walter.

Collections include those of Charles Feldman, Hedda Hopper, and Joseph Rauh.

The transcript of Arthur Miller's HUAC testimony is contained in "Investigation of the Unauthorized Use of United States Passports—Part 4."

Additional information comes from: Lillian Hellman, *Scoundrel Time*; Elia Kazan, *A Life*; Arthur Miller, *Timebends*; Arthur Miller and Inge Morath, *In the Country*; Victor Navasky, *Naming Names*; Norman Rosten, *Marilyn: An Untold Story*; Frederick Ungeheuer with Lewis and Ethel Hurlbut, *Roxbury Remembered*; Robert Vaughn, *Only Victims: A Study of Show Business Blacklisting*.

CHAPTER ELEVEN

Chapter Eleven is based on letters and memos by Hugh Beaumont, Lloyd Garrison, Vivien Leigh, Arthur Miller, Laurence Olivier, Joseph Rauh, and Harry Sokolov.

Collections include those of Charles Feldman, Joseph Rauh, Irene Selznick (Boston University), and Tennessee Williams.

My sense of Laurence Olivier's character owes much to conversations with Orson Welles and Kenneth Tynan.

The best portrait by far of the filming of *The Prince and the Showgirl* is Colin Clark's *The Prince, The Showgirl and Me*. Also invaluable is Jack Cardiff's memoir, *Magic Hour: The Life of a Cameraman*.

Additional information comes from: Joshua Greene, *Milton's Marilyn*; Fred Lawrence Guiles, *Legend*; Radie Harris, *Radie's World*; Anthony Holden, *Olivier*; Laurence Olivier, *Confessions of an Actor*; Laurence Olivier, *On Acting*; Tarquin Olivier, *My Father Laurence Olivier*; Sandra Shevey, *The Marilyn Scandal*; Donald Spoto, *Marilyn Monroe*; Susan Strasberg, *Marilyn and Me*; Kenneth Tynan, *Curtains*; Hugo Vickers, *Vivien Leigh*; Geoffrey Wansell, *Terence Rattigan*; W. J. Weatherby, *Conversations with Marilyn*.

CHAPTER TWELVE

Chapter Twelve is based on letters and memos by Hugh Beaumont, Kermit Bloomgarden, Charles Feldman, Lloyd Garrison, Harold Halperin, Lillian Hellman, Arthur Miller, Joseph Rauh, and Harry Sokolov.

Collections include those of Kermit Bloomgarden, Charles Feldman, Arthur Miller, and Joseph Rauh. Also important are Marilyn Monroe's Twentieth Century–Fox legal files.

Additional information on *The Prince and the Showgirl* comes from the works listed for Chapter Eleven.

CHAPTER THIRTEEN

Chapter Thirteen is based on letters and memos by Herb Brenner, Charles Feldman, Frank Ferguson, Lloyd Garrison, Richard S. Harris, John Huston, Harry McIntyre, Arthur Miller, Robert H. Montgomery, Jr., Joseph Moskowitz, Joseph Rauh, May Reis, Lew Schreiber, Frank Taylor, Spyros Skouras, Harry Sokolov, and George Stephenson.

Collections include those of John Huston, Arthur Miller, and Joseph Rauh. Also important are Marilyn Monroe's Twentieth Century–Fox legal files. Drafts of "I Don't Need You Anymore" are on deposit in the Arthur Miller collection at the University of Texas.

Additional information comes from: Tony Curtis, *Tony Curtis: The Autobiography*; Radie Harris, *Radie's World*; Laurence Olivier, *Confessions of an Actor*; Laurence Olivier, *On Acting*; Lena Pepitone, *Marilyn Monroe Confidential*; Norman Rosten, *Marilyn: An Untold Story*; Susan Strasberg, *Marilyn and Me*; Maurice Zolotow, *Billy Wilder in Hollywood*.

CHAPTER FOURTEEN

Chapter Fourteen is based on letters and memos by Buddy Adler, Harold Bow, Herb Brenner, Ned Brown, Ted Cain, George Chasin, Jack Codd, George Cukor, Bill D'Arcy,

Frank Ferguson, H. William Fitelson, Ralph Greenson, Richard S. Harris, John Huston, Elia Kazan, Marianne Kris, Irving Lazar, Harry McIntyre, Arthur Miller, Robert H. Montgomery, Jr., Joseph Rauh, Sid Rogell, Lew Schreiber, Abe Steinberg, Frank Taylor, Jerry Wald, Peter Witt, and Darryl Zanuck.

Collections include those of Brooks Atkinson (Lincoln Center), Kermit Bloomgarden, Montgomery Clift (Lincoln Center), George Cukor (Academy of Motion Picture Arts and Sciences), Robert Downing (University of Texas), Anna Freud (Library of Congress), Ralph Greenson, John Huston, Paul Osborn (State Historical Society of Wisconsin), and Joseph Rauh.

Also important are Elia Kazan's, Arthur Miller's, and Marilyn Monroe's Twentieth Century–Fox legal files, as well as the production files and daily production reports for *Let's Make Love*.

Additional information comes from: Cheryl Crawford, *My Fifty Years in the Theater*; Catherine David, *Simone Signoret*; Lawrence Grobel, *The Hustons*; Hervé Hamon and Patrick Rotman, *Yves Montand: You See I Haven't Forgotten*; Elia Kazan, *A Life*; Gavin Lambert, *On Cukor*; Robert Lewis, *Slings and Arrows*; Arthur Miller, *Timebends*; Berniece Baker Miracle and Mona Rae Miracle, *My Sister Marilyn*; Lena Pepitone, *Marilyn Monroe Confidential*; Simone Signoret, *Nostalgia Isn't What It Used to Be*; Susan Strasberg, *Marilyn and Me*; Maurice Zolotow, *Billy Wilder in Hollywood*.

CHAPTER FIFTEEN

Chapter Fifteen is based on letters and memos by John Bodnar, Harry Brand, George Chasin, George Cukor, Frank Ferguson, Ralph Greenson, David Hall, Richard S. Harris, Gladys Hill, John Huston, Vivien Leigh, Arthur Miller, Joseph Rauh, Sid Rogell, Lew Schreiber, Paula Strasberg, Frank Taylor, Marietta Tree, Jerry Wald, and Max Youngstein.

Collections include those of George Cukor, Anna Freud, Hedda Hopper, John Huston, and Joseph Rauh. Also important are Marilyn Monroe's Twentieth Century–Fox legal files, as well as the production files and daily production reports for *Let's Make Love*.

Additional information comes from: Eve Arnold, *Marilyn Monroe*; Catherine David, *Simone Signoret*; Hervé Hamon and Patrick Rotman, *Yves Montand: You See I Haven't Forgotten*; James Goode, *The Making of The Misfits*; Lawrence Grobel, *The Hustons*; Fred Lawrence Guiles, *Legend*; James Haspiel, *Marilyn: The Ultimate Look at the Legend*; Elia Kazan, *A Life*; John Kobal, *People Will Talk*; Alice McIntyre, "Making the Misfits," *Esquire*, March 1961; Arthur Miller, *Timebends*; Lena Pepitone, *Marilyn Monroe Confidential*; Norman Rosten, *Marilyn: An Untold Story*; Simone Signoret, *Nostalgia Isn't What It Used to Be*.

CHAPTER SIXTEEN

Chapter Sixteen is based on letters and memos by David Brown, Jack Codd, George Cukor, Joseph V. DiMauro, Charles Feldman, Frank Ferguson, Aaron R. Frosch, Bob Goldstein, Ralph Greenson, Gladys Hill, John Huston, Marianne Kris, C. S. Landau, Irving Lazar, Owen McLean, W. C. Michel, Arthur Miller, Joseph Rauh, Milton Rudin, Lew Schreiber, Spyros Skouras, Harry Sokolov, Ted Strauss, Frank Taylor, and Jerry Wald.

Collections include those of George Cukor, Charles Feldman, Anna Freud, Ralph Greenson, and John Huston. Also important are Lee Strasberg's and Marilyn Monroe's Twentieth Century–Fox legal files, as well as the production file for *Something's Got to Give*.

Additional information comes from: Eve Arnold, *Marilyn Monroe*; Philip Dunne, *Take Two*; James Hilty, *Robert Kennedy: Brother Protector*; Berniece Baker Miracle and Mona Rae Miracle, *My Sister Marilyn*; Eunice Murray, *Marilyn: The Last Months*; Lena Pepitone, *Marilyn Monroe Confidential*; Norman Rosten, *Marilyn: An Untold Story*; Edward Wagenknecht, ed., *Marilyn Monroe*; Nathan Weiss and Jack Brodsky, *The Cleopatra Papers*. Monroe's letter to Dr. Greenson is quoted in full in Donald Spoto, *Marilyn Monroe*.

CHAPTER SEVENTEEN

Chapter Seventeen is based on letters and memos of Alvah Bessie, George Cukor, Phil Feldman, Frank Ferguson, Anna Freud, Ralph Greenson, Stan Hough, Vivien Leigh, Peter Levathes, F. L. Metzler, Arthur Miller, W. C. Michel, Marilyn Monroe, Jesse R. O'Malley, Larry Rice, and Milton Rudin.

Collections include those of Alvah Bessie (State Historical Society of Wisconsin), George Cukor, Robert Downing, Anna Freud, Ralph Greenson, Hedda Hopper, Arthur Miller, and Joseph Rauh. Also important are Marilyn Monroe's Twentieth Century–Fox legal files, as well as the production file and daily production reports for *Something's Got to Give*.

Additional information comes from: George Barris, *Marilyn*; Joshua Greene, *Milton's Marilyn*; Elia Kazan, *A Life*; Arthur Miller, *Timebends*, Eunice Murray, *Marilyn: The Last Months*; Victor Navasky, *Naming Names*; Richard Reeves, *President Kennedy: Profile of Power*; Norman Rosten, *Marilyn: An Untold Story*; Arthur M. Schlesinger, Jr., *Robert Kennedy and his Times*; Bert Stern, "The Last Sitting," *Vogue*, September 1982; Susan Strasberg, *Marilyn and Me*; Edward Wagenknecht, ed. *Marilyn Monroe*; Nathan Weiss and Jack Brodsky, *The Cleopatra Papers*; Earl Wilson, *Show Business Laid Bare*; Earl Wilson, *The Show Business Nobody Knows*; Elizabeth Young-Bruehl, *Anna Freud: A Biography*.

Acknowledgments

To Betty A. Prashker, my editor at Crown Publishers in New York, I owe a tremendous debt of gratitude. We have done two books together, and I have learned from her in countless ways. I have benefited from Betty's wisdom at every stage of this project. The insight and care with which she guided this biography from the day I first had the idea to the very last draft of the manuscript have contributed immeasurably to whatever strengths it may have. I am deeply grateful for the opportunity to work with her. She is a great inspiration both as a woman and a friend.

Ion Trewin, at Weidenfeld & Nicolson in London, did everything possible to make this book a reality. Of particular importance were his ideas about the shape the story ought to take. His questions are always probing and astute, and he has a fantastic ability to help focus a project. I am enormously fortunate to have him as one of the mainstays of my writing life.

Allegra Huston was my editor at Weidenfeld for many years. She took time from her own projects to come back and work on this book with me. I cannot begin to thank her properly for agreeing to do that. Without Allegra's incomparable sense of structure, this biography would be something very different indeed. I can't imagine doing a book without her. Her thinking continues to amaze me with its clarity and originality. She is also the most beloved of friends.

And then there is Lois Wallace, my agent, my friend, and my most trusted adviser. Without Lois, none of this would be possible. She has the courage to say no—as well as yes. As an agent, Lois is without peer. As a friend, she has stood the test of time.

Also at Crown Publishers, I would like to thank all the people who have worked with such skill and dedication on my books. In particular I must single out Tina Constable and Andrew Martin, who have worked so effectively and with such care on my behalf.

I have been equally fortunate at Weidenfeld & Nicolson, where, after five books, I always know that I am in safe hands. From *Orson Welles* on, the wonderful staff at Weidenfeld has done everything possible to publish my books with flair and intelligence. I am very grateful.

Whitney Cookman designed the Crown jacket and Nick Castle did the Weidenfeld jacket. I am grateful to both for their brilliant work.

Thanks also to my London agent, Bill Hamilton, and my Paris agent, Michelle Lapautre, for their efforts on my behalf. And to Tony Cartano, my editor at Editions Albin Michel in Paris, I give my thanks for his support of this project.

I would like to thank the many people who so generously provided the information I needed to write this book. They include: Nan Abell, Charles Bell, Alan Brawn, Ann Caiger, Virginia Kaye Chilewich, Frank Corsaro, Judith Dike, Dr. Norman Farberow, Elsa Feminella, Esther Flores, Edwin Guthman, Jane Harvey, Eva Heilweil, Alfred Hayes, Jr., Marietta Hayes, Kathy Henderson, Gladys Irvis, Evelyn Keyes, Hope Lange, Esther Maltz, Charles Marcus, Edith Marcus, George Masters, Nancy McKechnie, Ross Miller, Dr. Jay Nagdimon, Walter Neville, Edward Parone, Elaine Pike, Howard Prouty, Tony Randall, Mary Ellen Rogan, Merel Rogers, Patricia Rosten, Sarah Samis, Meta Shaw, Sam Shaw, Senator George Smathers, Barbara Smith-LaBorde, Mickey Song, Marjorie Stengel, Shirlee Strahm, Theodore Strauss, Frank Taylor, Faye Thompson, Eli Wallach, and Brian Woo.

I also drew on past interviews with Henry Hathaway, Patrick O'Neal, Hermes Pan, Kenneth Tynan, Orson Welles, and Maurice Zolotow.

Many thanks to the archives, libraries, and historical societies, where I collected the material for this book: Vassar College, Special Collections, Poughkeepsie, New York; Academy of Motion Picture Arts and Sciences, Los Angeles, California; State Historical Society of Wisconsin, Archives Division, Wisconsin Center for Film and Theater Research, Madison, Wisconsin; UCLA, Special Collections, Los Angeles, California; UCLA, Film Collections, Los Angeles, California;

University of Texas at Austin, Harry Ransom Humanities Research Center, Special Collections, Austin, Texas; American Film Institute, Louis B. Mayer Library, Special Collections, Los Angeles, California; Library of Congress, Special Collections, Washington, D.C.; The John Gray Park Library at the Kent School, Kent, Connecticut; The Lincoln Center Library for the Performing Arts, New York, New York; and Boston University, Mugar Memorial Library, Special Collections, Boston, Massachusetts.

Finally, special thanks to Steve Boucher, for patience beyond the call of duty.

And most of all, I must thank my husband, David. He is the light at the very center of my life and the reason for everything good in it.

Index